Treatment of Alcoholism and Other Addictions

Treatment of Alcoholism and Other Addictions

A Self-Psychology Approach

Jerome D. Levin, Ph.D.

Jason Aronson Inc.
Northvale, New Jersey
London

Library of Congress Cataloging-in-Publication Data

Levin, Jerome D. (Jerome David)
    Treatment of alcoholism and other addictions.

    1. Bibliography: p.
    Includes index.
1. Alcoholism—Treatment.   2. Substance abuse—
Treatment.   3. Psychotherapy.   4. Self.   I. Title.
[DNLM: 1. Alcoholism—therapy   2. Ego.   3. Psychotherapy
—methods.   4. Self Concept.   5. Substance Dependence
—therapy.   WM 420 L6645t]
RC565.L434   1987   616.86'1   87-19563
ISBN 0-87668-947-0

Manufactured in the United States of America.

To Suffolk,
who missed many walks
so this book could be written

And malt does more than Milton can
To justify God's ways to man.

—*A. E. Houseman*

The road of excess leads to the palace of wisdom.

—*William Blake*

We are all more human than anything else.

—*Harry Stack Sullivan*

Contents

Preface

This book describes the psychological treatment of alcoholism and other addictions. Although it draws on many treatment approaches and has been influenced by several theories of addiction, it essentially uses the self psychology developed by Heinz Kohut and his students to understand the dynamics of alcoholism and other addictions and to derive a rational therapy for these diseases. The psychoanalytic tradition has also made a much greater contribution to the understanding and treatment of the addictions than is usually recognized and acknowledged.

This book is addressed to a wide audience: alcoholism counselors, social workers, psychologists, psychotherapists, psychoanalysts, nurses, physicians, and students of these disciplines, who bring different kinds of knowledge, skills, and experience to it. The information provided here will enable the reader to engage in psychodynamically oriented alcoholism counseling and self-psychological psychotherapy of the addictions.

Alcoholism affects mind, body, and relationships; thus, this text brings together material from medicine, biology, chemistry, psychology, sociology, counseling, and psychoanalysis. In order to facilitate the learning of some of the more complex material, discussions may appear in several chapters from different points of view. For example, Kohut's developmental theory is discussed in Chapters 1, 6, and 8. Readers will gain a comprehensive knowledge of alcoholism and addiction and will learn an effective treatment approach for these insidious and often fatal diseases.

Acknowledgments

I have always admired Chaucer's clerk, who "would gladly learn and gladly teach." If this book successfully and gladly teaches, it is because I have gladly learned from excellent teachers. I gratefully acknowledge their influence on me and on this work. From Morse Peckham, Ph.D., formerly of the University of Pennsylvania English department, I learned how literature reveals the unconscious; from Raymond Kilbansky, Ph.D., of the McGill University philosophy department, I learned that critical thinking is both a moral and a logical task; from my training analyst, Alvin Wolf, Ph.D., I learned how to feel without fear; and from a trio of truly remarkable clinical teachers and supervisors, I learned how to do therapy. Wilfred Haber, Ph.D., late Professor of Rehabilitation Counseling at New York University, brought passion to the therapeutic encounter, while my first analytic supervisor, Claude Miller, M.D., of the American Institute for Psychoanalysis and Psychotherapy (AIPP), brought humor. Marjorie White, Ph.D., also of AIPP, brought the empathic insights of self psychology to the therapeutic encounter. Passion, humor, and empathy—one could do worse. I would also like to acknowledge my debt to Hendrik Ruitenbeck, Ph.D., Al Brok, Ph.D., and Louis Getoff, Ph.D., all of AIPP, and to Eugene Glynn, M.D., of the Youth Service League, from whom I also learned a great deal.

Appreciation is also due to my students at Marymount Manhattan College, AIPP, the Postgraduate Center for Mental Health, and the New School for Social Research, who read and commented on sections of this book, as did a number of my supervisees. Their feedback was invaluable. I would also like to thank Peter Hartocollis, M.D., Ph.D., Chairman of the Department of Psychiatry at the University of Patras, for taking time out of a very busy schedule to read most of the manuscript, and for his support and encouragement. Judith Katsin, Ph.D., former Director of the Employee Assistance Program at Brookhaven National Laboratory, was another early and enthusiastic reader. Our clinical discussions and her comprehensive knowledge of substance abuse helped shape my thinking on addiction. My greatest debt, however, is to my patients.

Special thanks are due to my publisher, Jason Aronson, who supported this project from the time he heard of it, and to Joan Langs, my editor at Aronson, who helped shape and sharpen my efforts. Sharon Casey typed the manuscript; her assistance is appreciated. I would also like to thank Carol Buckley, CAC, for reading the manuscript and making many helpful suggestions.

I had the good fortune to grow up in a home that encouraged learning. From my earliest years, my intellectual and aesthetic interests were enthusiastically supported by my parents, Edith and Nathan, and by my aunts, Ella, Reba, and Hilda. I am grateful to all of them.

Finally, this book would never have been written without the support and infinite patience of my wife, Ginny. I thank her for enduring seemingly endless weekends of neglect—which hopefully are a thing of the past—and for much else.

CHAPTER 1

About Self Psychology

PSYCHOLOGICAL TREATMENT OF ALCOHOLISM AND ADDICTION

Alcoholism is more than a mental affliction and often requires medical as well as psychological treatment. Alcoholics Anonymous (AA) views the process as broadly pathological when it describes alcoholism as a "mental, physical, and spiritual disease." Whether or not we agree with this description, there is no question that alcoholism adversely affects every aspect of the alcoholic's being and that treatment must address every aspect of this pervasive damage.

Psychological treatment aims to replace addiction with relationship and to use this emotional bond to promote integration and growth. The multifaceted psychological treatment of alcoholism includes the following components: (1) diagnosing the disorder, (2) educating patients about the diagnosis so that they can use the knowledge to stop drinking, and (3) ameliorating the psychological and emotional derangement causing or resulting from the alcoholism. The first treatment component requires an understanding of the mental and physical effects of alcoholism. The second requires both the ability to effectively confront the patient's inevitable denial and the therapeutic tact to know when to do it. The third component requires an understanding of the alcoholic's inner experience and of the dynamics of the disorder, as well as a command of the repertoire of therapeutic interventions. *Self psychology* offers relatively little direct assistance with the first two steps, but it makes a vital contribution to the third, reparative, part of the task, and throws considerable light on diagnosis and confrontation. What, then, is self psychology?

KOHUT AND SELF PSYCHOLOGY

Self psychology is a body of psychoanalytic theory and psychotherapeutic technique developed by Heinz Kohut (1971, 1972, 1977, 1984) and his students. Kohut's self psychology is drawn from and incorporates much of the psychoanalytic tradition. In fact, Kohut considered himself and his theory an integral part of that tradition. Kohut developed his insights into the nature of the self and the treatment of self-pathology while working with a group of severely disturbed patients who suffered from what he called the *narcissistic personality disorders*. These patients suffered primarily from a developmental arrest—a failure to develop a normal self—rather than from unresolved intrapsychic conflict. Kohut viewed addictive behavior as an attempt to deal with narcissistic disturbance. Late in his life, he used the insights derived from treating these narcissistic personality disorders to develop a more general view of humans and of psychopathology. This theory, which subsumed the traditional psychoanalytic model, he called *self psychology*.

ADDICTION AS A DISTURBANCE IN
THE EXPERIENCE OF THE SELF

There are many reasons to consider alcoholism a disorder of the self. Alcoholism is, by definition, a form of *self*-destruction by *self*-poisoning, of suicide on the installment plan—a fact which strongly implies that alcoholism is a form of *self*-pathology. The alcoholic's notorious *self*-absorption is frequently highlighted both in popular accounts and in the scientific literature. In fact, one of AA's definitions of alcoholism is "self-will run riot."

Psychoanalysts are referring to another aspect of the same phenomenon when they say that "alcohol has become the alcoholic's sole love object, alcohol here experienced as part of self." *Narcissism* is love of oneself. In the Greek legend, Narcissus was a beautiful youth who fell in love with his own image reflected in the surface of a pond. He perished in his self-infatuation. The legend warns us that there is something dangerous about self-love. Yet without it we would also perish. Thus, there is a healthy form of self-love, from which self-esteem and feelings of well-being emanate; and there is an unhealthy form of self-love, which alienates us from our fellows and is ultimately damaging to the very self that loves itself. The first is healthy narcissism and the second is pathological narcissism. Developing a healthy form of self-love is one of the most difficult of the life tasks. As Rabbi Hillel (1957) said, "If I am not for myself, who will be for me? If I am only for myself, what am I?"

Alcoholics have failed to find a satisfactory way of loving themselves and are simultaneously self-absorbed and self-destructive. There is something paradoxical here. Alcoholics, who are, in some sense, overinvested and overinvolved with themselves, are known to take extremely poor care of themselves. They suffer a deficiency in the normal adult capacity for self-care. John Mack (1981) and Edward Khantzian (1981) have detailed the alcoholic's lack of self-care skills.

Alcoholics not only find it difficult to love themselves in a healthy manner; they also are insecure in the very possession of a self. Narcissus had to continually look at his reflection to make sure that he still existed. The same is true for the alcoholic: Alcoholics have to be self-absorbed to make sure that they are still alive. Their sense of self is so tenuous that they live constantly on the edge of psychic annihilation. Their barely cohesive selves may fragment at any time. Thus, alcoholics suffer from at least four kinds of self-pathology: (1) they are self-destructive; (2) they lack certain components of the self that mediate self-care and maintain self-esteem; (3) they are overly self-involved; and (4) their very sense of being, their self-concepts or representations, are fragile and in jeopardy. Since so many observers, from so many points of view, have pointed to an abnormality in alcoholics' relationship to themselves, it seems reasonable to postulate a relationship between alcoholism and pathological narcissism. We shall do so.

Kohut delineates a developmental sequence of the stages through which the self passes in route to its mature form. One of Kohut's stages is that of the *archaic self*, which manifests many of the characteristics of adult alcoholics. In some sense, the alcoholic is functioning at the stage of the archaic self. The alcoholic may be developmentally arrested, or *fixated*, in the stage of the archaic self. In that case, a causal relationship is apparent between the pathological narcissism (fixation at the stage of the archaic self) and the alcoholism. If, on the other hand, the manifestations of the archaic self are evident only after the development of the addiction, then the regression and pathological narcissism are viewed as a consequence of the alcoholism. To cover both possibilities, we shall say that the alcoholic is fixated/regressed to the stage of the archaic self, to pathological narcissism. Thus, Kohut's theory gives us a conceptual structure by which to understand the disturbance in the self concomitant with alcoholism.

SELF PSYCHOLOGY AS A BRIDGE BETWEEN THE COUNSELING AND PSYCHOANALYTIC TRADITIONS

Carl Rogers has had an enormous influence on counseling theory and practice. His *client-centered* therapy is another tradition of psychological treatment that is vitally concerned with the deformation and development of the self. Self psychology thus provides a bridge between the counseling and the psychoanalytic traditions. Although their language and many of their basic assumptions are radically different, Kohut and Rogers share an emphasis on the self and its actualization. As we shall see, the two theorists come from radically different theoretical and treatment traditions but arrive at a common core of formulations: (1) the importance of empathic understanding and unconditional acceptance of the patient; (2) the need for "mirroring" of the self by the environment; and (3) the concept of cure as the development of a *cohesive self* (Kohut) or as *self-actualization* (Rogers).

Rogers and Kohut share a view of human nature that is more optimistic than that of Freud; both diminish the role of intrapsychic conflict while emphasizing the need to provide a growth-promoting psychological environment for the client (Rogers) or patient (Kohut). In a sense, both Rogers and Kohut believe that the flowers will bloom if they receive sufficient water and sunlight, and their therapeutic approaches provide these. There are important differences, however, in how they do it.

BILL WILSON, AA, AND NARCISSISTIC DISTURBANCE

Bill Wilson, the cofounder and chief theorist of AA, the highly successful self-help movement for alcoholics, also emphasizes disturbances in the self as central to the etiology of alcoholism. Wilson taught that remediation of these disturbances is the core of the rehabilitation of the alcoholic. It is probably no accident that a *self*-help group is the best known and one of the most successful therapies for the treatment of alcoholism. As we shall see, it offers both help for the self and self-help.

Both Rogers's and Kohut's approaches to the psychology of the self make valuable contributions to the understanding and treatment of addictive behavior. Freud and the classical analysts recognized intrapsychic conflict aplenty in both active and recovering alcoholics. This book makes use of the insights of these theorists in a way that is not merely eclectic, but synthesizes their insights and ours into a coherent view of alcoholism and of its psychological treatment. Sir Isaac Newton is reputed to have said, "We see so far because we stand on the shoulders of giants." If indeed we do see further into alcoholism, it is because we stand on the shoulders of Sigmund Freud and Bill Wilson; of Carl Rogers and Heinz Kohut.

HISTORY OF CONCEPTS OF THE SELF

What is this *self* of which Rogers, Kohut, and many other psychological theorists speak? The status of the concept of self has been highly controversial in the history of psychology. *Psyche*, the Greek root from which the words *psychology* and *psychological* are derived, can be translated as mind, spirit, or soul. The same is true of the German word *geist*. The term *self* came to share in this ambiguity, and the concept of a self became merged with the concept of a soul.

In fact, our concept of self is a linear descendent of the "faculty psychology" of the premodern era, which attempted to characterize and list the attributes of the self, or soul. As such, the concept of self was scientifically tainted by its association with the idea of a soul. *Self* in this sense is a philosophical or, more pejoratively from a scientific point of view, metaphysical concept, and as such it was rejected by the new "scientific," or experimental, psychology of the nineteenth century. Although one school of the new psychology, the introspectionists, wished to give a scientific account of inner, subjective experience, even they rejected the concept of a self as vague and unscientific. The early Freud used the term *ego*—literally, the "I"—to mean the self, but he never really defined the term. He used *ego* not as a technical term, but rather as a synonym for *self*. He was appealing to ordinary language usage to justify his use of the term. Later, *ego* evolved into a technical term for Freud, denoting one of the three agencies of the mind. Unfortunately, his use of *ego* was inconsistent; sometimes he used the word to mean the "I" and sometimes to mean an agency of the mind.

Until Kohut arrived, the mainstream of psychoanalytic thought, like academic psychology, tended to reject the self as an unscientific concept. With the exception of the radical behaviorists, however, psychologists still recognized the need for a term denoting the inner, subjective experience of continuity and identity, however illusory that experience might be, and the concept of self slowly reentered the realm of respectable scientific discourse. It is perhaps no accident that the English word *self* comes from an Anglo-Saxon root meaning "the same." A scientific psychology needs a way to talk about, and to explain, the human experience of being the same person.

Thinkers as diverse as the British object relations school of psychoanalytic thought, the European phenomenological school, and the American ego psychological school have found it necessary to give a "scientific" account of the self. The object relations theorists went so far as to speak of a "hidden self" (Guntrip 1968, 1971) and of "true" and "false" selves (Winnicott 1960); the phenomenologists, who made the experiences of the self the object of their science, spoke of a "transcendental ego" (Husserl 1929), while the American ego psychologists referred to "self-representations" and their viscissitudes (Hartmann 1964, Jacobson 1964, Kernberg 1975) or to "identity" (Erikson 1950, 1968). Even Freud (1940) wrote of the "unification of the ego" as the goal of psychoanalytic psychotherapy.

Psychoanalysis has always been about integration of split-off, repressed, and disavowed aspects of self. Freud's unification of the ego was not so very different from Kohut's cohesion of the self. Their conceptual schemes and their views of what needs to be integrated or adhered are different, but their underlying notions of the tasks of therapy are not as different as they might at first appear. It is no accident that Freud's last creative efforts (1938, 1940) produced *Moses and Monotheism* and a paper on splitting of the ego. If polytheism is the projection of unintegrated aspects of self, then monotheism is the projection of the wish to be unitary and whole; in the end, Freud implicitly linked psychoanalysis and one latent meaning of monotheism.

The goal of both is the healing of splits in the ego, or, in Kohut's terms, cohesion of the self.

Rogers (1951, 1961) views the self as a subset of the totality of the organism's experience; parts of the organism's ongoing processes become conscious through symbolizations, which are experienced as a *gestalt,* or unity. Kohut views the self as a center of initiative which is experienced as coherent in space and enduring in time. Rogers sees psychopathology as the result of a constriction of the self in which too little of the totality of organismic experience is symbolized and made conscious. Kohut considers most psychopathology to be the result of an insufficient cohesion of the self.

Each of these thinkers was trying to do justice to the indisputable datum that man experiences himself as both a coherent whole and a disparate assembly of disjunctive feelings and experiences. One is reminded of the man who complained to his physician, "Doctor, my head hurts, my feet ache, my throat is sore, my bowels are upset, and to tell the truth, I myself don't feel so well either." It is this "I myself" that is the focus of the self psychologists in their accounts both of normal development and functioning and of psychopathology. No thinker has played a greater role than Carl Rogers in the rehabilitation of *self* and *self-concept* as scientific terms. Let us explore his theory and therapy in greater detail.

CARL ROGERS AND CLIENT-CENTERED COUNSELING

For our purposes, Rogers's greatest contribution is attitudinal. More than any other theorist, with the possible exception of Kohut, he has emphasized the curative powers of unconditional acceptance and empathic understanding. Rogers is being discussed in this psychoanalytically oriented text, not only because his influence on the counseling profession makes him a logical bridge between counseling and psychoanalysis, but preeminently because we believe that it is the relationship that cures and that Rogers is correct in his description of the parameters of a curative therapeutic relationship. However much they may emphasize other curative factors in the psychotherapeutic process—catharsis, derepression, or interpretations of unconscious conflict—the great psychotherapists have always known this. (See Freud's [1912b, 1913a] discussion of the importance of rapport in his papers on technique; Ralph Greenson's [1965] discussion of the importance of the working alliance in classical psychoanalysis; and Kohut's [1984] discussion of how analysis cures in his posthumous book on that topic.)

Rogers not only delineates curative attitudes; he makes explicit the relationship between unconditional acceptance by the other and unconditional acceptance of the self by the self. Regard by others results in self-regard. The self, previously impoverished and constricted by fear, becomes able to encompass progressively more of the disavowed and repressed. The self becomes not only more extensive, but also stronger—in Kohut's terms, more cohesive.

Rogers does not believe that self-acceptance and heightened self-regard result in increased interpersonal conflict. On the contrary, he believes that heightened self-regard increases socialized behavior and reduces aggression against others. Kohut, from a different theoretical perspective and using different language, is basically agreeing with Rogers when he argues that narcissism (self-love) and object love (love of others) do not have a reciprocal relationship in which more of one means less of the other, but rather are parallel phenomena which have "independent lines of development."

The counselor's unconditional acceptance of the client is nowhere more important than in working with the addicted, particularly the alcoholic. By the time alcoholics reach our clinics or our offices, they have long been scorned and rejected. Worse, they have internalized this scorn and rejection, and however defended by bluster and bravado, they hate themselves. Further, they have usually become expert at provoking rejections by others, thus confirming their worthlessness and providing a rationale for more drinking. The therapist's unconditional acceptance at least provides a possibility that this vicious cycle will be broken. AA has long known this. AA literature, folk wisdom, and testimonials are replete with hymns of gratitude for the *acceptance* that the alcoholic finds in AA. Attendance at any AA meeting will provide evidence of the centrality of acceptance in AA's self-understanding of its efficacy.

Rogers's Theory of the Self

Rogers (1959, p. 200) defines the self as

> the organized, consistent conceptual gestalt composed of perceptions of the characteristics of the 'I' or 'me' and the perceptions of the relationships of the 'I' or 'me' to others and to various aspects of life. . . . It is a gestalt which is available to awareness though not necessarily in awareness. It is a fluid and changing gestalt, a process, but at any given moment . . . a specific entity.

In other words, the self is the conscious and preconscious self-concept. Rogers's more inclusive theoretical structure is the organism, which he defines as the totality of experience—private, unique, and always changing. This private world is the *phenomenal field*. The self is that very small portion of experience which reaches consciousness, often in a distorted form, through symbolization. The phenomenal field can never be completely known; important experiences (experience is always inward, whatever its source, for Rogers) are denied entry into the self, into potential self-awareness, because awareness of them would lower self-regard. They would diminish self-regard because others (particularly parents and other early caretakers) did not accept these aspects of us. The result is a kind of repression, although Rogers does not use this word. How does the self "know" what not to admit to symbolization and consciousness? This is a reframing of the old question: How does Freud's psychic censor know what to exclude if it is unconscious? Rogers's answer is that the self has a kind of subliminal awareness, which he calls *subception*, which allows the self to reject elements of experience without becoming aware of them.

For Rogers, the purpose of existence is self-actualization, and self-actualization is the sole force motivating behavior. Pathology is anything that impedes self-actualization. Although his system is much more complex, Kohut in many ways agrees with this analysis of psychopathology. In his terms, classical psychopathology dealt with "guilty man," while his psychopathology deals preeminently with "tragic man," man as unfulfilled, not self-actualized. No better example of "tragic man," the unactualized self, can be found than the alcoholic—man self-poisoned and self-defiled.

If pathology is constriction of self and failure of self-actualization, what then is the "cure"? In what should the treatment consist? For Rogers, the "cure" lies in the progressive incorporation of the totality of experience into the self. It is counselors' unconditional acceptance of clients, their genuineness (that is, their acceptance of their own selves and feelings), and empathic understanding that make possible this progressive enrichment of the self. The counselor conveys empathic acceptance by "reflecting" the client's responses, thereby conveying understanding and implying acceptance.

When Kohut speaks of the importance of "mirroring," both developmentally and in treatment, he is talking about essentially the same thing. To have one's feelings empathically reflected is to be mirrored. It is vital that the counselor understand that excluded aspects of experience are not limited to forbidden aggressive and sexual desires, but include the self's needs for control of the environment, for acceptance, for relationship, and for self-actualization. In short, the content of Rogers's disavowed aspects of experience include what Kohut called the needs of the narcissistic sector of the personality. These needs include the need for empathic understanding; to have one's existence, one's ambitions, and one's ideals confirmed; for power; and for powerful others.

Both Rogers and Kohut tend to deemphasize the importance of insight, self-knowledge, and self-awareness to the cure. Not that they neglect these factors; on the contrary, both seek to promote such insight. Late in their respective lives, however, both theorists came to realize that self-knowledge is not enough.

What is needed is a change in *being*. For Rogers, not all self-actualization need be conscious; and for Kohut, the process of internalization of selected aspects of the therapist's activities change the self in vital ways that are at least as important as increased self-awareness. We believe that *both* the experience of therapy and the gain in self-knowledge are responsible for the change in the patient. A great deal of therapy works by indirection, and both Rogers and Kohut know this. Alcoholic clients in particular need a certain kind of experience as well as increased self-knowledge. It is our job to provide it.

Rogers contrasts the ideal self and the actual self, the self that we would like to be and the self as experienced. When there is too great a gap between them, when the ideal self and the actual self are too incongruent, self-regard plummets. One goal of Rogerian therapy is to increase congruence between the ideal and the actual self. Alcoholics experience extreme discrepancy between ideal self and actual self. The contrast is often so unbearable that the alcoholic drinks to blot out this tormenting awareness.

Despite Rogers's insight into the centrality of acceptance by others and of self-regard for both normal development and pathogenesis, his work does not provide the conceptual clarity into the nature of narcissistic pathology that Kohut's more complex scheme yields. Kohut also elaborates the patient–therapist relationship in ways that Rogers does not. The remainder of this text will therefore focus on Kohutian self psychology.

KOHUT'S THEORY OF THE SELF

In the course of Kohut's career, he worked with a group of severely disturbed patients who suffered from what he called narcissistic personality disorders. These patients were neither psychotic, out of contact with reality, nor neurotic, suffering from conflict between repressed desires and conscience. They seemed to lack a firm sense of self, yet they had the ability to enter into a stable relationship with the analyst. Psychotic patients are rarely able to do this. However, Kohut's patients did not react to him as neurotic patients typically do. Instead they formed what Kohut first called the "narcissistic" and later called the "self–object" transferences; that is, they related to their analysts as if the analysts were parts of them. Kohut classifies these relationships as either *mirror transferences*, in which the patients treated their analysts as if they were an extension of themselves, or *idealizing transferences*, in which the patients acted as if they were part of the analyst, whom they perceived as omnipotent.

After studying these forms of therapeutic relationships, Kohut was able to trace the development of the self from a state of fragmentation to an archaic (primitive), cohesive self to a mature self. The narcissistic patients appeared to be fixated at the developmental stage of the archaic self. Kohut then elaborated a therapeutic strategy for treating narcissistic personalities. In Chapter 6, we will argue that alcoholics are most frequently either fixated at or have regressed to this stage of the archaic self. This is a form of pathological narcissism or of self-pathology. Kohut believes that such fixations result from failures of empathic relating (mirroring) by primary caretakers very early in life.

Kohut (1977b) wrote explicitly about addiction, which he saw as a futile attempt to repair developmental deficits in the self. If this is indeed the case, then the rational treatment of addiction is the repair of these deficits. Kohut's self psychology is a modification of psychoanalytic psychotherapy designed to do just that. It therefore has great utility in the treatment of alcoholism. The details of Kohut's theory of the self and his treatment techniques will be discussed later; however, a few words on the applicability of self psychology to the treatment of alcoholism are in order at this point.

Certainly, not all alcoholics suffer from narcissistic personality disorders; however, narcissistic disturbances are extremely common in alcoholics. Their self-cohesion is tenuous and easily threatened, subjecting them to panic anxiety. They tend to relate to others, including counselors and therapists, along the lines described by Kohut in his discussion of the narcissistic transferences. They are subject to "empty" depressions because

they lack what Kohut called "psychic structure," internal resources for maintaining self-esteem. Finally, they often resist
giving up alcohol not so much because they want to drink as
because they experience the inability to drink safely as an intolerable defect. We can thus understand much of alcoholic behavior and denial as a defense against narcissistic decompensa-
tion—the fragmentation of the self, which would mean psychic
annihilation. Our treatment of the active alcoholic must therefore be informed by this understanding of their narcissistic
vulnerability, although self-psychological treatment techniques
are not particularly useful at this stage of treatment.

Self psychology also helps us understand the centrality of
control for alcoholics: they are trying to exercise omnipotent
control over their self-objects, the world experienced as part of
themselves, which is characteristic of the stage of the archaic
self. AA has long understood the alcoholic's need for control and
has tried to treat it in an educational manner through its slogans,
"Live and let live" and "Let go and let God." As we shall see in
Chapter 6, self psychology treats the pathological need for
control in quite a different way. It is only after the alcoholic has
achieved stable sobriety, however, that we can make use of
Kohut's insights into treatment to help the alcoholic "fill in" the
missing psychic structure, thereby repairing disabling deficits in
the self.

Thus, although Kohut's self psychology is not the only
fruitful way to look at alcoholism, it does indeed provide both
an understanding of the addictive process and some tools for
treating it. Before we can make full use of Kohut's contribution,
however, we must first learn about the physiology and psychology of alcoholism and what we can do to arrest the addictive
process—to help the active alcoholic stop drinking.

CHAPTER 2

About Alcohol

One of the reasons that the study of alcoholism is intrinsically and boundlessly fascinating is its complexity. The physical sciences, the biological sciences, and the social sciences are necessary to illuminate that strange and baffling phenomenon— the slow, relentless self-poisoning of a human being—that we call alcoholism. Alcohol is a chemical and a drug; it is contained in a vast range of fermented fluids; it is consumed by people; it affects their bodies and minds in ways not fully understood. Drinkers of alcohol have personalities, are members of families, live in societies, and are influenced by cultures. We will need to look at the chemical and drug, at its physical and psychological effects, at the people who drink it, and at the families, societies, and cultures that those people live in. Let us begin with the chemical and drug, with alcohol itself.

WHAT IS ALCOHOL? WHAT DOES IT DO?

Alcohol is a chemical compound. It has pharmacological properties; that is, it is a drug. Actually, there are many alcohols. The kind of alcohol that we drink is *ethyl alcohol*, or *ethanol*. It is a member of a class of chemicals that are characterized by carbon chains linked to hydroxyl ions; its empirical formula is C_2H_5OH; it is a relatively small molecule, perfectly soluble in water and soluble to a lesser extent in fat.

What about the drug ethyl alcohol? Before the chemical can become the drug, it must be present in a beverage, ingested, and absorbed. It then asserts its effects on the body. Let us trace this process.

FERMENTATION AND THE PRODUCTION OF ALCOHOLIC BEVERAGES

Alcohol (henceforth, *alcohol*, unless otherwise noted, means ethyl alcohol) is produced by the fermentation of substances containing sugar by enzymes produced by the microorganism yeast. Yeast spores are present in the air. Therefore, a sugar solution left at room temperature for a few days will ferment— that is, turn into alcohol and carbon dioxide. The chemical equation for this reaction is as follows:

$$C_6H_{12}O_6 \xrightarrow{\text{Zymase}} 2C_2H_5OH + 2CO_2 + 20 \text{ kg. kcal.}$$

Glucose or Fructose → Alcohol + Carbon Dioxide + Heat

If grape juice is kept at room temperature, it will turn into wine as yeast spores settle in the juice and begin to produce their enzymes. Primitive people probably discovered this by accident, and in this sense, human use of alcohol is serendipitous. This serendipity soon resulted in planned production. The development of reliable and replicable techniques for the production of beverage alcohol is one of the earliest technological achievements of humans. Almost every known culture discovered or developed a form of alcohol production, and every substance that can be fermented has been made into a beverage. Perhaps this early development of techniques for alcohol production, with its inherent potential for both good and evil, is emblematic of the double-edged nature of all technological progress. From this point of view, ambivalence toward alcohol is a manifestation of ambivalence toward technology.

Distillation, which became popular in the fifteenth century, is a way of removing water from the fermented product, thereby increasing the concentration of alcohol. As we have noted, wine is fermented grape juice. Beer is fermented malt to which hops have been added as a flavoring. Brandy is the distillate of fermented grapes; bourbon is the distillate of fermented corn; rye whiskey, the distillate of fermented rye; vodka, of fermented potatoes; and sake, of fermented rice. The concentration of alcohol in distilled products is measured in *proof*. A proof is half a percent by volume. Hence, pure, or "absolute" alcohol is 200 proof. The alcohol content of beer and wine is generally reported as percent of alcohol by volume.

The fermentation process results not only in alcohol, but in a variety of by-products. These are collectively known as *congeners*. They are present in very small amounts and do not play a major role in the effect produced by alcoholic beverages. Beverage alcohol contains ethyl alcohol, other alcohols, water, congeners, and sometimes flavorings, colorings, and carbon dioxide.

INGESTION AND ABSORPTION OF ALCOHOL

Alcohol usually goes from the bottle into the glass, although "serious" drinkers may omit this step. Alcohol thence goes into the mouth; part of the enjoyment drinkers derive from drinking comes from the gustatory and olfactory sensations that accompany the passage of alcohol past the lips and through the mouth. When alcohol is swallowed, it passes through the pharynx, descends the esophagus, and enters the stomach. It is important to note that alcohol is an irritant to the tissues with which it comes in contact. This may also be true of the congeners. It is not surprising, therefore, that prolonged, heavy, particularly abusive consumption of alcohol is associated with an increased risk of disease in those tissues. It is believed that such prolonged, heavy drinking may be an etiological factor in diseases of the lips, mouth, pharynx, esophagus, and stomach.

Alcohol requires no digestion. It is absorbed into the body and exerts it influence without changing. This, along with its small molecular size, makes alcohol readily and rapidly absorbable. The actual rate of absorption depends on the concentration of alcohol in the stomach and in the bloodstream, and on the stomach contents. Alcohol consumed when the stomach is empty "hits" the drinker much harder than alcohol taken after eating. Approximately 20 percent of the alcohol consumed is absorbed in the stomach, with the remaining 80 percent being absorbed in the small intestine. Very little alcohol descends further into the digestive tract.

Alcohol then rapidly enters the bloodstream and is transported to and affects every cell in the body. Alcohol's small molecule and solubility render it readily transportable across cell membranes; the resulting ubiquity of its distribution is the reason that alcohol abuse produces such widespread havoc in the body. Of all the actions of alcohol on cells and tissues, its effect on the nervous system is of the greatest importance. Alcohol's effect on the nervous system produces both the objective, observable behavioral changes that follow its consumption and the inward, subjective changes in thoughts and feelings that the user experiences. It is the action of alcohol on the nervous system that makes one "high."

ALCOHOL'S EFFECT:
WHAT PRODUCES THE HIGH?

The effect of alcohol on the nervous system, and its primary physiological effect, is the graded depression of synaptic transmission. By "graded depression" we mean that some parts of the central nervous system (CNS) are more sensitive to the effects of alcohol than are others, and their rates of synaptic transmission will thus become depressed at lower doses.

Chemically—that is, based on its molecular structure—ethanol belongs to the class of alcohols. Pharmacologically, ethanol is classified as a sedative-hypnotic, this classification being based on its effect on the nervous system. Sedative-hypnotics are central nervous system depressants. As the dosage increases, they are increasingly sedative. The sedative-hypnotics include the barbiturates—the "minor" tranquilizers, such as diazepam (Valium)—and the general anesthetics.

The sedative-hypnotics, including alcohol, initially depress the inhibitory synapses of the brain. Since the negation of a negative is a positive, the depression of the inhibitory synapses is excitatory. It is for this reason that alcohol is sometimes misclassified as a stimulant, although it is a depressant. Behaviorally, this disinhibition may manifest itself in high spirits and a devil-may-care attitude which may be subjectively experienced as euphoria. Anxiety is concomitantly reduced, especially in inhibited people. It is for this reason that the superego has been defined as that part of the psyche which is soluble in alcohol. It is these sensations, the euphoria and the carefreeness, that many drinkers are seeking. Excitatory synapses are soon also depressed, however, and the behavioral and experiential effects of the alcohol catch up with its pharmacological effect, which has been depressive all along.

Alcohol is addictive both in the sense that the drinker develops tolerance to the drug and requires more and more to get the same effect and in the sense that withdrawal symptoms are experienced after cessation of heavy and/or prolonged drinking. Alcohol also disturbs the normal sleep pattern, decreasing the amount of time spent dreaming.

METABOLISM OF ALCOHOL

Metabolism is the sum of the chemical processes and energy exchanges that take place within an organism. Metabolic processes take place in every cell and tissue of the body; however, the liver does a great deal of this metabolic work. In particular, the liver performs most "specialty" metabolic processes, such as the metabolism of drugs and hormones. Alcohol is almost entirely metabolized by the liver, where it is chemically converted into metabolites and energy. The metabolites, or break down products, are then eliminated from the body. The metabolism of alcohol is to be distinguished from its pharmacological effects. The metabolism of alcohol is a process by which it is changed and eliminated from the body; its pharmacological action is the result of the effects of the intact alcohol molecule on the functioning of the neuron.

The metabolism of alcohol by the liver takes place in several steps. These steps occur within the individual liver cells, the *hepatocytes*, which contain *nicotinamide-adenine dinucleotide* (NAD) and *alcohol dehydrogenase* (ADH). The first is a cofactor; it "reacts" with the alcohol. The second is an enzyme; it facilitates that reaction. The reaction converts the alcohol into *acetaldehyde*. When alcohol is converted into acetaldehyde, a hydrogen ion is split off and transferred to the NAD. This process takes place only in the presence of a specific enzyme which facilitates the removal of a hydrogen atom from the alcohol molecule; the enzyme is thus called *alcohol dehydrogenase*. It is found in significant quantities only in the hepatocytes. The amount of ADH, which is fixed, sets the maximum rate at which alcohol is normally metabolized. This rate is independent of the concentration of alcohol in the blood, and is approximately the volume of alcohol contained in one drink per hour.

The acetaldehyde is then converted by the enzyme aldehyde dehydrogenase into acetate. NAD once again acts as a hydrogen acceptor. The drug disulfiram, sold under the trade name Antabuse, blocks the conversion of acetaldehyde to acetate, leading to the accumulation of acetaldehyde, which is highly toxic. This property of disulfiram has led to its use in the treatment of alcoholism. The Antabuse user cannot drink alcohol without becoming acutely and severely ill. Depending on the dosage of the Antabuse, the Antabuse–alcohol reaction ranges from unpleasant to potentially lethal.

Acetate, which is the end product of the second stage of alcohol metabolism, in turn enters into a complex series of metabolic reactions known as the *Krebs cycle*. The Krebs cycle is the final common pathway for the conversion of sugars, fatty acids, and amino acids into energy. It is not unique to the metabolism of alcohol; however, it is the means by which energy is derived from alcohol. The acetate is "burned" during the Krebs cycle. Since energy is derived from it, alcohol is, in this limited sense, a food. These are "empty" calories, however; alcohol provides nothing that the body can use to build new tissue.

The conversion of NAD, which is important as a hydrogen acceptor in many metabolic processes, into NADH during alcohol metabolism significantly changes the chemical environment of the liver. There is now less NAD available for metabolism of other substances by the liver. When alcohol consumption is heavy, the ratio of NAD to NADH remains altered. These changes in chemistry impair normal biochemical activities of the liver, which may result in a variety of diseases. The metabolism of carbohydrates and fats is affected by the altered NAD to NADH ratio.

Other enzymes in the hepatocytes can facilitate the conversion of alcohol to acetaldehyde. They normally play a minor role in the metabolism of alcohol. With heavy, prolonged drinking, however, these "alternate pathways" come to play a significant role. They are overflow valves, so to speak, which are called into play when the primary valve, metabolism by ADH, is overburdened. There are two alternate pathways: metabolism of alcohol by the enzyme catalase, in which the cofactor is hydrogen peroxide; and metabolism by the microsomal ethanol oxidizing system (MEOS). Both change alcohol to acetaldehyde. The MEOS is involved in the metabolism of many drugs, as well as naturally occuring substances, including hormones. Repeated heavy drinking induces—that is, produces more of— the enzymes involved in the MEOS. (This is not true of ADH.) This induction of the MEOS means that alcohol is metabolized more rapidly by the heavy drinker, and this is one of the bases of the development of tolerance for alcohol. The other basis of tolerance is the accommodation of the neurons themselves to the alcohol. Since the MEOS also metabolizes other drugs, cross-tolerance results. Barbiturates and general anesthetics are among the drugs to which cross-tolerance develops.

Approximately 95 percent of ingested alcohol is absorbed and metabolized as just described. The end products, carbon dioxide and water, are eliminated by the lungs and kidneys. Some 5 percent of the alcohol is eliminated unmetabolized in the urine and in respired air; this exhalation of unchanged alcohol is the reason that breath mints do little to conceal alcohol consumption.

SOMATIC ILLNESSES ASSOCIATED WITH ALCOHOL ABUSE

Alcohol abuse can cause damage to any part of the body. This damage may be direct, the consequence of the ubiquitously distributed alcohol's effect on a particular cell, tissue, organ, or system; or, it may be indirect, the consequence of alcohol's profound alteration of the body's internal chemical environment. The most common sites of damage are the nervous system, the liver, and the blood. The gastrointestinal (GI) system, the heart, the muscles, and the reproductive organs may also be damaged.

Nervous System

The structure of the nervous system is extremely complex. However, for our purpose, which is to understand the effects of alcohol abuse on that system, a radically simplified description will suffice. The nervous system consists of two main divisions: the central nervous system (CNS) and the peripheral nervous system (PNS). The CNS comprises the brain and spinal cord, while the PNS consists of the nerves connecting the brain and spinal cord to the muscles, glands, and sense organs. Alcohol affects each of these parts of the nervous system. Alcohol abuse can damage all or any part of this complex system.

Functionally, the nervous system can be viewed as a mechanism for the reception, transmission, and interpretation of information from both the external and internal environments. It then originates and transmits responses to that information. Alcohol abuse can derange all of these functions. Alcohol depresses the control centers of the cerebral cortex, resulting in disinhibition; alcohol in higher doses depresses the cerebellum, producing slurred speech and staggering gait; alcohol in yet higher doses can depress the respiratory centers of the medulla, resulting in death.

Alcohol's primary pharmacological action is the depression of synaptic transmission in the CNS. The possible deleterious neurological effects of prolonged, heavy drinking are manifold. Some of these effects are the result of alcohol's addictive properties, including (1) the development of *tolerance*—requiring progressively larger doses to "get the same high"; (2) the development of psychological dependence; (3) the development of physiological dependence; and (4) withdrawal symptoms of varying severity. Other possible neurological sequelae of chronic alcoholism include diffuse damage to the brain, degeneration of specific structures within the brain, damage associated with the nutritional deficiencies so often concomitant with alcoholism, and damage to the PNS. Additionally, alcohol abuse impairs both cognitive functioning and normal sleep; these impairments may occur in the absence of gross neurological changes. The neurological sequelae of alcoholism are sometimes transient and reversible; unfortunately, they are also sometimes permanent and irreversible.

Tolerance, Dependence, and Withdrawal

The nervous system accommodates, becomes less sensitive to, the effects of alcohol. The mechanism of this accommodation is unknown, but its practical consequences may include increased alcohol consumption by drinkers as they seek to reexperience the old "high." Since, as we have noted, alcohol induces the MEOS enzymes, prolonged heavy drinking also results in the liver's metabolizing alcohol more rapidly. These effects are additive. They set up an addictive cycle in which the drinker has to drink more to get the same effect, while the increased alcohol consumption builds further neuronal tolerance and induces more MEOS enzymes. Thus, the alcoholic drinker is in a situation analogous to that of the laboratory rat who must run ever faster on a treadmill to receive the same reward. In advanced alcoholism, a point is reached at which the integrity of the nervous system is compromised and tolerance to alcohol decreases. Liver damage may also intervene at this point, lowering the rate of metabolism of alcohol. Advanced, chronic drinkers frequently report such a loss of tolerance.

Long before they become physiologically dependent on alcohol, drinkers may come to rely on alcohol to relax, to assuage anxiety, to self-medicate depression, to speak in public, to have sex, or to function comfortably in social situations. A drinker who cannot function without alcohol has become psychologically dependent on alcohol. To that extent, the drinker is "hooked." It is not uncommon to hear a patient say, without irony, "Doctor, I'm so nervous that I just can't drive my car without having a drink." Psychological dependence on alcohol may or may not progress into physiological dependence. It may be limited, as in the case of the nervous public speaker who must get a "little high" before a semiannual speaking engagement; or it may be all encompassing, as in the case of the alcoholic who can neither love, work, nor play without alcohol.

Physiological dependency is defined rather simply. If withdrawal symptoms accompany the cessation of drinking, then the drinker is physiologically dependent. Alcohol is a CNS depressant. Prolonged heavy alcohol use chronically depresses the CNS, which becomes accustomed to functioning in a depressed state. If the depressant is removed, the rebound effect causes the CNS to become hyperactive. It is as if a coiled spring were suddenly released. Withdrawal symptoms range from anxiety and tremulousness to hallucinations and convulsions. Alcohol withdrawal can be fatal. The physiologically dependent drinker must continue to drink to prevent the occurrence of withdrawal symptoms. His position is the reverse of that of the man who banged his head against the wall because it felt so good when he stopped; physiologically dependent drinkers drink because it feels so awful when they stop.

Withdrawal reactions are difficult to predict. Generally speaking, the longer the duration of the binge, and the greater the quantity of absolute alcohol consumed, the greater the risk of a serious withdrawal reaction. Although mild withdrawal symptoms may occur even after a few days of steady drinking, serious withdrawal symptoms are not common until the drinker has consumed at least a pint of whiskey (ten drinks) or its equivalent per day for at least ten days (Butz 1982). The symptoms begin several hours to several days after the last drink. They tend to peak between the second and fourth day, the third day being most commonly reported as the worst; they generally abate, at least in their acute manifestation, within a week. Three stages of withdrawal, of progressively greater severity, are generally recognized, although most withdrawals do not progress to the third stage. The first stage is characterized by tremulousness, restlessness, appetite loss, insomnia, anxiety, and intense feelings of apprehensiveness. Patients may describe themselves as ready to jump out of their skin. Pulse and respiration are rapid. Most withdrawals do not progress beyond this stage, which is extremely uncomfortable but not, in itself, dangerous. The primary danger is that the patient will drink to relieve the pain.

The second stage of withdrawal is marked by intensification of symptoms: The tremors become more severe; the patient "shakes inside"; pulse, respiration, and blood pressure continue to elevate, and the anxiety and dread intensify. During this stage the patient may suffer alcoholic hallucinosis, described by one patient as the "audiovisuals." These hallucinations do not have any prognostic significance; they are not indicative of schizophrenia or other psychoses. Patients experiencing alcoholic hallucinosis are usually oriented to time, place, and person and in relatively appropriate contact with reality. They are, however, extremely frightened. They require, and usually respond well to, reassurance. The hallucinations are a physiological phenomenon, but their content is expressive of emotional and intrapsychic conflict and, like all hallucinations, can be analyzed in the same manner as dreams. The clinician should try to understand the meaning of the hallucination for the patient. Grand mal seizures may also occur during withdrawal from alcohol. They are a rebound phenomenon and should not be misdiagnosed as epilepsy. The danger here is of self-injury during the seizure. Rarely, status epilepticus, a life-threatening condition of continuous seizures, develops.

The third, and most serious, stage of withdrawal is known as *delirium tremens*, or the DTs. During DTs, the previous symptoms worsen; the withdrawing alcoholic enters a state of abject terror. Hallucinations, often of small crawling animals or insects, become persecutory and are now tactile as well as visual and auditory; psychomotor agitation becomes intense; the pulse becomes even more rapid, blood pressure may continue to rise, and fever may develop; orientation is lost; confusion and paranoia set in; and contact with reality is lost. Even with the best care, a significant mortality rate is associated with DTs.

Detoxification is the medical treatment of alcohol withdrawal. Withdrawal is treated in a variety of ways, but almost all involve the use of sedative drugs, which are then titrated downward over several days to a week, until they are discontinued. Currently, the most popular drugs for use during detoxification are the minor tranquilizers chlordiazepoxide hydrochloride (Librium) and diazepam (Valium). These drugs can be addicting, and their use must be time limited. Treatment of vitamin, mineral, and other nutritional deficiencies is vital. Anticonvulsive medication may also be used. Close supervision, good nursing care, and emotional support are vital.

Withdrawal from alcohol can be *dangerous*. The question of how and where detoxification should be carried out is a medical decision. It should be made by a physician experienced in and knowledgeable about alcoholism and the management of withdrawal; it should *never* be made by a nonmedical therapist. Referral for medical evaluation is always appropriate for the alcoholic patient, who has been using a highly toxic substance indiscriminately. Detoxification can sometimes be carried out in an outpatient setting, with or without medication. If the patient has an intact social support system, the risks associated with outpatient detoxification are lessened. If the alcoholic is debilitated, however, or if the intoxication has been prolonged, or if there is a history of seizures or DTs, detoxification should be carried out in an inpatient setting. It is usually best to be conservative in these matters and to recommend hospitalization if there is any doubt about the safety of outpatient withdrawal. Simply put, better safe than sorry.

Wernicke's Syndrome and Korsakoff's Psychosis

Alcohol's interaction with the human nervous system is complex. The slowing of synaptic transmission, first in inhibitory and then in excitatory synapses, is responsible for both the subjective, inner experience—"the high"—and the objective, behavioral effects of drinking; further, the neurons accommodate to the presence of ethanol, possibly resulting in physiological dependence and withdrawal symptoms. Alcohol used abusively can have at least three additional deleterious effects on the nervous system: (1) damage from the toxic effects of the alcohol itself; (2) poisoning of brain cells by toxins circulating in the blood as a result of the failure of a diseased liver to metabolize them; and (3) damage to the nervous system as a result of nutritional deficits concomitant with alcoholism. Wernicke's syndrome and Korsakoff's psychosis result from such a nutritional deficiency—specifically, from a lack of vitamin B_1 or thiamine.

Wernicke's syndrome is an acute condition initially characterized by confusion, delirium, and hyperactivity. Frequently, the patient also suffers from peripheral neuropathy. Wernicke's syndrome is a nutritional deficiency disease. If caught in time, it is rapidly and dramatically reversible by the administration of thiamine. Complete recovery is often achieved. Although Wernicke's syndrome will occur whenever there is severe thiamine deficiency from any cause, its occurrence is overwhelmingly associated with advanced alcoholism.

Korsakoff's psychosis is a chronic condition which is believed to be a residual of Wernicke's syndrome. That is, Korsakoff's psychosis is the long-term result of brain damage caused by thiamine deficiency. These patients have severe short-term memory deficits, which they attempt to conceal by filling in the gaps. This *confabulation* is primarily an unconscious process, a defense against catastrophic anxiety. These patients lack insight and suffer from impaired judgment. There may be a general intellectual deterioration. Some patients with Korsakoff's psychosis fully recover with thiamine therapy and abstinence from alcohol; however, partial recovery is much more common, and some patients do not improve at all. In street parlance, Korsakoff's psychosis is called "wet brain," a term which may also refer to alcoholic dementia.

Other nutritional deficiencies, particularly of niacin, are also common. Extreme niacin deficiency causes *pellagra*, a condition characterized by skin lesions ("wine sores"), psychiatric symptoms, and brain damage. Vitamin and other nutritional deficits are so common in alcoholism that the nutritional status of all alcoholic patients, including functioning, middle-class ones, should be evaluated and appropriate remediation instituted.

Peripheral Neuropathy

Just as damage to nerve tracts in the CNS occurs as a result of the nutritional deficiencies associated with advanced alcoholism, such damage may occur in the peripheral nerves. This is also believed to be primarily the effect of thiamine deficiency. The direct toxic effects of alcohol itself also play a role in the etiology of peripheral neuropathy. Symptoms range from sensory abnormalities and gait disturbances to foot drop and paralysis. Since the distance from the feet to the spinal cord is greater than the distance from the hands to the spinal cord, symptoms in the feet and legs usually occur first. Muscle wasting may also occur. Advanced cases may involve the autonomic as well as the somatic peripheral systems.

Since alcoholic peripheral neuropathy is not uncommon, therapists treating alcoholism will encounter patients suffering from this disorder. Alcoholic polyneuropathy, as it is also known, is treated by abstinence from alcohol and massive dosages of the B vitamins. If the drinking continues, further nerve degeneration is inevitable.

Degenerative Diseases of the Brain

In addition to brain damage caused by avitaminosis associated with alcoholism—Wernicke-Korsakoff's syndrome and alcoholic pellagra—alcohol itself can damage nervous tissue. The mechanism by which alcohol damages nervous tissue is not entirely known, but several factors seem to be operative. First, alcohol may induce a form of autoimmune response in the brain. Second, alcohol causes red blood cells (RBCs) to agglutinate—clump, or sludge—and these agglutinated cells have trouble getting through the tiny blood vessels, the capillaries, of the brain. The sludged RBCs block and sometimes break the capillaries of the brain. The result is a series of microstrokes which, cumulatively, may result in considerable necrosis—death of brain tissue. Third, alcohol disrupts protein synthesis in the brain, which, if severe enough, also results in necrosis. Because CNS neurons do not regenerate, once they are lost, they are lost forever. The result is a premature senility.

When the processes just discussed result in diffuse damage to the cerbral cortex, an alcoholic chronic brain syndrome develops. This form of dementia is denoted *alcoholic dementia*, or sometimes *alcoholic deterioration*. This syndrome is marked by confusion, memory loss, and general intellectual deterioration. Personality changes, including emotional lability and paranoia, are common. There is considerable evidence that subclinical cortical shrinkage is common in alcoholic populations. Thus, the neurological requisites of recovery from alcoholism, the capacities to learn and to control impulses, may be compromised by the alcoholism itself. If the alcoholic continues to drink, the deterioration usually continues.

Other parts of the brain may also degenerate. when the damage is to the pons, the result is *central pontine myelinolysis*, a condition marked by rapid deterioration and death. When the damage is primarily to the corpus callosum, the nerve fibers connecting the right and left cerebral hemispheres, the result is *Marchiafava-Bignami disease*. When the damage is to the cerebellum, the result is cerebellar degeneration, with symptoms of unsteady gait and slurred speech. Nutritional factors may play a role in these conditions. The optic nerve and other parts of the visual system may also be affected, resulting in *alcoholic amblyopia*. This condition is characterized by blurred vision and blind spots. Once again, abstinence from alcohol and remediation of nutritional deficits is the treatment.

Effect on Learning

Alcohol interferes with the synthesis of proteins within the neurons. It is believed that messenger ribonucleic acid (mRNA), a cytoplasmic protein, plays a role in the encoding of new information. It is precisely the normal biochemical processes by which RNA is built and modified that are deranged by alcohol. The synthesis and processing of other cytoproteins are also negatively influenced by alcohol. When the alcohol abuse is mild, the derangement is of function only, and no cell destruction takes place. Nevertheless, there are cognitive deficits; learning is impaired. There is evidence that mice and other experimental animals require more trials to learn a maze following alcohol ingestion. This effect persists for an extended period of time after the mouse's last drink. Psychological testing has demonstrated that similar effects can, and frequently do, occur in human beings. These alcohol-related learning decrements have obvious practical significance in treating the active or recently sober alcoholic. It is prudent for the therapist to assume that the active alcoholic, however socially intact, is suffering from some degree of cognitive deficit. If the alcohol abuse persists and becomes severe, the intracellular derangement may progress until it affects not only function, but also structure, and the neurons die.

Sleep Disturbances

Sleep disturbances are extremely common during both active drinking and alcoholism recovery. Alcoholics, both active and recovering, frequently complain of an inability to fall asleep, of restless or tormented sleep, of disturbing or anxiety-filled dreams, and less frequently of early-morning awakening. Although psychological factors undoubtedly play a role in these disturbances, we know that the pharmacological effect of the alcohol is also a powerful determinant of these abnormalities.

Alcohol disturbs the normal sleep cycle. It reduces the amount of both slow-wave and rapid eye movement (REM) sleep. When a person is deprived of slow-wave and/or REM sleep, there is a rebound effect on the subsequent nights and the sleeper tries to make up the lost slow-wave and REM sleep. This happens when alcohol abuse ceases. At first REM rebound predominates, and the newly sober alcoholic complains of restless, tormented sleep. Complaints of insomnia and frequent awakening during the night are also common. There is evidence that the neurotransmitter serotonin is used by a part of the brain stem called the *raphe nuclei* to induce and maintain sleep. Alcohol is known to profoundly alter the metabolism of serotonin. Additionally, the metabolism of other neurotransmitters in the biogenic amine family, which are believed to mediate REM sleep, are also affected by alcohol. The practical meaning of all this is that there is a physiological basis for the wide-ranging sleep disturbances of alcoholism. Of equal importance is the fact that these abnormalities continue long into sobriety.

Subacute Alcohol Withdrawal Syndrome

Subacute alcohol withdrawal syndrome, also known as attenuated, or prolonged, withdrawal syndrome, is characterized by the cognitive deficits, sleep disturbances, and concomitant emotional dysphoria which occur during at least the first year of sobriety. It might be viewed as a "shake-down period," during which the nervous system is reestablishing its health. The emotional dysphoria which sometimes accompanies this healing process can serve as a "drink signal." If this signal is acted upon, the recovery is aborted and the alcoholism resumes. The duration and severity of the subacute alcohol withdrawal syndrome varies widely; generally, though, the heavier and more prolonged the drinking, the greater and more intense the attenuated withdrawal syndrome. Recent evidence suggests that prolonged withdrawal symptoms are far more common, disabling, and lasting than previously suspected. Psychotherapeutic interventions during the first year of sobriety must take into account this syndrome and its possible effects on the patient's feelings and behavior.

Hepatic Encephalopathy

Liver disease is a not uncommon complication of alcoholism. If the damage is severe, the liver might not be able to do its metabolic work. This results in the presence of toxins in the blood stream, which then carries them to the brain. Ammonia seems to be the main culprit. Its effects include confusion, drowsiness, and in severe cases, unresponsiveness. The patient may develop a characteristic "flapping" tremor. Treatment includes appropriate measures to remedy the underlying liver pathology and restriction of protein intake. From a psychotherapeutic viewpoint, it is important to be aware that ambulatory alcoholics with liver disease may be subject to periodic confusion from ammonia intoxification.

Trauma

Alcoholics are prone to head injury from automobile and other accidents, falls while drunk, and fights. Thus, alcoholics presenting themselves for treatment of their alcoholism may be suffering from slow intracranial bleeding resulting from their injuries. These subdural hematomas may cause fatal brain damage. The confusion and other symptoms of such injuries are often mistaken for withdrawal symptoms or the effects of intoxication.

Blackouts

Blackouts, or alcoholic amnesias, are memory losses during drinking episodes. In effect, the drinker has a temporary loss of the capacity for recent memory. Such loss can be partial ("greyouts") or total. Such "holes" in memory during drinking episodes are presumably caused by alcohol's power to disrupt protein synthesis in the neuron. Blackouts are a rather common symptom of problem drinking. "Social drinkers" have also been known to occasionally experience them. They are frequently casually dismissed by the drinker; however, they are considered by many authorities (e.g. Jellinek 1952, 1960) to be prodromal signs of alcoholism. This casual dismissal may conceal profound apprehensiveness on the part of the drinker. Blackouts can be psychologically interpreted as a failure of the synthesizing powers of the ego; experientially, they are disruptions in the experiences of the self. They are often a source of great anxiety and guilt for the drinker, who does not know what happened during the blank period. Unfortunately, such guilt and remorse may have a basis in reality, since auto accidents and serious crimes have been known to occur during blackouts.

The Liver

Alcoholic liver disease is a complex phenomenon. At one time it was believed to be a consequence of the poor nutrition associated with severe alcoholism. We now know this to be untrue: Alcohol abuse alone can cause both functional and structural derangement of the liver. Heavy drinking alters the inner environment of the hepatocyte in fundamental ways: The liver begins to use hydrogen as its fuel instead of fat, its normal fuel. This leads to a buildup of fat within the hepatocyte, resulting in the first stage of alcoholic liver disease, *alcoholic fatty liver*. This accumulation of fat is, in itself, usually asymptomatic. Sometimes there is abdominal pain or discomfort. As the liver swells, it may grow large enough to be felt by the drinker. If the drinking ceases, the liver will repair itself.

The disease process does not necessarily stop here, however. An active inflammatory process may ensue. This is alcoholic hepatitis, the second stage of alcoholic liver disease. When alcoholic liver disease progresses to the stage of alcoholic hepatitis, cell destruction occurs and the liver is, to some extent, permanently damaged. It is not clear why fatty liver is universal in chronic alcoholics, but only a minority develop alcoholic hepatitis. The symptoms of alcoholic hepatitis include liver swelling, jaundice, hepatic pain, and fever. The condition is extremely serious; if its progress is not reversed, it can be fatal.

The treatment is total abstinence from alcohol and vigorous supportive medical care.

The active inflammatory process of alcoholic hepatitis destroys a varying number of liver cells. These cells do not regenerate; on the contrary, they are replaced by fiber. This infiltration of the liver by fiber is called *alcoholic cirrhosis*, or *Laennec's cirrhosis*. During this third stage of alcoholic liver disease, the ability of the liver to perform its wide-ranging metabolic functions is compromised, and irreversible structural changes alter the architecture of the liver, which now has a hard time doing its job. As a result, the chemistry of the body may be deranged. Additionally, the fibrousness of the cirrhotic liver interferes with the flow of blood and other fluids through that organ. Thus, there is chemical change and mechanical blockage.

Treatment of alcoholic cirrhosis is total abstinence from alcohol, a modified diet, and a variety of medical and sometimes surgical interventions. If the patient continues to drink, further episodes of alcoholic hepatitis usually occur, worsening the cirrhosis. Unabated, this process is fatal. If the alcoholic stops drinking, the outcome is variable. Alcoholics, even those who are recovered, are also at increased risk for cancer of the liver.

The Digestive System

Alcohol is an irritant, and constant irritation can damage tissue. Alcohol irritates the lips, tongue, mouth, and pharynx through or over which it passes. The chronic alcoholic is at increased risk of cancer of all of these organs. The heavy smoking which so frequently accompanies alcoholism undoubtedly also plays a role in the etiology of these cancers.

The zinc deficiency sometimes associated with chronic alcoholism may lessen the taste acuity of the tongue, futher diminishing appetite and worsening an already existing malnutrition. The esophagus may be the site of hemorrhage, the result of back pressure of the blocked hepatoportal circulation secondary to cirrhosis, and it may be ruptured by violent vomiting.

Alcoholism is associated with increased risk of esophageal cancer.

Heavy consumption of alcohol can result in gastritis, a common complaint among chronic alcoholics. There is also evidence that chronic alcoholism contributes to the formation of peptic ulcers and is associated with greater risk of stomach cancer.

The damage to the small intestine caused by chronic alcohol abuse is usually functional. However, derangement of enzymatic activity and intestinal function can cause severe problems. Prolonged heavy drinking results in malabsorption of minerals, folic acid, vitamin B_{12}, fat, and other substances. This malabsorption may cause nutritional deficiencies in well-fed alcoholics. Alcohol abuse also increases the motility of the intestine, causing diarrhea.

Alcoholism can also damage the pancreas, resulting in pancreatitis, a not uncommon complication of alcoholism. Patients with acute pancreatitis are nauseated, vomiting, and in great pain. They seldom continue drinking. Acute pancreatitis usually responds to supportive medical treatment. More serious is underlying damage leading to chronic pancreatitis, a condition in which functioning tissue is replaced with fiber and the pancreas has difficulty performing its tasks. If the patient abstains from drinking, chronic pancreatitis can usually be managed medically. If the patient continues to drink, however, the prognosis is very poor.

The Blood

Alcohol abuse can derange the process by which the red blood cells (RBCs), the white blood cells (WBCs), and the platelets mature and enter the blood stream. These pathogenic processes result in anemia, diminished resistance to disease, and increased risk of hemorrhage, respectively. Anemia is the most common, and hence the most clinically important, of these alcohol-related hematological abnormalities. Alcohol-related illnesses may accelerate the destruction of RBCs, exacerbating the anemia. The treatment for alcohol-induced anemia is total abstinence from alcohol, in addition to nutritional repair, particularly supplementation of folic acid.

The body's immune system consists primarily of the WBCs, which fight bacterial infection, and antibodies, special serum proteins which defend against viral infection. Alcoholism can result in leukopenia—poverty of WBCs—which leaves the alcoholic vulnerable to infection. Given the effects of alcohol on protein synthesis, it is also likely that the antibody system is adversely affected by alcohol abuse. Chronic alcoholics are thus prime candidates for infection. A deficiency in the number of platelets in the blood is also likely to occur. This deficiency slows clotting time and increases the risk of hemorrhage. Once again, the treatment is folic acid supplementation and abstinence from alcohol.

The Heart

The heart is a muscle, on which alcohol produces a direct toxic effect. Alcohol adversely affects the internal metabolism of the heart muscle cell. The eventual result of repeated episodes of such transient toxicity may be alcoholic cardiomyopathy. In effect, the heart muscle is replaced with fat and fiber; it enlarges and becomes flabby. The result is a characteristic type of congestive heart failure. Alcoholic cardiomyopathy is slow and insidious. The prognosis depends upon the extent of damage. The treatment includes both complete, permanent abstinence from alcohol and the use of standard medical measures for the control of congestive heart failure.

Hyperlipidemia—abnormally high levels of fat in the blood secondary to the altered chemistry of the hepatocytes—increases the risk of atherosclerotic cardiovascular disease. This significantly increases the chronic alcoholic's risk of heart disease. Additionally, alcohol in sufficient quantities raises blood pressure. Therefore, alcohol abuse contributes to hypertension, or high blood pressure, which in turn increases the risk of both heart attack and stroke. Alcoholics who suffer from moderate hypertension often experience a "miraculous" return of normal blood pressure when they achieve stable sobriety.

The Skeletal Muscles

The skeletal muscles can be damaged in much the same way as cardiac muscle by chronic alcohol abuse. Acute alcoholic myopathy is a syndrome of muscle pain, tenderness, and swelling following binge drinking. The muscles of the pelvic and shoulder girdles, as well as the leg and arm muscles adjacent to these girdles, are most likely to be affected. Chronic alcoholic myopathy is a slow wasting of these muscles, without pain or tenderness. It is characterized by progressive muscle weakness. If the patient abstains from alcohol, slow recovery is the rule.

Alcohol-induced Anxiety and Depression

People often drink to alleviate depression and anxiety. This is true of the occasional "relief drinker" as well as the "problem drinker" and the alcoholic. As we have noted, alcohol is actually a pharmacological depressant: It worsens the depression. The early disinhibitory effects of alcohol are deceptive, since the initial euphoria is followed by a down. The pharmacological depression of the nervous system produces an anesthetic effect, which is experienced as cessation of pain, especially emotional pain. Therefore, the drinker experiences neither the preimbibing depression nor the pharmacological depression. Additionally, the drinking may be an aggressive act that serves to externalize anger which had been turned against the self, thereby, at least temporarily, alleviating the depression. Unfortunately, this aggression is usually followed by guilt, which deepens the depression. Thus, alcohol does not cure depression; it merely masks it. Inevitably, along with the hangover, the depression, now worsened by the depressing effects of the alcohol itself and sometimes by guilt, returns in spades. In alcoholic drinking, the drinker ultimately no longer finds cessation of pain, let alone euphoria. Nevertheless, the futile search for the old effect may continue indefinitely. The drinker may occasionally reexperience relief from depression, and learning theory indicates that this "intermittent reinforcement" is an extremely powerful maintainer of this dysfunctional drinking. In short, alcohol is a terrible antidepressant.

What about the tranquilizing, antianxiety effects of alcohol? In small quantities (up to three drinks), alcohol's depression of synaptic transmission exerts a tranquilizing effect. Subjectively, it dampens anxiety. The initial effects of low doses of alcohol—inhibition of inhibitory neural circuits—result in feelings of being carefree, exuberant, devil-may-care, and free of anxiety. Alcohol is especially effective in assuaging, or at least putting in temporary abeyance, anxiety caused by the superego—the anxiety produced by guilt over forbidden impulses and desires. Further, the anesthetic effect of alcohol results in a general reduction in anxiety. However, the subjective reports of the anxiety-reducing effects of alcohol indicate a much greater perception of reduction in anxiety than do experimental measures of the objective correlatives of anxiety (e.g., measures of galvanic skin resistance or of heart rate). In fact, some of the data indicate an increase in objective signs of anxiety. To make matters worse, the habitual drinker soon accommodates to the anxiety-reducing effects of the alcohol and requires progressively greater quantities to achieve the same relief of anxiety. Further, the anesthetizing effects of the alcohol soon wear off, leaving the drinker with the same conflicts, along with a physical and emotional hangover and concomitant guilt.

In doses exceeding three drinks, alcohol actually causes anxiety. There is nothing subjective or psychological in this process; it is a purely biochemical phenomenon. Alcohol causes the release of adrenalin-like substances, the catecholamines, which mediate sympathetic nervous system arousal—the fight-or-flight reaction. Subjectively, sympathetic arousal is experienced as anxiety. Thus the habitual drinker, who drinks to decrease anxiety, is actually drinking to reduce the anxiety caused by the alcohol already drunk to reduce anxiety. This cycle may be repeated endlessly. In this respect, heavy drinkers drink because they drink—truly a case of a dog chasing his tail, a quintessential exercise in futility. The rebound effect of the alcohol-depressed nervous system worsens the next day's anxiety.

In summary, if alcohol is a very poor antidepressant, it is an absolutely miserable tranquilizer, except in very small doses,

infrequently used. Drunk frequently and heavily, it is the an-
tithesis of a tranquilizer: It is an anxiety-*inducing* drug.

The Reproductive System

As the porter in *Macbeth* observed, alcohol "provokes the
desire but takes away the performance." According to Masters
and Johnson (1970), the most common cause of sexual dysfunction is excessive drinking. Alcohol does help some people to
overcome sexual repression, and, in low doses, alcohol undoubtedly increases sexual pleasure for many people. However, objective measures clearly demonstrate that alcohol, in more than
minimal quantities, decreases sexual performance. Measures of
penile tumescence show an inverse, nearly linear, relationship
between the quantity of alcohol ingested and the firmness of
erection. An experiment (Wilson and Lawson 1978) in which a
measuring device was inserted into the vaginas of volunteer
female college students indicated a similar inverse relationship
between quantity of alcohol ingested and vaginal pulse pressure
(a measure of sexual arousal). Both difficulties in achieving
orgasm and less satisfying orgasm are linearly related to the
quantity of alcohol ingested. Subjective reports do not necessarily agree with these findings, but the evidence is that for both
men and women, the more alcohol consumed, the more difficult
the consummation of the sexual act becomes.

In women, prolonged, excessive drinking may damage the
ovaries. Impotence is an extremely common complaint among
male alcoholics. Alcohol is directly toxic to the gonads. Liver
disease can also contribute to sexual dysfunction. Testicular
atrophy is not uncommon in chronic alcoholics. Feminization
may result from the abnormally high levels of blood estrogen
found in some male alcoholics. The feminized alcoholic has
enlarged breasts (gynecomastia), loss of body hair, and thinned,
softened skin.

Alcoholic impotence often remits spontaneously with abstinence. This is not always the case, however. The physical damage may be too great or the emotional inhibition too deep.
Sobriety sometimes results in impotence in men who were po-

tent while drinking. Alcohol-induced sexual dysfunction in both sexes is treated by total abstinence from alcohol. Psychological impotence or frigidity is treated by Masters and Johnson–type behavioral techniques and/or insight-oriented psychotherapy to resolve intrapsychic conflict.

Damage to the Fetus

Women who drink alcoholically during pregnancy risk damaging their unborn children. Ethanol readily crosses the placenta and affects the fetus. Infants have been born with alcohol on their breath. Since rapidly dividing cells are especially vulnerable to the toxic effects of alcohol, it is not surprising that heavy alcohol consumption by the mother can damage the fetus. The result is *fetal alcohol syndrome*. These babies are born small, often with various facial abnormalities and with varying degrees of brain damage. Sometimes the heart is also abnormal. These children have a variety of emotional and learning problems. Even with the best remediation and social rehabilitation, they remain gravely damaged. It is not known why some children of alcoholic mothers are born normal while others are affected, but is is known that the risk is related to dose. The greater the maternal alcohol consumption, the greater the risk of fetal alcohol syndrome.

There is also evidence, both in humans and in experimental animals, that moderate (the equivalent of two drinks a day) alcohol ingestion decreases the average size of the neonate. Although there is no reason to believe that an occasional glass of wine or beer will damage the fetus, it is wisest to abstain from alcohol during pregnancy. Heavy drinking doubtlessly exposes the fetus to great risk. Evidence in both humans and experimental animals indicates that the children born of recovering alcoholics are *not* at increased risk of abnormality.

CHAPTER 3

What Is Alcoholism?

THE DISEASE CONCEPT OF ALCOHOLISM

One reasonable conclusion that can be drawn from a perusal of the alcoholism literature is that nobody knows what alcoholism is. An equally reasonable conclusion is that everybody knows what alcoholism is, but they just don't agree. It is as if alcoholism were the elephant and the researchers the blind men in the parable. Depending on where they make contact with the beast, the researchers define it as trunk-like or ear-like or tail-like, when it is really a large, thick-skinned mammal with a trunk and ears and a tail. It is almost as if the integration of the parts into a cohesive whole is just as deficient in the theoretical speculations about alcoholism as is the integration of the aspects of being into a cohesive self in the individual alcoholic.

We still argue about whether alcoholism is a form of moral turpitude, a bad habit, or a disease. Depending on their perspective, people see it as a product of the devil, of the culture, of the body, or of the mind. All of these positions have their defenders. Clearly, something more than perspective is involved here; values also enter into these definitions and interpretations of alcoholism. Definitions are partly decisions; they are prescriptive as well as descriptive.

Let us suppose that we accept the viewpoint of most contemporary writers that alcoholism is a disease. Does that solve the problem? No, not at all. As Jellinek (1960) demonstrated, the disease concept of alcoholism is neither a clear nor a unitary concept. If alcoholism is a disease, then is it a physical disease? An emotional disease? A mental disease? All three? At the advanced stage, in which the patient may have a history of DTs, cirrhosis, or brain damage, there is no question that the patient has a disease—indeed, diseases—that are physical, diseases of the body. But is this physical disease the alcoholism? It seems more reasonable to say that these diseases are the consequences of the excessive drinking and secondary to it, although they may contribute to further excessive drinking by impairing the biological equipment necessary for the inhibition of impulsive behavior.

In what sense, then, if at all, is this excessive drinking itself a disease? Is it a genetic or a metabolic affliction? Is it an emotional disorder? If there is an emotional disorder, is it a result of the excessive drinking, or its cause? Or as this question is sometimes put, is there a "prealcoholic" personality? A vast and vexed literature is devoted to answering these questions— all of it inconclusive. Similarly, the literature is extensive on the distinction between "problem drinking" and alcoholism. When does the drinker cross what AA calls "the invisible line"? Again confusion and uncertainty. The issue of definition seems inexorably linked with the question of etiology. Yet there is no reason why this should be so. We define many things whose causes we do not know with certainty. There is no reason not to do so with alcoholism.

For practical purposes, alcoholism can be defined as drinking more than is good for you over an extended period of time. This definition comprises three essential elements: (1) the drinking does serious harm of various sorts to the drinker; (2) the drinking continues despite its harmful consequences (that is, it is compulsive); and (3) the harmful drinking continues over an extended period of time. For our purpose, the essential characteristic of alcoholic drinking is its compulsiveness. The drinker continues to drink regardless of consequences to health, relationships, emotional stability, or financial well being. The problem drinker also does harm to self and others by drinking, but the damage is usually not so severe and the behavior is less chronic.

The distinction is difficult to make, but it is of some clinical importance. Problem drinkers sometimes become social drinkers; alcoholics do not. Of course, this is tautological: If you can drink without doing serious harm to yourself or your environment, then you are not alcoholic, although you might have had problems connected with your drinking; conversely, if you cannot drink without seriously harming yourself, then you are alcoholic. The key issue is the ability to drink safely—that is, without returning to compulsive drinking. Unfortunately, we have no way of knowing which problem drinkers will become social drinkers and which will become alcoholic.

Epidemiological findings as to the prevalence and distribution of alcoholism depend on the definition of alcoholism used. This is a research question, however, and not our primary concern here. The question of definition is also clinically important, but in a different way. This *is* our concern. In cutting the Gordian knot of the problem of the proper definition of alcoholism, we will make several decisions. First, the question of etiology will be held in abeyance, and our definition will be purely descriptive. Regardless of their cause or causes, certain behaviors will be defined as alcoholic and others not. Second, we will assume that any behavior as dysfunctional and self-destructive as alcoholism is a disease. For an organism to destroy itself is pathological regardless of the source of this pathology. In these prescriptive acts we are accepting the stances of both the World Health Organization (WHO) and the American Psychiatric Association (APA); both define alcoholism as a disease or behavioral disorder, and both remain agnostic as to the etiology of the disease. Elsewhere in this book, we argue that alcoholism, in its psychological aspect, is a form of self-pathology. But here we simply want to describe it in order to recognize it.

Definitions of Alcoholism

The purpose of a working clinical definition is to diagnose. Undoubtedly, there are alcoholisms, each of which comprises a different mix of biological, cultural, and psychological factors. Since the goal of primary treatment of all these alcoholisms is to help the patient stop drinking, the first step must be diagnosis of the problem, and to this end descriptive definitions are helpful. Therefore, let us look at the WHO and APA definitions.

WHO

The WHO defines alcoholism as

> a chronic behavioral disorder manifested by repeated drinking of alcoholic beverages in excess of the dietary and social uses of the community and to the extent that it interferes with the drinker's health or his social or economic functioning. . . . Alcoholics are those excessive drinkers whose dependence upon alcohol has attained such a degree that it shows a noticeable mental disturbance or an interference with their bodily and mental health, their interpersonal relations, and their smooth social and economic functioning, or who show the prodromal signs of such developments.

This is a clear and useful definition which stresses both cultural deviancy and damage to the drinker. It can be used as a rough index for diagnostic purposes.

APA

The APA has published a series of Diagnostic and Statistical Manuals of Mental Disorders (DSMs). The current one, the *DSM-III*, was published in 1980. In it is a category of "substance use disorders." These disorders are classified according to their severity as either "substance abuse" or "substance dependence." The pathological use of alcohol is treated similarly. Since the DSM-III definitions of alcohol abuse and alcohol dependence provide very clear guidelines for the diagnosis of alcoholism, they will be cited at length.

Diagnostic criteria for alcohol abuse. The essential feature of Alcohol Abuse is a pattern of pathological use of at least a month that causes impairment in social or occupational functioning.

A. *Pattern of pathological alcohol use*: Need for daily use of alcohol for adequate functioning; inability to cut down or stop drinking; repeated efforts to control or reduce excess drinking by "going on the wagon" . . . or restricting drinking to certain times of the day; binges (remaining intoxicated throughout the day for at least two days); occasional consumption of a fifth of spirits (or its equivalent); amnesiac periods for events occurring while intoxicated; continuation of drinking despite a serious physical disorder that the individual knows is exacerbated by alcohol use; drinking of non-beverage alcohol.

B. *Impairment in social or occupational functioning due to alcohol use*: e.g., violence while intoxicated, absence from work, loss of job, legal difficulties (e.g., arrest for intoxicated behavior, traffic accidents while intoxicated), arguments or difficulties with family or friends because of excessive alcohol use.

C. *Duration of disturbance* of at least one month. The essential features of *Alcohol Dependence* are either a pattern of pathological alcohol use or impairment in social or occupational functioning due to alcohol, *and* either tolerance or withdrawal. Alcohol Dependence has also been called *Alcoholism*.

These definitions are extremely useful for the clinician; they are simple, clear, and provide behavioral criteria upon which to base a diagnosis of alcoholism. According to this APA definition, alcoholism entails physiological involvement. In that way it is similar to Jellinek's category of *gamma* alcoholism, which will be discussed shortly.

CLASSIFICATIONS OF ALCOHOLISM AND ALCOHOLICS

Alcoholisms and types of alcoholics can be classified according to clusters of personality traits, presumed dynamics, or drinking behaviors. Some students of alcoholism regard these classification schemes as misguided and diversionary, as distinctions without a difference. In a sense they are right. It's all the same shit, and if you drink enough of it, you will get hooked regardless of your age, gender, psychiatric diagnosis or lack of one, personality, or cultural background. However, this "hard-nosed" traditional alcoholism-counseling orientation is unpleasantly "know nothing" and hardly scientific. For all of their limitations, the attempts at classification have been important historically, and they do shed light on our obscure topic. In addition to the vexed but important distinction between problem drinking and alcoholism, illuminating typologies have been constructed by Jellinek, Knight, Blane, and Winokur. Jellinek distinguishes among drinking patterns, Knight among personality types, Blane among dynamics, and Winokur among psychiatric diagnoses or their absence.

Jellinek's Alpha, Beta, Delta, Gamma, and Epsilon Types

The Disease Concept of Alcoholism (1960) was a groundbreaking book. In it, E. M. Jellinek made the disease concept of alcoholism scientifically respectable by taking a very careful look at each of the possible ways of understanding alcoholism as an illness. He evaluated meanings of alcoholism as a disease in light of the available empirical evidence and weighed the conceptual strength of each meaning. Two major findings emerged.

The first was the concept of alcoholism as a progressive disease, culminating in loss of control—that is, the inability to stop drinking once having begun. Jellinek derived this view of alcoholism largely from the responses to a questionnaire he submitted to a sample of AA members about their drinking histories. Few pieces of survey research have had such influence. Almost every alcohol rehabilitation program uses a large chart of Jellinek's stages of progression to teach the disease concept of alcoholism. According to this scheme, alcoholism progresses from "occasional relief drinking" to "obsessive drinking continuing in vicious cycles," having passed through such stages as "onset of blackouts," "grandiose and aggressive behavior," "family and friends avoided," and "indefinable fears." The order of progression is seen as invariant.

This concept of alcoholism as a progressive, fatal disease is canonical in AA. Subsequent research (Park 1973, Vaillant 1983) has shown that neither progression in general nor Jellinek's particular order of progression are inevitable or invariant. Jellinek's basic finding holds, however. For most problem drinkers, things do not get better; if they continue to drink, things get worse, and they get worse in pretty much the way that the respondents to Jellinek's questionnaire said that they do.

Jellinek's second major contribution is his taxonomic system. Again, it has its limitations, and drinkers sometimes move from one category to another. One might say that it has cross-sectional validity, but that its longitudinal validity is in question. That is, at any given time all alcoholics will fall into one of the categories, but any given alcoholic may move across categories with the passage of time.

Jellinek's categories are denoted *alpha, beta, gamma, delta,* and *epsilon* alcoholisms. *Alpha* alcoholism is characterized by the presence of symptoms such as hangovers or blackouts and by psychological, but not physical, dependence. The alpha alcoholic is the person who needs alcohol on a regular basis and who becomes anxious if alcohol is not available. However, these alcoholics will not experience withdrawal symptoms upon cessation of drinking. Alpha alcoholism is not necessarily progressive. In fact, in Jellinek's formulation it is not, and indeed some drinkers remain psychologically dependent on alcohol for a lifetime without physically or mentally deteriorating or becoming physically dependent. We now know, however, that some alphas do deteriorate and wind up in other categories, usually gamma. Jellinek did not consider alpha alcoholism a "true disease."

Beta alcoholism is characterized by physical symptoms such as ulcers or liver disease, but not by physical dependence. Typical beta alcoholics are heavy, often beer, drinkers, who continue to function socially and economically in a fairly adequate way as they continue to self-inflict somatic injury. The beta alcoholic's drinking remains stable in terms of quantity consumed and the relative absence of psychological and social symptomatology. Although beta alcoholism is not a progressive disease, it too is a form of pathological drinking. There is something manifestly crazy about continuing to inflict bodily damage on oneself in this way. Again, Jellinek did not consider beta alcoholism a true disease, and he thought that betas remained betas; we now know that some betas move into other forms of alcoholism, chiefly gamma.

According to Jellinek, *gamma* alcoholism is the form of alcoholism most prevalent in this country. Almost all members of AA are thought to be gamma alcoholics. Gamma alcoholics are both symptomatic and physically dependent (at least in the late stages). They suffer emotional and psychological impairment; their social and economic functioning is compromised; and they develop tolerance to alcohol and experience withdrawal symptoms if they stop drinking. Clearly, they are sick people, and Jellinek considered gamma alcoholism a true disease. Gamma alcoholics include but are not limited to the chronic alcoholics seen in alcoholism clinics and detoxification facilities. It was from his study of the drinking histories of AA members derived from his questionnaire in the AA publication the *Grapevine* that Jellinek developed and described the category of gamma alcoholism as a chronic, progressive disease. He asserted that gamma alcoholism was characterized by "loss of control." That is, once the gamma alcoholic picks up a drink, there is no way of knowing when or how the drinking will stop. "Loss of control" refers to this unpredictability; it does not necessarily imply that gamma alcoholics will always get in trouble if they take a drink. Nevertheless, this unpredictability means that the gamma alcoholic cannot drink safely. This is clinically important. The therapist must often point out to patients that they don't know what will happen if they drink again, and the fact that nothing bad happened the last time they drank does not change this. As AA puts it, "It's the first drink that gets you drunk." This is true for the gamma alcoholic, as is the AA slogan, "One drink is too many, but a thousand isn't enough." The issue of loss of control is scientifically controversial, as is the disease concept. In our experience, however, it is true enough for those who are deeply into booze. They are genuine alcohol addicts. Therefore, this book takes a strong stance that abstinence, not controlled drinking, is the preferred, indeed the only rational, treatment for gamma alcoholism. The trick is to distinguish the gammas from the problem drinkers who may settle down into less dysfunctional drinking patterns. In general, the more symptomatic and the worse the history, the more likely it is that the patient is a gamma. A history of repeated withdrawal crises confirms it. In terms of the APA's DSM-III, the gamma alcoholic is suffering from "alcohol dependency."

Delta alcoholism is characterized by physical dependence, but few or no symptoms. Jellinek believes that alcoholism in heavy wine-drinking countries such as France is largely delta alcoholism. Deltas do not lose control; that is, they do not get drunk or violent or pass out, but they cannot stop drinking without experiencing withdrawal symptoms.

Jellinek's last category is *epsilon* alcoholism. Epsilon alcoholism is binge drinking, which the old psychiatric literature called *dipsomania*. The epsilon drinker goes on binges, often for reasons not apparent to self or others, but which usually end in collapse. They then don't drink until the next binge. The interval between binges may be weeks or months or years. It may remain constant; it may vary widely; or it may systematically decrease. In the latter case, the epsilon drinker eventually becomes a gamma. The epsilon alcoholic is also known as a "periodic."

Jellinek's categories are useful. However, it is the experience of many clinicians that a number of alpha, beta, and epsilon drinkers become gamma alcoholics. Of course, not all do. In each case, the alcohol is doing serious harm to mind or body. Therefore, at least temporary abstinence must be the treatment goal. For the gamma alcoholic, permanent abstinence is the treatment goal.

Knight's Essential and Reactive Alcoholics

Jellinek was a biostatistician and epidemiologist who became an alcohologist. Not surprisingly, he came up with a typology based on drinking behavior. Robert Knight was a psychoanalyst whose research interests were in borderline personality structure, which he was one of the first to describe, and in alcoholism. His classification system is essentially developmental; that is, he classifies alcoholism according to the developmental level of the alcoholic. His dichotomous scheme is based on many years of work with institutionalized alcoholics at the Menninger Clinic. By definition, the cases he saw were severe. Within this severity, Knight (1937, 1938) distinguished between "essential alcoholics" and "reactive alcoholics."

The essential alcoholics were the patients who never really established themselves in life. They had trouble from adolescence onward. They were often financially and emotionally dependent on their families; they had spotty educational and work histories, with very little evidence of accomplishment or achievement. Their object relations were at the need-gratifying level; they had failed to complete the normal developmental task of separation-individuation. Knight described them in more traditional psychoanalytic terms as oral characters, who had not reached the "mastery of the object" characteristic of the anal stage of psychosexual development. These essential alcoholics were unable to drink alcohol normally from the beginning. Fixation at and intense conflict around separation-individuation is characteristic of borderline personalities, so called because their level of psychopathology is between neurosis and psychosis. They are severely ill, but not overtly psychotic. The essential alcoholics were those who had a borderline character structure, and Knight believed that it was impossible for them to ever drink safely. Therefore, their treatment goal was permanent, complete abstinence from alcohol.

The reactive alcoholics, on the other hand, were those who had managed some life successes. They had achieved economic independence and often had considerable education and vocational attainments behind them. They had generally succeeded in marrying and establishing families. The quality of their object relations had once been fairly adequate, even if now gravely impaired by their drinking. Most of them had a period of "social drinking" before crossing that "invisible line" into alcoholism. Knight saw their addiction as a reaction to life stresses or to losses. From our perspective, Knight's reactives look for the most part like narcissistic personality disorders. Knight thought that some of these people could return to normal or controlled drinking once their psychological conflicts had been resolved or ameliorated. Experience often proves otherwise.

Knight (1938) pioneered the psychoanalytic treatment of alcoholism. It is important to note that he did so within a controlled environment in which patients could not drink. Knight's distinction is essentially between those severely addicted alcoholics who are afflicted with a borderline personality structure and those who suffer from narcissistic pathology. Essential alcoholics' massive developmental arrests render them extremely difficult to treat. They make up the population of many chronic alcoholic wards. Reactive alcoholics are much more functional, but they too suffer from grave psychopathology, albeit of a different type. Later in this book, it will be argued that they are fixated at, or have regressed to, the stage of the archaic self. Much of this book is devoted to the treatment of these reactive alcoholics. Knight's insights into the dynamics of alcoholism will be discussed in the summary of psychoanalytic theories of alcoholism later in this chapter.

Blane's Dependent, Counterdependent, and Dependent-Counterdependent Alcoholics

H. Blane (1968) developed a system of classifying alcoholics based on clinical experience. His system uses a differential distinct from Knight's. He is a subscriber to the dependency-conflict theory of the dynamics of male alcoholism and he divides the (male) alcoholic population according to the way in which they handle their dependency needs. In Blane's view, no alcoholic meets dependency needs in a healthy way. In *The Personality of the Alcoholic: The Guise of Dependency* (1968) Blane divides alcoholics into dependent, counterdependent, and dependent-counterdependent types.

The dependent alcoholics are openly dependent on others for financial and other forms of support. Theirs is not a healthy adult interdependence. Blane's dependent alcoholics are very similar to Knight's essential alcoholics. Blane believed their prognosis to be poor. The counterdependents handle their dependency needs by denial and reaction formation. They are the "two-fisted drinkers" who "don't need anybody." They are the people who are prone to break up the bar and give similar evidence of their "independence." Some of them are overtly sociopathic, and Blane believed that their prognosis was also poor. This is no doubt true among the more sociopathic of this group; however, some counterdependents can be successfully treated psychotherapeutically by a tactful and empathic understanding of the fear underlying their defiant defense. The trick is to find a face-saving way of keeping them in treatment. The third group, the dependent-counterdependents, are those alcoholics for whom the conflict around dependency is active and intense. They are in the most pain and therefore the most amenable to treatment. There is no question that dependency conflicts are played out in alcoholic behavior, and Blane's typology is of considerable clinical utility. The alcoholism therapist will certainly be called upon to treat dependent, counterdependent, and dependent-counterdependent patients, and it is sometimes useful to think of them in these terms.

Winokur's Primary, Sociopathic, and Depressive Alcoholics

Winokur and colleagues (1970, 1971) distinguished between primary alcoholism and secondary alcoholism. Actually, Winokur's typology is trichotomous: primary alcoholism, depressive alcoholism, and sociopathic alcoholism. However, both depressive alcoholism and sociopathic alcoholism are secondary to something else; namely, depression and sociopathy. Primary alcoholics are those whose alcoholism is not preceded by a major psychiatric illness. Secondary alcoholics are those whose alcoholism follows a major psychiatric illness, by which Winokur generally meant a major affective disorder, most often a unipolar depression.

This is a distinction of great clinical importance. Both primary and secondary alcoholics may be seriously depressed; however, the depression associated with primary alcoholism will remit with treatment of the alcoholism by abstinence and appropriate psychotherapeutic intervention, while that associated with secondary alcoholism will not. AA participation also helps alleviate depression associated with primary alcoholism. This is not the case with patients suffering from secondary alcoholism. Their affective disorders are not a consequence of their alcoholism, which is an attempt at self-medication of depression, and treatment of the alcoholism will not cure it. On the contrary, the major affective disorder must be treated psychopharmacologically as well as psychotherapeutically. Secondary alcoholism is more common in women.

Winokur also drew attention to another important differential—that between primary alcoholism and alcoholism secondary to sociopathy. Primary alcoholics, while they are active drinkers, may display some sociopathic behavior, but they are not sociopaths; sociopaths, on the other hand, are often heavy drinkers without necessarily being alcoholic. Winokur's alcoholism secondary to sociopathy overlaps with Blane's counterdependent alcoholism. Both are generally found in men, and both are extremely difficult to treat.

Summary

Alcoholism in itself is not a personality disorder, nor is it a manifestation of another psychiatric condition. Rather, it is a primary disorder, characterized by drinking to a point at which the drinker and the environment are seriously damaged. It is a disease insofar as it is compulsive and not under the control of the drinker. Alcoholisms can be classified in many ways, and the classifications we have reviewed have great clinical utility; however, alcohol abuse is the overriding characteristic common to each and all of these categories. Personality disorders are certainly associated with alcoholism, but they are not themselves the alcoholism, however much the alcoholism may be a futile attempt to treat the personality disturbance. The alcoholism, the drinking itself, must be addressed before the patient can improve.

WHAT DO WE KNOW ABOUT ALCOHOLISM?

The best answer to the above question is, Not much. In terms of solid, empirically verified, replicated data, surprisingly little is known about alcoholism. Aside from physiological and some rather uncertain demographic findings, we possess very few hard facts. There are some studies that purport to demonstrate a genetic component of, a predisposition to, alcoholism; there are a handful of replicated empirical psychological findings; there are less than half a dozen longitudinal studies; and there is a limited body of fact about special populations suffering from alcoholism. Let us look at what is known in each of these areas.

Evidence for a Genetic Factor in Alcoholism

Family studies (Amark 1951, Bleuler 1955, Pitts and Winokur 1966) consistently show an increased incidence of alcoholism in relatives (parents and siblings) of alcoholics in comparison with various control groups or with the general population. Such studies show a greater risk for male relatives (fathers and brothers) than for female relatives (mothers and sisters) and a higher risk for both male and female relatives than for control groups. These findings do not throw any light on how the alcoholism is transmitted—whether by culture, by learning, or by genetic factors. However, they do establish that children of alcoholics are at risk for alcoholism.

Studies of twins have also contributed to the evidence for a genetic factor in alcoholism. These studies calculate the concordance between identical (monozygotic) and fraternal (dizygotic) twins. The *concordance rate* is the percentage of twins sharing a given trait or condition. In this case, the percentage of alcoholic twins whose twin is also alcoholic is calculated for populations of both identical and fraternal twins. These concordance rates are then compared. Identical twins are the product of the same fertilized egg, or zygote—hence monozygotic—while fraternal twins are the product of different fertilized zygotes—hence dizygotic. A higher concordance among monozygotic than dizygotic twins is therefore taken as evidence of a genetic factor in the transmission of the trait or condition under study. In the case of alcoholism, the results consistently show that identical twins of alcoholics have a significantly higher incidence of alcoholism than do fraternal twins of alcoholics. In a typical study, Kaij (1960), using only male twins, found a concordance of 53.5 percent in monozygotic twins and a concordance of 28.3 percent in dizygotic twins. These studies strongly suggest a genetic factor in at least some forms of alcoholism. Too much should not be made of this evidence, however. Environmental factors, including the fact that identical twins are more likely to be treated alike, confound such studies.

One of the most suggestive of the genetic studies was conducted by Goodwin and his associates (1973) in Denmark. They followed children of alcoholics who were adopted at or shortly after birth and raised by nonalcoholic parents. These children had a 25 percent rate of alcoholism (contrasted with a 17 percent rate for children of alcoholics raised by those alcoholics). A Swedish study (Cloninger 1983) essentially confirmed these findings. The Cloninger study found early onset, severe alcoholism to be most heritable, while late onset, less severe alcoholism seems to be more environmentally mediated. These results cannot be readily argued away, and they do indeed suggest a genetic factor in alcoholism, or at least in this particular alcoholic population.

Alcohologists have argued about what, if anything, is inherited in alcoholism, and a variety of suggestions have been made. The alcoholics in the Danish study were Winokurian primary alcoholics, and Winokur has argued that there is a genetically transmitted "depressive spectrum illness" which places women at risk for unipolar depression and men at risk for alcoholism or sociopathy. He seems to argue that a common mechanism predisposes one to these diseases, but he does not specify what it might be.

Self psychology understands these manifestations of depressive spectrum illness as consequences of failure to acquire sufficient psychic structure through internalization. Such a failure could result from constitutional or environmental factors or from a combination of both. Others (Tarter 1981, Tarter, Alterman, and Edwards 1985) have pointed to the association between childhood hyperactivity and adult alcoholism, found in the Danish study and elsewhere, as a clue to what might be transmitted. However, hyperactivity has not been consistently found in the childhoods of alcoholics.

Another approach has involved animal studies in which strains of mice have been bred who will drink alcohol, which is not a normal mouse predilection. This too suggests something genetic in drinking behavior.

No firm conclusions can be drawn from all this, but the best evidence we have, which is fragmentary and based on small samples, indicates that a predisposition to some forms of alcoholism appears to be inherited. Most probably, alcoholisms can be arranged in a continuum ranging from those in which constitutional factors play little or no etiological role to those in which constitutional factors play a vital role. From a clinical standpoint, the most important finding of these studies is the fact that children of alcoholics are at extremely high risk for alcoholism, although this is not necessarily, and certainly not exclusively, on a genetic basis. Treatment is not substantially affected by the presence or absence of constitutional factors in the etiology of a particular alcoholic's alcoholism.

EMPIRICAL PSYCHOLOGICAL FINDINGS

There are few consistent empirical psychological findings in alcoholism research. We do have a few facts that hold up across studies and across populations. Unfortunately, almost all of the studies we do have are about male alcoholism. Further, they are for the most part about the characteristics of men after they have become alcoholic; that is, insofar as they are descriptive of the "alcoholic personality," they are descriptive of the clinical alcoholic personality, not the prealcoholic personality. Given these limitations, we do know the following about alcoholics: (1) they have elevated psychopathic deviancy scores on the Minnesota Multiphasic Personality Inventory (MMPI), (2) they are field dependent on a variety of measures, (3) they have low self-esteem, (4) they have impoverished self-concepts, (5) they manifest various symptoms of ego weakness, (6) they frequently have a confused or weak sense of sexual identity, and (7) they are stimulus augmenters.

MMPI Elevated Pd

The MMPI is a 550-item self-report which is widely used in both personality assessment and personality research. Subjects respond to each item by indicating if it is true of them. Like all self-reports, it is limited by subjects' lack of self-knowledge and by their conscious and unconscious desires to "fake good" or to "fake bad." The subjects' responses to the items are reported as scores on eleven scales, including Psychopathic Deviate, Depression, Hypomania, Masculinity-Femininity, Hypochondriasis, Paranoia, and Psychasthenia (neurosis).

The most consistent and frequently replicated MMPI finding among alcoholic populations is significant elevation of the Psychopathic Deviate (Pd) scale score. This finding dates back to a 1943 study by Hewitt of an early AA group in Minneapolis. Subsequent MMPI studies of a wide variety of alcoholic populations have also reported elevated Pd.

What does this mean? A number of Pd items refer to excessive drinking, while others refer to situations likely to be associated with heavy drinking. Are the elevated Pd findings trivial then? Not necessarily. When later investigators (MacAndrew 1965, MacAndrew and Geertsma 1963) modified the Pd scale to eliminate these items, the findings of elevated Pd held. The most reasonable interpretation of the elevated Pd scores is that alcoholics tend to have a devil-may-care attitude, or at least they say that they do. This could be interpreted as a tendency toward mildly sociopathic behavior. Self psychology sees this as a manifestation of regression to, or fixation at, the stage of the archaic grandiose self in alcoholism.

Interestingly, Pd scores do not fall much with sobriety. Research (Cox 1979, Sadava 1978) has shown that it is the abnormal personality measure most resistant to change with continuing sobriety, psychotherapeutic treatment, and AA participation. Perhaps, once an operator, always an operator. Within limits, this tendency can be a strength in our society. Further, we know that at least some prealcoholics show elevated Pd on the MMPI. We know this because the University of Minnesota once required entering freshmen to take the MMPI, and Kammeier and colleagues (1973) back-checked the MMPIs of University graduates admitted to the University Hospital for treatment of alcoholism. These alcoholics had shown elevated Pd scores twenty years earlier when they were college freshmen. Thus, something extremely persistent and characteristic of (male) alcoholics is measured by this scale. It is antecedent to the alcoholism, accompanies it in its active phase, and persists with recovery. This finding may well be a manifestation of narcissistic personality disorder.

The other consistent MMPI finding in alcoholics is elevated Depression (D). Although the elevation of D is generally not as high as the elevation of Pd, it is still at abnormal levels. Unlike elevated Pd, elevated D does remit with enduring sobriety. The prealcoholic University of Minnesota students scored high on the Hypomanic, not on the D, scale as freshmen, but they had elevated scores on the D scale when admitted to the hospital for treatment of their alcoholism. It could be argued that their hypomania was both a manifestation of narcissistic pathology— that is, of split-off and unintegrated archaic grandiosity—and a defense against underlying depression caused by inner emptiness consequent upon failure to adequately internalize objects and structure. So interpreted, these data support the self-psychology view of the dynamics of alcoholism.

Field Dependence

The second important and consistent finding is that alcoholics tend to be field dependent. *Field dependence* refers to the way in which people organize their perceptive fields. The field-dependent person relies on the environment, on external cues, rather than on introceptive, internal cues in orienting himself in space. The field-independent person does the opposite.

The concept of field dependence–field independence as a relatively enduring individual difference was developed by Witkin and his associates in the 1950s. Field dependence–field independence is a cognitive style, a way of structuring the experiential world. These cognitive styles manifest in both the characteristic ways in which a person establishes spatial orientation and in the acuity of figure and ground discrimination.

Witkin and Oltman (1967) argued that field dependence was but one manifestation of a global style, whereas field independence was but one manifestation of an articulated style. The field-dependent person experiences events globally and diffusely, with the surrounding field determining the way in which those events are organized. In contrast, the field-independent person experiences events analytically, segmentally, and sequentially, with the surrounding field having little influence on the way in which those events are organized. The field-dependent person is less differentiated from the environment, at least in terms of perceptual organization. From the point of view of self psychology, the field-dependent person experiences the world as a self-object to a much greater degree than does the field-independent person. Although field dependence–independence is a dichotomous distinction, it is actually a continuous variable with field dependence at one extreme and field independence at the other. Most people fall somewhere in between.

Ever since the original 1959 study by Witkin and colleagues, alcoholic populations have consistently been found to score as field dependent. Further, field dependency persists into recovery, and sober alcoholics remain field dependent, although the degree of field dependency decreases with continuing sobriety. (We are talking here about statistical averages and not about individual alcoholics, who may be field independent.)

What does all this mean? We are not sure. Unfortunately, no longitudinal studies have measured field dependence–independence prior to the onset of alcoholism; therefore, we do not know if field dependence is a factor in the etiology of alcoholism or if it is a consequence of alcoholism, or both. We do know that field-dependent subjects have less articulated and less differentiated body concepts, as measured by the Draw-a-Person test, than do field-independent subjects (Irgens-Jensen 1971). Further, field dependence is correlated with susceptibility to social influence. Field dependents look to the social environment to determine their feelings. It is probably this trait to which AA refers when it speaks of alcoholics being "people pleasers." Witkin and Oltman (1967) believe that field dependency is correlated with interpersonal dependency; other researchers disagree. Some authorities think that field dependence in alcoholics is the result of brain damage, because people with organic brain damage are field dependent. There is no proof of this, however. It is of some interest that hyperactive children, who are postulated to be minimally brain damaged, are field dependent, and the few longitudinal studies we have suggest that alcoholics tend to be hyperactive as children. People grow more field independent as they mature and become less so as they age; it is as if life were a process of progressive differentiation which eventually reverses itself as dedifferentiation ensues. However, the field dependence of alcoholics is independent of age.

What we can conclude is that alcoholics, whether as cause or as consequence, whether through a failure to differentiate or through dedifferentiation, whether by fixation or by regression, are relatively undifferentiated from the physical and social environment, an environment they tend to experience as a self-object, and that this trait persists into sobriety. This lends credence to the theory that fixation at or regression to pathological narcissism is characteristic of full-blown alcoholism.

Impoverished Self-concept

Elevated MMPI Pd and field dependency are the most consistently replicated findings in alcoholic populations. Several others, however, surface with considerable regularity in the research literature. One of these is impoverishment of the self-concept. The self-concept is one's conscious image of oneself. It is related, but not identical, to the self-representation, an endopsychic structure which may be unconscious, preconscious, or conscious. As such, the self-concept is an empirical psychological, rather than a psychoanalytical, construct. It is usually measured by some form of self-report.

One of the most illuminating of the self-concept studies was done by Ralph Conners in 1962, using an adjective checklist. Active alcoholics checked very few adjectives as descriptive of themselves. The self-concepts of these barely sober alcoholics could be characterized as lacking extensivity and as impoverished. The adjectives that they did check were either what sociologists call primary traits—those that are functional in primary groups such as adolescent peer groups—or neurotic traits, such as "anxious" or "depressed." They did not check "secondary characteristics"—those necessary to function successfully in the impersonal organizations of the modern marketplace. The primary traits are global and diffuse, such as "nice guy" or "soft hearted." The secondary traits are specific and delimited, such as "active," "interests wide," and "logical." In other words, the alcoholics thought of themselves as having traits that would enable them to enter into relationships characterized by lack of differentiation, but not as having traits that would enable them to enter the segmental, differentiated relationships characteristic of the workplace; their self-concepts were impoverished, depressed, and diffuse. The primary relationship they sought was similar to that of the infant to the mother.

Notably, when Conners tested a group of recovering alcoholics sober for three years in AA, he found that their self-concepts were radically different from those of the active alcoholics. The recovering alcoholics checked many adjectives; their self-concepts were far more extensive than those of the active alcoholics. The neurotic traits found in the actives' checklists were not present, and secondary traits were included, but the primary traits characteristic of the active alcoholics' self-concepts also appeared in the self-concepts of the recovering alcoholics. Although this is a cross-sectional rather than a longitudinal study, it is highly suggestive of the persistence of narcissistic problems in recovering alcoholics. The present author (1981) found a similar persistence of diffuseness, operationalized in several ways, into sobriety in a sample of well-educated, middle-class alcoholics.

Impoverishment of the self-concept appears regularly in the literature on the alcoholic personality. It is unquestionably characteristic of the "clinical alcoholic personality"; whether it is true of the prealcoholic personality is not known. The constriction of self-concept in alcoholics may be the result of either a regression or a fixation. Self psychology sees the lack of extension of the self-concept as evidence of failure to adequately internalize objects and structure, resulting in an "empty self," and sees the primary traits or diffuseness as manifestations of the persistence of self–object relating. This impoverishment of the self has been replicated in many studies, but we do not have sound evidence that it is a premorbid alcoholic trait; it may well be a consequence of the alcoholism and the alcoholic life-style. It is probably both causal and consequential.

Closely related to this impoverishment of the self-concept is low self-esteem. This is also a consistent finding in a wide range of alcoholic populations. Here, self psychology would view the alcoholism as an attempt to increase self-esteem by fusion with an ideal, omnipotent self-object, the alcohol itself.

Ego Weakness

Many personality studies, including research using both objective and projective instruments, have found evidence of "ego weakness" in alcoholics. By *ego weakness* these researchers mean impulsivity, the inability to delay gratification, low affect tolerance, a propensity toward panic-level anxiety and prolonged depression, and an unclear, confused sense of identity. Again the self psychologist would view the ego weakness as resulting from a failure of internalization and fixation at or regression to the stage of the grandiose self. As AA puts it, the alcoholic oscillates between "the Great I Am and Poor Me," between reactive grandiosity and empty depression, both characteristics of pathological narcissism.

There is considerable evidence of tendencies toward confused sexual identity among alcoholics. Irgens-Jensen (1971) gave Norwegian merchant seamen the Draw-A-Person test. He found that those who were judged to be "problem drinkers" by a psychological interviewer, drew figures with many pathological features. These features can be interpreted as evidence of poorly differentiated, confused body images and of insecure gender identity. Many other studies of clinical alcoholics using interviews, objective tests, and projective techniques have also demonstrated poorly differentiated body images and confused or insecure gender identity. Once again, regression to or fixation at the stage of the grandiose self found in pathological narcissism accounts for the data. Developmentally, sexual identity is not firmly established at the stage of the grandiose self. Further, there is considerable evidence that alcoholics suffer a great deal of sexual role conflict. The problem here is not lack of gender identity, but rather conflict over "masculine" strivings in female alcoholics (see Wilsnack's 1973 Thematic Apperception Test (TAT) studies, from which she concluded that women drink to feel more "feminine") and conflict over "feminine" characteristics in male alcoholics. These conflicts are, of course, endemic in our society during this period of changing role expectations. It may be that those who suffer the most severe sex role conflicts turn to alcohol to attenuate this anxiety.

Stimulus Augmentation

The final significant finding in alcoholic populations is stimulus augmentation. The concept of stimulus augmentation-stimulus reduction was developed in 1967 by Petrie, who studied the ways in which subjects responded to the pressure of a wooden block pressed against their hands out of their sight. It was found that the perception of the size of the block and the intensity of the pressure ranged along a continuum from those who perceived the block as greatly magnified and the pressure as highly intense, who were denoted *stimulus augmenters*, to those who perceived the block as smaller and the pressure as less than it was, who were denoted *stimulus reducers*. What evidence we have shows that alcoholics are either stimulus augmenters or moderates, tending toward stimulus augmentation. Since stimulus augmentation–reduction is a relatively stable personality characteristic, this tendency may point to something either constitutional or acquired in alcoholics that leads them to experience stimuli in a particularly intense way. This would help explain their apparent lack of affect tolerance; the affects they experience may well be more intense. Similarly, their intolerance of external stress may have the same source.

From a developmental standpoint, stimulus augmentation would be seen as the consequence of a failure to internalize the functions of the mother as a stimulus barrier. In self psychology terms, there has been a traumatic failure by early self-objects (mother and other care takers experienced as part of the self) to provide adequate stage-appropriate care. The result is a failure to internalize the stimulus-containing and anxiety-modulating functions of the self-object.

ANTHROPOLOGICAL EVIDENCE

The anthropological contributions we will look at are large-scale cross-cultural studies; they are noteworthy, but they risk generalizations that are highly inferential and far removed from direct observation. Although these methodological flaws restrict our confidence in their results, the studies are of great heuristic value and offer important insights into the dynamics of alcoholism.

Horton

The earliest and best known is D. Horton's 1943 study based on data from 56 cultures. Horton tested several hypotheses relating drinking behavior, especially drunkenness, to psy-chocultural variables. His basic hypothesis was that alcohol is anxiety reducing and that the cultures with the highest levels of anxiety will display the most drunkenness. He understood anx-iety in several ways: (1) anxiety about lack of supplies, which he called subsistence anxiety, and (2) anxiety attributable to cul-tural disapproval of drunkenness, which he called counteranx-iety. According to this hypothesis, the amount of drunkenness in a culture will be directly proportional to the level of subsistence anxiety and inversely proportional to the level of counteranx-iety. The data showed that there is a direct relationship between the level of subsistence anxiety and drunkenness. There was no relationship between drunkenness and counteranxiety.

Field

P. Field (1962) reanalyzed Horton's data and came to a different conclusion. He saw a relationship, not between subsis-tence anxiety and drunkenness, but between lack of social struc-ture and drunkenness. That is, he saw that the societies with the poorest and least reliable sources of supply were the societies which had the least highly developed social structure, and he attributed the drunkenness, not to subsistence anxiety, but to weak or absent social structure and the accompanying lack of social control.

Another way of looking at this interpretation of the data from the 56 cultures would be to say that societies with the greatest amount of drunkenness were societies that suffered the greatest degree of what Durkheim (1897) called *anomie*, the absence of social norms. For self psychology, Field's interpreta-tion of the data is both interesting and suggestive. Self psychol-ogy postulates that the addict, including the alcoholic, suffers from a lack of "psychic structure." Since psychic structure must be internalized from the outside, from the environment, it would be entirely reasonable to predict that societies lacking firm social structures would be deficient in the kind of parenting that becomes internalized as psychic structure; these societies would therefore have high rates of drunkenness.

Klausner

S. Klausner (1964) looked at the relationship between sacred ritual drinking and secular ceremonial drinking. Sociologists had pointed out that observant Jews, who do a great deal of carefully controlled ritual drinking as part of religious ceremonies, have a very low rate of alcoholism. Wondering whether this relationship held for other cultures, Klausner looked at the relationship between sacred drinking and secular drinking cross-culturally. He found no relationship.

Klausner then speculated about the symbolic meaning of alcohol. He noted that alcohol symbolizes blood in many religious rites and frequently serves as a sacrificial offering. This suggested that the cultures that held blood to be most sacred would be the ones with the most successful social controls of drunkenness. The abuse of the sacred would be unacceptable to both the culture and its members. Klausner further hypothesized that cultures that regarded blood as sacred would have the strongest menstrual taboos. Therefore, the societies with the strongest menstrual taboos should have the lowest rates of drunkenness. The data supported this ingenious hypothesis. Of course, one could postulate that both the strong menstrual taboos and the low rates of drunkenness are manifestations of powerful systems of social control. This study has an important clinical implication—namely, that the clinician should be alert to the symbolic meaning(s) of alcohol for the patient. The symbolic meanings of alcohol are highly variable, the most common being milk, mother, magic fluid, source of power, blood, and semen.

Child, Bacon, and Barry

The most important of the anthropological studies was done by Child, Bacon, and Barry in 1965. They studied 138 primitive societies and demonstrated that drunkenness was positively correlated with punishment or deprivation of dependency needs, and with cultural pressures toward individual achievement. Although drunkenness is not necessarily alcoholism, this anthropological finding lends powerful support to one of the major psychodynamic theories of alcoholism, the dependency-conflict theory. Their conclusion was that societies that frustrate dependency needs while demanding independence, individual achievement, and self-reliance, and that also give social sanction to secular drinking, have high rates of drunkenness. Ours is such a society.

Self psychology interprets this study as evidence that societies that do not allow sufficient opportunity for self-object relating, that overemphasize separateness at the cost of relatedness, and that permit or encourage drinking as a culturally sanctioned method of covertly allowing such self-object relating will be the ones with the highest rates of alcoholism. Thus, Child's study can be interpreted as both supporting the traditional psychodynamic dependency-conflict theory of alcoholism and supporting the insights of self psychology into the dynamics of addiction.

McClelland

D. McClelland and his students (1972) took a different approach to the cross-cultural study of drinking behavior. He studied folktales in primitive societies to determine their psychological attitudes toward drinking. He found that "cultures which do not institutionally stress maleness are the ones that drink." McClelland reasoned that unstructured societies with low male solidarity do not provide sufficient social support for men to mediate the conflict between achievement and obedience. This is not too different from the discovery by Child and colleagues that societies that drink heavily frustrate dependency needs. However, McClelland argues that men solve their conflicts between achievement and obedience by drinking in order to feel powerful, and that this feeling of power gives the drinker the feeling or illusion that he can achieve whatever he wants without having to fear punishment for disobedience. McClelland theorized that men drink in order to feel powerful.

LONGITUDINAL STUDIES

Most of the findings just discussed, the Loper-Kammeier MMPI studies (1973) being the exception, are "post" findings—findings about the clinical alcoholic personality. In order to determine what, if anything, is characteristic of the prealcoholic personality, we need longitudinal studies, which follow a population sample from childhood through adulthood. Such longitudinal studies allow us to look back on the childhood characteristics of those who later become alcoholic. There are very few such studies. Besides the MMPI studies, there are essentially four: (1) the McCord and McCord study of Cambridge, Massachusetts, blue-collar boys; (2) Robbins's study of child guidance clinic clients; (3) Jones's Oakland Growth Study, which includes more middle-class subjects and which includes girls; and (4) Vaillant's study of Harvard graduates and Cambridge working-class men.

By and large, the longitudinal studies show that prealcoholics, those who later become alcoholic, were outwardly confident, nonconformist, rebellious, acting-out children and adolescents. Their personality profiles are similar to those of predelinquent or mildly delinquent youngsters. They tended to be restless, active, perhaps hyperactive, and, quite possibly, angry. This is true of the Loper-Kammeier psychopathically deviant, hypomanic middle-class college students, of McCord and McCord's working-class boys, of Jones's lower-middle- and middle-middle-class junior high school boys and girls, of Robbins's child guidance clinic clients, and of Vaillant's Harvard students. In short, all of these prealcoholics resembled Blane's counterdependent alcoholics and, to a lesser extent, Winokur's sociopathic alcoholics, rather than the depressed, anxious, dependent clinical alcoholics lacking in self-esteem who are found in so many studies. The picture also lends support to Tarter's (1981, 1985) retrospective studies, which found a high correlation between childhood hyperactivity and adult alcoholism.

What does this mean? Vaillant asserts that it vitiates the dependency-conflict theory of the etiology of alcoholism. The other authors disagree; they hold that the childhood profiles of their alcoholic subjects reflect a reaction formation against deep-seated dependency conflicts. Considering the open dependence and neediness of many adult alcoholics, this view seems plausible. It is well known that juvenile delinquency in both its mild and severe forms, as well as acting out in general, may be a symptom of "masked depression." It may also be an expression of and defense against underlying anxiety. Here the hyperactivity (Tarter 1981), the hypomania (Loper et al. 1973), and the psychopathic deviancy (Kammeier et al. 1973) are all seen as manifestations of a "manic defense" against massive underlying depression.

Self psychology considers that depression an "empty" depression, caused by a failure of "transmuting internalization" resulting from impoverished or disturbed early object (or self-object) relations. The manic defense may also act as a defense against overwhelming repressed rage, which finds partial expression in the acting out. Therefore, the presence of an "empty depression" does not preclude the presence of an "angry depression," which we understand as narcissistic rage turned against the self. The hyperactive, hypomanic, unrestrained, shallow life-style which these researchers found to be characteristic of the prealcoholics in their samples is pathognomonic of the narcissistic personality disorders.

McCord and McCord

W. McCord and J. McCord (1960) followed a population of white, predominately Irish Catholic, working-class boys, who were at risk for delinquency, from their childhoods into their 30s. They collected data from the boys' latency years in the 1930s through their early adulthoods in the 1950s. McCord and McCord described the childhood personalities of those who later became alcoholic as, " . . . outwardly self-confident, undisturbed by abnormal fears, indifferent toward their siblings, and disapproving of their mothers, . . . evidencing unrestrained aggression, sadism, sexual anxiety, and activity rather than passivity." The McCords' study has thus been referred to as "the little bastards" study. The McCords found that these active, aggressive children became dependent, passive, self-pitying, and grandiose after they developed alcoholism. They felt victimized by society. The McCords theorized that this childhood pattern is a reaction formation to intense unresolved dependency conflict resulting from inconsistent, erratic satisfaction of childhood dependency needs.

Vaillant (1983) holds that the McCords explain away their actual findings on the basis of a theory. The point is important because it relates to the issue of the role of emotional factors in the etiology of alcoholism. Vaillant's criticisms are not convincing. The McCords did not have an antecedent theory into which they attempted to force their data, and they did have a great deal of highly specific data on the family lives of these children which supported their interpretation. Without question, the disturbed early object (or self-object) relations which the McCords found would predispose children to the narcissistic disturbances which we believe are at least concomitant with, if not etiological to, alcoholism.

Robbins

Robbins's (1962) study was based on a population of child guidance clinic clients, many of whom were referred for antisocial behavior. Her findings on the childhood personalities of future alcoholics were very similar to those of the McCords. The boys who later became alcoholic were more active (or hyperactive), acted out more, and were more aggressive than the study's population as a whole, but were less so than those who later became sociopathic.

Jones

M. C. Jones (1968, 1971) followed Oakland, California students from junior high school into adulthood. Hers is the only longitudinal study that includes women. Her sample was small, but her findings on the boys who later became alcoholic were virtually identical to those of the McCords and Robbins. The girls who later became heavy drinkers were "expressive, attractive, . . . and buoyant"—that is, they too tended to high levels of activity. Jones's findings are especially significant because her subjects were more middle class; they were not considered to be at risk for delinquency, nor were they in trouble at the time they were initially studied.

Vaillant

The most recent and the largest longitudinal study was reported by G. E. Vaillant in his book *The Natural History of Alcoholism* (1983). Vaillant reported on two relatively large research samples. One consisted of Harvard University students who were followed from their sophomore year into their 50s; the other consisted of "core city" working-class subjects who were followed from their childhoods into their 30s. What Vaillant found was that childhood and adolescent emotional problems and overtly disturbed childhoods did not predict (correlate with) adult alcoholism in either sample, although such childhood disturbance did predict (correlate with) adult mental illness. He found that ethnicity (Irish or Northern European ancestry) and parental alcoholism did predict (correlate with) adult alcoholism. From this he argued that the clinical alcoholic personality is the result of drinking, not of premorbid personality factors. It does not seem possible that parental alcoholism could fail to result in disturbed early object relations, however well the consequences of such disturbances may be defended against.

Vaillant also argues that adult alcoholics retrospectively falsify the degree of pathology in their childhood environments in order to rationalize their drinking. Our experience is that there is rationalization aplenty, but that retrospective idealization of their childhoods is at least as characteristic of adult alcoholic patients as is retrospective devaluation or denial of whatever may have been positive in their childhoods. Vaillant's data cannot be argued away, but his interpretation of it is not persuasive.

SPECIFIC POPULATIONS

There is a growing literature on specific alcoholic populations: women, blacks, Hispanics, American Indians, ghetto dwellers, professionals, teenagers, and the elderly. Very little is actually known, however. We will survey this literature in a superficial way. The interested reader is referred to articles and books on specific populations.

Women

The largest body of literature concerns women. Alcoholism was once considered almost exclusively a male disease; we now know that this is not the case. We also know that alcoholic women are more likely to suffer from depression than are alcoholic men; that is, women are more likely to be Winokurian depressive alcoholics than are men, and they are less likely to be Winokurian sociopathic alcoholics. They are more likely to drink to alleviate intolerable feelings of worthlessness, and it appears that they suffer even more than male alcoholics from devastatingly low levels of self-esteem. H. T. Blane (1968) postulated that women drink to deal with feelings of inferiority, whereas men drink to deal with repressed dependency needs; the research data supports this.

S. C. Wilsnack (1973, 1974) theorized that women drink to alleviate sex role conflict and to feel more feminine. There is considerable research evidence (Sandmaier 1981) that female alcoholics have a higher-than-average rate of gynecological problems, but it is not clear if this increases sex role conflict or makes them feel less feminine or if it is an etiological factor in their alcoholism. We also know that women are more likely to become iatrogenically cross-addicted to the minor tranquilizers. Winokur's (1970, 1971) data on the relatively high incidence of depressive illness in alcoholic women is compelling; the other findings are more questionable. Women do have more difficulty maintaining self-esteem in our society. They may self-medicate depression with alcohol, and this self-medication may be an important factor in the etiology of female alcoholism. Certainly women are subjected to many narcissistic wounds in a sexist society, and this may contribute to narcissistic vulnerability. However, women's narcissistic problems have historically been expressed in personality disorders rather than in behavioral disorders such as alcoholism. There is some evidence that this is changing as sex roles change. What is certain is that more women are being diagnosed as alcoholic and treated for alcoholism than have been in the past. Whether this means that female alcoholism is actually more common, or simply that it is "coming out of the closet," is not clear.

Wilsnack's (1974) research using the TAT, a projective technique in which subjects are asked to make up stories in response to a picture on a stimulus card, demonstrated that women who drank heavily in a simulated social situation drank to feel more "feminine"—or at least their stories, which were assumed to be projections of their inner feelings, dealt with "feminine" material and themes. Wilsnack therefore hypothesized that problem drinking in women is correlated with sex role conflict. Perhaps, but though other studies tend to confirm her hypothesis, Wilsnack's data is too fragmentary to permit any broad conclusions.

Adolescents, Blacks, Hispanics, and the Elderly

The data (Cahalan et al. 1969, Harris 1971) on adolescent drinking indicates that problem drinking in youth is extremely common and that it is not predictive of adult alcoholism. Moderate drinking, rather than abstinence, is the usual treatment goal with this population.

The data (Harris 1971 et al.) on blacks who drink show that black males have approximately the same rate of alcoholism as white males, but that black women have substantially higher rates of alcoholism than do white women. Since black women are often forced to become breadwinners in single-parent homes, this finding is consistent with Wilsnack's hypothesis. It is at least possible that black women forced into "male" roles drink to feel more "feminine." There can be no doubt that alcoholism in the black urban poor and in demoralized populations, such as the American Indians, is connected with feelings of hopelessness and helplessness. It serves as both a passive-aggressive expression of rage and a means of anesthetizing that rage. Hispanic male alcoholics are postulated to have a unique drinking problem pattern related to machismo, but there is little research evidence for this, and the degree of truth, if any, residing in this stereotype is not known.

The most important finding about alcoholism in the elderly is that it exists. Some alcoholics in this age group are the survivors of a lifelong career of alcohol abuse, but others are newly recruited to the ranks of the alcoholic by their inability to handle object loss and the narcissistic blow inflicted by retirement. Since relatively small quantities of alcohol may seriously physically damage the elderly, it is especially important that this syndrome be recognized and treated. We once treated a retired woman librarian in her 70s who had developed late-onset alcoholism when she could not adjust to retirement. She was a classic "old maid"—prim, proper, and rather supercilious. She responded to treatment, became sober, and joined AA, where she met a hell-raising retired sailor who had been in more beds in more ports than she had books in her library. They fell in love, married, and lived happily for eight years, until he died of a heart attack. She is still sober and active in AA.

The specific-population literature tends not to be very helpful clinically. Its main contribution has been to make mental health workers aware that alcoholism is not exclusively a disease of social outcasts and middle-aged, red-nosed, Irish men. Sensitivity to culture, gender, age, environmental stress, and the effects of economic deprivation and racial discrimination on patients, alcoholic or not, is essential if a psychotherapist is to be effective and empathic. The specific-population literature deserves our gratitude for increasing our sensitivity to these issues and to the existence of alcoholism in these populations, but thus far this literature has contributed relatively little of substance to our understanding of alcoholism.

THEORIES ABOUT ALCOHOLISM

In this section we will first review psychoanalytic theories about alcoholism and then present three main theories of its etiology. After we have discussed these theories in an expository manner, we will see how they might be restated in the language of self psychology. What this book is suggesting is neither that all alcoholics suffer from narcissistic personality disorders, which is clearly contrary to fact, nor that all psychopathology is narcissistic pathology, as the more radical of the self psychologists maintain. Rather, narcissistic problems often play a decisive role in the etiology of alcoholism, and the alcoholic process inflicts deep and lasting narcissistic wounds which frequently eventuate in a regression, if a fixation did not already exist, to at least some degree of pathological narcissism. This, we maintain, is the usual final outcome of severe alcoholism, and treatment must address itself to its remediation. Helping the alcoholic find a way to maintain a reasonably constant, sufficiently high level of self-esteem and a reasonably secure self-cohesion without resort to alcohol is the key issue in treatment. It is for this reason that the previously reviewed empirical findings and the theoretical positions described next are evalutated in terms of their support for this theory and restated in the language of self psychology.

Psychoanalytic Theories

Freud

The earliest psychoanalytic insight into alcoholism, and into addiction in general, is contained in a letter from Sigmund Freud (1985) to his friend Wilhelm Fliess. Freud writes, "It has occurred to me that masturbation is the one great habit that is a 'primary addiction,' and that the other addictions, for alcohol, morphine, etc., only enter into life as a substitute and replacement for it." Thus, masturbation is the "model" addiction, upon which all later addictions are based. Substance addictions are substitutes for and reenactments of the addiction to masturbation.

In Freud's view, infantile masturbation is both compelling and guilt-inducing. It is often forbidden by parents or other care takers, and the child comes to internalize this prohibition. A struggle ensues between the wish for instinctual gratification and the internalized prohibition. The struggle not to masturbate is almost always lost; the pleasures of genital, or for that matter pregenital (oral and anal), masturbation are too great. However, the return to masturbation is accompanied by guilt and by the diminished self-esteem which accompanies the failure to carry through a resolution. Masturbation may then be used as a way of assuaging this anxiety, thus beginning a vicious cycle. This familiar sequence is indeed the pattern of much addictive behavior. From this point of view, addictions are not only displacements and reenactments of the original addiction to masturbation, but are also attempts to master, through repetition, the traumatic loss of self-esteem just described.

This theory of Freud's is very much a product of the nineteenth century, a period of obsession with masturbation and the alleged damage it caused. Masturbation may have represented an escape from social control, one which an increasingly bureaucratized and rationalized society could not tolerate. We now know that infantile masturbation plays an important role in the process of separation-individuation and that it is a vehicle through which the child establishes autonomy and confirms the cohesion of self. If this is the case, and if later addictions are symbolic reenactments of the first addiction, then addiction must serve the same purposes of reassurance of the cohesion of the self and the establishment of autonomy.

Freud returned to this theory of addiction many years later, in his essay *Dostoevsky and Parricide* (1928). In it he analyzed the great Russian novelist's compulsive (addictive) gambling. Playing on the word "play" Freud traces Dostoevsky's compulsion back to an addiction to masturbation, but he adds the insight that the addiction also serves as a means of self-punishment for the original forbidden wish. Thus, it is the *conflict* around masturbation that is reenacted in the conflict which accompanies the addictive behavior. This use of addiction for self-punishment is certainly not uncommon.

Although Freud's theory was not intended to be a basis for the interpretation, "Your drinking is nothing but jerking off," his insight has some validity. Alcohol addiction is indeed a deadend path, like masturbation as an exclusive form of sexual activity, and Freud's theory has the further merit of highlighting the narcissistic nature of addiction. In masturbation, one's love object is oneself, or one's genital, or, at best, one's fantasy of another object; similarly, in the addictions there is a regression (or fixation) to a state in which there is no human object. The addict's love object becomes the abused substance itself, which is experienced either as an extension of the self or as an omnipotent self-object into which the addict merges. In the case of the alcoholic, the apparent love object is alcohol, but the actual love object is the self.

Freud's theory highlights another aspect of the narcissistic pathology inherent in the addictions—namely, the loss of self-esteem the masturbator or addict experiences when giving in to the addiction. This loss of self-esteem in turn requires more of the addictive substance or activity to attempt to raise the lowered self-esteem, thus establishing an addictive cycle. Freud's insight into the self-punishing potential of addiction is also on target. Freud's late theory of the "repetition compulsion" also throws light on the addictions, but Freud did not mention addiction as a manifestation of repetition compulsion.

Abraham

K. Abraham, one of Freud's early students, published the first psychoanalytic paper on alcoholism, "The Psychological Relation Between Sexuality and Alcoholism" in 1908. In it he states that, "alcoholism is a nervous and sexual perversion." When he speaks of perversion, he is referring to oral regressive and homoerotic tendencies. Abraham based his theory on analyses of male alcoholics and on his observation that men become openly physically affectionate in the camaraderie of the beer hall. He inferred that heavy drinking allows the expression of forbidden homosexual wishes and postulated that alcohol addicts have especially intense conflicts around repressed homosexuality. In emphasizing the regression to orality in alcoholism,

Abraham is not only calling attention to the oral ingestion of the drink; he is pointing out the parallel between drunken stupor and the warmth and security felt by the satiated infant. It is this state of satiation that the alcoholic craves.

From the point of view of self psychology, Abraham's theory is suggestive. Freud postulated that one mechanism of male homosexuality was "narcissistic object choice," or loving someone like oneself—in fact, loving another man in the way that mother loved you, rather than loving someone like mother. Hence homosexuality is self-love once removed, and a commonality between intense homosexual feelings, repressed or otherwise, and alcoholism would not be surprising if both were expressive of narcissistic regression. Be this as it may, it is certainly the case that conflicts around repressed homosexuality are extremely common in alcoholics. Further, the oral and the narcissistic stages are developmentally close, and a theory of narcissistic regression is not far from a theory of oral regression in alcoholism.

Glover

E. Glover (1928), an English analyst, emphasizes the aggression in alcoholism. Although he does not use the term, he was the first to call attention to the "fuck you martini". Glover, from the viewpoint of classical analysis, speaks of "oral rage" and "anal sadism"; the self psychologist would understand the same phenomena as expressions of narcissistic rage and the self-punishment in alcoholism as narcissistic rage turned against the self.

Rado

S. Rado (1933) was the first to point to the similarity between alcoholism and manic-depressive psychosis, with the alcoholic cycle of elation during the "high" and depression during the hangover paralleling the manic-depressive cycle. Rado relates both the mood alterations of manic-depressive illness and the alcoholic pattern of highs and lows to the cycle of infantile hunger and satiation. He sees the key issue in the addictions as a disturbance in the regulation of self-esteem, a conclusion with which self psychology wholeheartedly agrees.

Knight

R. D. Knight (1937), whose typology of alcoholism we have already discussed, emphasizes the depressive aspects of the alcoholic personality. Frustrated orality results in repressed rage, and hence in depression. The self-psychological approach to alcoholism owes much to Knight. He was the first to highlight the borderline, deeply regressed nature of alcoholic psychopathology. Self psychology would understand the chronic depression of which he speaks as both an "empty" depression and an "angry" depression with the narcissistic rage turned against the self.

Fenichel

O. Fenichel, whose book *The Psychoanalytic Theory of the Neurosis* (1945) is almost canonical, also thought that oral dependence and frustration result in chronic depression in the alcoholic. He sees alcoholism as a maladaptive defense mechanism utilized to resolve neurotic conflict, especially conflict between dependence and the expression of anger.

It is to Fenichel that we owe the observation that "the super-ego has been defined as that part of the mind which is soluble in alcohol." Therefore, forbidden impulses can be indulged, and id-superego conflicts resolved by the use of alcohol. He was the first to explicitly refer to narcissistic regression in alcoholism. Although he is speaking from the point of view of classical analysis and emphasizes the expression of forbidden wishes rather than narcissistic pathology per se, those wishes are for narcissistic as well as instinctual gratification, and there is nothing in his formulation with which self psychology would disagree.

Menninger

K. Menninger (1938), who emphasizes the self-destructiveness of alcoholism more than do many theorists, calls alcoholism a form of "chronic suicide." It is a self-destructive aggression against the self as punishment for hostile, agressive feelings which are unacceptable to the self. Alcohol makes manageable the conflict between passive, erotic dependence on and resentment of the ambivalently experienced father. Although this is hardly a self-psychological formulation of the problem of alcoholism, self psychology would agree with Menninger's assessment of the self-destructiveness of alcoholism but would understand that self-destructiveness rather differently.

Szasz

T. Szasz (1958) views addictions as counterphobic activities. The drinker drinks to confront and master intolerable fears, including the fear of being addicted. There is a defiance of fate implicit in this counterphobic behavior. Szasz's theory is insightful, although self psychology sees this counterphobic defense as serving a different purpose. To the self psychologist, the fear is of psychic annihilation and oblivion, which represents both regressive fragmentation of the self and engulfment of the self by the symbiotic mother. The alcoholic's tenuous self-cohesion gives a certain reality to these fears. Experientially, both are death. Thus, alcoholics self-inflict death in order to master fear of death. So seen, alcoholics are mythic heroes who descend to the underworld and emerge intact—at least that is their hope. The alcoholic's defensive grandiosity is fed by participation in this unconscious drama.

Recent Psychoanalytic Formulations

More recent psychoanalytic theorists, including Wurmser (1978), Kernberg (1975), Khantzian (1981), and Hartocollis (1968), have emphasized impairments in ego functioning, lack of affect tolerance and affect regression, and the use of primitive (borderline) defense mechanisms, including splitting and denial. Self psychology sees the same things, but explains them differently, in terms of deficits in the self resulting from failures of internalization. Thus, the major psychoanalytic theories of alcoholism are surprisingly consistent with the point of view of self psychology: that alcoholism is a regression to or fixation at pathological narcissism.

JUNG AND THE FOUNDING OF AA

Jung, who broke with Freud and is not usually considered an analyst, had an important, albeit indirect, role in the founding of AA and a strong influence on one of its founders, Bill Wilson. It seems highly improbable that a Swiss psychiatrist whose writings are often obscure should have influenced an American self-help organization. He did, however, and it is an interesting story, which has become part of the AA mythology.

Jung had treated a patient known in the AA literature as Roland H. He was a successful American businessman who had come to Jung for treatment of his alcoholism. He had undergone a seemingly successful Jungian analysis with the master himself and had left Zurich certain that he was cured. He felt that he had such deep self-understanding that he would never again have trouble with booze. In a short time he returned to Jung, drunk and in despair. Jung told him that there was no hope. Roland H. asked if there was none at all, and Jung replied that only a major personality reorganization driven by a powerful emotion—in essence, a "conversion experience"—could save him. Roland H. left, still in deep despair, but Jung's words had touched something within him.

He did what AA would later call "hitting bottom" and in his despair he reached out for help. He did indeed have a "conversion experience," joining the Oxford Group, an upper-middle-class revival movement popular in the 1920s and 30s. He became and remained sober. The Oxford movement espoused a set of "spiritual steps" which their members followed. These steps became the basis of AA's Twelve Steps. Roland H. spread the good word to his friend and fellow drunk Ebby Thacker, who also became sober. Ebby in turn went to visit his drinking buddy, Bill Wilson, who was drunk. Ebby told Bill the story of his meeting Roland and joining the Oxford movement. Bill Wilson entered a hospital to dry out, where he experienced some sort of "peak" or mystical experience. When he left the hospital, he too joined the Oxford movement, and remained sober.

Bill gradually pulled away from the Oxford movement, although he borrowed a great deal from it. He began to work with drunks on his own. Shortly thereafter, he joined with another drunk, Bob Smith, whom he had helped to become sober, and AA was born. Ebby Thacker didn't make it; he died in Rockland State Hospital of alcoholism. Many years later, Bill Wilson wrote to Jung telling him the story, and Jung replied that Roland's

> craving for alcohol was the equivalent on a low level of the spiritual thirst of our being for wholeness, expressed in medieval language: the union with God . . . You see, "alcohol" in Latin is "spiritus" and you use the same word for the highest religious experience as well as for the most depraving poison. The helpful formula therefore is: *spiritus contra spiritum.*

In the language of self psychology, the cure lies in the merger with an omnipotent self-object. This strongly suggests that narcissistic pathology is at the root of alcoholism.

Major Theories of Alcoholism

In this section we will outline three major theories of the dynamics of alcoholism: the dependency-conflict theory, the need-for-power theory, and the epistemological-error theory. The first is the prevailing psychoanalytic theory which runs like a thread through the work of most of the analytic writers just discussed; the second is the creation of a social-psychologically oriented personality theorist; and the third, a cybernetic theory in which alcoholism is seen as a disturbance in information flow. It is our contention that all three of these major theories can be subsumed under the theory that narcissistic regression/fixation is the salient psychological characteristic of alcoholism. The way in which it can do so will be explained in Chapter 6.

There is another major theory of the etiology of alcoholism that is not considered in any detail in this book. This is the learning theory—the contention that alcoholism is learned and, like any behavior, can be accounted for by an examination of the contingencies of reinforcement that accompany that behavior.

Learning theory and its variations deal with these contingencies of reinforcement, pointing out that the reduction of anxiety and other dysphoric feelings upon the ingestion of alcohol is reinforcing, while the negative consequences of excessive alcohol ingestion are not immediately punishing, so that the ill effects of drinking are only weakly associated with taking the drink. Self psychology does not disagree with these formulations and certainly concurs with the idea that such learning takes place and that the therapist should be aware of it. This theory does not explain all aspects of the etiology of alcoholism, however, and self psychology does not base much of its therapeutic strategy upon it.

The Dependency-Conflict Theory

The dependency-conflict theory of alcoholism states that alcoholics are people who have not succeeded in establishing, or at least in maintaining, healthy patterns of interdependence. This much is certainly true. However, this theory further states that their failure to establish such forms of adult mutuality is the principal etiological factor in their alcoholism. This is more controversial.

In its naive form, the theory states that alcoholics are socially, psychologically, and often economically dependent. Holders of this form of the theory cite the openly dependent behavior of many alcoholics, oblivious to the many alcoholics who are *not* openly dependent. They also run afoul of the dilemma that the open dependence of some alcoholics may as easily be a consequence as a cause of their disease.

The more sophisticated form of the theory states that alcoholics are people who suffer particularly acute conflict over how to meet their dependency needs and who have turned to alcohol in an attempt to resolve this largely or entirely unconscious conflict. Subscribers to this theory believe that these dependency needs, and the necessity of meeting them in psychologically and socially acceptable ways, is inherent in the human condition. It is not dependency in itself that is pathological, but rather certain ways of being dependent. They are correct. As we have seen, this more sophisticated form of the theory has been held by many students of alcoholism, including Blane, Knight, Menninger, Child, Bacon, and the McCords. The more psychodynamic of these theorists turn the screw a bit by pointing out that the conflict is exacerbated by the fact that alcoholics are often enraged at those upon whom they are dependent.

The dependency-conflict theory of the etiology of alcoholism is largely based on the observation that alcohol provides a socially acceptable way of meeting dependency needs, of being dependent, without appearing to do so. It builds on this observation to conclude that people who cannot openly acknowledge their dependency needs, who supress or repress them, are particularly prone to meeting those needs in a veiled manner through the consumption of alcohol. If they belong to a culture or subculture that sanctions heavy drinking, this is even more likely to occur. In our society, at least until recently, such a denial of the need for support and love from others was more characteristic of men. Our society also tended to be more approving, or at least less censorious, of heavy drinking, and even drunkenness, in men. Therefore, the dependency-conflict theory of alcoholism is essentially a theory of male alcoholism. From the perspective of this theory alcoholism is a form of pseudo-self-sufficiency.

The empirical evidence for the dependency-conflict comes from three sources: (1) clinical evidence, (2) anthropological evidence, and (3) evidence provided by longitudinal studies. Clinical evidence is of two kinds: (1) statistical research using various objective measures, and (2) case studies. The evidence from the objective studies is mixed. Most of the psychoanalytic theorists who stress the centrality of dependency conflicts in the dynamics of alcoholism base their conclusions on in-depth case studies.

Dependency conflicts are often powerfully revealed in the analysis of alcoholics. The clinical work of Blane, Knight, and many others supports the belief that highly intense dependency conflicts are common in alcoholics. Whether or not such conflicts are etiological is less clear. The anthropological work of Barry, Child, and Bacon has already been discussed. As they interpret their data, societies that drink heavily are those that frustrate dependency needs. But can we infer from this that a similar dynamic is etiological in alcoholism in our culture? The McCords interpreted the data from their longitudinal study of alcoholism as supporting the dependency-conflict theory. Others have interpreted their data differently. The hypothesis most consistent with their data and with the evidence of hyperactive and undercontrolled behavior in prealcoholics is that alcoholism is one outcome of a reaction formation against unacceptable dependency needs. All in all, the evidence for the dependency-conflict theory of the dynamics of alcoholism is compelling enough that it cannot be ignored. Apparently, there is something about dependency, and about the conflict it engenders, that is implicated in alcoholism. It is our contention that regression to or fixation at pathological narcissism is a better way to conceptualize and to explain the phenomena that the dependency theory attempts to account for.

The Need-for-Power Theory

David McClelland (1972) originated the theory that men drink to feel powerful. He specifies that the kind of power that men seek in alcohol is personal (egoistic) power and not socialized power; that is, the power is sought for the satisfaction of purely personal needs. McClelland and his associates studied why men drink, and the psychological motives for drinking, over a period of ten years. Their studies cut across cultures and social class and ranged from examination of anthropological data to carefully controlled experimental studies.

McClelland studied under the personality theorist H. Murray, who developed the TAT, a series of pictures about which subjects are asked to tell stories about what had happened, what is happening, and what is going to happen. As is the case for all projective techniques of personality assessment, the underlying assumption of the TAT is that the subject projects aspects of self into the production. In Murray's original formulation of the TAT technique, the subjects' stories were evaluated in terms of the "needs and presses" expressed, which were assumed to be characteristic of the story teller's personality. McClelland has made extensive use of the TAT in his research.

His findings are based on an analysis of the folk tales of many cultures and on a series of experiments in which subjects were asked to tell stories to TAT cards while sober, after which they were offered drinks, and were then asked to tell a new set of stories. He found a correlation between cultures that drink heavily and cultures that tell stories with personal-power themes. His experimental evidence showed that the men who told TAT stories of personalized power while sober were the men who drank the most during the experiment, and that the consumption of alcohol increased the incidence of themes of personal power, with a concomitant decrease in themes of socialized power in both moderate and heavy drinkers. On the basis of this evidence, and the absence of dependency or oral themes in the sober stories of the heavy drinkers, and the absence of an increase in oral or oral-dependent themes with the consumption of alcohol, McClelland concluded that the dependency-conflict theory of the dynamics of alcoholism did not hold, and proposed his countertheory that men drink to feel personally powerful and that alcoholics are men with a particularly strong need to feel powerful, which they meet by drinking.

In fact, McClelland's power theory and the dependency-conflict theory may not be so far apart. After all, the need to feel powerful must come out of feelings of powerlessness, and to be powerless is necessarily to be dependent. It is of some interest that Bill Wilson, in discussing the "proper form of dependence," used the example of being dependent on electrical *power* as an example of healthy dependence. In any case, the theory of regression/fixation to pathological narcissism presented in Chapter 6 reconciles the two theories and shows that both the conflict over the wish to be orally dependent and the abnormal need for personal power are manifestations of a narcissistic disturbance.

The Epistemological-Error Theory

G. Bateson, an anthropologist, has advanced a theory of alcoholism. Bateson, who has written on schizophrenia and on alcoholism, sees mental illness as disturbed communication. In Bateson's view, this disturbance in communication is both a cause of mental illness and the essential quality of the illness itself.

Communication is the exchange of information. Bateson has been influenced by cybernetics—scientific information theory. His principal work on mental illness is *Communication: The Social Matrix of Psychiatry* (1951). Bateson is also the principal author of the double-bind theory of the etiology of schizophrenia. Because he has drawn so heavily on information theory in his studies of psychopathological conditions, it is not surprising that his essay on alcoholism is titled "The Cybernetics of 'Self': A Theory of Alcoholism" (1971).

Bateson asserts that the self as it is usually construed—is "reified," experienced as a thing rather than as a process, and set in opposition to a disjunctive world. He considers this an illusion or, as he would prefer to put it, an epistemological error. There is no substantial self apart from its world; rather, the self is interrelational, the pattern of its communications with its world. Bateson believes that Western culture makes this kind of cognitive, or epistemological, error in its understanding of self, world, and their interrelationship, and that the alcoholic is caught in a particularly intense form of this error. Bateson is interested in the unreflective assumptions, sometimes conscious but generally unconscious, that people use to "construe" a world. These largely unconscious assumptions are a cognitive structure that we impose on experience in our efforts to organize and make sense of that experience. They are our unspoken ontologies and epistemologies—that is, our understandings of and assumptions about the nature of reality and of how we know that reality. There is a dialectical relationship between our assumptions about the nature of reality and how we come to know that reality, and how we will experience that reality.

Cognitive structures tend to be self-validating; they distort the data that filter through them. Bateson is here echoing the philosopher Immanuel Kant (1781) who taught that we are not passive recipients of sensory data and information about the world; on the contrary, we are active organizers of that sensory data and of data from the "inner"sense. We are constitutive of our experience of both self and world. The poet Wordsworth

(1850) phrased the same point somewhat differently when he said, "The world is half perceived and half created." For Kant, the action of the human mind in constituting knowledge is invariant; it is, so to speak, prewired, and it is the same for all humans. This is not true for Bateson, who believes that one's ontology-epistemology is personally and culturally determined. Different cognitive structures, or epistemologies, result in different ways of construing the world. For Bateson, the alcoholic is suffering from cognitive error, from a false epistemology. Instead of being part of a (feedback) loop, the alcoholic gets looped. What is the nature of this epistemological error?

It is the error, first promulgated by the seventeenth-century philosopher René Descartes, that there is subject, the "Self" which knows an object or objects "out there." This view leads to a radical disjunction between self and world that does not really exist. The "real" reality is a feedback loop in which information, or, in Bateson's words, "transformations of differences," flow; and self and object are nodal points in that flow, mutually interactive and mutually interdependent. The radical disjunction of self and world predisposes one with this epistemology to "objectify"—that is, treat as objects—both the world and the people in it. This results in an attempt to control totally the world and the objects in it, as if the destruction of the objects would have no effect on the destroyer since they have nothing to do with him. This leads to a kind of sadomasochistic relationship to the world and pseudo-self-sufficiency. Shades of pathological narcissism! From a radically different theoretical base, Bateson has arrived at a description of the alcoholic attempting to exercise omnipotent control over the environment, as pseudoindependent, as incapable of true mutuality or interdependence.

Here we have a paradox: The apparent disjunction of self and world actually leads to experiencing the world as an extension of the self, over which the individual is attempting to impose sadistic control. Precisely because there are no true independent objects out there—no independent centers of initiative—the individual treats the world and those in it as self-objects, as parts of the grandiose self. An interactional, information-flow model of reality simultaneously connects knower and known, and makes the known a center of independent, or better interdependent, initiative, and does not lend itself to efforts at omnipotent control. It contains less epistemological error.

The sober alcoholic does not construe the world in this way. Alcohol offers a corrective to epistemological error; alcohol breaks down the barriers between self and world—here experienced as an object to be exploited—and reestablishes the alcoholic's interconnection with and interdependence on those objects. In other words, alcohol dedifferentiates self and object representations. If such differentiations are too rigid, if the ego boundaries are too impermeable, then the alcohol will be corrective. In Bateson's view, no matter how regressive the psychological consequences of this pharmacological process are, they result in a world picture that is, in some sense, more "true" or more correct, in that it allows the alcoholic to experience the self as a part of, rather than apart from, the world. Alcoholism is then an attempt to correct an epistemological error. Unfortunately, the pharmacological qualities of alcohol are such that the attempt is ultimately futile.

If the alcoholic's sobriety is in some way "wrong," as Bateson believes, then the usual advice to "use will power" to remain sober is disastrous. There is no way for the alcoholic to remain sober without changing the epistemology of the sober state. The battle between the alcoholic's "will," another reification of the self, and the bottle sets up what Bateson calls a "symmetrical" relationship—that is, one that is basically competitive—when what the alcoholic needs is a "complementary" relationship, which would give a feeling of being in relationship with rather than in opposition to. The genius of AA is that it offers precisely such a complementary relationship: The alcoholic is related to a power, the "higher power" of AA, in a mutually sustaining (complementary), rather than symmetrical (competitive), way. In terms of self psychology, the alcoholic has moved from a *mirror transference* (the need for omnipotent control and domination) relationship with the world to an *idealizing transference* (a participation in the power of an omnipotent object) relationship with the world (see Chapter 6).

If Bateson is correct, then alcoholism is an attempt to correct pathological narcissism, not by working through the need for self-objects, which would compound epistemological error, but by pharmacologically dedifferentiating overly rigid ego boundaries. The cure lies in finding a healthy way of meeting the need for self-object relationships. Bateson believes that AA participation is one way of meeting those needs.

CHAPTER 4

Counseling the Active Alcoholic

Active alcoholism is not easily arrested. It has a dynamic of its own that operates independently of the personality, the psychopathology, the social milieu, and the culture of the drinker. It is a primary disorder that must be dealt with before any psychopathology antecedent to or consequent upon the alcoholism can be remediated. The sheer pharmacological impact of continuing alcohol consumption will vitiate most or all of the psychological work that takes place between the therapist and the patient. Yet the patient has been unable to stop drinking without such psychological intervention. No wonder working with active alcoholics is such a notoriously frustrating pursuit. Further, the social, interpersonal, and psychological consequences of continued abusive drinking are so devastating that a downward spiral of alcohol abuse, damage resulting from that alcohol abuse, and more alcohol abuse to make the pain tolerable is almost ensured. To further complicate matters, it is impossible to effectively treat any somatic pathology secondary to the alcoholism without halting the addictive process.

What all this means is that, for all practical purposes, alcoholism cannot be regarded as a symptom of anything else during its active phase. Later insight into the dynamics of their addictions becomes therapeutic for alcoholics, but, as AA maintains, knowing the reasons for one's drinking and what, if anything, that drinking is symptomatic of is not necessary for the achievement of sobriety—and achievement of sobriety is what it's all about. This is not to say that insight is not intrinsically valuable or that it never plays a role in the achievement of sobriety. But the treatment for alcoholism is the cessation of drinking. One must put the fire out before the house can be rebuilt. What can the therapist do to facilitate the patient's attainment of sobriety?

The therapist must diagnose, confront, and educate. The diagnosis is sometimes blatantly obvious, but often, particularly in outpatient psychotherapy, it is so far from obvious that it is missed altogether. Common is the alcoholic who has been treated for everything but alcoholism. The opposite error, misevaluation of alcoholism that is secondary to some form of severe undiagnosed and untreated psychopathology, such as biological depression, is also common. Thus, diagnosis is a vital, and far from easy, task.

The definitions discussed in the previous chapter give us diagnostic criteria, but they do not make the diagnosis. It is also possible to misdiagnose occasional drunkenness as alcoholism. Some overzealous therapists see alcoholism in every sip of wine. Diametrically opposite treatment errors are also endemic in handling the confrontation stage of therapy. On one hand, some analytically oriented practitioners attempt to maintain a stance of "technical neutrality" when what is needed is an active stance that the patient cannot improve until the drinking stops. On the other hand, premature and unempathic confrontation of the addiction may drive the patient away before any progress has been made. The educational phase of the counseling is also strewn with pitfalls, ranging from the danger of being didactic at the cost of failing to help the patient deal with sobriety-threatening feelings to the danger of leaving patients in ignorance of things they need to know about their illness because the therapist is afraid of "stepping out of role" by teaching the basic facts of alcoholism.

What can therapists do to pass safely between Scylla and Charybdis not once but thrice as they steer the drinker to sobriety? Unfortunately, there are no adequate navigational charts, but we do know that before we can effectively do any of this, we must establish a strong enough bond with the drinker for relationship to replace rum in maintaining the drinker's equilibrium. The rest is experience and therapeutic tack. The liaison role is also important: Counselors and therapists refer patients for detoxification and/or inpatient rehabilitation, and help patients affiliate with self-help groups.

Let us look in more detail at the process of counseling the active alcoholic. We will do so by tracing the progress of two cases: a treatment success and a treatment failure. The first case, that of Kirk, is instructive in several ways: The diagnosis was far from obvious; insight played a major role in the client's getting sober; and the improvement in the client's emotional condition with sobriety was dramatic. The second case, that of Norman, demonstrates, regrettably, that creative and informed counseling, AA affiliation, and an excellent inpatient rehabilitation program are not always sufficient for some patients to achieve sobriety. These are the unfortunates whom we do not yet know how to treat successfully.

KIRK: A SUCCESS STORY

Kirk, a tall, articulate man in his mid-20s, entered psychotherapy because he was chronically depressed. He presented no readily discernible signs of alcoholism or of problem drinking. Although a careful history was taken and the patient answered detailed questions about his use of drugs and alcohol, nothing indicative of an alcohol problem was forthcoming.

Neither was there anything in his background to suggest a drinking problem.

He was the third son of a prominent lawyer, with whom he had an intense and stormy relationship. The father had practiced criminal law during most of his career, which included Kirk's formative years. In the first session, Kirk told the therapist that his father had 500 suits. His father loomed large in Kirk's mind. Kirk's mother first emerged as a foil to the father, with whom she fought frequently and violently. The brothers, outwardly successful professionals, were 7 and 12 years older than Kirk. They were emotionally troubled and unhappy individuals.

Kirk remembered himself as a lonely, self-conscious, overweight, socially awkward child. He had felt alienated and isolated—different and unrelated—during most of his childhood. As he put it, "The cliques were already formed when I got to kindergarten." These feelings had continued into adulthood and were still present when Kirk entered treatment. Feelings of estrangement, uniqueness, and alienation are well-nigh universally reported by alcoholics. Although the report of such feelings should alert us to the possibility of addiction, they are not confined to alcoholics, and a diagnosis cannot be made on the basis of these feelings. It is extremely doubtful that alcoholics describing such childhood feelings are engaging in retrospective falsification. Kirk felt this sense of being different with exquisite intensity. He seemed to have experienced little support or concern from his self-involved and volatile parents. Kirk's brothers had served as a buffer between Kirk and his increasingly disturbed parents. He remembered that he and his brothers would cry out "battle stations" when their father returned from work each night. Although this was supposed to be a joke, there was real fear not far beneath it. When his oldest brother left for prep school and then college, Kirk felt bereft and abandoned.

When the last brother left, the fear turned to terror as Kirk became the sole witness to his parents' openly erotic and often violent fighting. He became more and more actively involved in these quarrels.

The one bright light during Kirk's toddler and school age years was his relationship with Maggie, the family's black housekeeper. Maggie took care of Kirk's physical needs, comforted him, and gave him love. In short, she acted like a mother to him. As Kirk remembered it, he received more attention from Maggie than from both his parents combined. An island of sanity in an ocean of irrationality, she gave him the feeling that he was important to somebody.

At age 8, Kirk was sent to summer sleep-away camp, and when he returned, Maggie was gone. He never really recovered from this trauma. His longing for her was so deep that he searched for her. Several years later, he took the subway to the slum district where she lived and knocked at her door. Although they reestablished some contact which continued into Kirk's adolescence, the old feeling of closeness and security was never regained. Not long after Maggie's disappearance, Kirk's parents had transferred him out of the public school, where he finally felt reasonably comfortable, into a high-pressure private day school. Although he begged them to allow him to stay in the public school, they were adamant, and Kirk had never forgiven his parents for this decision.

After the middle brother's departure, Kirk's parents increasingly involved him in their sexualized fighting. They seemed to need an audience. He was forced to play voyeur to their exhibitionists. This was one of the sources of Kirk's feelings of being a spectator rather than a participant in life. Kirk was not always merely a spectator, however; he once tried to stab his father to protect his mother and on another occasion tried to stab himself. Although this kind of craziness is not uncommon in the childhoods of chil-

dren of alcoholics, there was nothing to suggest parental alcoholism or even problem drinking in Kirk's accounts. Later, when Kirk became sober himself, it
became crystal clear that his mother was and continued to be alcoholic. The contrast between the parents' social standing, the father's occupational attainments, and the lower-depths quality of much of their
home life did not escape the therapist, who inquired
about drug and alcohol use. Although Kirk conceded
that "Mother certainly likes a drink," he maintained
that his parents were normal social drinkers and were
not drug users, with the exception of the "occasional"
use of Valium. The counselor for the moment accepted that the parents' sadomasochistic behavior was
not drug or alcohol related.

Given the histrionic quality of so much of his
home life and his voyeuristic role in it, it was not
surprising that Kirk developed an encyclopedic
knowledge of Hollywood movies. He also learned to
shoot his own movies, making a number of high-qual-
ity films during his adolescence. His parents encouraged and lent financial support to this interest. Kirk
also developed an interest in all things related to black
culture, especially black music. He sublimated his
love for Maggie into a highly developed social conscience and sensitivity to the plight of the underdog,
with whom he identified.

Kirk had a miserable time during his preteen
years. He became fat and remained fat until he was
out of college. Food was the one thing that made him
feel safe and secure. Maggie had been a good cook. At
times Kirk was close to obesity. This compulsive overeating was his first addiction, and it caused him a great
deal of unhappiness. He was only slightly overweight
when he began treatment. Kirk seemed to have gone
through high school in a fog. He mentioned considerable pot smoking but made it sound like not atypical

teenage behavior. Unlike his brothers, he did not attend an "Ivy League" college; his father was furious about this "lack of ambition." In college Kirk majored in film, but did not do particularly well. For reasons that were not clear, he ceased to be creative in that medium. In the years since graduation he had worked in menial clerical jobs. At one point his father had insisted on getting him "a real job with a future." He did not last long.

Kirk had never had many friends. The few childhood friends that he did have were girls. His mother discouraged this once he reached puberty, while his father made obscene remarks about whether Kirk had "gotten into any of their pussies yet." Kirk was horrified. While he was in treatment, his middle brother had a daughter. His mother remarked that she would have to get the baby a diaphragm. Kirk was upset by this ungrandmotherly remark. This sort of naivete and shocked reaction to predictable behavior was characteristic of Kirk.

Kirk's love life had been focused almost entirely in the pick-up singles scene, where he engaged in anonymous, impersonal sex when he could get it. Kirk's father had frequently called Kirk's mother a cock-sucker in front of Kirk, and Kirk, identifying with his mother and obeying his father's not-too-covert command, did some of that too. At the time he entered treatment, he was "in love" with a "prom queen type" who was going with someone else, but who led him on in a sadistic manner. This was one of the reasons that he was so acutely depressed. Drug and alcohol abuse is certainly not unknown in the singles scene, but Kirk denied that he drank much during his frequent forays into singles bars.

Kirk had few friends, although he was prone to engage in rescue operations in which he tried to help people in trouble. He was particularly involved with an elderly couple who lived in a neighboring apartment. The husband appeared to be psychotic. This couple went from crisis to crisis, and Kirk had taken them to psychiatric emergency rooms a number of times. His rescue efforts provided him with a kind of pseudointimacy. They were essentially unconscious reenactments of his attempts to rescue his mother from his father. Although his human relationships were either superficial or deeply conflicted, he did have a significant relationship with his two dogs, April and Lorna. He not only loved them; he felt loved by them. This was not true, at least to the same extent, in any of his other relationships. He prayed each night for God to protect Mommy and Daddy, April and Lorna. If the first part of this prayer was perfunctory, the second was not.

Although not conventionally religious, Kirk expressed an uncritical belief in God; he prayed each evening. When his mother, who was socially active in a wealthy Reform Jewish congregation, told him that she did not believe in God, Kirk was shocked and angry at her cynicism and hypocrisy. This strong reaction to a perfectly transparent aspect of his mother's character was reminiscent of his reaction to his mother's diaphragm remark. Both were reflections of his intense need for an object worthy of idealization. Kirk had had no opportunity for age-appropriate idealizing while he was growing up. Since he had missed out on this normal developmental stage, he was suffering from a deficit in this area. Kirk's childish credulity left him vulnerable, and it would have been easy for a therapist to play into Kirk's childishness and childlikeness instead of helping him mature.

Kirk's history and current functioning were indicative of serious psychopathology. His object relations were impoverished; his vocational functioning was marginal; and he was deeply depressed. Before long, he confided that he frequently thought of suicide, although he had no concrete plans to and had never attempted it. Kirk's ability to talk about rather than act on his despair probably saved his life. It was not without significance that Kirk's one enduring social activity was his attendance at meetings of the burial society which his extended family had established to provide final resting places for its members. Thoughts of rest comforted this deeply troubled young man.

Kirk's initial diagnosis, in terms of the criteria set forth in DSM- III, was dysthymic disorder (depressive neurosis). It later became clear that Kirk experienced periods of intense excitement, which led the therapist to consider a diagnosis of manic-depressive disorder. Some of the father's behavior also suggested manic-depression, and the therapist considered a psychiatric referral for pharmacological treatment of the depression and possible manic-depression. Only later did the accurate primary diagnosis of alcoholism ("alcohol dependence" in the terminology of DSM- III) become clear. At that time, it became possible to determine that Kirk also suffered from a personality disorder which had both schizoid and narcissistic qualities. This realization was a long way in the future, however. The initial focus of treatment was psychotherapy to alleviate the depression.

During the early sessions, Kirk seemed consumed by his feelings toward his powerful and difficult father. Mother was not much mentioned. Ultimately, the mother's alcoholism and pill addiction became clear, but there was no indication of her drinking problem during the early months of Kirk's therapy. Denial of other people's alcoholism is almost as common as denial of one's own alcoholism. Kirk got some relief from pouring out his feelings and developed a strong and trusting bond with the therapist, but his depression did not significantly improve during the early months of therapy. Depression that does not improve with appropriate treatment is often caused by alcoholism.

The Relationship Intensifies

Relationship is the sine qua non of therapy. Without relationship, nothing happens. Patients vary widely in their ability to enter into a relationship with a therapist. Not only do patients differ from one another in this regard, but the same patient will evidence different capacities to enter into the therapeutic relationship at different stages of treatment. Deepening and broadening the patient's capacity to relate to the therapist is a primary goal of the therapy. It is not an end in itself, but rather a means by which the patient may learn a new way of establishing and maintaining contact with, of touching and being touched by, others. It is the patients who are able to become intensely involved with their therapists who are most likely to succeed in treatment.

Kirk entered treatment starved for meaningful human contact. He had almost never had anybody *really* listen to him or treat him as an "end in himself," rather than as an object to be manipulated for their gratification. His current human relationships could hardly have been more empty or more frustrating, and Kirk was unconsciously perpetuating this situation, largely out of fear. Fortunately, his fear was not so intense that he could not overcome it, given sufficiently favorable conditions. Therapy provided just such conditions, and Kirk formed a strong therapeutic bond almost at once. Hunger for relationship proved stronger than fear of relationship. Unfortunately, this is not always so, and many people starve in the midst of plenty, being unable to partake of the banquet of life. Perhaps Kirk's early relationship with Maggie saved him. Perhaps it was his drive for health that allowed him to move past his fear. Whatever it was, he still wanted to be listened to, to be heard, to be responded to in a nonmanipulative manner, and he was willing to take a risk to get that. (In Chapters 7 and 8, we will examine the concepts of therapeutic alliance and transference.)

Kirk desperately needed not to be impinged upon, to be left alone in the presence of an empathic other, to be understood rather than acted upon. The English analyst D. Winnicott (1952) has written about the deleterious effects of overstimulation, of nonempathic "impingement" upon infants and children. Kohut also stresses the dangers to normal development of unempathic overstimulation in childhood. Kirk was a conspicuous example of the effects of such developmental damage. Thus, the therapist's task was clear. Kirk needed to be, and to feel, taken seriously as a person in his own right. The therapist did just that and Kirk responded by becoming attached to the therapy and to the therapist. This attachment may very well have saved his life in the worst moments of his depression.

Many students of counseling and psychotherapy fear that they "aren't giving the patient anything" if they restrict their activity to active listening. This is not the case; for a patient such as Kirk, it is an enormous gift. However, active listening is not easy; on the contrary, it can be extremely difficult to stay with the patient in the way that the patient needs to be stayed with. A beginning therapist must learn to deal with the anxiety induced in not intervening more actively.

For a long time, Kirk was transmitting, not receiving, and that was fine. As time went on, Kirk entered into an idealizing transference. (This Kohutian concept will be elaborated on in Chapter 8.) In an idealizing transference, the patient puts the therapist on a pedestal. The need to idealize parents is a normal developmental stage of which Kirk had been deprived. He now idealized the therapist. Idealizing transferences can be extremely uncomfortable for the therapist, but worry not; as surely as the night follows the day, disillusionment follows idealization. To be therapeutic rather than traumatic, this disillusionment must be gradual and phase-appropriate. As long as the patient needs to see the therapist as perfect, the therapist must not do anything to deliberately create disillusionment. Idealization can be a means of controlling the idealized object, and this sometimes must be interpreted to the client. Such an interpretation is usually a mistake, however, especially early in the treatment. Kirk, who felt powerless and empty, needed to participate in the omnipotence and plentitude he attributed to the therapist. This idealization permitted Kirk to develop enough trust to ultimately tell the therapist, and more importantly to tell himself, how much he was drinking.

The Diagnosis of Alcoholism

Denial is never complete. Addicts know at some level that they are destroying themselves. Fear prevents this knowledge from becoming fully conscious. Auxiliary defenses, such as rationalization and projection, are brought into the battle to not know; they support the denial. According to traditional psychoanalytic theory, defense is a function of the ego, the executive organ of the psychic apparatus; however, this does not mean that a defense is necessarily conscious. On the contrary, defenses are primarily unconscious, although they can operate on the unconscious, preconscious, and conscious levels. Often they operate on all three levels simultaneously. Freud made a distinction between the dynamic and the descriptive unconscious. We are unaware of both unconscious and preconscious material; descriptively, both are unconscious. However, we can become aware of preconscious material by an act of attention or recall; it is more or less retrievable by an act of will. This is not so for the material and mechanisms within the unconscious, which are repressed and retrievable only by derepression induced by life events or therapeutically achieved through analysis. This is the dynamic unconscious. Although alcoholic denial has conscious and preconscious aspects, it is principally an act of the dynamic unconscious.

Awareness that they are using denial is not available to alcoholic clients through an act of will. On the contrary, treatment must lay bare this unconscious defense and the terrifying secret behind it. This is why confrontational techniques so often fail. On the conscious level, alcoholic denial manifests in dissimulation and evasiveness; on the preconscious level, alcoholic denial manifests in self-deception; on the dynamic unconscious level, it manifests in panic terror of return of the repressed, which would confront the alcoholic with nearness to death and the necessity of giving up that which cannot be lived without. To further complicate the situation, the pharmacological effects of alcohol contribute a measure of oblivion and forgetfulness which reinforces the psychodynamically motivated psychological denial.

Like all alcoholics, Kirk was in denial on all of these levels. His denial encompassed not only his own alcoholism, but also his mother's. Kirk had started drinking in his high school years. Like many teenagers, he experimented with marijuana. By his senior year of prep school he was getting high every day, but it was never his drug of choice. He also "experimented" with the hallucinogens, lysergic acid diethylamide (LSD) and mescaline. The Kirk who was restless and "hyper," perhaps suffering from frightening hypomanic tendencies, preferred the sedating effects of alcohol; whereas the Kirk who was sexually inhibited preferred the disinhibiting effects of alcohol. His preference for alcohol was also an identification with his mother. This was both an identification with the aggressor and an identification with a source, however erratic, of support and nurturance.

Kirk's drinking became more frequent during his college years and the quantity consumed escalated. By the time he graduated, Kirk was a daily drinker. He drank to allow himself some instinctual gratification with his pick-ups from the bars. He needed to drink even more to gratify his homosexual impulses, which were even more unacceptable to his "straight" self. By the time he was out of college six months, he was getting drunk every night. He began to experience memory gaps (blackouts), was increasingly ill in the mornings, and suffered increasingly from guilt, re-morse, self-reproach, and depression. However, Kirk could not allow himself to see the connection between his drinking and his increasing misery. Here the psy-chological defense of isolation—of keeping thoughts separate and unrelated to each other so that their causal relationship will not become apparent—was used to support alcoholic denial. Kirk's conscious be-lief was that alcohol provided him with harmless plea-sure and that it was ancillary to the "fun" he was having in his nightly escapades. Thus, Kirk was "being honest" when he told the therapist that he enjoyed drinking but that it was not a problem.

One effect of psychodynamic psychotherapy is to increase awareness. When Kirk entered therapy his denial was almost complete. Treatment changed this, mostly indirectly. As Kirk increasingly trusted, ad-mired, and even loved the therapist, he became less guarded and more able to disclose details of his life. In so doing, Kirk became aware of much that he had not previously known, even if most of the material was, technically, conscious. It now had more emotional reality and more connectedness with the rest of Kirk's mental life. Dialogue vivifies. The sort of modified "free association" used by the therapist brought some previously unconscious material to Kirk's awareness. Although the therapist offered few interpretations, he asked questions and sought more specificity and detail.

On a descriptive level, it became increasingly clear that Kirk drank a great deal, and frequently. This in itself was not sufficient evidence for a diagnosis of alcoholism, but it alerted the therapist to the possibility of such a diagnosis. The more Kirk disclosed about his life, the more this possibility became a probability. Paradoxically, it was Kirk's very denial that allowed him to provide the information that the therapist needed to diagnose his alcoholism. The same facts that spelled alcohol abuse to the therapist spelled recreational drinking to Kirk. At another, unconscious, level, Kirk "knew" that he had a drinking problem and he wanted the therapist to know. A neurotic has been defined as a person who cannot keep a secret; fortunately, Kirk was neurotic enough to be unable, ultimately, to keep this secret from either the therapist or himself.

Another effect of the therapy was to put Kirk in closer contact with his feelings. He thus became increasingly aware of the pain associated with his drinking. One of the unconscious motives of Kirk's denial of his own alcoholism was protection from the pain of having to acknowledge his mother's. Retrospective idealization of alcoholic parents is common in their children. This was true in Kirk's case. Kirk's idealization of the therapist gave him an alternate idealized object with which to fuse and enabled him to risk losing his mother as an ideal object, thus loosening his defensive structure. Alcohol had served as a source of omnipotent power with which he could fuse; it too was an ideal object. His relationship with the therapist allowed Kirk more freedom to risk losing his most important love object, his closest friend, alcohol. In technical terms (see Chapter 8), Kirk had a self-object relationship with alcohol in which alcohol served as an ideal, perfect, omnipotent object with which he merged, thereby participating in that perfection and power. This relationship was replicated in his relationship with the therapist;

having replaced the first relationship, the one with alcohol, before he actually had to relinquish it, he became willing to risk this loss. In revealing more and more of his drinking behavior, Kirk was taking that risk. Relationship and rum before relationship instead of rum. Kirk was telling the therapist that he was an alcoholic before he was able to tell himself. He felt safer that way and could simultaneously deny and not deny. This maneuver worked for him.

Session by session, the evidence of Kirk's alcoholism increased. Such classic tipoffs as Monday morning absences from work, a puffy face, and red eyes began to surface, but it was his reporting of frequent memory lapses, of blackouts, that convinced the therapist of Kirk's alcoholism. Kirk did not come in and report that he had had a blackout; rather, he would hesitantly recount such incidents as waking up in bed with somebody he did not recognize and did not remember having brought home. By then Kirk was talking of his mother's frequent drunkenness and dependence on tranquilizers to help her "function" when she wasn't drinking. The presence of alcoholism in a family, particularly in one or both parents, increases the likelihood that the patient is alcoholic. The final piece of evidence was Kirk's reporting that he had found himself suddenly awakening in a subway train in a dangerous neighborhood at three in the morning without any inkling of how he had gotten there. This was different and more dangerous than the other memory lapses. There was no longer any doubt about the diagnosis; the therapeutic relationship was solid; the therapist decided to make his move.

Confronting Kirk with His Alcoholism

The therapist told Kirk that he had had an alcohol-induced blackout. He further informed him that blackouts were dangerous symptoms that were often indicative of alcoholism. The therapist described blackouts to Kirk and, in so doing, told him a good deal about alcoholism. Confrontation overlaps education. Ignorance is the handmaiden of denial, just as knowledge is the handmaiden of insight. Rational explanation will not replace the psychological work of overcoming emotionally powerful resistance, but it does facilitate that work.

Part of being sane is knowing how to be sane. For the alcoholic patients, knowing the effects of alcohol and understanding that they must abstain from it if they are to get well is a vital part of knowing how to be sane. Alcoholic patients make sure that they remain ignorant of the facts of alcoholism; part of the therapist's work is to see that they do not remain so. Kirk's therapist spent considerable time discussing blackouts with him; he then confronted Kirk with a detailed account of his blackouts and other alcoholic symptoms. He told Kirk that the evidence pointed to a serious drinking problem and that he needed to do something about it. Kirk looked blank and left without responding. The therapist doubted that he had "gotten through," but he was wrong. Kirk offered no overt response, and consciously he would have denied that he had a drinking problem, but at a deeper level he had heard the therapist and knew that this was not the case. His unconscious responded with a dream. The dream was not about alcoholism or drinking, but it was an augury of a psychic reorganization that would result in stable sobriety for Kirk.

Kirk's Dream

Very early in treatment, Kirk had reported the following dream:

"I was walking along the street. A violent wind began to blow. I felt like I would be swept away. Just as I was about to lose my footing and fly off, I reached

out in desperation and barely managed to grasp hold
of a nearby fence. The wind started to blow me away
and I was swept off my feet. My body was flying
upward. I was barely able to maintain my grasp. At
the end I was literally holding on by my fingertips as
my body was about to be torn loose and carried away.
I woke sweating and trembling."

This dream had many meanings, but the therapist understood it as a visual representation of Kirk's
existential position—barely holding on by his fingertips as the winds of psychosis threatened to sweep him
away. The therapist continued to think of Kirk as on
the verge of annihilation by the emotional storms
within. His hold on reality was tenuous and his links
with the earth could snap any time. In psychoanalytic
theory, the first dream reported is held to have special
significance, expressing the patient's basic conflict.
Kirk's basic conflict was between the unconscious
wish to fly away, to succumb to mania, to get and
remain "high," and the counterstruggle to remain on
earth, to stay sane, to not get "high," however tenuous
his grasp on that fence.

Patients tell us their dreams because they are
important to them. Alcohol (and other drugs) alter the
basic mechanisms of sleep and dream regulation, but
these physiological changes do not exhaust or necessarily determine the content or meaning of the alcoholic's dreams. As Freud (1900) noted, the mental
apparatus uses the organic factors determinative of
dream content to express its wishes and conflicts.
Therefore, the therapist should listen to a dream just
as to any material—to understand it and its meaning
for that patient at that time. This does not mean that
dream interpretation is an important part of our work
with active alcoholics, but neither should such material be neglected or rejected. The manifest content of
Kirk's initial dream was interpreted, as was the dream

that he reported after the therapist confronted him with his alcoholism.

Kirk came to the session following the confrontation looking less distressed than the therapist had ever seen him. He did not make reference to the preceding session. Rather, he said, "I had a dream. Would you like to hear it?" Many alcoholism counselors, viewing this as diversionary and avoidant of the real issue, would have directed the session back to Kirk's drinking. But this maneuver is bad technique. It cuts the patient off before it is known if reporting of a dream, or of anything else for that matter, is relevant or not. There are situations in which the reporting of a dream serves as a defense against dealing with important issues; in such cases it *is* entirely appropriate, and indeed mandatory, that the therapist point this out to the patient. However, patients, alcoholic or not, *must* be listened to first. Therefore, the therapist nodded, and Kirk proceeded to describe the following dream:

"I was walking with my mother. We were going across town. A bus came along. We ran for it, but the door closed just as we reached it. I realized that we had a chance to catch the bus at the next corner, which was the last stop before the bus expressed. I thought, if we don't make that bus we will never get there. I told Mother to run and started running myself. I put on a desperate burst of speed; I was running flat out, using the last ounce of strength I had. I reached the bus just as the doors were closing and almost threw myself aboard. The doors closed. As we pulled away, I looked around and saw Mother on the street; she had missed the bus. I had left her behind."

This was a dream about separation-individuation, about Kirk's finally escaping his mother, her alcoholism and pill addiction, and her masochism. Kirk was leaving his mother behind in two senses—both as a real and troubled person in his daily life and, even more important, as a part of his mental world, an internal object, a pathological introject. Kirk, whose sense of self was none too firm and whose boundaries were none too clear, had taken a big step towards disidentification with his mother and her alcoholism. No emotional battle is won once and for all. Naturally, Kirk's unhealthy identification with his mother was not resolved instantly and permanently, but a Rubicon had been crossed and Kirk's relationship with the mother in his head and the mother in his life was never the same again.

The therapist elicited Kirk's associations and re-flected the accompanying affects. He was struck by the contrast between Kirk's loss of contact with the ground in the first dream and his landing on his feet on the bus in the second dream. Every dream reported in treat-ment is also a transference dream; that is, one of its meanings concerns the relationship between the thera-pist and the patient. At the very least, every dream is a communication from the patient to the therapist. It was not without significance that the bus that Kirk boarded with his last breath was going toward the therapist's office. Freud maintained that the only way we can relinquish an object is to make it part of ourselves. Kirk's mother was all too much a part of him, and he was able to begin to relinquish, to move away from, his mother only when he had replaced her with the thera-pist, both as a participant in their "real" relationship and as an internal object. At this level the dream was "about" leaving Mother for the therapist, leaving alco-holic drinking for sobriety. Although neither Kirk nor the therapist knew it then, Kirk had taken his last drink. He has now been sober for nearly ten years.

The Therapist Educates

Kirk's education about the effects of alcoholic drinking on the body, mind, and spirit had commenced during the confrontation. It was to continue for a long time. The salient fact at this stage was that although alcohol might mask depression, it actually deepened and worsened it. The therapist also told Kirk that many people self-medicate their depression with alcohol and that he would be less depressed if he stopped drinking, although he might not be immediately aware of it.

Education about alcoholism is often accomplished in an inpatient rehabilitation center, but many alcoholic patients do not attend such programs. Therapists must therefore be prepared to tell patients about alcoholism in such a way that they can hear and understand the information. Since there is resistance to this information, it must be presented simply, clearly and frequently. Education about their disease provides alcoholics with a cognitive structure that reduces anxiety, lessens guilt, and makes sense of their experiences.

Kirk proved to be a quick learner. He had already learned enough to bring about the psychic reorganization that resulted in his dream, and he learned a great deal more in subsequent months. The next educational step would have been to tell Kirk about AA, but this was something he found out for himself.

Kirk Joins AA

Kirk arrived for his next session looking rather sheepish. The therapist intended to inquire about his reaction to their discussion of the destructiveness of Kirk's drinking if Kirk did not raise the topic. The session started off in an unexpected way.

"I went to my parents' Passover seder. It was horrible. Everybody except my father was drunk. I had decided not to drink for a while because of the blackouts, so I was sober. I guess I hadn't seen my family when I was sober for a long time. My oldest brother drank glass after glass of wine and he became louder and louder, making less and less sense. His girlfriend couldn't even stand up. My middle brother wasn't much better, and he kept saying vile things about my parents. My mother got to the point where she was slurring her words. Then she started to bait my father. He cursed her, and finally they got into a shoving match. He looked like he was going to hit her until I said, "Daddy stop it." It was awful, awful; it was my childhood all over again. I thought, "Next year in Bellevue," and I walked out.*

"I realized that my whole family was alcoholic. I didn't much care about any of them except my mother. It really hurt to think of her as a drunk. She didn't give me as much support as I would have wanted, but she was okay in her way. I started to cry; suddenly I thought, my therapist is right—I am an alcoholic too. Funny, but that didn't hurt in the same way as thinking about my mother being alcoholic. In fact, it was sort of a relief. I cried some more, deep sobs this time.

"I don't know where I got the idea, but I decided to go to an AA meeting. They hold meetings in the church at my corner, and I had seen their sign many times. I guess maybe going there had been in the back of my mind for a long time. I walked into the meeting. It was wonderful. I cried all the way through. I felt at home. I felt safe. Some time in the course of the meeting I thought, a seder is supposed to be about everyman's journey from slavery to freedom—I heard that in a sermon when I was a kid—my family's seder sure wasn't that, but this meeting is about *my* journey from slavery to freedom. I didn't want to live the way I had been living; I didn't want to drink anymore; I didn't want to take pills any more. As they say in AA, I had hit bottom. I walked out feeling exhausted, a little

*The seder ends with the line, "Next year in Jerusalem."

empty, but clean. I don't think that I'm going to drink again—"a day at a time"—but I'm scared. I don't know how to live any other way than the way I've been living. Can you help me learn?"

Kirk started to cry, and the therapist's eyes got a bit wet too. The massive emotional reorganization that Kirk underwent between his blackout on the subway train and the session just reported is characteristic of many recoveries from alcoholism and addiction. Bill Wilson, the cofounder of AA, who had a "conversion experience" of his own, frequently quoted William James's (1902) discussion of such experiences in *The Varieties of Religious Experience*. According to James, conversion experiences are of two kinds: Damascus conversion experiences (an allusion to the conversion of St. Paul on the road to Damascus)—sudden bursts of illumination; and educational conversion experiences—slower, less dramatic changes in values and perspectives. Bill's physician, William Silkworth, who came to occupy an important place in the AA legend, understood Bill's experience as a massive psychic reorganization. Jung, among others, believed that some such emotional cataclysm was necessary to reverse the powerfully regressive currents of alcohol addiction, to break the icy grip of the repetition compulsion pulling the addict toward death. It is not an accident that the Salvation Army has long ensconced itself on skid row. Bill Wilson wisely distrusted Damascus conversion experiences, although he valued his own; he thought that the educational conversion experience, which he tried to institutionalize in AA, was a much safer and more trustworthy substructure on which to build sobriety.

Many psychotherapists are uncomfortable with such formulations. They smack of mysticism and irrationality. Experience has shown, however, that Jung and Bill Wilson are basically correct on this issue. Insight is important, but it is the realignment of emotional forces which provides the energy to change the suicidal pattern of addiction. Such a realignment may be sudden, in the pattern of the Damascus experience, or gradual, in the pattern of the educational experience. Usually it is both. There is nothing mystical about this; it is a matter both of freeing up energies lost to repression or bound to pathological introjects and of providing enough security for the anabolic forces of the psyche and the patient's own drive for health to take over. Powerful emotion is a necessary, if not always sufficient, condition of recovery. To paraphrase Kant, insight without passion is impotent; passion without insight is useless.

Kirk had had a kind of Damascus experience which convinced him, at least for the moment, that drinking meant death, and which enabled him, at some deeply unconscious level, to choose to live rather than to die. The slow work of the educational conversion, of securing the insight and emotional realignment he had gained in his moments of illumination at the seder and at the AA meeting, now began. It would take many years of therapy and many hundreds of AA meetings to secure and expand upon Kirk's realization that he was an alcoholic. It was most certainly not to be a story of linear progression; quite the contrary, it was to be two steps forward and one step back, with an occasional two steps back, but Kirk never again experienced suicidal depression, nor was he ever tormented by a desire to drink.

NORMAN: A TREATMENT FAILURE

Norman had been referred by the therapist who was treating his wife. There was no question about the diagnosis, at least not on the part of the wife or her therapist, who described him as drunk more often than he was sober, an unquestionable alcoholic. Norman, a stolid man in his mid-40s, evidenced a lack of education in his diction, vocabulary, and style. He was abrupt, surly, and obviously resented being in the therapist's office. It wasn't until months later that the therapist learned that Norman had studied classical Greek in college, had a knowledge of ancient philosophy and literature, and was a published composer.

Since Norman was obviously there under duress, the therapist acknowledged this. He decided that the situation was hopeless unless he could elicit from Norman some desire to participate. Appearances to the contrary, this was not beyond the realm of possibility. Patients who come for therapy under external pressure sometimes actually wish to be there. They may or may not be aware of this wish. Such referrals are common in alcoholism counseling; patients are often referred by concerned relatives or by employee assistance programs (EAPs), which may require that a worker either attend sessions or lose his job. Some therapists stress the necessity of "therapeutic leverage"—otherwise known as having the patient by the short hairs—in working with active alcoholics. Other therapists are not particularly comfortable with this arrangement. However, it must be said that it is frequently effective. These patients still have a lot to lose; they are what AA calls "high-bottom drunks." The very fact that they have jobs that someone is trying to save for them can indicate ego strength. In their case, the AA motto "Bring the body and the mind will follow" frequently holds true. However, it might also be said that far more alcoholic patients recover without the use of such therapeutic leverage than with it.

Norman was in treatment under duress, but possibly he also wanted something for himself. The therapist encouraged Norman to talk about whatever that might be, and Norman responded with a torrent of rage against his wife, whom he saw as a cold, critical, rigid hypocrite. The therapist, deciding to go with the

material he had, encouraged Norman to elaborate on
his wife's deficiencies, real or imagined. This was
somewhat manipulative on the part of the therapist,
but he really didn't know how much reality might be
behind Norman's complaints, and at least Norman
was interested in expressing himself on this subject.
Minimally, the therapist would learn something about
Norman's feelings, even if Norman's attack was simply a response to a perceived threat to his drinking (a
possibility that did not escape the therapist). Norman
almost instantly became talkative. As he poured out
his dissatisfaction with his wife, the therapist acknowledged Norman's feelings. Norman seemed somewhat
less defensive by the end of the hour and even evidenced some positive feelings toward therapy. He
had come prepared to be attacked; instead he had
been listened to. He surprised the therapist by readily
agreeing to return for a second session. As he walked
out he turned and said, "That miserable cunt is right
about one thing: I do drink too much."

During the next session, the therapist asked Norman about his comment. Norman said little, except to
mutter that he wouldn't drink so much if "she didn't
bitch so much." When attempts to explore this were
met with sullen silence, the therapist backed off and
decided to take a history. Norman was also resistant to
this, and information was obtained slowly and in a
fragmented, disconnected form. Norman preferred to
talk about the "fucking bitch" rather than about himself. The history emerged over several months.

Norman was the only child of urban, working-
class parents. He described his father as a "nonentity"
and his mother as a "pain in the ass," which was also
one of his favorite appellations for his wife. Norman
was not a positive thinker. Like so many active alcoholics, Norman did not make it easy for a therapist to
remain nonjudgmental and understanding. His therapist had his share of difficulties remaining "attuned" to
his client, who described virtually every person in his

life as some sort of asshole, and characterized every experience by noting that "it sucked" or "it was a crock of shit." The adjectives exhausted the fund of gutter vituperation. Such countertransferential difficulties are well-nigh ubiquitous in therapists who work with alcoholics. Although the unrelenting negativity, which usually includes the therapy and the therapist, is a genuine expression of the client's *weltanschauung*, the name of the game is to elicit rejection, or at least something that can be interpreted as rejection, so that the rottenness of the world will be reconfirmed and the next drink justified. If the therapist remembers this, the annoyance will dissipate.

Norman had few memories of his early years. He did recall that his maternal grandmother, a forbidding, self-absorbed, old-world autocrat, had lived with them and that she had been largely responsible for rearing him. His earliest memory was of her yelling at him. He experienced his wife as a reincarnation of this harsh and critical grandmother. The family had little money, and Norman conveyed a sense of marginality in his description of their existence. His mother worked and he had little contact with her, but he remembered her as an endless complainer. His complaining was in part an identification with her. His father's main contact with him seemed to be to beat him "only on the ass" when provoked to do so by the mother or grandmother. The therapist considered the impact of this on the transference: Norman would experience therapy as being sent by his wife (grandmother) to be beaten by the therapist (father). This was interpreted to Norman, but he dismissed it.

Norman's school experience was also unhappy. He was a poor student who had never felt a part of things. He had barely gotten through elementary and junior high school. He was a frequent visitor to the guidance office and would be beaten at home if his parents found out that he had been in trouble in school. He remembered no friends, hated sports and played them poorly, and had virtually no interests; he had clearly been a depressed and miserable child. When he discovered marijuana in ninth grade, he was a sitting duck for the development of a heavy habit.

Fortunately, he also developed an interest in jazz music at this time. He learned to play the clarinet in school and his parents, who had a little more money by then, offered him private lessons. Despite Norman's reluctance to say anything positive about himself, it was clear that he had been a talented jazz clarinetist. He was soon playing in jazz combos. For the first time in his life he felt a part of something, accepted and competent. The world by which he felt accepted was drug oriented, and Norman loved it. By the time he was fifteen, he was smoking pot daily and drinking heavily on the weekends. Seldom was he not high on one or the other.

Norman did better in high school. He relished his status as a jazz musician. He still had no "real" friends, but he had drinking companions and smoking buddies. He was accepted by the older musicians with whom he played on weekends. His intelligence enabled him to function through a drug-induced haze, and his grades were "not bad." According to Norman, most of his classmates were stoned most of the time, so his drug use attracted no particular attention. His grandmother died during his senior year, and Norman remembered thinking that "that parasite won't be looking over my shoulder any more."

Norman finished high school without incident and went on to college because "my fucking old man insisted, but it didn't mean anything to me. I studied that liberal arts crap because it was the easiest thing." There was a clear discrepancy between Norman's perception of his parents as totally uncaring and their paying for music lessons and insisting on his going to college. Whereas Kirk had retrospectively idealized his markedly disturbed, inadequate mother, Norman's retrospective distortions were all in the negative direction. For both, the distortions were defenses against intolerable emotional pain and justifications of highly emotionally invested world views.

Norman lived at home and commuted to a free public college. Although he described himself as indifferent, unmotivated, and uncaring, it slowly emerged that Norman had at one time had a fine command of classical Greek and a broad knowledge of Greek literature. This was an odd major for a student who was only attending college to please his father. Norman dismissed his academic accomplishments: "It was all a crock of shit anyway." It was difficult to tell what Greek literature had meant to Norman—perhaps escape from and rebellion against his parents' working-class values and life-style. Had oedipal guilt prevented his pursuing this interest or enjoying his success in it? Or was he so overwhelmed by separation anxiety that he had to turn his back on the world of culture? Or was he punishing himself for death wishes against his grandmother?

Norman's academic career peaked in his junior year. His grades fell precipitously in his senior year and he barely graduated. Although he refused to see the connection, the evidence was that his drinking and drugging had caught up with him. He started to have the morning shakes and became more anxious, and in the middle of his senior year he began to experience panic attacks. The attacks always occurred in the morning and always followed a night of drinking. He went to a physician and was given a prescription for Valium. It alleviated his anxiety. Before long he had learned the trick of getting prescriptions from a number of physicians. He was soon addicted to the pills and was always either drinking or taking Valium, when he was not doing both. Although Norman's anxiety attacks had many psychodynamic determinants, their immediate etiology was physiological: the effect of heavy alcohol consumption (see Chapter 2). There was no time when he was chemical-free.

Norman must have recognized that he was disabled by his drug use because he dropped a plan to study classics in graduate school, played less and less music, and took the safest, easiest civil-service job he could find. He was working at a similar job when he came for therapy twenty years later. Norman reluctantly disclosed that during his college years and for several years thereafter, he had composed music, some of which had been played in public performances. But Norman disavowed or dismissed his accomplishments. Perhaps it was too painful to think about what might have been.

Kohut might have described this as a failure to integrate the phase-appropriate grandiosity and exhibitionism of the archaic, nuclear self into the ambitions pole of the mature, bipolar self. In other words, Norman had repressed the claims of infantile grandiosity without sublimating or absorbing the energy and vitality associated with that grandiosity. Whatever portion of archaic grandiosity had not been repressed was dissociated and unavailable to Norman for the pursuit of adult ambitions and mature goals. It was separated from the core of Norman's self by what Kohut describes as the *vertical split*. This dissociated archaic grandiosity manifested as a false self (Winnicott 1960) which assumed the form of insane and self-destructive bravado: "Nothing can touch me"; "Alcohol can't destroy me." Here, repressed and split-off archaic grandiosity supports the illusion of omnipotence and the defense of denial. According to Kohut, such a state of affairs comes about as a result of deeply disturbed early object—or more accurately, self-object—relations. Kohut prescribes psychoanalysis for such a narcissistic disturbance. Of course, this treatment was not possible in Norman's case; the treatment for active alcoholism is psychodynamically informed alcoholism counseling, not psychoanalysis. What the therapist can do is to take an interest in the patient's interests. Therefore, Norman's therapist tried to rekindle Norman's interest in music, but this proved impossible. It was as though alcohol had so thoroughly extinguished the spark of creativity that there was nothing left to be reignited. If rage is a frequent countertransferential concomitant of alcoholism counseling, so is sadness. (For a discussion of Kohut's metapsychology, see Chapter 6. For a discussion of Kohut's treatment methods, see Chapter 8.)

During his 20s, Norman lived a dual life, going through the motions in an undemanding civil service job slightly zonked on Valium or marijuana as he anxiously waited for 5:00, when his "real" life began. As happens to all addicts, his life became progressively narrower and emptier. His interests and ambitions fell by the wayside. Just before he reached total collapse he met a woman, Ann, in a club where he was playing and married her soon after. She too was heavily involved in drugs and was probably schizophrenic. The therapist got the sense that Norman had really loved her. Their ten-year marriage was one long agony. During this time Ann had several "breakdowns" which necessitated hospitalizations. Shortly after the last hospitalization, Ann either killed herself or accidentally took an overdose of medicine that her psychiatrist had prescribed. Norman expressed his bitter hatred toward psychiatrists, psychiatric hospitals, and especially psychotropic medication. He believed that the medicine had not only been the "poison" that killed her, but that it had also destroyed her as a person long before she overdosed. The therapist could not judge the accuracy of Norman's perceptions of the effects of psychotropic medication on Ann and there may very well have been considerable reality behind them; however, it was clear that Norman was *splitting*. The psychotropic medication became the bad mother (breast, milk), while alcohol became the good mother. The split defended his addiction.

Norman was also hospitalized on a psychiatric ward during this period for detoxification from alcohol and Valium. The experience became another source of his hatred for psychiatrists. He felt he had been dehumanized and "treated like a crazy" during this hospitalization, and he had never gotten over his bitterness about it. Given his experiences, it was a wonder that Norman had consented to see a mental health professional of any sort.

Somewhere between their respective breakdowns, Norman and Ann managed to conceive a child, Ann. She was 3 years old when her mother died. Norman cleaned himself up after the death of his wife. He was depressed and bitter, but he drank much less and did not return to the Valium. He moved in with his parents and went to work while his mother took care of the child. Before long he met a woman in his office and courted her. They soon married. Norman had married Barbara for convenience and to have a mother for his child. He never expressed any positive feelings toward her. He characterized her as "not particularly good looking," "lousy in bed," and "a horror" who "didn't like to drink." The last-mentioned character trait did not endear Barbara to Norman, who once married, lost little time in returning to alcohol. He conceded that his second wife "took good care of the kid." It was a good thing she did. Norman hardly ever mentioned his daughter and was markedly lacking in warmth toward her. He had a cat that he expressed more interest in, but he didn't really take care of her either. The marriage worsened. Norman drank more and became increasingly hostile. Finally his wife told him to get help or leave. That was the point at which he arrived in the therapist's office.

The Diagnosis

Norman was clearly alcoholic. In terms of the DSM-III classifications of mental illnesses, Norman suffered from alcohol dependency. He also met the criterion for cannabis dependency. Additionally, he was readdicted to minor tranquilizers.

In terms of Jellinek's typology of the alcoholisms, Norman was a gamma alcoholic. According to Blane's classificatory scheme, Norman was somewhere between a dependent and an independent-dependent alcoholic, but closer to the dependent type. In Knight's terminology, Norman was more of an essential than a reactive alcoholic. In Winokurian terms he was a primary alcoholic, although the possibility that he was a secondary (depressive) alcoholic could not be entirely ruled out.

At one level, Norman's diagnosis was clear: Even he did not seriously dispute the fact that he was addicted to alcohol. What he did dispute was the seriousness of that addiction and the value of treating it. At another level, however, his diagnosis was not at all clear. Two questions arose. The first concerned the nature of his depression; the second concerned the nature of the personality disturbance that seemed to be antecedent to his alcoholism and that most certainly had not changed. If he was drinking to self-medicate a biogenic unipolar depression, then that depression needed to be treated with antidepressant medication. On the other hand, his depression was not helped by his alcoholism; on the contrary, it was exacerbated by it. In other words, was Norman a Winokurian primary alcoholic, or secondary alcoholic? The answer had practical implications for treatment.

From his history, it appeared that Norman was depressed before he was addicted; however it was questionable that this was the kind of depression that would respond to antidepressant medication. The therapist considered a referral to a psychiatrist, but in view of Norman's hatred for psychiatrists and psychotropic medication, he did not. In any event, Norman would have to be sober and drug free before his depression could possibly lift. The question was whether or not antidepressant medication could help toward that goal. Given the circumstances, this was a diagnostic and treatment question that was never answered.

Norman was also suffering from a narcissistic personality disturbance which antedated his addiction, but he lacked the strengths often displayed by patients with such personality disorders. It seemed more likely that his narcissistic problems were expressions of borderline pathology. His multiple addictions, depression, rage, and contempt for virtually everything and everybody were consistent with this diagnosis. He used the borderline defenses (Kernberg 1975) of denial, splitting, omnipotence, devaluation, and primitive projection. His vocational history and level of object relations were also consistent with this diagnosis. The therapist therefore diagnosed him as a borderline personality with schizoid, depressive, and narcissistic features, in addition to his alcohol and cannabis dependency.

The Therapeutic Relationship

Norman never really related. Yet he attended session after session. He came on time, sullenly and resentfully, but he came. Whatever the outside pressure on him to attend, it was assumed that he must have been getting something for himself from the therapeutic relationship. Patients do not last six months in therapy if they are merely attending to get their husbands or wives off their backs, although they may maintain that they are doing so in the service of a pseudoself-sufficiency. It was not clear, however, what the meaning of the therapeutic relationship might be for Norman. He sat through sessions depressed and apathetic. He rarely volunteered anything and only became animated when he was discussing his wife's unreasonableness and hostility. Occasionally he spontaneously discussed his work, describing how stupid and boring it was and how he hated everything about it: "The whole fucking office sucks; it's all a farce; I hate it."

For the most part, Norman was silent. Silence has many meanings. It can be a moment of reliving or living for the first time the preverbal attunement of mother and infant; it can be a reliving of anal withholding during a struggle over toilet training; it can be an expression of resistance; it can be a manifestation of a new peacefulness. Freud maintained that the patient was thinking about the therapist during periods of silence. The therapist inquired into this possibility, but he drew a blank. Norman never spontaneously expressed any feelings about the therapist and attempts to elicit such feelings were unproductive. What else could Norman's silence mean? It could have been an unconscious way of showing the therapist how he, Norman, had felt in the unresponsive environment of his childhood, a turning of a passive experience into an active one; it could have been a passive-aggressive expression of hostility and anger toward the therapist; and it could have been a way of avoiding talking about his addictions. It was probably all three, but the last possibility, avoidance of discussing the addictions, is *always* one meaning of silence in active addicts. The therapist received no response when he interpreted this to Norman.

The therapy proceeded fitfully, with periods of silence, slow revelation of Norman's history in response to active digging by the therapist, and occasional outbursts of rage at Norman's wife and work. Clearly, free association was not the technique of choice in this situation. It rarely is with active alcoholics. The therapist became increasingly active, preventing the silences from enveloping the therapeutic process. After about three months of therapy Norman decided that "that asshole bitch can leave whenever she wants; I'm not going any fucking place." After this pronouncement, Norman stated that he was coming to therapy for himself and not for "her." This indeed sounded like progress and the therapist said so, going on to inquire about what Norman wanted for himself. Norman replied in a combination of moan and shout, "How the fuck should I know." This was the only time that Norman had openly expressed anger toward the therapist. As therapy proceeded, it became apparent that Norman's continuing ventilation of wrath at his wife was not productive. It was also clear that he was drinking at least as much as he had been when he began therapy. As the therapist switched the focus of therapy to Norman's drinking, Norman became increasingly apathetic. He contributed less and less to the sessions and even slept through one of them. The therapist changed his stance from one of active listening to one of active educating and confronting. The therapy had always had aspects of both, but it was now clear that the only hope was that Norman would be able to hear a consistent, calm, concerned, nonpunitive voice speaking to him about the misery he was inflicting on himself.

The therapist must speak with the voice of reality, not of the superego. This is not always easy with active alcoholics, who provoke and frustrate. A therapist's best defense against inappropriately expressing such countertransferential feelings is self-awareness. Norman's therapist felt abundantly frustrated and provoked. He accepted these feelings and got on with the work. He used the sessions to talk about alcoholism and the necessity for Norman to do something about his drinking. Norman was unresponsive.

Actually, Norman had developed a bond with the therapist. It was a dependent relationship, but it was a relationship. Norman's "dependency," which was denied and defended against, was far from a negative phenomenon. Developmentally regressed it certainly was, but only it gave the treatment any chance at all. Would Norman listen to the therapist? Once again, relationship was the key. As AA says, "Bring the body and the mind will follow." Nothing can happen if the patient doesn't attend the sessions, and Norman's dependency accomplished that much. As we shall see, there was sufficient relationship for Norman to turn to the therapist for concrete help in stopping drinking when he finally became overtly desperate. The despair had been there all along; Norman's belligerent cynicism and hostility was really one prolonged scream for love.

Confrontation and Education

Norman "knew" that he was alcoholic; what he needed to be confronted with was the necessity of doing something about it. He needed to learn that his drinking and drugging were making his emotional pain worse, and something could indeed be done about it and was worth doing. This knowledge would not in itself alleviate his masochistic need to injure and possibly destroy himself, but it would at least impart an intellectual awareness of what alcohol was doing to him—or better, what he was doing to himself with alcohol.

The therapist tried to educate Norman about alcoholism. He taught the disease concept of alcoholism; he listed the effects alcohol was having on Norman's mind, his emotions, and his body. He stressed the role of alcohol in causing depression and told Norman that there was no way of knowing what was under the chemicals unless he stopped taking them. Norman replied that he was "crazy anyway." The therapist countered, "You think that you drink because you're crazy. Did it ever occur to you that you're crazy because you drink?" Norman replied, "So I'm not crazy, what difference does it make?" The therapist thought about terminating. He told himself, "Try to understand and not to judge." He inwardly laughed at himself for his sanctimonious thinking and returned to the work with Norman.

It was clear that Norman was deteriorating. The therapist told Norman that he had to stop drinking if he wanted to continue therapy. Amazingly, Norman agreed. The relationship *had* become important enough for Norman to at least verbally agree to stop drinking in order to preserve it. The therapist told Norman that he had to go to AA. He had been talking about AA for months, but now he insisted that Norman go to a meeting. He did. He got drunk on the way home. The therapist arranged for a "sponsor" to take Norman to another AA meeting. Norman went to the meetings for a while. Although he drank less, he was seldom sober. He started drinking heavily again and then stopped attending the AA meetings. Certain that Norman could not stop on his own, the therapist introduced the topic of inpatient rehabilitation. Knowing of Norman's fear of psychiatric hospitals, he explained the difference between alcoholic rehabilitation programs and psychiatric programs. He urged Norman to accept the referral and tried to convince him that the investment in himself was worth while. The therapeutic approach was now frankly persuasive and directive.

Despite the fact that the process was blurred by an alcoholic fog, Norman had learned a great deal in his six months of therapy. He had heard more than he had wanted to. He knew about alcohol's effects; he knew that he had to stop drinking and drugging if he was to have any chance at all, although he didn't know how to do that; he knew about AA and about inpatient rehabilitation programs. This knowledge threw him into a panic. To borrow a line from AA, the therapy had "ruined his drinking"; the thought that he really had to stop drinking increasingly intruded into his consciousness and terrified him. He couldn't envision life without booze and pot, and now he knew he couldn't live with them either. He responded to the panic induced by this insight by going on a week-long, round-the-clock binge. Finally his body couldn't stand any more, and he hit a "bottom" of sorts. Feeling that he couldn't live without alcohol and that he couldn't live with it, he was a serious suicide risk. Fortunately, he was able to reach out in the depths of his despair and ask for help. He got it.

Detoxification and Rehabilitation

When he finally called for help, Norman was too defeated and terrified to lie about the extent of his drinking. The therapist referred Norman to an experienced internist who could admit patients to the hospital for detoxification and medical treatment. The hospital employed a full-time alcoholism counselor, whose task it was to educate and break down denial in detoxifying patients, who were presumably in sufficient crisis to hear what is said. Although the therapist had little doubt that hospitalization would be required, the actual decision to detoxify Norman in or out of the hospital would be made by the medical specialist. Norman was in enough pain to readily agree to see the internist, but he failed to keep the appointment. The next day he called in even worse shape. The therapist told him to come in immediately. He arrived semidrunk and disheveled. The therapist accompanied Norman to the office of the internist, who agreed that Norman, by now nearly comatose, required inpatient treatment for detoxification. The therapist put Norman in a cab, directing the driver to take him to admitting. Norman never got there. After several more days of this approach-avoidance behavior, Norman finally admitted himself to the hospital.

By then Norman was very ill. He remained on a medical unit for 10 days, at the end of which time he agreed to enter a 30-day alcoholic rehabilitation program that was housed outside a psychiatric hospital. Sick as he was, it took the combined efforts of the hospital counselor, the internist, and his therapist to persuade Norman to enter the program. The therapist was surprised when Norman admitted himself to the rehabilitation unit without incident.

It could be argued that the therapist's personal involvement in Norman's detoxification was infantilizing and ultimately harmful. The drama that surrounded Norman's hospital admission gave Norman power and control without his having to take the responsibility for getting treatment. Many alcoholism counselors would consider such "coddling" antitherapeutic, and most analytically oriented therapists would maintain that such "direct feeding" hopelessly contaminates the transference. There is another, perhaps more realistic, side to this issue, however. It is reminiscent of the comment of a clinical supervisor to a student therapist who refused to hospitalize a suicidal patient because the threat was "a transference acting out." The supervisor said, "You can't do dynamics with a corpse." In a crisis you respond to a crisis. Alcoholism counseling sometimes seems like an endless series of such crises, but generally they are infrequent enough to be manageable. Obviously, each situation must be judged on its individual merits, and the therapist should have clients do as much on their own as possible. Further, one difficult patient should not be allowed to adversely impinge upon an entire caseload. As far as transference and dynamics are concerned, it is not the case that such active involvement by therapists with alcoholic patients is counterproductive or antitherapeutic. Quite the contrary, many a sustained recovery has started with a tremulous patient clinging to a therapist as they sped to an emergency room.

In the rehabilitation program, Norman received a thorough education about alcohol and alcoholism at a time when his capacity for learning was less impaired than it had been. He was required to attend AA meetings daily and was thereby given exposure to a program that could provide a basis for permanent recovery. He also had an opportunity to express his feelings in group therapy, individual counseling, and psychodrama. He was encouraged to take part in recreation therapy, rap sessions, nutrition education, and other therapeutic activities. It was a time to heal and to learn about his disease and about himself. As the weeks went on, he was given passes so that he could gradually readjust to the world outside. Along with his fellow patients, Norman was taken to outside AA meetings by visiting sponsors. The rehabilitation program did all it could reasonably do to provide an environment conducive to emotional learning while giving patients time to internalize controls and to become accustomed to sobriety. In Norman's case, its efforts were unsuccessful.

Discharge and Relapse

Most patients leave a rehabilitation program feeling chastened, frightened, and somewhat optimistic. The period after discharge is always a crucial one. Discharge means separation, and separation engenders anxiety. Discharge means the end of external control, and the absence of external control engenders anxiety. Discharge means having to deal with the world and dealing with the world evokes anxiety; discharge means that alcohol is available, and the availability of alcohol means anxiety. Nevertheless, most discharged patients manage to take enough away with them to remain sober for weeks, months, or even years. Some remain permanently sober. Norman got drunk in the bar across the street from the rehab five minutes after his discharge. We do not know why, although we can speculate. Suffice to say that the regressive pull of his disease was stronger than Norman's drive for health; Thanatos was stronger than Eros; symbiosis overwhelmed differentiation; the lack of psychic structure was too all-encompassing; the rage was too great; the internal objects too "bad." "Gee, Officer Krupke . . . ."

Norman was drunk when he arrived at his first postrehab counseling session. He had been drinking since discharge. The therapist suggested that he re-enter the hospital for a second detoxification. Norman refused, insisting that he could stop on his own. Surprisingly, he did. He returned for the next session sober. The therapist told Norman that he would not see him for any future sessions if he had been drinking that day and that he would have to pay for any such sessions. Norman agreed. His recent drinking was interpreted—understood—as a panic reaction to his discharge. The therapist told him that many people, feeling overwhelmed when they leave the hospital, react by drinking, but he emphasized that Norman had a decent chance of maintaining sobriety if he remained in AA and continued in therapy.

Norman called two days later to say that he was drinking again. He had not attended any AA meetings. Norman was told to stop drinking, to go to AA meetings, and to return to the hospital if he was unable to stop drinking. Norman managed to stop once more and he did go to a few AA meetings, only to repeat the pattern. During the following months Norman did not comply with any treatment recommendations. He couldn't, or wouldn't, attend either AA meetings or the rehab program's aftercare group; he wouldn't talk to his AA sponsor; and he refused a psychiatric referral. He attended his psychotherapy sessions, but he usually arrived after drinking. The therapist refused to see him. He would return the next week and sleep through the session or sit resentful and silent. The sessions must have meant something to Norman or he would not have continued to attend them; however, it was clear that the treatment was not working.

Termination

The therapist decided that therapy was simply providing enough support for Norman to "slip" from drinking episode to drinking episode. The therapist had become an enabler—one, usually a parent or spouse, who enables the alcoholic to drink. Enablement may be emotional or financial or both. The therapeutic relationship should be maintained in most cases, for it provides some hope. When the treatment has come to support the addiction, however, and no other meaningful work is taking place, that support must be withdrawn and therapy ended until the patient stops drinking. The decision to terminate is a serious one, for it may result in suicide. However, if the therapy is enabling the drinking without accomplishing any meaningful psychological work, then the therapist is involved in complicity in suicide, albeit a slow suicide, anyway. The choice is never easy.

In Norman's case, the therapist decided to terminate. The therapist told Norman that he could not attain stable sobriety with the assistance of weekly or even twice-weekly sessions alone and that nothing else could improve until he achieved sobriety. He emphasized that Norman had a progressive, fatal disease and was visibly deteriorating. The therapist urged Norman to recommit himself to the rehabilitation program. When Norman refused, the therapist told him that he could not continue to see him because the treatment was simply sustaining his alcoholic drinking, but that he was welcome back when he stopped drinking and was ready to follow the therapist's rec-

ommendations, including attendance at AA meetings.
The therapist stated that he would continue to stand
ready to assist Norman in obtaining admission to a
detoxification or rehabilitation program. Norman
said, "I've had enough of this shit anyway," and left.
The therapist never heard from him again.

The therapist knew that Norman had successfully
completed the rehab program. As long as he was an
inpatient, he was sober. Norman did not drink on
passes. The therapist theorized that Norman experienced the rehab program as a mother, with whom he
merged. This union filled the same needs for Norman
that alcohol and drugs did. He was unable to deal with
separation from that program-mother. His resistance
to participation in AA, in the aftercare program, and in
therapy was really an expression of Norman's fear of a
wished-for but dreaded merger, experienced as engulfment, with these symbolic mothers. Unfortunately,
this could not be usefully interpreted to Norman.

When we apparently fail with a patient, we do
not really know whether or not we have helped that
patient. It is possible that our work will become an
ingredient in a future recovery; it is also possible that
the patient will deteriorate to the point of severe disablement or death. Unfortunately, Norman seemed
headed in the latter direction.

TREATING ACTIVE ALCOHOLICS

In this section we will discuss some topics that were touched
upon in the case histories, including cross-addiction, referral for
detoxification and rehabilitation, self-help groups, abstinence
versus controlled drinking as a treatment goal, "hitting bottom,"
and the role of insight in achieving sobriety. We will also discuss
the use of "interventions" and the use of group and family
therapy with alcoholic patients.

Cross-addiction

Today it is rare to encounter an alcoholic who is not cross-addicted. This is especially true of patients under 35 years of age. Alcoholics are particularly prone to taking other sedating drugs, such as the barbiturates. Alcohol and cocaine is also a popular combination, and marijuana smoking is all but ubiquitous among the young. Cocaine addicts frequently use alcohol to "come down" and become "hooked" on it also. Conversely, it is not uncommon for alcoholics to self-medicate the depression consequent upon alcohol abuse with cocaine. "Speed" (amphetamines) is used for the same purpose, and hallucinogens are in widespread use. More rarely the therapist will encounter patients cross-addicted to heroin or morphine, which are also sedating drugs, or to methadone, the synthetic used to wean addicts off heroin. Therapists must therefore be informed about the physiological and psychological effects of these drugs and must be alert to the possibility of their use by alcoholic patients. It is not possible to safely use any drug once addiction to another drug has become established. Therefore, alcoholic patients must be educated to the fact that the use of any mood-altering drug, with the exception of properly prescribed psychotropic medications, will sooner or later result in a resumption of active alcoholism.

Referral for Detoxification and Rehabilitation

Therapists working with active alcoholics and substance abusers must be familiar with the detoxification and rehabilitation programs in their areas. They must know about admission criteria, financial requirements for admission, the nature of the program, and the quality of the staff. The therapist should tour several of the local facilities and develop relationships with key staff members, especially admissions personnel. The quality of programs change, and one that was once excellent may decline, while a previously mediocre or poor program may develop into a successful one. The therapist needs to keep abreast of these changes. It is unwise to refer a patient to a facility of which the therapist does not have personal knowledge.

Decisions about where and how to detoxify a patient from alcohol or other drugs are *always* medical decisions. Nonmedical therapists should be extremely conservative and refer the patient for medical evaluation if there is the slightest potential for difficulties during withdrawal. Referral for inpatient rehabilitation is a therapist's decision. In general, the more damaged the patient, the more prolonged the addiction, and the more recurrent the relapse history, the more likely it is that the patient will benefit from a period in a rehabilitation facility. At the very least, they provide a safe environment in which feelings may be explored, experienced, and expressed while some drug-free time is being bought for healing and reorganization.

Whenever a therapist makes a referral, the transference is altered. Patients may perceive the referring person as lacking in power and magic potency; they may feel grateful or resentful or angry. Therefore, it is *vital* that the therapist explore, uncover, and help the patient experience, express, and work through feelings about the referral. Failure to do this usually results in losing the patient.

Self-help Groups

The first of the self-help groups is AA. The therapist needs knowledge by acquaintance, as well as knowledge about, AA. The AA literature is recommended, especially *Alcoholics Anonymous* (the "Big Book") and *Twelve Steps and Twelve Traditions* (Alcoholics Anonymous World Services 1955, 1957). The therapist should learn the steps and the AA slogans. They are useful in relating to both stably sober patients and active alcoholics. The AA concepts of "A day at a time" and "The first drink gets you drunk" are particularly useful in helping active alcoholics deal with their addiction. AA has a reservoir of experience in dealing with alcohol addicts, and there is much that therapists can learn from it. The therapist should attend open AA meetings, at which professionals and other nonalcoholics are welcome. Do so even if you yourself are "recovering" and a program member—you will be there for a different purpose and will experience it differently. Although AA participation is not the best route to sobriety for all patients, it remains the best single bet for achieving and maintaining sobriety for most alcoholics. It is especially helpful during the first year of sobriety.

The therapist may find it necessary to translate AA's "spiritual" side into more secular terms for those patients who dislike AA's spiritual style. For example, AA's third step, "Made a decision to turn our will and our lives over to the care of God *as we understand Him*," can be secularized into "Let it happen." AA's "higher power" can be interpreted as the AA group itself.

AA participation is a parallel process to psychodynamic psychotherapy. One does not replace the other. In working with active alcoholics and during early sobriety, there is usually no serious conflict between the patient's participation in AA and participation in therapy. What conflict there is centers around AA's tendency to teach supression of strong affects, particularly of the so-called negative emotions such as anger, and the therapist's attempts to help patients experience all of their feelings. This is rarely an insurmountable problem for either therapist or patient. Later in therapy, however, AA's extensive encouragement of the use of reaction formation–style defenses can indeed conflict with the goals and methods of psychoanalytic psychotherapy. The use of a self-psychology approach minimizes this conflict, but does not eliminate it.

The therapist needs to learn to use AA as a resource without either denigrating it as a nonprofessional inspirational movement or becoming an uncritical apostle. The therapist needs to become aware of and work through feelings about self-help groups.

Some patients will reject AA, whereas others will become "true believers." In general, the more schizoid or paranoid the patient, the more likely it is that AA will not work. Borderline patients usually do not do as well in AA as do those with the more intact narcissistic personalities. Nevertheless, an AA referral is always worth a try with active alcoholics.

One might ask how AA works. The dynamics of the AA program are discussed in Chapters 6 and 7, but for the moment we might be content with AA's answer to this question: "AA works fine."

There are many other self-help groups, most of which model themselves on AA and adapt the AA Twelve Steps. Alanon works with the alcoholic's significant others, and Alateen works with the teenage children of alcoholics. The populations served by Narcotics Anonymous (NA), Overeaters Anonymous (OA), and Adult Children of Alcoholics (ACOA) are apparent by their names. All of these groups are active and publish meeting books in cities and most rural areas across the country.

Abstinence versus Controlled Drinking as a Treatment Goal

The longer a patient has been drinking, the less likely it is that the patient will be able to return to social drinking. Many alcoholics have never been normal social drinkers. Very few patients are able to move from problem drinking of any duration and severity to normal social drinking. The goal of therapy with the vast majority of alcoholic patients must therefore be abstinence. There are some exceptions. Total abstinence is not a realistic goal with some adolescent substance abusers, who are prealcoholic in any case, nor is it a realistic goal with some late-middle-age problem drinkers—alcoholic patients who have been abusing alcohol for many years, but who have reached a relatively stable intrapsychic and interpersonal adjustment, and whose relationship to alcohol is also relatively stable. Abstinence remains the treatment of choice with these patients, but if it proves to be untenable, then it is necessary to help the adolescent deal with developmental issues or help the aging rummy minimize binges and express feelings, especially rage, in a more adaptive way. These are exceptions, however; complete abstinence must be the treatment goal with the overwhelming majority of active alcoholics.

Some behavioral psychologists disagree with this, opting instead to attempt to recondition their clients to drink normally by using a variety of classical conditioning, instrumental conditioning, social learning, and cognitive-behavioral techniques. The research evidence does not support the use of this approach, except with a few selected patients. The problem is that we do not know how to predict reliably which alcoholics can be successfully treated with these methods. Some behavioral therapists use various forms of aversive conditioning, in which drinking is paired with punishment in a classical conditioning paradigm, with the goal of abstinence. The research evidence is not conclusive on the efficacy of aversive conditioning in treating alcoholism, but it clearly takes extraordinarily motivated patients to subject themselves to this treatment.

Some psychoanalysts believe that an alcoholic patient should be able to drink normally after a successful analysis. We now know that there are some biological factors, such as the induction of the MEOS in the heptacytes, that mitigate against such an outcome and that analysis will not change; and it is amazing how unimportant, or even undesirable, drinking becomes to most successfully rehabilitated alcoholics. Kohut (1972) speaks of the traditional goal of analysis, ego autonomy—the rider off the horse in his metaphor: "where id (horse) was, there ego (rider) shall be"— as unrealistic and even undesirable in many treatment situations. He instead proposes ego dominance—the rider (ego) on the horse (id) but in control—as a more realistic and more appropriate goal of analytic therapy. Abstinence would be a form of ego dominance rather than ego autonomy.

What about the patient for whom alcohol meets vital psychological needs and who does not do well in sobriety? It is the purpose of psychological treatment to change this state of affairs, and it usually does. Very few patients are worse off when they are sober, and those who are worse off tend to be near-psychotic patients who need psychotropic medication to do the work that they hoped alcohol would do. With these exceptions, if the therapist helps the alcoholic mourn the loss of the alcohol, the alcoholic will not feel worse when sober. Quite the contrary, the overcoming of an addiction increases self-esteem and inevitably raises the patient's level of functioning.

Hitting Bottom

"Hitting bottom" is an AA phrase denoting a central AA concept: the idea that alcoholics cannot be reached until they are deeply hurt and in a state of despair. Alcoholics who are not in such a state are not considered candidates for rehabilitation. When alcoholics do not succeed in AA, it is said that they have not yet hit bottom. It is held that different alcoholics have different bottoms; there are high-bottom drunks (members) and low-bottom drunks (members). Although it seemingly contradicts the concept that the alcoholic must hit bottom, the AA program also compares alcoholism to a downward ride on an elevator, which the alcoholic may leave at any floor. The bottom floor is death. The concept of hitting bottom is tautological: If prospects become sober in AA, then they have hit bottom; if not, they failed because they have not hit bottom.

Despite its tautological nature, is there anything in the idea of hitting bottom? Since AA offers a kind of conversion experience, hitting bottom might be compared to the mystic's "dark night of the soul," which precedes the moment of illumination. There may very well be something in this; many recovering alcoholics do indeed report such dramatic experiences. A related concept is "ego deflation," a concept of H. Tiebout (1949, 1957), Bill Wilson's therapist. He believed that alcoholic grandiosity had to be punctured if the alcoholic was to have any chance at sobriety and that the moment of hitting bottom was the most propitious for this. If the ego deflation was successful, the alcoholic "surrendered," admitted his "powerlessness over his disease," and embraced the AA program. There is something punitive, even sadistic, in Tiebout's description of the "need for ego deflation" and the process of that deflation, but he is talking about pathological narcissism and one way, although not the analytic way, of dealing with that pathological narcissism.

The lesson for therapists in this is that despair, if it leads to insight, can be productive, and that being oversupportive can be counterproductive with active alcoholics. On the contrary, they often must be allowed to hit bottom, if that is where their drinking is taking them, before they become open to the possibility that sobriety might be preferable. This does not mean that therapists should not do everything in their power to assist patients in getting off that elevator on as high a floor as possible.

The Role of Insight in Achieving Sobriety

Insight has many facets. For active alcoholics, the crucial insight is that alcohol is hurting and not helping them, which may lead to the further insight that they must stop drinking. AA and some "hard-nosed" alcoholism counselors maintain that this is all the insight that is necessary. But even AA is not consistent on this, and some of the Twelve Steps aim at a broader insight. Many sorts of insight can contribute to an alcoholic patient's ultimately achieving sobriety. For example, Kirk's insight that he was identifying with his mother's masochism and self-destructive behavior, which he later realized was a part of her alcoholism, was important in enabling him to acknowledge and come to terms with his own alcoholism. For many alcoholics, psychological insight *is* important in achieving sobriety. Psychodynamically oriented counseling and psychotherapy, contrary to what some may believe, makes an important contribution to the treatment of alcoholism, including active alcoholism. The less severe the alcoholism and the less deteriorated the drinker, the more likely it is that psychological insight will help.

Interventions

Intervention has a specific meaning in alcoholism counseling. It refers not to the use of psychological interventions, such as clarification and interpretation, but rather to the carefully planned confrontation of active alcoholics with their alcoholism by significant others, including family members, friends, and professional associates. The desired outcome of such an intervention is for the alcoholic to enter a rehabilitation program, preceded by detoxification if necessary. An intervention is coordinated by a specialist, usually a recovering alcoholic, in conducting interventions. Major cities and many smaller ones have an ample supply of such "interventionists." Therapists are some-

times asked to participate in, and may sometimes initiate, such
interventions. Although it is not a "professional" technique, interventions are sometimes effective and the therapist should be
aware of the associated community resources.

The Use of Group Therapy

Group therapy is a popular modality in alcoholism treatment, particularly among alcoholism counselors. It is universally
used in inpatient rehabilitation programs. The aftercare group is
also a nearly universal component of alcohol rehabilitation unit
treatment strategies. Groups are also used for didactic purposes
to teach patients about alcohol and alcoholism.

There are many theoretical understandings of and ratio-
nales for the use of group therapy, and many ways of conducting groups. Our understanding of group dynamics has been
influenced by Freud's (1913b, 1921) theories of the identification of the group members with each other through the sharing
of an ego ideal and the sharing of guilt over common aggression;
by Bion's (1959) distinction between "work groups" and "common-assumption groups" and his elucidation of the regression in
and primitive mechanisms of common-assumption groups; and
by the empirical social-psychological studies of group behavior.
Our understanding has been preeminently influenced by the
application of self-psychological theory, including (1) the wish
for and fear of self-object merger; (2) the fear of psychic annihilation through such mergers; (3) the defenses against this wish;
(4) the need for and quest for mirroring; and (5) the formation
of mirror, twinship, and idealizing transferences between group
members and toward the leader. Self psychology also alerts us
to the issues of the need for control, of narcissistic vulnerability,
and of narcissistic rage in the behavior of the group. (The reader
is referred to the aforementioned works of Freud and Bion, to
the empirical social-psychological literature, and to Chapters 6
and 7 of this book.)

Despite the complexity of group dynamics, group therapy
for alcoholics often lacks a preconceived rationale, and understanding of the dynamics of the group interaction is generally

neither pursued nor valued. This is unfortunate, not to say potentially disastrous. The role of the group therapist is at least as difficult as the role of the individual therapist and should only be assumed by highly trained, skilled professionals, rather than by untrained or minimally trained "counselors," as is often the case in alcoholism rehab programs. How can group therapy be effectively used in the treatment of alcoholics?

Our concern here is primarily with the use of groups that are homogeneous, in the sense that all of the group members arc alcoholic, and all of the members are in the same "stage" of recovery or lack thereof. These groups are of maximum benefit to patients struggling to get sober and to recently sober patients. There is no reason that a stably sober patient should not be a member of a well-selected, well-led psychodynamically oriented outpatient psychotherapy group with a "mixed" population—mixed in the sense that the members carry different diagnoses. If recovering aloholics with several years of stable sobriety are judged to have sufficient ego strength to participate in such a group and would benefit from group treatment, then they are placed in a mixed, psychodynamically oriented group and treated like any other group member. (For a comprehensive guide to the dynamics of and leadership techniques for such groups, the reader is referred to Yalom's [1975] classic text.)

Active alcoholics are usually treated in inpatient groups. If an active alcoholic is to be treated in an outpatient group, homogeneous or heterogeneous, the alcoholism must be relatively mild and the patient must be willing and able to refrain from drinking on the day of the group. Several reasons are given for the use of groups in treating alcoholics. One is the intensity of the transferences that alcoholics are known to develop toward individual therapists. The use of a group is said to deliquesce and make manageable the intensity of the "alcoholic" transference. In particular, the alcoholic's intense repressed and largely unconscious hatred and rage—narcissistic, oral, anal, preoedipal, part-objectal, and so on—is unconsciously perceived by the alcoholic as potentially lethal to the therapist, an outcome to be avoided at all costs. The alcoholic may therefore run away, by emotionally withdrawing or by leaving treatment. The intensity of this "negative" transference threatens the treatment. In a group, an inchoate awareness of so much internalized rage may be much less threatening. Guilt can be shared, and if a group member or the leader should be "killed," all would not be lost; there would be other members remaining. The group leader can also demonstrate the alcoholic's tendency to use the primitive defenses such as splitting objects by pointing this out when it happens in the group. These benefits had been noted by psychoanalytic writers ranging from E. Simmel (1929), who managed a sanatorium for the treatment of alcoholism outside Berlin in the 1920s, to K. Menninger (1938) and R. P. Knight (1938), working in Kansas in the 1930s, to H. Krystal and H. Raskin (1970), writing of the alcoholic's self and object representations in the 1970s. These writers recommend a "team" approach rather than group therapy per se, but the rationale is the same.

The other justification for the preference for group treatment comes from the alcoholism counseling tradition. The rationale here is two-fold, or actually, two sides of the same coin: First, "it takes one to know one," and second, sharing a common experience is healing. The first can be used as an extremely powerful device to break down denial and unmask "bullshit"; the second makes the relinquishing of denial less painful, diminishes guilt, and is a balm to the narcissistic wounds that are an ineluctable concomitant of an alcoholic career. An additional reason that groups are preferred is that groups are settings in which primitive defenses such as splitting and projective identification quickly manifest themselves. In a group setting, these defenses can either be confronted and interpreted, or they can be supported in such a way that they protect without being overly destructive until the patient is strong enough to relinquish them. Further, the group frequently becomes an ideal object with which the alcoholic can merge in an idealizing transference, with less fear than might be experienced in establishing a similar transference in individual therapy.

Group therapy does not and should not replace individual treatment, however. These groups should not be led by undertrained personnel who are neither sufficiently aware of nor able to manage the depth of regression and the potential release of primitive aggression in a basic-assumption group. All too often these groups regress to the most primitive and barbaric mutual destruction in the name of "confrontation." There must be confrontation of denial of the alcoholism and of the rationalizations suppporting it; there must not be savage wounds to the members' self-esteem. By definition, group leaders have less control than individual therapists, but they do set the tone and limits of the group and retain considerable control over group members' behavior. Understanding the narcissistic vulnerability of the alcoholic patient and applying the principles of self psychology to the group interactions minimize the very real dangers of putting the patient through "confrontation" groups. The leader's relative lack of control *always* leads to disillusionment; this must be uncovered and interpreted. With proper safeguards, the inpatient group can be a very effective means of breaking down denial, reducing guilt, and giving the patient a safe area in which to experience and express feelings.

Further subdivisions of the already-homogeneous inpatient group are also common. The most frequently used are the adolescent alcoholic, the woman alcoholic, and the gay alcoholic groups, in which topics particularly relevant to these populations are stressed. These "special-interest" groups are also useful in providing additional safety for the discussion of sensitive issues. The more restricted and homogeneous the group, the greater the mutual identification of the members.

Inpatient rehab programs see themselves as, and sometimes are, "safe" places to "let it all hang out." They therefore often use treatment modalities that encourage a great deal of affective arousal and release. The most common is the psychodrama group. Led by a skilled facilitator, these groups are indeed effective for "decompression," allowing the barely sober alcoholic to discharge long-repressed emotions, which makes maintenance of sobriety immediately after discharge more likely. Psychodrama is also said to increase its participants' empathy for their significant others. However, there is no evidence that psychodrama groups produce structural change.

This brings us to the second-stage, or aftercare, group. These groups focus on alcohol and the problems of early sobriety. They alert their members to "drink signals," provide support and mutual identification, and serve as a safe place to express feelings. While all of this is indeed useful, these aftercare groups unfortunately also provide models for "slipping" and are often poorly led and too loosely structured. The third-stage group is a homogeneous group of recovering alcoholics which seeks to uncover and modify maladaptive defenses and which works far more psychodynamically. Preferable to a third-stage group is a heterogeneous, psychoanalytically oriented group if group treatment is indicated for a stably sober alcoholic.

Family Therapy

Family therapy is a popular modality for the treatment of alcoholism. In fact, alcoholism is said to be a "family disease." There is no question that a member's alcoholism powerfully affects the other family members. Indeed, the children of alcoholics are often tragically affected and afflicted by their parents' alcoholism. Despite the drinker's pernicious effect on the other family members, they often come to have an investment in the alcoholic's disease, but they are usually unaware of it. Family systems theory looks at the way in which a family maintains its homeostasis—its equilibrium—be that equilibrium benign or malignant. Systems theory postulates that inertia causes any family system to resist change. Since an alcoholic's becoming sober is a profound change, it follows that this change will be resisted by the family members. Unfortunately, experience tends to confirm this theory. Family systems therapists look at who has the power, who has what effect on whom, who has what role, and how the role incarnation impacts on the other members and their roles. This thinking has been applied to the alcoholic family to describe a set of typical roles, one of which is the "parentified child," also known as the "hero."

Family therapists see the family together, and their interactions and interdependencies are worked with in a variety of ways, depending on the therapist's theoretical orientation. What the family therapist sees as systematic and interpersonal, the self psychologist sees as intrapsychic and representational. For example, the "enmeshed family" of family systems theory is understood by the self psychologist as lack of self–object differentiation in the intrapsychic representational worlds of the family members. Family systems theory and self psychology are complementary and examine the same phenomena, although they understand these phenomena differently. A valuable contribution of family therapy to the treatment of alcoholism is its insights that any disturbance in the family system will be resisted, and that any change in one of its members will importantly impact on all of the other family members. An alcoholic family member's becoming sober will affect the entire system, and a radical readjustment of roles and relationships, which may be far from welcome although this is almost always denied, will take place. Family therapy sessions help the family understand the ways in which the alcoholic family member's drinking affected their family system and the impact that sobriety is now having on that system. Family therapy is usually perceived by alcohol rehab programs as a valuable treatment modality. In the case of the adolescent substance abuser, family therapy is regarded as a necessity, along with group and individual therapy.

Family systems theory has also alerted us to the frequent psychopathology of the enablers in the family. Their problems can be addressed in family therapy or in individual therapy; both are frequently used. The danger of the family therapy approach is that it can easily turn into a blaming of the victims of the alcoholic's aggression, when in fact they may have had very few options and perceived none. The case comes to mind of the wife with a number of small children and no income who stays with an alcoholic husband. She undoubtedly also has emotional reasons for staying with him, but reality considerations are often paramount and should not be disregarded or discounted in working with such a woman. This may seem obvious, but to overzealous systems theorists and practitioners, it often is not. Another danger of overzealous family therapy is that its active, intrusive style may push the recovering alcoholic toward his family when this may be the last thing that that alcoholic needs. Families are and have always been "mixed bags," and some of them are best left. Overzealous family therapists can do much harm trying to "fix it" when it is unfixable or best left unfixed. If these caveats are observed, family therapy can be of help to alcoholic patients. Psychotherapists who work with patients in individual therapy should be familiar with family systems theory and use it to understand how their patient's families impact upon them.

"GOD IS IN THE QUIET ROOM": ONE PATIENT'S EXPERIENCE IN A REHABILITATION UNIT

The experience of a psychiatric hospitalization or an alcoholic rehabilitation program is often traumatic. It is a crucial event in an alcoholic career. How the alcoholic reacts at this nodal point frequently determines whether sobriety is achieved. It is therefore worthwhile to look at this experience from the alcoholic's perspective. We will do this by following one inpatient experience.

The patient initiated psychotherapy after four years of sobriety primarily because he was unhappy in his career choice and felt trapped. Like so many recovering alcoholics, he had wished to become an alcoholism counselor. But it had been a wrong choice for him; he hated it. As a result of psychotherapy, he entered a graduate program in business administration and is now happily employed in a stock brokerage firm. Some of his other problems proved more recalcitrant, but on the whole he did well. During therapy he recounted his experience in the psychiatric hospital that had served as his rehab. Having been in the field, he "spoke the language"; his story appears here as he reported it during the first weeks of his therapy.

Doctor, I'm coming to you because I'm not getting as much out of my sobriety as I would like, but my present unhappiness is paradise compared to what it was like when I was drinking. I've been thinking about that a lot since I called to make this appointment. It's just about four years to the day since I entered the University Hospital psychiatric clinic. I was a drinker and a failure at many things as far back as I can remember—well, not quite, but at least since I went to college. After many years of this I really fell apart and finally went to AA. It wasn't easy but I managed to stay sober for two and a half years. Then I had a fight with my girlfriend and picked up a drink. I'm sure you've heard that alcoholism is a progressive disease; believe me, it is. It was sheer hell once I picked up that drink. I would go on a binge, either not go to work or go to work with the "shakes," not go home, sleep in fleabag hotels, wake up shaking in the middle of the night, reach for the bottle or run past the other bums to find an open bar; then I would go to a few AA meetings, get sober for a while, make some excuses, and go back to work. After a few days I would pick up a drink again and it would be worse than ever. It—or maybe I should say *I*—was crazy; I had been in AA and I knew what to do, but I couldn't do it; I had a place to live, a house with some friends, but I didn't go there. Instead I went to those lower-depths hotels when I was drinking.

Things got worse; the sober periods became shorter and the drinking became almost constant. I just couldn't get my feet on the ground. I wanted to stay sober but I just couldn't do it. Finally I became desperately ill—physically and mentally. I went to my regular doctor—the kind who takes your temperature instead of showing you the dirty pictures. That's supposed to be funny; don't you ever smile, Doctor? I told him I was going mad. He arranged for me to enter the hospital. First I got drunk and went to my job, where I resigned with a melodramatic flourish. I drank some more and blacked out.

The next thing I remember I was in an office signing myself into the mental hospital. I had taken only nine months to change from a somewhat dissatisfied, somewhat anxious, but functional human being into a stumbling wreck of a zombie who couldn't even

remember how he got to the funny farm. I had managed to find a new girl friend during that period. I did
that by staying away from her when I was drinking
heavily; that meant she hadn't been seeing much of
me. Fortunately she had known me during my sober
years, and I guess she had some hope that I would stop
drinking. I asked the admitting doctor if I could call
her before I went up to my floor. The resident looked
disapproving, but he gave me permission. When two
attendants appeared, I really started shaking. What
the hell had I done? I had signed myself into a bughouse. I wanted a drink; I wanted a thousand drinks; I
wanted to leave. It was too late! I had signed away my
"freedom." The attendants, who looked preppy,
started to lead me to the elevator. I told them that I
had permission to make a call, and they let me. Permission to make a call! Jesus Christ, what had I gotten
myself into? I called my girl friend and told her I had
signed myself into the "flight deck," as the bughouse is
called in AA. She said "Wonderful; that's the best thing
you could have done." I knew she meant it suppor-
tively, but her comment didn't feel supportive. I gathered that she had been less than delighted with my
condition during the past few months. I thought of
saying, "Gee, thanks"; instead I said "I love you"—
we're still together—and stumbled somewhat tearfully
toward the elevator.

The tweedy attendants were firm although
friendly, but somehow they looked like concentration
camp guards to me. One of them took out his key to
open the elevator door, and as that door shut behind
me I heard the clang of all the dungeon doors that
have ever closed upon a previously free man resound
in my ears. You raised your eyebrows, Doctor; don't
you know you're supposed to be a mirror? Think I'm
histrionic, eh? Of course I know that I threw away my
freedom, but that wasn't the way it felt then. By the
time that elevator door shut, I was quaking inside and

probably outside as well. One of the attendants pushed a button and up we went.

The elevator opened and we were on the "floor"; it was dark and gloomy. Once the elevator closed I was locked in. For the next month I did not leave there without an attendant opening that door and escorting me wherever I was going. Have you ever been locked up? If you're writing that the patient suffered a narcissistic wound in being hospitalized, you're right in spades. Four years later, I still shudder at those locked elevators. Yes, you can put down claustrophobia too. I felt bewildered. I couldn't remember how I had gotten there; I didn't know what had happened to the day. It was now night and apparently it was late, since nobody was around. The attendants led me to my room. It was actually a reasonably cheerful and comfortable room, but I didn't notice it then. What I did see were the bars on the windows. A shiver ran down my spine.

The attendants told me that the doctor was coming to examine me in much the same tone they might have used to announce that God was coming to see me. I was told to take a shower to prepare for the examination. That made me feel dirty, and I probably was. I wondered if I smelled. I felt some resentment, but far more fear. The sense of being locked in was fading, and I even felt a little secure behind those locked doors and barred windows, but by then my blood alcohol level must have been falling and I was feeling more and more shaky. Every nerve was screaming for a drink and so was I. I managed to shower and put on the hospital gown I had been given. It was not easy, with rubbery legs and arms that wouldn't quite work smoothly either.

"The doctor," who turned out to be two very young residents, arrived. They acted very seriously, as if to make sure that nobody treated them like kids. If you've read Kernberg, you know that I was using

devaluation as a defense, just like I'm doing now.
Don't you ever smile? Well, I needed to devalue them;
they frightened me. At that point everything did.
They asked a seemingly endless series of questions,
just as the admitting doctor had. I felt that they were
students practicing on me. They weren't exactly great
at establishing rapport, and I sure needed some rapport. I must have been in pretty bad shape because I
had a hard time answering those questions and I'm a
real smart guy. I thought, "Oh shit, I really did it this
time; I'm brain damaged." Mercifully, the residents
switched from a psychiatric to a medical mode and
gave me a very thorough physical exam. I found it
reassuring. Although I didn't like being poked and
jabbed, I guess I felt cared for.

I had been drinking two quarts of rye a day for
quite a while, and you might say that I was more than
a little worried about my health. You'd better get your
eyebrows analyzed, Doctor; they're not under ego
control. I wasn't a light case, and two quarts a day it
was. That I did remember to tell the residents. The
examination ended; I was given some medicine and
fell into a sleep of sorts.

I woke feeling like death. A nurse came in and
told me to dress and come to the "dayroom." By now
every nerve in my body was screaming and all I could
think of was a drink. I left my room and entered a
bustling world of patients and staff. I unsteadily made
my way down a seemingly endless corridor and entered the dayroom. I was struck by the fact that the
people there didn't look like patients, however patients are supposed to look; they just looked like people. Pretty well-dressed ones at that. I found this reassuring; maybe this wasn't such a bad funny farm after
all.

I was taken to see my "regular doctor," a
Dr. Kruse. Although he was a resident too, he looked
grown up and somehow very medical. He was very

authoritarian, or at least that's the way that I perceived him. He told me that he was detoxifying me from alcohol and that I would be given pentobarbital in decreasing dosages for five days and then nothing; that I would see him three times a week; and that I could stay in bed and not participate in the floor activities for the next two days. I found him so intimidating that I forced myself to tell him that alcohol strips the body of B vitamins and that I should be given vitamins. I don't even know if that's true. Is it? At any rate, Kruse prescribed the vitamins and I felt a little more, very little more, in control. Pathetic, isn't it? Still, being able to ask for something and get it helped.

Then I panicked. Five more days and then no alcohol and no medicine. I literally didn't think I would survive. I didn't even have to deal with a drugless state for five more days, yet I was already going up the walls. At that moment I turned to my AA experience and decided that this was going to be tough, very tough, but that I would deal with it a day, an hour, a minute at a time, and I did. My two and a half years in AA were not wasted; I used the program to get through the hospital experience and to get all that I could from it. I also decided not to stay in bed for three days, but to participate in the hospital program from the start. This desperate attempt to retain a little dignity in front of Kruse and my decision to use AA's day-at-a-time concept to do what I had to do to face drug-freeness were important events in my recovery. I know it sounds corny, but it was at that point that I started to fight to get well and somehow, sick as I was, I knew it then. Knowing it was almost as important as doing it, because knowing it changed how I felt about myself a very little, but vital, bit. Nothing like an "observing ego," eh Doctor? Smiled that time, didn't you? As soon as I was capable of it, I tried to understand what was happening to me as it happened.

Sure, this was a defense against feelings, and I can intellectualize forever, but this trying to understand also helped me a great deal. If it did nothing else, even if all the insight was pseudoinsight, it increased my self-esteem. Interesting patient, aren't I?

These vestigial feelings of self-worth and of having a coping strategy didn't last long. In fact, they didn't even last until I left Dr. Kruse's office. As I walked up that endless corridor to the dayroom, I was in a panic and I mean a *panic*. My skin crawled; my breath came hard and then seemed to come not at all until it started to come all too rapidly and I started to hyperventilate; my palms dripped sweat; my heart pounded wildly; the vessels in my temples pulsed and felt like they would pop; my legs quivered; my hands shook; my vision blurred; the lights seemed to dim. Somehow I reached the nurses' station. Ever have a panic attack, Doctor? Do you know Edvard Munch's painting *The Scream*? I see you do. Well, that's just what it's like. Oh, why am I explaining—you're human, aren't you? "Nothing human is alien to me," eh? I must stop mocking you. It's part of my cool, detached, arrogant, yet proper and polite persona, a facade that I used as a defense in the hospital just like I'm doing now. I didn't tell you about that. In the hospital I was polite and very controlled—under the shaking, that is. I mean, I liked to look in control. Pathetic, wasn't it? But I already said that. I was also superintellectual. Technical terms poured from my lips like I had four PhDs. Back to that word—pathetic—that really was pathetic, and I say that without self-pity. It's repetitious, but it's apt.

At the nurses' station I was given my pentobarbital. It took a little while until it hit; but when it did, it was wonderful. It was like two double-double Seven-and-Sevens. I soon felt drunk, and I loved it. Somewhere I knew that this was but a reprieve which would come to an end, but that didn't much matter—I felt too good.

That pentobarbital really hit me hard. Soon I was staggering and slurring my words. Pat, the big, snappish, tough-sounding black nurse who had given me the medicine tried to talk me into going to bed. I said, "No. I want to participate in the hospital program, and the doctor said that I could if I wanted to." She relented and I staggered from the nursing station to the dayroom, literally bouncing off the walls. An alcoholic rehab would have kept me in bed at that point. I'm glad that the hospital took some risk of my injuring myself and let me stagger around for a few days. Like, I said, discovering the will to fight, wherever that came from, made the difference.

It's a mystery, isn't it? Why did I choose life instead of death at that point? I don't know, but I did. God? The anabolic forces of the universe? A massive psychic reorganization? Symbiotic union with the hospital? Who knows, but it happened. Somehow I was able to say to myself, "I fucked up, but I'm going to do it differently this time; I'm going to build on bedrock instead of sand, a minute or a second at a time." Somehow, somewhere I knew then that I could, although of course there were many moments of panic and despair in the process. Perhaps I was drawing on a deeply buried repository of all the love I had received in my life. Again, I don't know. But I had decided to fight to build on solid ground this time. To do that I decided to use everything the hospital had to offer and get everything I could from the experience. Kind of goody-goody, eh? Of course, I was also casting myself in a heroic role, and part of me enjoyed it. But so what? Why shouldn't I have given myself some "fringe benefits" by way of enjoying my private version of the myth of death and rebirth. Funny, I never thought of it that way before—being in therapy does have its uses.

So I bounded and staggered into the dayroom. I was very drugged. Sitting there were a very angry-looking bear of a bearded, middle-aged man and a seventyish, stylishly dressed woman—Bill and Sadie. Bill was slapping down cards from a tarot deck on a table top with great force and looked every bit the conjurer. I wobbled across the room, introduced myself, and said, "Will you overlook my ataxia and dysarthria? They are induced by the medication I'm taking." I remembered those terms from my grand-father's stroke. Sadie looked blank; Bill said "Sure, kid" and slammed the tarot cards harder. I lunged into a jargon-filled discussion of my condition. Bill said, "Sit down and let me get a reading of your cards." I felt accepted, but I remained standing. You look amused, Doctor. I told you I was playing the most pleasant of gracious intellectuals who knew more or less everything and was willing to share it with all. "Gladly learn and gladly teach," eh? As they say in AA, I was being a "people pleaser" in my own strange way. Bill and Sadie took it all in stride and again invited me to join them at the card table. This time I did.

I was slurring badly enough that it would have been difficult to understand me even if I was making sense, which I almost certainly wasn't. That didn't seem to bother Bill and Sadie. As we say in AA, we ran our stories. Bill, a lecturer on communications at a local college, was manic-depressive. He said he was in the hospital because his wife was afraid of him. Look-ing into the almost infinitely deep pools of hatred and rage in his eyes, I understood why, but I was too drugged to feel afraid. Sadie said she was 67 years old and in her third hospitalization for depression. She was very much the lady, and I thought it was funny when she told me that her doctor during her last hospitalization 20 years ago had told her to buy a set of cheap dishes and break them all. I couldn't picture her doing that. That old internalized anger doesn't do much for people. Looking back on it, it almost killed me. I didn't know that then.

Just as Bill, Sadie, and I were getting acquainted, a chime rang. I'll always be able to hear that chime. It rang for meals, for meds, for activities, for bedtime, for everything. Structure for the structureless, I suppose. Comfort in routine. Comfort or not, I got to hate those chimes. This particular chime called us to activities. The dayroom had filled with about twenty people, but I hadn't noticed. We were lined up and marched—at least that was the way it felt—to the locked elevators. The attendants were actually kind and friendly, but I still experienced them as prison guards, which in part they were. Being escorted everywhere through locked doors was humiliating. There is just no other word for it. I staggered as the others walked. We were taken up to the top floor, which had a gym, game rooms, and a screened-in roof garden. The younger patients played volleyball while the older patients played in the game room. I didn't feel capable of doing anything, so I went out on the roof garden and looked down at the traffic far below through the wire mesh. At least its not barbed, I thought, as my depression rose like waves through the waning pentobarbital.

For the next four or five days I followed the hospital routine, participating in what I could. There was individual therapy with Dr. Kruse, group therapy, recreational therapy, occupational therapy, dance therapy, and community meetings. As the withdrawal medication was titrated down, my anxiety returned and once again moved toward panic proportions. The slurring and staggering gave way to a sort of spasticity. My arms and legs would jump up, much as though I was a dancer in the dance of the toy soldiers. It was embarrassing, although it was hard to feel embarrassed in the totally accepting atmosphere of the floor. It was also disabling. Without warning, an arm or leg would fly up.

I remember sitting and playing bridge with Bill, Sadie, and "the Princess," a wealthy, very uptight woman who had gotten herself hooked on pills and had attempted suicide. I had had my last dose of pentobarbital about three hours before. I could feel the drug losing its effect. I was excited about being drug free and terrified at the same time. Suddenly the day room grew bright and the objects in it sharply defined. It was as if the lights had gone on in a dark theater. I was fascinated. So this was what the world was supposed to look like. Then I was dealt a hand. As I picked it up, my arm involuntarily snapped over my head and the cards flew. The heightened illumination of the room now seemed sinister. My thoughts raced. I thought, I'm going mad. This is the madhouse. I'm losing my mind. I'll never get out of here. I felt sheer terror. I felt I wasn't going to recover; I felt it was all over. Yet I picked up those cards with those spastic arms and bid one trump. Made the hand, too. I wanted to talk about what was going on inside of me, but I was afraid to. My thoughts kept speeding up and became more and more confused. I jumped up and ran to my room, where I collapsed on the bed in a state of utter despair. I know part of it was physiological, but I must have been close to madness that night.

I finally fell into a deeply troubled sleep. After I don't know how long, I woke to one of the strangest sensations I have ever felt. There were waves of force emanating from the center of my abdomen, traveling through my body, and smashing against my skin. Rhythmic and relentless wave succeeded wave. It felt like I would shatter, that the waves would break me into pieces. The impact of the waves against the surface of my body was so strong that I feared that I would fly off the bed. I reached up and grasped on to the bars of the bed above my head and held on for dear life. Smash, smash, smash, they kept coming, relentlessly, inexorably. I thought of screaming out, but I didn't. Suddenly a thought occurred to me: Holy shit, that's my anger, my rage, *my*, *my*, *my* anger coming out. This is not something happening to me; it is me—it's my rage. I held on to that thought as my last tie to reality. I repeated to myself over and over again, "It's my anger and nothing else." It was my Copernican revolution, though I certainly didn't think of it that way while it was happening. What I mean is that that thought changed the center of things for me. It was I who was doing this thing, not some outside force. This was another pivotal point in my recovery, just as important as my decision to fight. It took a long while for the waves of pressure to stop shattering themselves against my flesh, but the terror was gone. Finally I fell into a deep sleep, from which I awoke exhausted and drained, yet somehow freer than I had felt for a long time. Doctor, I suppose you'd classify what happened to me as a somatic delusion, and I suppose it was, but that doesn't really matter. What did matter was that I was able to use it to "own" my anger, or at least some of it.

The floor consisted of two long arms connected to a body consisting of the dayroom, the nurses' station, and the dining room. My room was at the end of one arm and Dr. Kruse's office was at the end of the other arm. The total distance was a full city block. During the days following the anger waves I paced those arms, the corridors, obsessively. Whenever I wasn't in a scheduled activity, I paced. You are probably thinking that I was going in and out of mother's arms to her breasts, the nurses' station. Perhaps you're right on that, but I sure didn't experience it that way. It's probably of some significance that I forgot to mention that my mother was dying, or at least was supposed to die during my final round-the-clock binge and was still critical when I entered the hospital.

Responded to that one, didn't you, Doctor? As it turned out, Mother unexpectedly survived, but her illness must have had something to do with that final binge. Lost the girl friend, losing the mother, eh? Let me tell you something strange: One of the things I am most grateful to AA for is that it taught me how to mourn. Maybe that doesn't make much sense, and I don't know how it happened, but after my nine-month slip, when I returned to AA I was somehow able to mourn another loss, that of my father. That was an old loss and I somehow think that my failure to come to terms with my feelings about him and his death were connected to my slip, although the occasion, if not the cause, of that slip was girl friend trouble. Gratitude for being able to mourn. That's really crazy isn't it? I don't really believe that; I know it isn't crazy. It's just that I'm embarrassed by the depth of my feelings. AA puts a lot of emphasis on gratitude: gratitude for sobriety; gratitude for the program itself. Sure, sometimes that gratitude is defensive, another form of denial, a reaction formation, but sometimes it's genuine—and that's been an important part of my recovery. Melanie Klein would understand that, wouldn't she? Gratitude for the good breast making possible reparation for spoiling that good breast and turning it into the bad breast—working through the depressive position— that's what AA is all about. Read the Steps. It may sound like I'm intellectualizing again, but I'm not, even if I'm showing off a bit. I really am choked up right now, thinking of all I have to be grateful for.

As the days passed, the spastic jerking of my extremities became less and less frequent. I still paced, but now the focus of my concerns had shifted. I became hypochondriacal and drove Pat, the nurse, crazy demanding blood pressure readings. The ubiquitous chimes summoned us to have our blood pressures taken three times a day shortly after they had summoned us for meds. Pat did not take kindly to my pestering. She rebuffed me harshly and gruffly. I thought of her as the ogre of the floor. During my hypochondriacal phase I was also very aware of my anger.

At times it was so intense that I thought it might break me in half, but never after the anger-wave hallucination did I experience it as external. It was an objectless anger. Is there free-floating rage like there's free-floating anxiety? I guess there is; I had it. So overwhelming was it's intensity and the intensity of some of my other feelings, especially my fear, that all I could do was to self-consciously constrict my experience of the world to an instant at a time. More and more constricted did my world become until I was living in a succession of infinitesimal flecks of time, an infinitesimal at a time, so to speak. I did not dare to live even five minutes ahead or look five minutes behind; it engendered too much fear. Similarly, I constricted my spatial world to tiny patches of perceived space. I mean this quite literally; when my anxiety was high enough I could feel my world shrinking toward an instant and a point. It was like a camera in my head was being focused more and more narrowly. This was being in the here-and-now with a vengeance.

I remember being in the gym, totally overwhelmed by rage and fear and something like despair as I stared at the punching bag. Suddenly my visual field narrowed to a patch of pebbly brown; this was about 10 percent voluntary and 90 percent involuntary. I tried to open my visual field, but it didn't happen. I thought, well you really did it this time; you're stimulus bound now. Then I thought, so be it; I'll be stimulus bound, and I started pounding that patch of pebbly brown with the pent-up rage of a lifetime. When I stopped, wringing wet and exhausted, my point world gradually expanded to encompass the gym and my fellow patients. That was scope enough for me. I knew that something impor-

tant had happened, but oddly I didn't feel much relief.
That came considerably later. I spent many more
hours punching that bag. It helped.

Another way my hypochondria, and doubtless
the withdrawal too, manifested itself was in blinding
headaches. They fed my obsessional worry about high
blood pressure. I ran from nurse to nurse trying to get
aspirin. I tried to manipulate Dr. Kruse into prescrib-
ing medicine. Forget it. If I stood on my head, there
was no way that hospital was going to give me anything but a vitamin tablet once I was detoxified.

I've often wondered what my experience would
have been in an alcoholic rehab unit instead of a
psychiatric hospital. Fortunately the hospital I was in
was very "hip" on alcoholism; witness their reluctance
to give me drugs. At least half of the patients who
came and went during my month-long stay on the
floor were drug or alcohol cases, whatever else may
have been wrong with them. Popular problem, eh? I
worked in an alcohol rehab after I became a counselor, so I know what they're like. I learned the psychoanalytic "lingo" from one of the social workers on
the unit. We were the mavericks of that staff. I missed
the alcohol education that I would have received in an
alcohol rehab, but on the whole my hospitalization
really worked. Since I already had AA exposure, the
psychiatric hospital was probably best for me. Alcohol rehabs are less humiliating and less frightening,
but they are also kind of doctrinaire. I don't like that.
My hospital did a terrific job of creating a therapeutic
community on the floor. For all of the inevitable
aloneness, there was a real feeling of shared adventure
and closeness on that floor. At least I felt that at times.
I also liked the hospital's emphasis on being honest
about your feelings and expressing them. It wasn't AA,
but its values were similar. I know that I have a lot of
negative feelings about that hospital and about being

treated like a prisoner. But my positive feelings aren't all a reaction formation or a form of denial either.

Paradoxically, my period of being "stimulus bound," as I thought of it, coincided with my increasing involvement in the life of the floor. It was almost cinematic the way my scope of focus would spatially, and to a lesser extent temporally, expand and contract. During my relatively expansive periods, my relationships with Bill, Sadie, and the Princess, Jan, became more and more important. There was a real bond around that bridge table, a bond not without its conflicts and disturbances. I became increasingly afraid of Bill. He really looked like he might kill everyone on the floor. Sitting across from him at the bridge table was no easy thing. His psychiatrist was trying to get him to take a major tranquilizer. He was threatening to sign himself out if the doctor insisted that he take it. I finally got up my courage and told him I thought he was dangerous and that he should take that medicine. Amazingly, he agreed. After that we became closer, and I was initiated into the tarot card mystique. When I was given a good reading I felt elated. A recovery is made of many tiny steps, like those infinitesimals I spoke of, that accrete into something substantial and solid. Telling Bill he was dangerous was such a step for me.

Sadie was a truly lovely person who had had a lot of loss in her life. I wished so hard that she would break those fucking dishes. The Princess could be arrogant, but she was bright and witty. I enjoyed her. She had been in the hospital for a long time and was scheduled for discharge. She went on pass and took an overdose of Valium while she was out. Her suicide gesture greatly upset me; I thought maybe nobody gets out of here intact. I was surprised when the Princess was discharged as planned. I often wonder what happened to her. She was replaced by an overtly psychotic patient. When I told him I was in for alcohol abuse, he said, "Oh, that. I stopped drinking years ago and joined AA. Look at me now." This frightened and discouraged me more than the Princess's suicide attempt. At about the same time, a middle-aged man was brought in on a stretcher. He had also attempted suicide. He turned out to be a physician whose son had been killed in a South American political upheaval. He clearly did not want to live. The sadness in his eyes was as profound as the anger in Bill's eyes. He was a charming and worldly man whose charm and worldliness were automatic and mechanically empty. He insisted on leaving the hospital after a week and was discharged against medical advice. I was sure he was going to his death.

During my "social period" in the hospital, I felt a great need for the approbation of my fellow patients. After I confronted Bill, I seemed to regress. He improved on his medicine and was gone from the floor on pass more and more frequently. The Princess was leaving. Although I liked her, Sadie was limited companionship. I felt isolated and alone. I became even more of a people pleaser; I felt that I needed the approval of every person in that hospital. In fact, I just plain needed everybody in that place. Under my formal, helpful, intellectual, polite facade, I was enraged at the people leaving and distrusted the newcomers. My facade clearly turned some people off, particularly Pat.

The floor held community meetings each evening. Generally I didn't much participate. The night the Princess left and Bill's discharge date was set, I was particularly forlorn. Left behind in the madhouse. At the community meeting some blowhard took the floor and monopolized the meeting in a way that really annoyed me. It seems ridiculous now. I've become quite good at telling people to go fuck themselves, but then I couldn't risk alienating anybody, including that asshole. I should tell you that a psychotic medical student had been brought in that day. She kept repeating "E equals MC squared." In the course of the day she became more and more disorganized. They put her in the quiet room, an isolation cell used for out-of-control patients. This terrified me. Other patients, particularly Ruth, a provocative, street-wise teenager, had been put in the "quiet room." But this was for short periods, sort of like sending a kid to her room. The quiet room held a peculiar fascination for me. I was utterly terrified by it. I suppose I was afraid of losing control, but unconsciously wished to at the same time. Fear of confinement permeated every fiber of my being. The quiet room was a prison within a prison. I identified with Julie and her "E equals MC squared," and by that night all of my terrors were focused on the quiet room. So at that community meeting I was not only desperately into people pleasing, but terrified of losing control lest I be put into the quiet room. At one level I knew this was ridiculous, but my terror wouldn't go away.

So there I was listening to that long-winded asshole ramble on. Suddenly I knew I had to say something. I was slumped down into a couch almost as if I wanted to bury myself in it. It took every bit of strength I had to force myself to sit up. I was sweating and shaking. Finally I managed to say, "I don't like what you're doing. You're taking over this meeting. Sit down and shut up." My body almost convulsed, but I had done it. I relaxed and sank back into the couch. That was one of the most significant accomplishments of my life; it took more courage and there was more fear to go through to say those few words than has been the case in some seemingly much more significant accomplishments. At the end of the meeting, Pat came over and put her arm around me and said, "You did good." I shan't forget that.

Speaking up at the community meeting opened things up to me. Julie, the medical student, grew increasingly agitated. I thought she was reacting to being locked in the quiet room. Put in the quiet room because she was agitated; agitated because she was put in the quiet room. At least that's the way it seemed to me. I would look through the window of her locked door. The staff stopped me from doing this. Julie became more frantic. Finally they "snowed" her, put her out with massive doses of tranquilizers. Now she lay unconscious on the floor of the quiet room, with her arm raised and splinted as intravenous solution dripped into it. I thought, "God, they're killing her." I became totally absorbed in her fate and my identification with it. The quiet room became a symbol for all that I feared and dreaded, yet perhaps secretly wanted—after all, hadn't I rendered myself unconscious with a drug, alcohol? Hadn't I sought death? Another new insight; I hadn't thought of that before. That day in my session with Kruse, I said, "I'm afraid of you. You have too much power." The reference was to Julie, but I was also thinking of myself. This comment to Dr. Kruse was also important in my recovery. Difficult, but not as difficult as speaking at the community meeting. Maybe courage is cumulative and each instance of it makes the succeeding one a little easier.

Another way in which I opened up was by running my story. I had learned to do this in AA, and I had been doing it to some extent since I entered the hospital. But now I ran my story to everybody who would listen and to some who didn't. I did it in group therapy; I did it at the community meetings; I did it with the staff; I did it with my fellow patients. Each time I told my story I learned something new. I suppose you would call that "working through." I knew that I was boring people and taking advantage of a captive audience, but I didn't care; I did what I had to do and it helped.

I also opened up physically, with my body. I had never been very involved in recreation therapy. I had played volleyball only with the greatest reluctance and only when pushed by the recreation therapist. I played fearfully, self-protectively, holding my body tight and closed. Naturally my playing was awful. A few days after that community meeting I was cajoled into playing volleyball. This time it was different. I could feel the energy flowing through my body. I became the game. I felt myself leaping into the air. I felt myself coming down hard. I felt myself taking risks. The closeness, the tightness, the self-protectiveness fell away. It was wonderful. They say that how you play the game is a picture of yourself; it's true. I was not self-conscious while it was happening, but afterwards I processed what had occurred, and that helped too; it was part of my changing my self-image.

I had a somewhat similar experience in occupational therapy. At first I was reluctant to do anything because of my physical condition. Besides, I looked upon "arts and crafts," let alone "basket weaving," as I thought of it, with derision. But I said to myself, Fuck it; I'll do this garbage since I've decided to "work" the hospital for all it's worth. So commitment won over arrogance. I struggled for weeks to make a mosaic ashtray. At first it was almost impossible to do because my hands shook so both from the withdrawal and from anxiety. I finally finished the thing. I couldn't believe the way I was reacting; I felt ecstatic. What was important about this was that it convinced me that I could function in the face of and in spite of anxiety. I told Pat that the ashtray was "an external and visible sign of an internal and invisible grace." She treated this bit of pretension with the contempt it deserved, but the idea behind it was valid enough. I've recalled making that ashtray many times when I thought I couldn't do something because of emotional pain, and sometimes I was then able to do it. I still have that ashtray and I no longer smoke.

Julie stayed "snowed out" for days, and I kept returning to that window to stare at her prostrate body until a staff member chased me away, much like a child compulsively putting his tongue to a sore loose tooth. Finally she regained her feet, although she was still very much out of it. One of the staff told me, "It's okay. She needs to regress." I oscillated between thinking that this was a rationalization of what they had done to her and that it reflected a deep empathy. I guess that reflected my ambivalence toward the hospital—mistreated and understood at the same time. A few days later Julie was released from the quiet room. She and Ruth immediately became friends. I remember one exchange between them. Julie asked, "Why is this nuthouse different from all other nuthouses?" Ruth, perfectly seriously, answered, "It's the real McCoy." For some reason I loved the medical student and the street kid for this exchange.

I was getting better. I was given a pass to leave the hospital. As I walked out of the hospital and tried to walk down the street, I felt a magnetic force drawing me back to the hospital. I don't mean this metaphorically; I mean I actually felt pulled back to the hospital. Another quasipsychotic episode, I suppose. I thought, no, this can't be happening. But it was. It really felt like the force would pull me back. I fought it and succeeded in breaking loose. No doubt a projection of my desire to cling to the mother, eh Doctor? Or was it the regressive, seductive pull of madness? Whatever it was, it sure was no joke then. A need to regress indeed. I had had enough regression; I feared it as much as I desired it. Fortunately the fear was slightly greater than the desire, and I escaped the regressive pull of the hospital and of madness. I started to run and didn't stop until I ran out of breath several blocks away. The pull was gone.

I felt a surge of joy. I was free. I bounded toward the park. I felt as if I had springs in my heels. It was a little like being on speed. Looking back on it, I was more than a little manic. I ran toward the polar bears in the zoo. They seemed glad to see me. We spoke for a while; at least I spoke to them. I felt a great sense of communion with the polar bears. My social worker friend told me that one of the psychoanalytic theorists had spoken of the toddler's "love affair with the world" when he starts separating from his mother. I suppose my feelings in the park were like that. Later that day I stubbed my toe, so to speak, and ran crying back to my mother-hospital. You know, AA's like that—a safe home base from which one can go into the world to take his lumps and return to be comforted. *Rapprochement*—that's what they call that stage. But we all need that, don't we? Funny, I never thought of AA that way before. After a while I left the park and went to my girlfriend's. Our relationship had just begun to get close when I started to avoid her during my heavy drinking, yet she had come to visit me several times in the hospital. Like most of those places, they strictly regulated phone calls and visits. It took a while to get phone privileges and even longer to be allowed visitors. They wanted us to "act in," to work out our shit right there in the hospital. When she was finally allowed to see me, Ann was very supportive and that meant a lot to me. I shared as much of the hospital experience with her as I was able to. I had an overwhelming fear of being impotent sober. If you've been to many AA meetings, Doctor, you know that's a very common fear. At her last visit I had spent an hour explaining to Ann that we couldn't make love for at least a year after I left the hospital because I couldn't afford to jeopardize my sobriety by putting any pressure on myself. I was perfectly serious. Five minutes

after I arrived in her apartment we were in bed.
Everything went fine.

Several hours later, I left Ann to go to an AA
meeting before returning to the hospital. I had come
down off my "pink cloud," but I was still feeling good.
That wasn't to last long. I was excited about going
back to my old group. I had bounced in and out of
that meeting during my nine months of drinking. Now
I was sober and hopeful. I walked into the meeting
and immediately felt estranged. I couldn't connect
with anything or anybody. It was horrible. I sat
through the meeting, but I really wasn't there. I felt
very far away. It was as if a thick, viscous fluid surrounded me and isolated me from the group. Again I
do not speak metaphorically. I could feel that viscous
medium intruding between me and the people in that
room. It prevented me from making human contact. It
was a little like being in an underwater movie. I must
have been distancing, but I sure didn't know it then. I
left in a state of deep despair. Whatever my ambivalence toward the hospital, I felt warmth and concern,
something like loving care there. I had counted on
finding that at my AA meeting, but it surely didn't
work. I have never felt as alone as I did on my return
to the hospital. I felt defeated and profoundly depressed. I wanted to give up.

During the following days I went through the
hospital routine mechanically. My friends had been
discharged, which made me feel even more forlorn
and abandoned. For some reason I didn't talk about
my experience at the AA meeting back at the hospital.
Although Julie was out of the quiet room, I still obsessed about that incarnation of evil, as it seemed to
me. My discharge was approaching. I was given
another pass. I didn't want to use it, but I did. With
great reluctance I decided to try a new AA group. This
one was a few blocks from the hospital and met, as it

turned out fittingly, at the Church of Epiphany. I was
very shaky as I walked into that meeting. I didn't
really expect anything good to happen, but I felt that I
had to try to get back to AA anyway. The meeting
started with the preamble. "Alcoholics Anonymous is
a fellowship of men and women who share their experience, faith, and hope with each other. . . ." Something was happening. Those words sounded like pure
poetry to me. The speaker was a beautiful young
woman, intensely and vibrantly alive. Her vivacity
and sparkle certainly faciliated what was to happen to
me. Eros, I'll take all the help I can get from you. She
spoke of her years of drugging and drinking, of her
progressive spiritual and emotional death. Finally she
said, "I got to the point that I couldn't feel anything.
For no particular reason, I went on a trip across the
country with some drinking buddies. As we crossed
the country my feelings became more and more
frozen. We arrived at the Grand Canyon. I looked at it
and felt nothing. I knew that I should be responding
with awe and wonder to the sight before me, but I
couldn't. I had always loved nature; now that love,
like everything else about me, was dead. I decided to
take a picture of the magnificence spread before me,
so that if I ever unmelted I could look at the picture
and feel what I couldn't feel then."

At that moment something incredible happened
to me. I completely identified with the speaker. I
understood her frozen feelings; they were mine. I
understood her wish to preserve a precious moment in
the hope that some day she could adequately respond
with feelings of awe and wonder to it. Something
welled up in me. I began to sob, deep, strong, powerful sobs; they did not stop for the hour and a half that
the meeting lasted. As the speaker told her story—how
she had managed to stop drugging and drinking and
how her feelings had become unfrozen, my feelings

became unfrozen. I was still crying when I shook her hand and thanked her. I walked out of the meeting feeling happy. I couldn't even remember feeling happy.

As I walked down the street toward the hospital the tears were still flowing. Now they were tears of happiness and gratitude. I, who had been so formal and controlled and concerned to impress, walked past staring strollers with tears streaming, completely indifferent, indeed virtually oblivious, to their reactions. Doctor, do you know Edna St. Vincent Millay's poem *Renascence?* It tells of a young woman who has been buried; then the rain comes, washing her grave away and returning her to life. She becomes aware of "A fragrance such as never clings/To aught save happy living things . . ." I had always loved that poem; now I truly understood it. My tears were like that rain in the poem; they, like the rain, washed me out of the grave I had dug for myself with alcohol and emotional repression. I too smelled the fragrance that never clings to aught save happy living things.

I walked into the floor feeling buoyant. As I joined the perpetual rap session in the dayroom, a thought came to me: God is in the quiet room. I didn't know where it came from nor what I meant by it, but I vocalized it. I think it had something to do with feeling loved and connected and potentially loving myself. It seemed that whatever I had experienced at that AA meeting was also present in the quiet room. That's as close as I can get to understanding what I was trying to express in that phrase. What had happened at the meeting had something to do with receptivity, with being open and being able to hear. That part of it was a gift, from whom I do not know. When I left the hospital a week later, I was given a good-bye party, as all about-to-be-discharged patients were. At the party I was given a pastel drawing of my saying, "God is in the quiet room." I still have it.

I'm not much on theodicies and I can't do much with a young girl going mad as a manifestation of divine grace. I don't know who or what, if anything, is out there, and I haven't become religious in any formal sense—I don't belong to a church. So when I said "God is in the quiet room," I must have meant it in some metaphorical sense. But I did mean it. There was certainly denial in that statement, denial of evil and pain and sorrow, denial of all I hated about the hospital, denial of my rage at the waste my life had been, but there was something else in it too, something that liberated me to engage in the long, slow, up-and-down struggle for health. In AA we say that sobriety is an adventure; it certainly has been for me.

Well, Doctor, now that I've told you my story, let me tell you about why I came here. My fucking job is driving me crazy; I hate it. . . .

CHAPTER 5

Other Addictions and Their Treatment

In this chapter we will look at the pharmacological and behavioral effects of the more commonly abused drugs. Although it could be argued that such afflictions as compulsive gambling, compulsive overeating, and compulsive sexuality are also addictive states, this text will restrict itself to the chemical addictions. We will also look at the dynamics of drug addiction and see how self-pathology—narcissistic deficit and the addict's attempt to self-medicate that deficit—plays as least as large a role in the other addictions as it does in alcoholism. Treatment issues will also be discussed; however, all addictions are treated in essentially the same manner, and our discussion of the treatment of alcoholism will serve as a model for the treatment of the other addictions.

As is the case with alcoholism, the addiction must be diagnosed and confronted, the patient educated on the drug's effects, and the active addiction halted. A support system must be provided for the recovering addict, either through membership in a therapeutic community or through participation in a self-help group, such as NA. Only then can the slow work of reme-diating the structural deficits in the self through psychodynamic psychotherapy begin. It is these structural deficits and the ad-dict's maladaptive attempts to compensate for them that consti-tute the pathological narcissism so characteristic of the active addict.

The most commonly abused drugs are marijuana and hash-ish; CNS depressants, including the barbiturates, methaqualone (Quaalude), and the "minor" tranquilizers; CNS stimulants, in-cluding amphetamine (speed) and cocaine; the opiates and other narcotitc drugs, including opium, morphine, heroin, and methadone; and the psychedelic drugs, including mescaline and lysergic acid diethylamide (LSD).

Marijuana and Hashish

Marijuana and hashish—pot and hash—which share the psychoactive agent tetrahydrocannabinol (THC) are the second most widely used drugs, following alcohol, in western cultures. Marijuana differs from alcohol in that it is illegal, although this illegality is frequently ignored. As is the case with alcohol, many people use it without psychological or other difficulty and with-out becoming dependent. This is not always the case, however, and psychological addiction to THC in its various forms is quite common. What effect does THC have on the user, and how is this effect produced?

Marijuana use has a very long history. It was used as a mild intoxicant and sedative by a variety of peoples, and the fact that the plant grows wild made it easily accessible. However, mari-juana has not played near the central historical role that alcohol has. In the 1920s, "tea" became associated with jazz musicians and with the "lost generation," although this group of writers was second to none in their devotion to alcohol. Marijuana remained a drug of the ghetto and of bohemia until the 1960s when smoking grass became a badge of membership in the youth culture. During the intervening years Harry Anslinger, the U.S. Commissioner of Narcotics, had conducted a scare campaign attributing every kind of evil to marijuana smoking. Much of the public came to believe that pot smoking inevitably led to heroin addiction and a life of crime. This contributed to the hate which the youth rebellion elicited in many older Americans. As the decade progressed, however, pot smoking became more widespread. A movement to decriminalize it arose. By the 1970s, its use had spread throughout the country, and few were the younger members of the middle class who had not at least tried it. Today it is rare to encounter a patient under the age of 50 with addictive tendencies who has not "dabbled" with pot. Cross-addiction to alcohol and marijuana is extremely common.

Both marijuana and hashish are prepared from the hemp plant *cannabis sativa*. Marijuana is a mixture of the crushed leaves, stems, and flowers of male and female *cannabis* plant; hashish is the resin obtained from the flowering tops of the female plant. Hashish is considerably more potent than marijuana. The pharmacological and psychological effects of marijuana and hashish are almost entirely due to the action of Δ9-tetrahydrocannabinol (THC), although other cannabinols may be psychoactive. Marijuana and hashish are usually smoked, although they may be ingested. Gertrude Stein's friend, Alice B. Toklas, published a recipe for hashish cookies in her cookbook. Marijuana and hashish can be dissolved and injected, but this very dangerous procedure is rarely used. Marijuana, also known as "tea," "grass," and "pot," is usually rolled into a cigarette, or "joint," and smoked. Hashish is usually smoked in a pipe. Their psychological effects vary with set and setting.

In low doses, the effect of THC is similar to that of the sedative-hypnotic drugs; it induces feelings of relaxation, drowsiness, and well-being. The user often enters an anxiety-free, drifting state which resembles a pleasant daydream. Marijuana, unlike alcohol, does not disinhibit aggression. Many users report intensified perceptions and enhancement of sensory experience. They report that food tastes better, music is more acutely experienced, and sex is more enjoyable. In large doses the THC present in marijuana and hashish acts as a psychedelic, inducing hallucinations and changes in body image. In such large doses, toxic psychosis, in which the sense of identity is lost and depersonalization ensues, may occur. The user may feel paranoid. THC increases pulse rate and reddens the eyes. Despite a great deal of research, the mechanism by which THC exerts these effects is unknown. THC is metabolized primarily by the liver, and the metabolites are excreted in the urine and feces.

Frequent heavy marijuana use can result in psychological dependency. Whether or not physiological dependency develops is controversial, but it is known that THC is less addictive than alcohol. Nevertheless, abrupt cessation of prolonged heavy marijuana smoking can result in withdrawal symptoms, and tolerance does develop. Chronic marijuana use, especially in large amounts, is associated with respiratory illnesses, including bronchitis and asthma; with suppression of the body's immune system; and with reduced levels of testosterone. Prolonged heavy marijuana or hashish smoking is known to leave residues in the lungs, the long term-effects of which are unknown. THC has some medical applications. It reduces nausea in cancer patients undergoing chemotherapy, and it reduces intraocular pressure, suggesting that it might be useful in the treatment of glaucoma. THC, like all other psychoactive drugs, crosses the placental barrier and enters fetal tissues.

There is no solid empirical evidence on the preaddictive personality of marijuana or hashish addicts. Chronic use is associated with apathy, social withdrawal, and impairment of goal-directed behavior; impairment of short-term memory may also result. It is not known if these personality characteristics are etiological in marijuana addiction or if they are consequences of the use of the drug.

Experience indicates that borderline personality organization is far more often found in "pot heads" than in alcoholics. Apparently there is something in the sedated, dreamy withdrawal which pot can induce that attracts borderlines. Perhaps it quiets their rage. This does not mean that the narcissistic pathology so frequently seen in alcoholics is absent in pot heads, but it does mean that they are more likely to also suffer from the more severe ego impairments associated with what Kernberg (1975, 1976) calls the lower end of borderline pathology.

CNS Depressants

We are already familiar with one CNS depressant: alcohol. Alcohol is classified as a sedative-hypnotic—that is, a drug that disinhibits and relaxes in low doses and induces sleep in high doses. As do all CNS depressants, it exerts its pharmacological effects by a graded depression of synaptic transmission in the CNS. Sedative-hypnotics other than alcohol are classified as barbiturates and nonbarbiturates. Both classes of sedative-hypnotics are usually orally ingested. They may also be dissolved and injected, although this is extremely dangerous. Since these drugs initially depress inhibitory pathways, their effect in low doses is often a feeling of euphoria and well-being. As the dosage increases, they produce hypnotic effects. In yet higher doses they act as anesthetics, and still higher doses produce coma and death. They are not analgesics; that is, they do not reduce pain. On the street this class of drugs is known as "downers."

The Barbiturates

The *barbiturates* are a class of chemical compounds derived from barbituric acid. Structurally, the barbituric acid molecule is a ring, and the various barbiturates are prepared by adding side groups to that ring. The drugs vary in strength and in the duration of their action. The most common are pentobarbital (Nembutal); secobarbital (Seconal), amobarbital (Amytal), phenobarbital (Luminal), and thiopental (Pentothal). The primary medical use of the barbiturates is to induce sleep. They are also used for daytime sedation, as tranquilizers, for the relief of anxiety, for the prevention of epileptic seizures, and for induction of anesthesia. Their sleep-inducing effect derives from their selective depression of synaptic transmission; they will exert their strongest action on the parts of the brain that contain a great number of synapses. It happens that the parts of the brain that are involved in behavior arousal (the ascending reticular activating system [ARAS] and the diffuse thalamic projection system) have a great number of synapses. These pathways are therefore particularly susceptible to the action of the barbiturates. The barbiturates also depress the respiratory centers of the medulla, which can lead to death in cases of overdose.

The barbiturates are absorbed from the stomach and small intestine and enter the blood circulation, which distributes them to all tissues. The more fat soluble of these compounds readily cross the blood-brain barrier, whereas the more water-soluble ones do not cross as easily. Barbiturates produce their pharmacological action in the brain until they are redistributed to other tissues. The speed with which they are redistributed varies with the drug. Following redistribution to muscle and fat, they are metabolized by the liver and excreted by the kidneys. Barbiturates cross the placental barrier and have a depressant effect on the fetus. The long-term effects of such fetal depression are unknown. It is possible for a baby to be born addicted to barbiturates.

Barbiturate-induced sleep differs from normal sleep; slow-wave sleep is increased, and a corresponding decrease in rapid eye movement (REM) sleep is produced. A REM rebound occurs when the drug is withdrawn. Although relatively safe when properly presribed, the barbiturates are addictive both psychologically and physiologically. Tolerance develops as a result of both induction of enzymes in the liver and accommodation of the neurons in the brain to the drug. Severe and even life-threatening withdrawal effects can result from cessation of prolonged heavy use of barbiturates. The withdrawal effects are a result of the rebound effect (hyperactivity) which follows the cessation of any CNS depressant. Tolerance to depression of the respiratory center does not develop, however, so doses that a barbiturate addict might require to experience the desired sedation may be fatal.

Sedative-hypnotics are additive in their actions; that is, a combination of drugs will sum their effects. Often they produce a synergetic reaction, so that the combined effect of more than one sedative-hypnotic drug can be much greater than a simple summing of their effects. It is for this reason that a moderate dose of barbiturate combined with a moderate dose of alcohol, which would not be dangerous if their effects were simply additive, may result in death. Such deaths are not uncommon.

The effects of barbiturate abuse are very similar to those of alcohol abuse. As the user increases the dose, signs of "drunkenness," including cognitive and motor impairment, appear. Psychological dependency develops, followed by physiological dependency, and life becomes progressively impoverished as obtaining and using the drug becomes the most important activity in the addict's life. People who would be horrified at the thought of becoming alcoholic sometimes become barbiturate addicts. Such addicts are frequently women who start out using prescription drugs and gradually increase their intake. Persons who become addicted to "downers" are presumably attempting to compensate for the same structural defects in the self as are alcoholics, but we have only clinical evidence for this.

Cross-tolerance develops to all CNS depressants, and cross-addiction is extremely common. Such cross-addiction may develop to various kinds of downers or between alcohol and downers. AA speaks of "sedativism"—the use of downer drugs, including alcohol, to alleviate or at least mask dysphoric affects. In their view there is no difference between pill use and alcohol use. They refer to such use as "taking a martini in powered form."

There is a paucity of carefully controlled studies of downer addicts, but it is presumed that their personality characteristics are similar to those of "clinical" alcoholics. With the near ubiquity of cross-addiction, this question is of decreasing practical importance.

Nonbarbiturate Sedative-Hypotics

The commonly abused *nonbarbiturate* drugs are meprobamate, marketed as Miltown and Equanil; the benzodiazepines, including chlordiazepoxide (Librium), diazepam (Valium), flurazepam (Dalmane), clorazepate (Tranxene), and lorazepam (Ativan); and methaqualone, marketed as Quaalude.

Meprobamate. Meprobamate and related dicarbamate derivatives were introduced in the 1950s as "tranquilizers." The most popular of these drugs was Miltown, with Equanil a close second; derivatives were marketed under such trade names as Soalcen and Soma. These drugs were introduced to replace, or to offer an alternative to, the barbiturates. They were supposed to offer the advantages of the barbiturates—sedation and relief of anxiety—without the disadvantages—habituation and possible addiction. Experience has shown this to be a misapprehension. For all practical purposes, they perform the same services and carry the same risk as the barbiturates. Everything that has been said about the barbiturates applies to them.

The Benzodiazepines. The benzodiazepines, a class of sedative-hynotic drugs, are in widespread use. They are "minor" tranquilizers; that is, they have sedating and antianxiety effects, but they do not have antipsychotic properties like the "major" tranquilizers. The first of them, chlordiazepoxide (Librium), was introduced in 1960. The most popular is diazepam (Valium). Serax, Dalmane, Tranxene, and Ativan are also members of this family.

The benzodiazepines are structurally different from the barbiturates, but they are pharmacologically similar. They are somewhat more specific as antianxiety agents, and they are less hypnotic. It is postulated that their primary site of action is the hypothalamus rather than the ARAS. They depress the respiratory center less than do the barbiturates and are therefore less likely to produce fatal overdoses. They are almost always taken orally, are absorbed slowly, and are long acting. They produce the same feelings of disinhibition, euphoria, release from anxiety, and well-being as do other sedative-hynotics. Higher doses produce the same impairments in memory, judgment, cognitive functioning, and motor coordination.

Contrary to early reports, prolonged use does result in tolerance and physiological addiction. The withdrawal from these drugs, especially Valium, is particularly severe. Popular drugs of abuse, they are extremely popular with "sedativists." Cross-addiction to alcohol is more the rule than the exception, but tranquilizer addicts who do not drink are also seen. Psychological dependence short of addiction is almost epidemic. Like other prescription drugs, the minor tranquilizers are abused by many people who abhore "drug addicts." The ways in which tranquilizer abusers differ from alcoholics and barbiturate addicts is not known, but considering the prevalence of cross-addiction, it is probably a distinction without a difference.

Methaqualone. Methaqualone, marketed as Quaalude, Parest, Somnafac, and Sopor, enjoyed a vogue as a "love drug." It is actually a sedative-hypnotic of average strength and has no aphrodisiacal qualities. It is strikingly similar to the barbiturates in its psychological and behavioral effects. It too is popular with "sedativists" and it is one of the most popular of the street downs. In fact, it is more associated with a street style than are the minor tranquilizers. Prolonged heavy Quaalude use results in tolerance and physiological dependency.

CNS Stimulants

Although many types of drugs stimulate the nervous system in one way or another, we will restrict our discussion to the class of drugs known as *behavioral stimulants*, also denoted *CNS stimulants* and *psychomotor stimulants*. These drugs are distinguished from clinical antidepressants, such as Elavil; convulsants, such as strychnine; and general cellular stimulants, such as caffeine, which also exert a stimulant effect on the CNS but are rarely drugs of abuse. Methylphenidate (Ritalin), which is used to treat hyperactive children, is also a behavioral stimulant, but it, too, is rarely a drug of abuse.

The behavioral stimulants are among the most frequently abused drugs, and the amphetamines and cocaine are by far the most popular of these. They are used by dieters to reduce appetite, by students to stay up to study for exams, by the depressed to self-medicate their dysphoria, and by party-goers to get high. The recreational use of these drugs is controversial; it is both illegal and increasingly popular. An unknown percentage of these recreational users become hooked; these are the "speed freaks" and the "coke addicts." In low doses the behavioral stimulants elevate mood, produce euphoria, increase alertness, and reduce fatigue. In high doses they can produce irritability, tension, anxiety, psychotic behavior, and convulsions. How do the behavioral stimulants affect the nervous system?

Like a vast majority of psychoactive drugs, the CNS stimulants produce their effects in the synapses, the gaps separating the neurons. Chemicals called *neurotransmitters* carry the neural impulses, the information, across the synapses. Among the most important of the neurotransmitters are a class called *catecholamines*. Close relatives of adrenaline, the catecholamines also play a role in the peripheral nervous system, where they are involved in the state of behavioral arousal called the fight/flight/fright reaction. The behavioral stimulants act by increasing the amount of available norepinephrine (a catecholamine) in the synapses of the brain. They produce this effect by increasing the release of norepinephrine (NE) into the synapse by the presynaptic neuron. Amphetamine also "mimics" NE, directly stimulating the postsynaptic membrane. Cocaine blocks the "reuptake" of NE and of dopamine, a related neurotransmitter.

Once a neurotransmitter enters a synapse, it would continue acting forever unless something intervened. Two things can happen: (1) It can be actively pulled back into the presynaptic membrane, or, (2) it can be destroyed by enzymes in the synaptic cleft. Cocaine acts by blocking the first action, but this leaves the NE remaining in the synapse subject to the second action. It is postulated that the enzymatic destruction of NE and dopamine, rather than its preservation by reuptake, is responsible for the "crash," the intense depression, which follows a cocaine spree and for the "craving," which may persist for a long time.

The Amphetamines

Amphetamine is widely used. It has legitimate medical uses, and its relative, Ritalin, is used in the treatment of hyperactivity in children. Why a stimulant should be effective treatment for hyperactivity is something of a mystery. One theory that has been advanced to explain this paradox is that these children are depressed and that their hyperactivity is a manic attempt to ward off this depression.

Amphetamines have been widely used as diet pills because they supress appetite, but the body very quickly develops tolerance to this effect. The dosage must then be increased to achieve the same degree of appetite supression. Many people have been hooked on "uppers" in this way. There is no medically sound reason to use amphetamine for weight reduction. In the (not very) long run, they are ineffective, and they have considerable potential for abuse. Since the development of antidepressant drugs, which do not produce tolerance, amphetamines are rarely used for the medical treatment of depression. They are widely used as a euphorant, however, both recreationally and in the self-medication of depression. Amphetamine slightly improves psychomotor, intellectual, and athletic performance, and it is widely used for this purpose. As the dosage increases, fine motor control decreases and performance suffers.

In low doses, amphetamine (Benzedrine, or "bennies") is usually taken orally; 5 to 50 milligrams is considered a low to moderate dose. The amphetamine derivative dextroamphetamine (Dexedrine, or "dexies") is more potent, and methamphetamine (Methedrine, or "speed") is even more potent.

Amphetamine acts both peripherally and centrally. Peripherally, it mobilizes the fight/flight/fright reaction, the body's sympathetic response to threat. This results in increased blood sugar, decreased blood flow to internal organs, increased blood flow to muscles, increased respiration, and dilated pupils. Centrally, amphetamine increases mental alertness and elevates mood, an effect that is subjectively experienced as sharpness and euphoria. No wonder uppers so easily generate a craving to repeat the experience and are so notoriously psychologically addicting.

At higher doses, tremor, restlessness, agitation, and sleeplessness result. Serious "speed freaks" soon habituate to low to moderate dosages of these drugs, at which point they change the route of administration and inject the amphetamine into a vein. They also radically increase the dose. The result is a "rush," said to be a "whole-body orgasm" which no other experience can match. Tolerance soon builds to this effect also, and addicts engage in a futile search to reexperience the quintessential high they so vividly remember. Drug induced psychosis is produced by shooting high doses of amphetamine for any length of time. At these doses amphetamine produces a "model" psychosis which is strikingly similar to paranoid schizophrenia. Such users frequently see "narcs" (narcotic agents) in every tree. They may suffer hallucinations and delusions, and they may become dangerously aggressive. Antisocial behavior is common. Withdrawal results in prolonged sleep, radically increased appetite, and profound depression. The dysphoria following a prolonged amphetamine "run," or spree, may be intolerable, compelling the addict to take more of the drug.

Little is known of the personality traits of speed freaks, but they are presumed to be profoundly depressed individuals who self-medicate their depression and sense of inner deadness with uppers. From a self psychology point of view, they are attempting to ameliorate a paucity of psychic structure, which they experience as deadness and emptiness, through the use of stimulant drugs. The drug also serves as a self-object which performs from the outside functions, such as the regulation of self-esteem, that should be performed from the inside, and with which the drug addict fuses in order to participate in its omnipotent power. In effect there is an idealizing transference to the speed.

Cocaine

Cocaine is strikingly similar to amphetamine in its physiological and psychological effects, although its mechanism of action is pharmacologically distinct. Cocaine, a white powder, is administered in several ways. It may be sniffed and absorbed by the vessels of the nasal passages, a practice known as snorting; it may be treated with an alkali, usually sodium bicarbonate, and smoked, a practice known as freebasing; or it may be dissolved and injected directly into a vein, a practice known as shooting or mainlining. Cocaine can also be taken orally, although it is absorbed slowly and incompletely. Before the passage of the Federal Food and Drug Act (1914), cocaine was present in Coca Cola, and its stimulant effect helped make Coke popular. Cocaine is a far more powerful stimulant than amphetamine, and its effects far more dangerous. Shooting can be fatal, and deaths from freebasing are not unknown. Cocaine is a potent local anesthetic, and it is used for that purpose in ophthalmology and otolaryngology. It has no other current medical uses.

Freud discovered the euphoric properties of cocaine and wrote about them both privately in his correspondence with his fiancee, Martha, and publicly in professional journals. He called it a "wonder drug," uncritically praising its ability to alleviate low spirits. He himself used the drug for many years. Freud also discovered the anesthetic effects of cocaine, but his friend Kohler published the information first and received credit for discovering the use of cocaine for ophthalmological surgery. It is interesting to note that Freud was misled by ambition, by the need for narcissistic fulfillment, in his errorous judgment of cocaine. Freud's ambivalent feelings about cocaine play a considerable part in his (1900) masterpiece *The Interpretation of Dreams.* His analysis of his dreams reveals both pride in its discovery and guilt over hurting a friend to whom he has recommended it.

Cocaine is a very potent CNS stimulant, especially when it is freebased or injected. It produces all of the effects of amphetamine, only more so. It is far more likely to produce convulsions, and drug-induced psychoses occur at far lower doses. Further, cocaine is metabolized by the liver much more quickly than is amphetamine, and its effects last only a short time; it is thus highly addictive. Psychological habituation occurs readily; tolerance develops rapidly; the withdrawal crash is extremely painful; and craving is common even weeks and months after the last dose. Cocaine devotees frequently use alcohol to "come down" when they are "too" high and to medicate cocaine withdrawal crashes; cross-addiction is common. Alcohol actually worsens the depression, but it masks it. This is soon followed by a new round of freebasing or mainlining, and the cycle starts again.

Addicts thus attempt to exercise omnipotent control over their emotions, fine-tuning moods and affects. The result is that they dehumanize themselves into objects, the state of which is to be controlled by chemicals.

Cocaine is an "in" drug, extremely popular with young urban professionals, or "yuppies." Doubtless many of them use it recreationally without serious difficulty, but many become addicted. They are probably warding off feelings of inner emptiness, but the sheer pharmacological power of this drug is so great that it is virtually impossible to know what is "under" the addiction until the addict has cleaned up. Shooting cocaine is extremely dangerous; it may result in convulsions or death, and its continued use inevitably leads to paranoid psychosis. Cocaine is expensive, and its devotees frequently lose savings, homes, jobs, and relationships in supporting their habits. Many become dealers, involving themselves in a criminal life-style. Whether sociopathy antecedes addiction in a substantial number of these addicts is not known.

Opiates and Other Narcotics

The opiates are a group of drugs, natural and synthetic, that produce the same effects as opium does. Opium is a naturally occurring substance obtained from the opium poppy, *papaber somniferum*. Pharmacologically it is classified as a narcotic. Narcotics have *both* sedative *and* analgesic effects.

Opium has been used since antiquity for the relief of pain and the treatment of cough and diarrhea. It was also used recreationally, and addiction to it was well known in classical times. Opium was a highly sought-after substance and an important item of trade. Wars have been fought over it.

Opium, a crude extract, contains many chemicals, most of which are pharmacologically inert. In the nineteenth century, morphine, the active ingredient in opium, was isolated. Addiction to opiates was common in nineteenth-century America; opium and its principle derivatives were widely used in patent medicines, and until the Harris Act of 1914 put these substances under strict control, addiction to opium-containing patent medicines was pandemic. Although no longer legally available, the opiates continue to be widely abused.

Opium, the crude resin obtained from the opium poppy, contains many biologically inert compounds. These make up 75 percent of the resin. The remaining 25 percent is biologically active and consists primarily of two substances: morphine and codeine. Morphine is a powerful analgesic and a potent antidiarrhetic. Codeine shares its basic chemical structure with morphine, but it is much less potent. It is used primarily as a cough suppressant. Heroin, a synthetic derivative of morphine, originally developed to treat morphine addiction, is considerably more potent. Other important synthetic opiate narcotics are meperidine (Demerol), used as an analgesic, and dolophine (methadone), which is analgesic but not euphoric, and which is used to treat heroin addiction.

The opiates are variously administered. Inhalation is among the oldest of the methods. The resin may be smoked or its derivatives finely powdered and sniffed. The sniffing of finely powdered heroin, called snorting, is the usual introduction to the drug. The opiates may also be injected into the muscles, under the skin, or into the veins. The latter two methods—subcutaneous injection, or "skin popping" as it is called on the street, and intravenous injection, or "mainlining"—are popular with opiate addicts.

Although the reaction to opiates varies with dose, route of administration, drug, set, setting, and previous drug experience, most people experience a sense of euphoria and well-being, warmth and contentment, and great power. These feelings may be followed by an enjoyable dream-like state and by sleep. There may or may not be a "rush," an initial intense experience said to be similar to, but more powerful than, a sexual orgasm. This "rush" is more likely to occur with heroin, which readily passes the blood-brain barrier, than with the other opiates, which do not. Analgesia, which is more an indifference to pain than a cessation of it, also occurs. Although the opiates are used medically to manage physical pain, they also make people indifferent to psychological pain, which accounts for much of their appeal.

Opiates reduce the motility of the gastrointestinal tract, resulting in constipation. By acting on the brain, morphine and its relatives decrease the size of the pupils of the eye to pin-points. These disparate effects—analgesia, euphoria, sedation, constipation, and pinpoint pupils—are the primary results of the administration of opiates. Opiates also depress the rate of respiration, so overdoses are dangerous.

The opiates act by binding with specific receptor sites in the brain and in the intestinal tract. These receptors appear to be designed specifically to receive the opiates. This seemed strange before the discovery of naturally occuring opiate-like substances, the *enkephalins*, which play complex and poorly understood roles in the body. In the CNS, these opiate receptors occur in the spinal cord, brain stem, thalamus, and limbic system.

Morphine and heroin are metabolized largely by the liver and excreted by the kidneys. They are metabolized rapidly, disappearing from the body in four to five hours, which means that narcotics addicts must constantly renew their supply. Tolerance to respiratory depressant, analgesic, euphoric, and sedative effects develop. Tolerance results from both induction of enzymes in the liver and adaptation by neurons in the CNS. Tolerance to pupil-constricting and constipating effects does not occur. Tolerance also builds to the rush, so that the user is forced to take more of the drug to get the same effect. Physical dependence may develop. Depending on the dose and the duration of the addiction, withdrawal from opiates can be quite painful, although not usually dangerous. Withdrawal symptoms include agitation, restlessness, craving, intense anxiety, fever, vomiting, severe flu-like pains, rapid breathing, chills and violent diarrhea. They last about a week.

Opiate addicts do not get good press. It is they who are referred to as "dope fiends" and "drug addicts." It is their addiction, especially to heroin, that is held to be responsible for much urban crime. There is indeed a correlation between crime and addiction, but the relationship is far from simple; the hopelessness of ghetto life may well be an intervening variable significantly influencing both of these behaviors. In any case, heroin addicts, whether poor black or middle-class black or white, do not receive much empathy in our society.

Heroin and other opiate addiction occurs in the middle and upper classes. Ironically, opiates are less damaging to the body than is alcohol, and an opiate addict with financial means and access to supplies may be able to live a socially acceptable life. In fact, long-term opiate addiction has few somatic consequences, and the deterioration associated with long-term alcohol use may not occur. On the other hand, the emotional impoverishment consequent on the other addictions also occurs with opiate addiction. Fortunate circumstances do not protect the opiate addict from such impoverishment.

We have little solid evidence about the personality correlatives of opiate addiction. It is believed to be a disease that primarily afflicts young men. Sociological factors are important, but they are not decisive. After all, only a small proportion of the economically and socially oppressed ever become addicted to opiates or any other drug. The most enlightening study of preaddictive personality was done by Chein and his associates (1964). In their book *The Road to H*, they demonstrated massive psychopathology in the preaddictive lives of young drug addicts. This pathology could be broadly characterized as borderline personality disorder, which included severe narcissistic damage and deficit. Sociopathy is also associated with opiate addiction, but it is not clear how much of this *follows* addiction to an expensive, illegal drug.

Treatment is difficult and is often undertaken in a "therapeutic community." Methadone maintenance, which substitutes a minimally euphoric opiate for heroin, is also widely used. Analytic treatment of opiate addiction is also possible and perhaps too seldom used. The knowledge of narcissistic pathology contributed by self psychology gives us a powerful weapon for the understanding and treatment of this affliction.

Psychedelic Drugs (Hallucinogenics)

The psychedelic drugs alter both sensory experience and consciousness. The experience induced by these drugs, called a "trip," includes hallucinations, altered experience of time, and changed self-perception. They may cause derealization and depersonalization. Chemically they differ widely, but all of them either mimic or modify the action of a neurotransmitter. Their effects are primarily psychological, although they do exert some somatic effects. They are not physiologically addicting, but they do produce tolerance, and they may induce psychological dependence in susceptible individuals. Because they induce psychotic-like states, they were thought to be psychotomimetic, producers of model psychosis. This is no longer thought to be the case, however, largely because the psychedelic user retains insight and is aware that the experience is the result of having taken the drug. Amphetamine is much more a psychotomimetic.

The long-term effects of the psychedelic drugs are unknown; however, prolonged repeated use has been suspected of causing brain damage. There is no hard evidence to support this, but heavy users may experience flashbacks (involuntary trips) months or years after their last dose of the drug. Addiction to these drugs is rare. Their use is usually self-limiting, and the addiction-prone will return to alcohol, pot, or uppers as their main drug of abuse. Bill Wilson, the cofounder of AA, is said to have experimented with psychedelic drugs toward the end of his life, but he neither became addicted to them nor returned to alcohol. The use of these drugs may lead to psychotic episodes in borderline patients, who sometimes decompensate under their influence. Whether such patients would have escaped psychosis if they had not used these drugs is a matter of conjecture. Although psychedelic drugs are now used much less commonly than they were in the 1960s and early 1970s, bad trips still account for a significant number of psychiatric hospital admissions.

The use of psychedelic drugs has a long history. They occur naturally in a variety of plants and herbs which have been used medically, recreationally, and ritually. They have been used to induce ecstatic or mystical states as part of religious rituals. The best known of these naturally occurring substances are the mystical mushrooms of Mexico, *Psilocybe mexicana,* and the peyote cactus, *Lophophora williamsii*, of the American southwest. The mushrooms contain psilocybin and psilocin, both of which have been synthesized and are available on the street. The "buttons" of the peyote cactus are chewed to obtain its active principle, mescaline, which has also been synthesized. Aldous Huxley (1954) wrote *The Doors of Perception*, a widely read book reporting his experience with mescaline. He regarded it as a shortcut to mystical insight. The drug enjoyed a vogue among rebellious youth in the sixties. Mescaline is strikingly similar to the neurotransmitter norepinephrine (NE) in its chemical structure. Like NE, mescaline induces behavioral arousal; but unlike NE it alters perception, changes the experience of time, and induces hallucinations.

LSD is an extremely potent synthetic hallucinant. It is the most widely used of this class of drugs. It is usually added to a sugar cube and taken orally. It too received a great deal of publicity in the sixties when its use was advocated by Timothy Leary and Richard Alpert, then Harvard University psychology professors. It is believed to act by altering synapses using the neurotransmitter serotonin in such a way that the sensitivity of the reticular formation to sensory information is augmented. Its psychological effects are similar to those of mescaline; however, unlike mescaline, it produces those effects in almost infinitesimal doses. The hallucinations and alterations of consciousness produced by LSD are said to be particularly intense and vivid. It too can produce bad trips, flashbacks, and psychological dependence. At one time it was thought to do genetic damage by breaking chromosomes, but studies of children of LSD users do not reveal an abnormal incidence of congential defects.

The most dangerous of the psychedelic drugs is phencyclidine, known as angel dust or hog. This drug, which has many nonpsychedelic effects, was originally developed as an anesthetic. A popular street drug, it is often mixed with other substances and can cause a variety of medical and psychiatric problems. Unlike the other psychedelics, an overdose of angel dust can be fatal. Its mode of action is unknown, but it does not resemble any known neurotransmitter and is not believed to act by mimicking one of them. Psychotic states and bad trips are frequent consequences of its use, and persistent psychosis may result from chronic use.

Patients rarely present themselves for treatment of addiction to psychedelics. Nor does treatment of other psychiatric and psychological conditions often reveal that the patient is addicted to hallucinants. Rather, what usually comes to the surface is that the use of psychedelics is a symptom of a polyaddictive syndrome. Some patients will take anything to escape themselves, and the cross-addicted almost always try hallucinants. Patients who do not have a drug problem who have experimented with psychedelic drugs will report such experiences in the course of analytic psychotherapy; the meaning of the experience for the patient is analyzed like anything else. On the other hand, patients who repeatedly take these drugs often conceal or minimize that use. Like other addicts, they protect their addictions. Chronic users of psychedelics suffer from serious emotional disabilities. As is usual in the addictions, it is difficult to tease out what is cause and what is effect.

DYNAMICS OF DRUG ADDICTION

Our model addiction is alcoholism, and virtually everything that has been said about the dynamics of addiction to alcohol applies to addiction of other drugs. We agree with Kohut that drug addiction, regardless of the substance abused, is a futile attempt to supply externally what is missing internally. What is missing is psychic structure. This failure of internalization, for whatever reasons, is the essence of vulnerability to drug addiction. Choice of drug is a complex interaction of exposure, availability, less specific sociocultural factors, and psychological need. In these days of well-nigh universal cross-addiction, choice of drug is seldom clear-cut and tells us less about the patient. Nevertheless, the intolerably anxious tend toward the "down" drugs: including, alcohol, barbiturates, and minor tranquilizers, whereas the intolerably empty and "dead" tend toward the "up" drugs amphetamine and cocaine. Opiates, with their rush followed by oblivion, appeal to both the anxious and the empty, while psychedelics make those who feel inwardly dead feel alive.

The common underlying factor in any addiction is the intolerability of the self to itself; something, anything, must be done to change that self so that it can be tolerated. Drugs are ideal for that purpose. They change moods, narcotize feelings, change self-perception, import either oblivion or the illusion of vitality, and give hope to the hopeless, self-esteem to the self-hating, and relief from psychic pain to the emotionally wounded. They give users a sense of power. The drug gives the illusion of magically controlling reality; it allows users to feel or be whatever they wish to feel or be. All of this sounds wonderful, and most people do indeed occasionally use drugs to modify consciousness. Unfortunately, none of this works for long, and the tragic progressive regression and impoverishment characteristic of alcoholism is equally characteristic of the other addictions.

As is the case with alcoholics, substance abusers start with varying degrees of psychopathology, but they all regress to a state of pathological narcissism. The drugs become either self-objects over which they exercise omnipotent control (that is, have a mirror transference to) or self-objects with whose omnipotence they merge (that is, develop an idealizing transference to). The drug may serve as an object as well as a self-object, and the identifications implicit in this object relationship may determine the meaning of the drug for the user. Drugs may also have all sorts of symbolic meanings, but their essential function is always that of the self-object who gives, at least the illusion of, control, power, and comfort. It is addicts' inability to perform for themselves what had been, or should have been, phase-appropriately performed for them by the self-objects of childhood—stimulus attenuation, modulation of anxiety, self-soothing, maintenance of a reasonably constant level of self-esteem, impulse control, and maintenance of self-cohesion—which leads them to turn to another self-object, the drug, to perform these functions. This is not to say that drugs are not "oral supplies," and in terms of psychosexual stages the addict has indeed regresssed to orality, but this is not the most salient point about this condition. Why this regression to orality? Fixation or regression to a developmental sore spot, yes—but it is the object relational, or better, the self-object relational, correlatives of orality which have gone awry, and that is where the difficulty lies.

Addicts have insecurely cohesive selves. The propensity of their selves to fragmentation renders them vulnerable to massive, undifferentiated panic-level anxiety. Addicts suffer a paucity of psychic structure, of good internal objects and well-metabolized internalizations of those objects' functions, which renders them vulnerable to intolerable feelings of emptiness, deadness, and hollowness. Massive anxiety and inward nothingness cannot be lived with indefinitely. Something must be done. Given the "right" environment, drugs are tried. Pharmacology does the rest, and addiction results. Being a pseudosolution, it is, as Kohut says, a "futile effort," doomed to failure. Everything gets worse, and the addict is soon locked into the addictive cycle.

Drug addiction differs from alcohol addiction in that it is illegal. The use of marijuana and cocaine is so widespread that their illegality has become somewhat technical. They remain illegal nevertheless, and people go to jail for using or selling them. Because of this illegality, it has been thought that drug addicts are more sociopathic than alcohol addicts. There is some empirical evidence for this, and although greater sociopathy and acting out do not make treatment any easier, they also do not change the basic dynamics. Cultural factors are important here. A physician who writes his own prescriptions for drugs may appear less sociopathic than a street dealer, yet both may suffer from striking similar psychic deficits and conflicts.

In addition to their greater sociopathy, drug addicts are generally thought to suffer from more severe psychopathology than alcohol addicts. They are held to suffer from borderline personality disorder in addition to severe narcissistic impairments. That is, they have even less self-cohesion than do narcissistic patients. Although this is by no means universally the case, drug addicts are frequently found to have borderline personality traits. They have not worked through the stage of separation-individuation. Paradoxically, the addict uses the drug to feel a sense of separateness, of pseudo-self-sufficient selfhood, *and* uses the drug to lose that very self in a merger with an omnipotent self-object. Here the drug is being used adaptively to work through separation-individuation. Chaotic life-style and primitive rage are the most prominent clinical manifestations of the borderline condition. Drug addicts manifest plenty of both. A great deal of borderline pathology centers around explosive oral, narcissistic, and anal rage as well as defenses against this rage. These defenses, which must be confronted in the treatment, include splitting, projective identification, and denial.

Drug abusers have even less self-cohesion than alcoholics and even more narcissistic vulnerability. Their self-esteem is inevitably abysmal. Treatment must aim at the amelioration of all of this—pharmacological regression, narcissistic pathology, and borderline rage. As with an alcoholic, the first step must be to confront the addict with the addiction and halt the pharmacological regression.

TREATING THE ACTIVE ADDICT

Just as with the alcoholic, who is after all but a special case of addiction, the therapist must diagnose, confront, and educate the substance abuser. Diagnosis of substance abuse is often easy enough, especially when that abuse is glaring. That is not always the case, however; many substance abusers are highly functional and successfully conceal their addictions. As is the case with alcoholics, drug addicts will reveal their addiction to themselves and to the therapist if they feel safe enough. Once again, relationship is the key.

The following behavioral signs aid in diagnosis: personality changes; irrational hostility; sudden deterioration of vocational and social performance; otherwise inexplicable onset of seclusiveness, social withdrawal, and paranoia; depression that does not remit with treatment; and frequent Monday absence from work or school. Any and all of them may be clinical manifestations of addiction. The behavioral or otherwise observable indications of addiction to a particular drug, such as the pinpoint pupils of the opiate addict, also aid in establishing a diagnosis of substance abuse. Repeated attendance of therapy sessions while "high" is diagnostic in itself.

In the past, the role of substance abuse in psychopathology, both as a primary disorder and as an exacerbating factor in and symptom of other mental disorders, has not been sufficently appreciated. This is changing. The DSM III (1980) recognizes both substance abuse and substance dependence as mental illnesses. These illnesses are widespread in our society. Failure to recognize and confront a patient's addiction results in therapeutic failure. As they say in the self-help groups, "You can't grow behind drugs." We must also guard against mistakenly diagnosing substance abuse. Recreational drug use is not addiction, and adolescent or young adult experimentation does not predict a tragic outcome.

Once the diagnosis is made, patients must be told that they will not get better until their addiction is dealt with. The behavioral, somatic, and psychological effects of the abuse must be explained to the patient and a plan to arrest the addiction worked out. Hospital detoxification, rehabilitation programs, and therapeutic communities are available to assist addicts who cannot stop on their own. Once the acting out has been quelled, the meaning of the drug for the patient and its role in the patient's psychic economy must be elucidated. Mourning for a lost love object and cherished self-object as well as for a lifestyle necessarily occurs if the addiction is overcome. Failure to so mourn leaves the addict tied to the addiction. The therapist must become a self-object that replaces the abused substance. Only then can the long, laborious process of remediating psychic deficits and resolving or rendering tolerable intrapsychic conflict be begun.

The addict's primitive rage and fear of engulfment complicate the treatment. Transference reactions are often primitive and intense. Addicts often run from treatment because they fear that their rage will kill the therapist. Alternately, they may project that rage onto the therapist and fear being killed. In either case, treatment will cease unless the therapist heads off flight by interpreting the addict's unconscious fear of killing or being killed. Similarly, the wish for merger may be so intense that the addict runs to avoid engulfment, which is experienced as psychic death. Indeed it is the death of the fully individuated self, and it is defended against by pseudo-self-sufficiency. This wish and fear must also be interpreted or the addict will flee. They may flee anyway. It is vital that the therapist's interpretations be phrased such that they can be heard. Be creative and down to earth; avoid technical language. Even therapists who remain highly attuned to the acting out of unconscious processes will not always be able to anticipate flight responses by active addicts. Feelings that the addiction is threatened may also lead to sudden termination, which is why it is so important that a strong relationship be established before confronting the addiction.

Until recently, therapeutic pessimism reigned in this field. Drug addiction was seen as nearly incurable. This pessimism is unwarranted. Addiction is indeed clung to tenaciously, but if the therapist can understand and address the fear, indeed the terror, which is primarily fear of annihilation of the self, that binds the addict to the addiction, then many will be enabled to overcome their addictions.

Most of the patients discussed in this book were cross-addicted, but their drug of choice was alcohol. Let us examine two cases in which the drug of choice was not alcohol.

Bill: A Marijuana Addict

Bill was an adolescent substance abuser, a condition notoriously difficult to treat. Although drug use as a manifestation of adolescent rebellion does not predict adult addiction, it is serious enough in its own right to merit our best efforts. Adolescent substance abuse not infrequently ends tragically and inevitably leaves residues of guilt along with educational and developmental deficits.

Bill had tried many drugs and liked them all, but his drug of choice was pot. From the age of 13 until he

arrived for treatment at age 16, he had smoked marijuana whenever he could get it. By age 15 he was
hooked. He had become psychologically dependent
on marijuana, and he became intensely uncomfortable, especially in social situations, if he could not get
it. His school performance was miserable, and he and
his parents were at war. The family was referred for
therapy by their physician when Bill reverted to pot
smoking after returning from a 6-month stay in a therapeutic community. At the mother's request, a family
session was scheduled.

The initial session was tension-filled. Bill looked
like a refugee from Haight-Ashbury, with his waist-
length hair, love beads, and Grateful Dead T-shirt. His
brother Bob, 2 years younger, looked like a clean-cut
"preppy." It was soon apparent that Bill and Bob were
cast as "bad boy" and "good boy," respectively, in the
family drama. Bill was sullen, withdrawn, and frightened. The parents looked bewildered and acted enraged. Bob looked on top of the world. Mother dominated the session. She engaged in one long tirade of
"rotten kid" as she described the grief that Bill had put
them through. She was extraordinarily involved in
Bill's life, and she and her husband had spent the past
4 years trying to change his behavior. She subtly denigrated the father and praised the younger brother. As
the session continued, it became clear that this was an
enmeshed family which the mother apparently dominated, but Bill really controlled.

The therapist pointed out that everything seemed
to revolve around Bill and that he had a great deal of
power in the family. The parents seemed startled by
this, but they were willing to consider it. This family
was open to therapeutic intervention; they were overwhelmed and looking for help, a prognostically favorable sign. The main problem was separation. Bill and
his mother were locked in a hostile symbiosis. The
therapist considered family therapy, decided that Bill

had had too much family and needed individual therapy to confirm his existence as a separate person. On the other hand, the family needed and wanted help. The therapist therefore suggested alternating two individual sessions with one family session, a useful treatment strategy with adolescent drug users. Immediately looking to establish some boundaries, the therapist told Bill that he needed individual work and that his individual sessions would be completely confidential. Bill agreed to participate, though evidently under duress.

As always, relationship was the key, and Bill was hungry for a nonsmothering relationship with an adult. He had a good deal going for him: He was bright; he was psychologically minded; his parents, for all their overinvolvement with him, cared deeply and were willing to look at themselves and to set limits for him; and, most important, Bill had developed the capacity for basic trust. Bill's psychopathology was thus less severe than that of many drug abusers, but it was far from negligible. He had not functioned for years and was still enmeshed in the drug culture.

Bill started therapy by announcing that he was having sex with a girl and wasn't using contraception. The therapist sidestepped this attempt at provocation and asked Bill if he knew what people who used the "rhythm method" were called. When Bill said no, the therapist answered, "Parents." Bill laughed and relaxed. He had expected a lecture. Bill continued his attempts to shock and provoke; they were ignored, and they gradually became less frequent. Bill started to talk about his experience in the therapeutic community (TC), which had been both traumatic and ego building.

Therapeutic Communities

Therapeutic communities (TCs) are "total institutions" (Goffman 1961); they exercise all-encompassing control over the lives of their members. They cut their members off from the larger society, which they replace with a closed community in which contingencies of reinforcement are self-consciously selected and administered. They may be extended treatment facilities, or they may constitute an alternative life-style. They have both utopian and totalitarian facets and are strongly ideological.

TCs arose in the 1960s as a method of treating drug addiction, which was seen as so intractable that only such a radical "therapy" could succeed in "curing" it. The first of these TCs was Synanon, founded by Chuck Deitrich, a former AA member. It built communities in California and had a "game club" in New York. Synanon received a great deal of publicity and was widely imitated, but it ultimately became corrupt and its leaders were convicted of criminal charges.

The "Synanon game" is a highly confrontational form of group therapy which aims at breaking down denial and at radical "ego deflation." It is an encounter group in which the members play hard ball. It endeavors to destroy the addict's grandiosity and to replace it with an identification—which is equally grandiose—with the group and its ethos. "The game" replaces the grandiose self with an idealized omnipotent parental imago. This archaic imago is the TC, in whose omnipotence the addict participates. The game does nothing to work through the grandiosity or to remediate deficits in psychic structure; instead it compensates for these deficits by merging the player with the group, which becomes the player's ego and self. It is a cure of sorts, but a cure at the price of individuality. Although both the "game" and life in the TC can be intensely painful, humiliation being a major "treatment" technique, they are also immensely supportive. As one patient put it, "You know, as depressed and rotten as I sometimes felt in Community X, I was never anxious. Only when I left did I start getting these anxiety attacks."

The game and the TC life-style mobilize enormous aggression and rage, for which there is ample opportunity for expression in the "game." Externalization of narcissistic rage undoubtedly takes pressure off the self and lessens depression, while being on the "hot seat" satisfies masochistic yearnings and alleviates guilt. Surviving such a rigorous "initiation" increases self-esteem. TCs do help addicts to overcome their addictions, but they do so by repressing the self, except as it may express itself through the collective self. Since this does stop the actual drug use, it may be life preserving in cases of malignant addiction, but this is not a treatment or solution acceptable to self psychology. Synanon repudiates "professionalism" of all types and is strictly a "peer treatment."

Synanon was the original TC and remains a powerful influence in the TC movement; however, many TCs are less authoritarian than Synanon, and many incorporate professional treatment into their programs. Such TCs are time-limited, extended-treatment facilities, with treatment lasting from six months to several years, which combine milieu therapy of a particularly intense type with encounter groups and psychotherapy, social work, and vocational counseling. They often include excellent remedial educational and vocational programs. They are far less ideological than Synanon, and they aim at reintegration of the addict into society rather than into an alternate life-style. Their quality varies enormously. Well-known examples are Odyssey House and Daytop Village.

The therapist dealing with addiction will encounter many addicts who have been through TCs. The therapist must understand that this is a powerful experience and must empathize both with the patient's allegiance to the TC and with the deep narcissistic wounds inflicted on the patient by that TC. This is logically, but not emotionally, contradictory. Some patients simply cannot get well—that is, stop using drugs—without the "total" approach of the TC, and the therapist needs to know what resources of this sort are available in the community. TCs, preferably the better managed, less authoritarian ones, are the treatment of choice for some recalcitrant cases of addiction, and the therapist must facilitate these patients' entry into such programs. Since much of their treatment philosophy and practice is anathema to self psychology, this is always a difficult therapeutic decision, but such radical therapy may be the only way to arrest an addiction. If at all possible, these patients should return to therapy after their reentry into society.

Bill's TC Experience

The TC in which Bill participated was one of the better ones. Its encounters were tempered with support, and Bill had suffered far less narcissistic injury than is usually the case. His TC assigned Bill a set of tasks of increasing difficulty and responsibility, which gave him an opportunity to learn to function drug free. Bill expressed considerable pride in his "promotions" from toilet cleaner to cook to office manager. All of this had been ego building for him. The TC had also forced him to deal with long-anesthetized feelings. After a period of isolation, they permitted "outside" contacts. Bill's parents attended the "Mommas and Papas group" and gained some insight into their enabling of Bill and some support through sharing with other parents. The TC also served as a container which insulated Bill from the drug culture and from substance abuse, buying some time for healing and growth. All of this constituted the positive side of Bill's experience, but the TC also imposed many punishments and regularly used humiliation as a disciplinary technique. Bill had been particularly hurt by "hair cutting," shaving of his head, as a punishment. When he entered treatment he was growing his hair as long as possible as a way of recovering from this symbolic castration.

A good deal of time was spent in therapy helping Bill to feel and express his rage against the "community"—a difficult process because the TC had become an ideal object. Instead of experiencing this rage, he had acted it out by leaving before completing the TC program and by returning to drugs. His post-TC use of marijuana as a way of saying "fuck you" to the TC was interpreted to him, as was the loss of self-esteem he felt as a "quitter."

Understanding Bill's Addiction

Bill's addiction was essentially a desperate attempt to maintain self-esteem. Since he hated himself for being addicted, this attempt was bound to fail. Bill had had early difficulties in school which worsened when he entered junior high school. He felt socially inadequate, had few friends, was afraid of girls, and was an academic failure. Pot seemed to be the answer to his prayers. As a user and later as a supplier, he had status in his peer culture, which enabled him to discount his academic failure and feel successful. The sedative-hypnotic and hallucinogenic effects of marijuana facilitated this self-deception. When its effects were insufficient, he would turn to mescaline and other drugs. He was quickly trapped.

This life-style was too deviant for the "straight" kids, and he "got in with the scum bags." The therapist said, "You felt like a scum bag, too." Bill first denied this, but gradually acknowledged it, which was a major step in his recovery. His addiction made academic functioning more and more difficult. Ultimately he could not perform in school at all. Since he needed a successful experience, he plunged even deeper into drugs and the drug culture, where he was a "big man." He was stoned more and more, functioning less and less. A vicious cycle had been established and there was no way out.

Conflict with his upwardly mobile parents escalated to mayhem. He was continually being punished, and he continually retaliated by drugging more and by "fucking up" in school. His father beat him and his mother screamed at him, but his downward plunge didn't abate. Finally drugs and only drugs, especially pot, which allowed him to dream dreams of glory and to feel socially and sexually adequate, made life tolerable, and there was literally no day during which he was not stoned. Various acts of minor delinquency supported his habit. Finally his parents forced him into the TC. Although Bill could not admit it, he was relieved. He insisted on leaving after six months of a year-long program. Bill returned to school labeled a "druggie." He was still filled with repressed rage and still academically overwhelmed. Neither his skill deficits nor his ego deficits had been remediated. Failure was inevitable. He soon returned to drugs and was brought to therapy. Fortunately, Bill had seen enough of the benefits of being drug free in the TC to want that for himself, but he didn't believe that he could function on the "outside" without drugs. He felt hopeless.

Feelings of Inadequacy and Deficits in the Self

The therapist interpreted Bill's hopelessness, but affirmed that there was a decent chance that he could "make it." Bill's feelings of inadequacy were an intensification, almost to the point of caricature, of normal adolescent self-doubt. His treatment was so focused on stopping the addiction and on here-and-now ego building that the genetic roots of his narcissistic vulnerability were never uncovered. From the nature of his difficulties, we can infer that his experiences with the self-objects of his childhood were traumatically inadequate, but the details of this inadequacy were never established. Bill's difficulties around separation indicated that he may have been traumatically rebuffed at the rapprochement subphase of separation-individuation (Mahler, Pine and Bergman 1975). It is clear that Bill felt enormous guilt over having let his parents down.

Bill's parents, who lacked formal education, were ambitious for their children. Bill felt that he had failed them, and the more he failed, the guiltier he felt; simultaneously he felt progressively angrier about this burden. He was aware that his parents' investment in his achievement was a form of vicarious fulfillment, and his resentment of it added to his sense of guilt. Although his parents had some concern for him as a separate person, they also treated him as an extension of themselves, a form of relating that Kohut (1971) called a *narcissistic cathexis*. In failing, he was separating from his parents; he was expressing his rage for being "used" for vicarious achievement and for much else; *and* he was maintaining his closeness to his uneducated parents by identifying with them. Thus, he both separated from and merged with his parents by failing in school. It would have been a "perfect" compromise solution for his conflicts over separation if it had not been accompanied by massive guilt. The therapist interpreted the emotional meaning of his school failure to Bill.

Classical psychoanalysis would see fear of oedipal victory in Bill's failure, and that was certainly there, but the insight of self psychology into fear of losing the self-object through individuation resonates clinically. Patients understand this far better than they do the oedipal aspects of achievement conflict, and they are far more able to work with it. The fear of and wish for an oedipal victory should be interpreted much later in the treatment and only when it clearly emerges from the material or manifests itself in the transference.

Bill's inadequacies were exacerbated and made inaccessible to efforts at remediation by early failures of internalization which renderd him vulnerable to massive anxiety and empty depression. Drugs alleviated both. This was interpreted to him, and Bill took a quantum leap in treatment when he felt safe enough to acknowledge and to verbalize his feelings of inadequacy. Once he had established an idealizing transference to the therapist, he felt enough connection to strength to acknowlege his weakness. He spoke of his feelings of inferiority in relation to "nice" girls, in relation to school, and toward "good" students. He told the therapist that he felt like a "dirt bag" and that he related only to "scum bags" and "douche bags." He connected his pot smoking to flight from these feelings of inferiority. All of this was liberating. His self-deficits, his lack of psychic structure, could not be so easily filled, but experiencing instead of acting out his fears was itself curative.

Issues of Separation

Pot was a self-object for Bill—it comforted him, soothed him, and raised his self-esteem. It did what a mother does for a small child. Pot smoking was simultaneously a separation from the parents—what could be more different from their conforming and upwardly mobile life-style?—and a fusion with a pharmacological representation of the omnipotent parental imago, the idealized archaic self-object. Bill was aware of the first part of this, the being different, the self-assertion of being a pot head; but he was not aware of the symbiosis, of the remerger, which the drug represented.

At a suitable juncture, the therapist noted, "Pot is your mother, and smoking makes you feel close to her." Bill replied, "You're crazy, man." The therapist went on to explain that Bill's recent return to drugs had been a way to feel "mothered" while rebelling against Mother. Bill understood this; "It's crazy, but you're right. Wait till I tell her, 'You're nothing but a joint, Ma.' Only it's the other way around, right?" Bill left the session smiling sheepishly. Bill and the therapist worked with this insight for a long time; it was demonstrated and illustrated with as much concreteness as possible.

Bill Gets Clean

During the first six months of therapy, Bill "slipped around." School was a major torment for him. After a period of apparent progress during which he became deeply committed to treatment, opened up emotionally, and decreased his smoking, he started cutting school and running around with an older boy who had a car and a supply of alcohol and marijuana. The boys got into a medley outside another school over a contested drug sale. Bill's parents were informed. In his words, "They went crazy." His father beat him and sought out Bill's "friend" and supplier, threatening to "kill him if he turns on my kid again." Bill's parents grounded him and insisted on the right to approve his friends thereafter.

Bill was angry with both his parents, "those total assholes." However, it soon became clear that he was relieved that his parents weren't going to allow him to lose control again. Their methods may have been questionable, but their limit setting was a vital ingredient in Bill's recovery. Bill chafed at their restrictions, but he felt secure. He upbraided his parents unceasingly during his sessions. The therapist maintained neutrality. Bill's rage gradually quieted. His father apologized for hitting him and started doing more things with him. Bill confessed to the therapist that he "sort of liked" his parents.

At that point Bill informed the therapist that he wanted to quit school and get a job. School was a losing proposition where only the "scumbags" would accept him, and they all used drugs. Bill didn't see any way to change his situation there. He asked the therapist to support his leaving school. They explored the issue carefully, and it gradually became clear that Bill could not function in school. He was stereotyped, and he was too far behind academically. The therapist decided to step out of the neutral analytic stance, which isn't of much use with active addicts in any case, and recommend to his parents that Bill be allowed to leave school and get a job. A family session was held, and surprisingly, they agreed. To Bill this meant that his parents were willing to let him be himself. He was enabled to leave a situation that lowered his self-esteem and enter one that enhanced it. Becoming involved in a patient's life in this manner is tricky. It changes the transference and it may go sour, but such "active" intervention is sometimes appropriate with addicts, especially younger ones. In this case it was.

Bill obtained a job in a factory warehouse and was soon one of the best workers there. He had found something at which he could succeed. His self-esteem rose immeasurably. Therapy focused on helping him not sabotage his success. All of the reasons that he might undermine himself were discussed. His pot smoking tapered off and then ceased all together. He started working more psychodynamically in therapy. He started a relationship with a girl for whom he had respect. He is studying for his high school equivalency diploma.

Bill's recovery was complex. Its essential ingredients were his relationship with the therapist, his parents' staying with him and setting limits for him, his parents' allowing him to individuate by leaving school, his own drive for health, and his success on the job. Bill has probably survived a troubled adolescence with relatively little residual damage. He still needs help to mature and he remains at risk for readdiction, but he has made significant strides in learning to maintain his self-esteem without resorting to drug use.

Carl: A Cocaine Addict

Carl was far more disturbed than Bill was. He had a long history of drug abuse and violent acting out. He began therapy after a drug-induced psychotic break. It was not at all clear that his psychosis was entirely drug related. He was referred by a hospital psychiatrist who had seen him in the emergency room.

Carl had been on a "coke spree." He had withdrawn to his room to freebase. After several days of wild ups and precipitous downs, Carl decided that he needed something stronger, so he began to intravenously inject the cocaine, thereby risking his life. After mainlining for another day, Carl picked up a rifle and began to fire it through the walls of the room. At age 28, Carl was still living with his parents; there were people in the house who might easily have been killed. His father disarmed him and he was brought to the emergency room. Carl claimed that the gun went off when his father tried to disarm him. The father claimed that Carl was trying to kill himself. Yet another version had it that he was trying to kill his father. The hospital psychiatrist thought that he might have been hallucinating when he started to fire the gun and later became suicidal or homicidal or both. The incident was never fully clarified.

Carl was not an average analytic patient. The question arose whether to treat him in outpatient psychotherapy at all. If he had still been actively psychotic, this form of treatment would have ben contraindicated. But his underlying personality structure was unknown. How vulnerable to psychosis was he, and, even more important, how prone to violence? Some assessment of these factors was necessary. The hospital psychiatrist thought that he was not dangerous when drug fee. He wanted treatment and was willing to come to sessions. Bizarre behavior is not unusual in substance abusers and does not in itself rule out psychotherapeutic intervention. The therapist decided to evaluate Carl. He proved to be tractable and motivated. He made an effort to be straightforward and honest. The therapist did not feel himself to be in danger, which would have been sufficient reason to reject Carl as a patient. He decided to try to treat Carl on a twice-weekly basis.

In a situation like this, it is best to have consultation before accepting the patient. Psychological testing can also be helpful. But in the end it is clinical judgment and the clinician's "gut feeling" which determine whether the patient is a reasonable treatment risk. Therapists should not accept patients of whom they are afraid. But bizarre behavior characterizes some severely disturbed substance abusers, many of whom do well in treatment.

Carl was a short, black man who looked and acted much younger than his age. He wore a vest which exhibited his heavily muscled arms and chest. He had a surface cockiness. He started the interview by announcing that he was not suicidal and had not been trying to kill himself. Taking his cue from Freud's (1925) essay *On Negation*, in which Freud notes that unsolicited denials are really affirmations, the therapist heard that Carl was suicidal. Carl's most striking characteristic was his immaturity. He not only lived at home; he worked for his father's truck rental business. He saw nothing odd in this. He considered himself independent and made a point of saying that he did not need anybody. This pseudo-self-sufficiency was a manifestation of the grandiose self and of pathological narcissism. Carl's assertion was so pathetically compensatory and so clearly contrary to fact that it called his reality testing into question. His father paid him far more than his skill level and erratic performance was worth. The family also paid Carl's debts to his dealer and to various finance companies. The father trusted him to handle large amounts of money. Carl had been stealing from the business for years. His father must have known this, but chose not to see it. Denial seemed to be this family's modus operandi.

Carl had been in trouble from an early age. He had been markedly rivalrous with his father and jealous of his father's closeness to his mother. He was envious of his older sister's academic and social success. He had tremendous feelings of rage toward his mother. He was tormented by feelings of inferiority and envy in his relations with just about everybody. He tried to compensate for this by being tough, and by the time he was in high school he was getting into serious trouble. He injured several boys in fights, and he assaulted a teacher. His parents always came to his rescue, and they succeeded in extricating him from many jams. Finally he was expelled. He went to work for his father and remained there. He was bright and learned quickly, but he was not sufficiently stable to make much of a contribution.

Carl had experimented with drugs and alcohol since his early teens. He was a setup for addiction. A friend turned him on to cocaine. It was love at first sight. He went from snorting to freebasing in short order; eventually he started shooting. He turned to dealing. His ability to make money easily and quickly fed his grandiosity. By the time he came to treatment, he was in debt to the "wrong people," a common outcome of dealing to support a habit. His fights were more serious now. Many were with "college punks," whom he secretly envied and feared. His fighting served to displace the aggression he unconsciously feared unleashing on his family. His hatred was hatred of them and of himself. His addiction was also an expression of this narcissistic rage toward his parents. When this was interpreted to him, Carl had trouble hearing it. Only slowly did he see how he used his addiction as a weapon.

Carl came close to killing several people, but his father bought his way out of trouble, thus increasing his feelings of omnipotence. He bought bigger and faster cars and motorcycles. Speed fascinated him; danger attracted him even more. He was in three near-fatal motorcycle crashes. He injected himself with steroids and testosterone to increase his muscle size and strength, thereby further increasing his feeling of invulnerability. He crashed again and had to spend months in bed. He resumed his use of cocaine as soon as he was able. He was using more and getting crazier. He got himself deeply into debt and didn't know how to get out of it. Finally he went on the spree that landed him in the hospital.

Diagnosis and Dynamics

Carl evidenced more sociopathy than did the other patients whose cases we will consider. His life-style was one prolonged acting out. He externalized his conflicts and looked for magical solutions in cocaine, steroids, violence, and speed. He courted death. In his grandiosity he thought that he was invulnerable and immortal. Everything he did was an attempt to increase arousal, to obtain more stimulation. He used stimulating drugs; he engaged in adrenaline-releasing activities—all a manic defense against suicidal depression, depression of unremitting blackness and bleakness. Carl felt dead, and all of his thrill-seeking behavior and chemical stimulation was an attempt to feel alive. Paradoxically, he sought death in order to experience life. He looked on the outside for what was really in the inside—deadness—and in this sense his quest was an externalization of an inner experience. Better to find death in the external world than to be dead in the internal world. The therapist interpreted this to him.

Along with his struggles to overcome his lack of aliveness, Carl managed to maintain only tenuous control of his nearly psychotic rage. His desperate need to prove himself could trigger that rage at any moment. Just as he had to prove that he was alive, he had to prove that he was not inferior. Carl's feelings of being unable to compete with his highly successful father still plagued him.

As was the case with Bill, we do not know the genesis of Carl's psychopathology. We do know that feelings of being alive come from being reacted to as a living thing. It was as if Carl had not been "quickened" by sufficient human contact during infancy. This may well have been the case. His obsessive focus on his father and virtual failure to mention his mother implied that something had been very wrong in his early relationship with her. He was probably understimulated, but it is also possible that he was overstimulated and his deadness was a defense against that overstimulation. There was a massive failure of internalization both of objects and of self-object functions, so that Carl wound up with a paucity of good internal objects and of psychic structure. He was fleeing from his psychological and experiential emptiness. The aliveness of good internal objects was absent. Empty meant dead. This deadness was also a defense against intolerable feelings of envy and rage. Playing dead is a phylogenetically ancient protection against external aggression; it no doubt served a similar purpose for Carl.

According to Kohut (1971), the integration of archaic grandiosity into the reality ego makes for vitality, energy, and feelings of aliveness. Carl had never integrated his grandiose self. On the contrary, his grandiosity was split off by what Kohut called the *vertical split* and primitively acted out. Whatever was left of this legacy of infantile omnipotence, with its potential for creativity and excitement, was repressed by what Kohut called the *horizontal split*. The reality ego was thereby impoverished and experienced itself as empty and dead. This was clinically manifested by Carl's frequent complaints of boredom.

The therapist interpreted Carl's boredom as a "drug signal." The failures of internalization, the defensive deadness, and the walling off of sources of energy were all exacerbated by Carl's addiction, which depleted neurotransmitters necessary for feeling vital and alive. Thus Carl's depression and his manic defense against it had both psychodynamic and pharmacological determinants. The dreadful mess he had made of his life added a reality-based component to his depression, as did the self-hatred that is inherent in any addiction.

According to the DSM-III, Carl would receive two diagnoses on Axis I: cocaine abuse and cyclothymic disorder. On Axis II, which delineates personality disorders, Carl could be diagnosed as having either a narcissistic or an antisocial personality disorder. On the basis of a somewhat higher level of object relations, the therapist diagnosed him as a narcissistic personality disorder.

Treatment

As is the case with any addiction, the first order of business was to arrest the addiction. The early sessions went well. The therapist took a reality-based, educational stance. He explained to Carl that much of his depression was a withdrawal symptom. Carl was too frightened by the shooting episode to do much acting out. To borrow an AA phrase, he had hit bottom. He was in enough pain to want help, although he couldn't admit it, and he struggled to talk about his feelings and about his life. He didn't really know how to proceed and needed a lot of direction from the therapist.

As Carl felt better he became more arrogant. The therapist warned him that he was setting himself up for a slip. It didn't matter; Carl started using again. He plummeted rapidly. The therapist talked him into admitting himself to a rehabilitation program. Carl lasted only two weeks, but he was detoxified, learned about his disease, and was introduced to Narcotics Anonymous (NA). NA is a twelve-step program modeled on AA. Although NA has not been as successful as AA, it has helped many. It helped Carl, although he didn't much like it and didn't attend many meetings.

Therapy was ego supportive for a long time. Issues like how to pay off the pusher and how to cope with boredom occupied these early sessions. Carl's age-inappropriate dependence on his parents was gingerly broached, as was his relationship to them. Carl lessened his burden of guilt by confessing that he had stolen from his father's business for years. His father's enabling and his apparent vicarious enjoyment of Carl's activities were also interpreted. When Carl denied this, the therapist dropped it.

Carl was very popular with women and this was something he could talk about. The therapist encouraged him. Somehow, with the aid of this mostly supportive and only occasionally interpretive psychotherapy and with minimal attendance at NA meetings, Carl managed to stay off cocaine. His few slips were rage reactions, or, as the therapist called them, temper tantrums. Carl laughed, but the slips became less frequent. After six months of abstinence, Carl abruptly terminated treatment, saying that everything was fine and he didn't need therapy any more.

Carl probably left because he feared his wish for closeness, indeed for merger, with the therapist and needed to maintain an illusion of self-sufficiency. The therapist sensed that interpretation would not save the case and decided to give Carl a gracious send-off. He recapitulated Carl's gains and wished him luck. This allowed Carl to separate without guilt, something his parents were apparently unable to do. Carl is still severely disturbed, but at least he is off cocaine. He can now benefit from self-psychological analytic psychotherapy.

Treating the Recovering Addict

Helping patients like Carl get "clean" is no easy task, but it is more directive and educational than dynamic. After a period of drug freeness, such patients need long-term psychodynamic work to remediate deficits in psychic structure and resolve psychic conflicts. There is essentially no difference between working with a stably sober alcoholic and working with a stably clean addict. The reader is therefore referred to the final chapter of this book, in which such treatment is discussed.

CHAPTER 6

A Self-Psychological Theory of Early Sobriety

THE EXPERIENTIAL WORLD OF THE NEWLY SOBER ALCOHOLIC

The recently sober alcoholic, whether freshly graduated from a detoxification program or painfully emerging from "tapering off" or "going cold turkey," is a person in crisis. This crisis may be the privotal point around which a recovery is organized. Newly sober alcoholics are simultaneously bereft of an all-pervasive defense, a magically powerful drug, an inner identity, a social role, and a "best friend." They are, although they may or may not consciously feel, denuded, terrified, depressed, vulnerable, insecure, fragile, and perhaps exhilarated. They are also most certainly ambivalent about sobriety. Moreover, they are at least potentially, and perhaps for the first time in years, in possession of realistic feelings of hope. These hopeful feelings may be expressed as euphoria, which reflects both the ego's response to escape from a life-threatening situation (alcohol addiction) and a manic defense against underlying depression and fear. AA refers to this stage of recovery as being on a "pink cloud." Although the pink cloud can be adaptive, it also increases the newly sober alcoholic's vulnerability to internal and external dangers. At this delicate juncture, the therapist's rather awe-inspiring task is to optimize the chances of a favorable resolution of this existential crisis. The question is, how can this best be done? It is to this question that this chapter is addressed.

Addictive drinking is an all-encompassing activity, affecting the body, the mind, and the spirit. Its cessation leaves an aching gulf: There are endless stretches of newly unstructured time; there is the need for a new "script"; there is the necessity of reestablishing damaged relationships; and, most important, there is the urgent task of learning to deal with feelings long anesthetized and conflicts long muted by alcohol. Further, these tasks must be undertaken by an organism whose nervous system has been assaulted and who is probably suffering from residual, although hopefully transient, neuropsychological deficits. Years of addictive drinking have left residual scars in all areas of the alcoholic's life: vocational, financial, interpersonal, and intrapsychic. Thus, a profound emotional reorganization must be undertaken by the weakened and beleaguered alcoholic. If ever an ego needed an ally, it is the ego of the newly sober alcoholic. Therefore, at this stage of recovery, the therapist's primary task is to provide external support for the alcoholic's ego. The analysis of maladaptive defenses must wait.

Let us sketch a "typical" early-sobriety alcoholic and then proceed to devise a rational therapy based on our knowledge of the likely state of his or her mind and body. First a caution. Although science seeks regularities and a scientific therapy bases its efforts to establish a rational treatment approach upon these observed regularities, each alcoholic is unique. Theory and research findings guide the therapist's observation, but they never supersede the concrete data emergent from the therapeutic interaction. Further, the therapist must be sensitive to the effects of culture, class, family, economic situation, race, gender, and life stage on the alcoholic's drinking career and current state of mind.

Physical Determinants

Alcohol can damage the nervous system. If the drinking has been heavy and prolonged, there is probably some continuing neurological dysfunction, even after the acute stage of withdrawal is over. These deficits may be due to the effect of alcohol per se, or they may be a reaction to its withdrawal. These neuropsychological dysfunctions are collectively known as the *subacute alcohol withdrawal syndrome* (Gross and Hastey 1976). Although the dysfunction may be minimal (subclinical), it is, to some extent, still operant at this stage. Some theorists (Ludwig and Wikler 1974) believe that the subacute alcohol withdrawal syndrome is related to "craving" for alcohol in early sobriety.

The syndrome manifests itself in tendencies toward concrete thinking, emotional lability, and sleep disturbances. Further, the capacity for new learning may be impaired. The condition is, in effect, an attenuated, transient organic brain syndrome. In Goldstein's (1939, 1941) terms, there is a temporary, partial loss of the abstract attitude. AA has long recognized this stage of recovery and refers to members in this state as "mokus."

The clinical implications are clear. The therapist must provide structure; interventions must be simple and clear; rapid shifts are to be avoided and repetition encouraged; and the patient's defenses against catastrophic anxiety (Goldstein 1939, 1941) must be supported and reinforced. The therapist also has an educational role since he or she can provide realistic hope that recovery will continue and that cognitive function will continue to improve for at least a year, at which time sleep patterns should also have returned to normal. The therapist should be alert to both the danger of and the possible organic basis of the dysphoria so often concomitant with early sobriety.

If no psychological basis is apparent, the mood swings and painful affects experienced in early sobriety can be interpreted to the patient as the effects of alcohol withdrawal, and assurance given that they will clear spontaneously if sobriety is maintained.

In some cases, however, the outlook is not so sanguine. If the patient shows marked and persistent cognitive deficits, there may be permanent brain damage. Fortunately, we see few such cases in outpatient settings. If the therapist suspects such damage, the patient should be referred for neurological evaluation and psychological testing. The Halstead battery will pinpoint the exact nature of the cognitive deficits. Patients with such deficits must be helped to compensate for their disabilities and to function at the highest level possible. They may also have to go through a mourning process for these losses, as described by Wright (1960). However, alcoholics seem to have scant awareness of even severe psychological disability consequent upon alcohol abuse. If denial is operative at this stage in the rehabilitative process, it is probably adaptive, and efforts should be directed toward teaching the patient how to make the best use of remaining capacities, rather than toward breaking down the denial.

The newly sober alcoholic may also be either recovering from or permanently impaired by other alcohol-related organic damage. Alcohol abuse can impair the function of any body tissue. Liver disease and anemia are the most common physical complications during early sobriety. If it has not been done as part of the detoxification program, it is mandatory that the patient have a complete physical examination with all appropriate laboratory tests, and that the results be communicated to the therapist. Given the high incidence of nutritional deficiency in alcoholics, it is also imperative that the patient receive nutritional counseling.

Psychological Determinants

There is considerable evidence (Sadava 1978, Barnes 1979, Cox 1979) that there is a "clinical" alcoholic personality. That is, alcoholics, at the point at which they present themselves for treatment, manifest considerable similarities in their psychological functioning. One way of understanding the clinical alcoholic personality is to view alcoholism as a process of progressive impoverishment and deindividuation; regardless of where they started, everyone in detox is in a similar psychological boat. For some, this common outcome reflects fixation at an early stage of psychological development; for others, it reflects regression from a more mature mode of functioning. The goal of treatment is a reversal of this process, leading to enrichment and individuation of the alcoholic's personality.

Regression/Fixation to Pathological Narcissism

The common point of regression/fixation is pathological narcissism, a construct which both makes sense of the empirical data and gives coherence to competing theories of the dynamics of alcoholism. It illuminates alcoholism in both men and women. Most theories of the dynamics of alcoholism have the disadvantage of applying to men only; they are theories of *male* alcoholism. When advanced alcoholism is understood as a narcissistic behavior disorder, the higher rates of male alcoholism are explained by sociological and cultural factors that favor the manifestation of narcissistic pathology in women in narcissistic personality rather than behavioral disorders. This formulation is consistent with the lower rates of "acting out" pathologies in women.

The Clinical Alcoholic Personality

The salient, and for the most part consistently replicated, empirical findings delineating a clinical alcoholic personality include elevation of the Psychopathic deviate (Pd) and Depression (D) scales of the MMPI, impoverishment of the self-concept, field dependence, confused gender identity, ego weakness, and stimulus augmentation. (See Chapter 3 for a detailed discussion of the evidence for the existence of a clinical alcoholic personality.) The best-known theories of the dynamics of alcoholism, which are also the theories with the greatest heuristic power, are the dependency-conflict theory (McCord and

McCord 1960, Blane 1968), the need-to-feel-powerful theory (McClelland et al. 1972), and the epistemological error theory (Bateson 1971). How can the concept of pathological narcissism illuminate these findings and these theories?

UNDERSTANDING THE NEWLY SOBER ALCOHOLIC

Some Developmental Considerations

Freudian Theory

Freud (1914b), in his seminal essay "On Narcissism: An Introduction," described a normal developmental process in which there is a progression from autoeroticism (love of isolated body parts) to narcissism (love of self) to object love (love of others). The infant first derives pleasure from body parts, experienced as yet as isolates, not as parts of a self; these sensory experiences are later integrated into a self, or ego, which is exprienced as tenuous and unclearly demarcated from the not-self (the world), and this ego is loved; and finally a portion of this primeval self-love, or *primary narcissism*, overflows and is projected out as object love. Thus, our instinctual energy is first invested in our own body parts, then invested in ourselves before the distinction between self and other has been established, and finally flows outward to emotionally invest (*cathect* in Freud's terminology) objects. Narcissistic libido becomes object libido.

According to Freud, disappointment in object love can lead to withdrawal of interest (libido) from the world and reinvestment of that libido in the self. Freud denoted this phenomenon *secondary narcissism* to distinguish it from the initial stage of life, which he denoted as *primary narcissism*. Freud postulated that normal self-esteem results from a reservoir of self-love which is retained from the stage of primary narcissism and which continues to exist alongside object love. He thought that secondary narcissism was the basic mechanism of psychotic withdrawal from the world, and that the psychotic delusion of the end of the world reflected the reality of the withdrawal of libido from the world of objects and its redirection onto a now impoverished and isolated self. Although most alcoholics do not carry their emotional withdrawal to the point of psychosis, the parallels between the emotional component of the alcoholic process and Freud's description of secondary narcissism are apparent.

Jacobson: Self and Object Representations

Later psychoanalytic theorists both built on and criticized Freud's work on narcissism. E. Jacobson (1964) thought that Freud's formulation lacked precision because he had failed to distinguish between ego, self, and self representation. Jacobson defined *ego* in accordance with Freud's 1923 structural hypothesis, which divided the mind into three "psychic organs": the id, the ego, and the superego. These components of the mind were defined by their functions. *Ego* functions include perception, judgment, motility, and defense. Jacobson reserves the term *ego* for this system within the mind in order to avoid the confusion that results if it is also used to denote the self, as it is by Freud and in ordinary usage. The *self*, on the other hand, is defined as the whole person of an individual, including body, psychic organization, and their respective parts. *Self representations* are defined as the unconscious, preconscious, and conscious endopsychic representations of the physical and mental self in the system ego. They are never purely conceptual but always have an affective quality.

Jacobson saw the initial stage of human development as an undifferentiated "psychosomatic" matrix, which she denoted as the *primal psychophysiological self*. This stage, in which neither self representations and object representations nor the (libidinal and aggressive) drives are yet differentiated, corresponds to Freud's stage of primary narcissism. However, Jacobson does not believe that it makes sense to speak of narcissism, or self-love, in a stage preceding the establishment and differentiation of self and object representations. Therefore, she defines narcissism as the libidinal cathexis of the self-representation. Analogously, object love is seen as the libidinal cathexis of an object representation. She conceptualizes severe psychopathology in terms of regressive refusion of self and object representations. Some blurring of self and object representations, entailing varying degrees of impairment in reality testing, is characteristic of chronic alcoholics during the period of early sobriety. This phenomenon probably reflects both organic and psychodynamic processes concomitant with the drinking career.

Kernberg: Object Relations

O. Kernberg (1975) used Jacobson's concept of self and object representations to delineate four stages in the development of object relations. He, too, starts with the undifferentiated matrix. In his second stage, self and object are not differentiated, but there are endopsychic structures, self-objects, that are affectively colored. Memory traces of gratification result in positive (libidinally cathected) self-object representations, while memory traces of frustrating experiences result in negative (aggressively cathected) self-object representations (self-objects) which do not differentiate between the I and the not-I, between self and world. In normal development, gratifying experiences predominate in early infancy.

Fixation at either of the first two stages results in psychosis. In the third stage, the self and object representations are differentiated, resulting in four endopsychic structures: a positive (libidinally cathected) self representation, a negative (aggressively cathected) self representation, a positive (libidinally cathected) object representation, and a negative (aggressively cathected) object representation. Self and object are now differentiated, but self and object representations reflecting gratifying and frustrating experiences are not yet integrated. Thus, the object (usually mother) who both gratifies and frustrates is experienced as two separate objects, the "good mother" and the "bad mother." Similarly, there is a "good self" and a "bad self," which are not experienced as the same self. Fixation at this stage, or regression to it, results in borderline (between neurosis and psychosis) pathology. Clinically, borderline personalities have severe difficulties in interpersonal relationships, chaotic emotional lives, and poor impulse control, and are prone to acting out. They characteristically use primitive defenses, especially splitting and projection, rather than the higher-level defense of repression. Many alcoholics regress to a borderline character structure, whereas some have never developed beyond this stage.

Kernberg's fourth stage involves the integration of positive and negative self and object representations. Successful completion of this process results in a stable self representation and in *object constancy*. Frustrations are tolerable because there are stable endopsychic representations (internal objects) of loving, albeit humanly flawed, caretakers. The attainment of object constancy indicates that there is a cathexis of the constant mental representation of the object regardless of the state of need. There is also a firm sense of identity. In Alfred North Whitehead's (1933) phrase, "there is memory of disaster survived," which gives strength in a present crisis. Unfortunately, most alcoholics in the early stages of recovery are not functioning at this psychological level.

In normal development, psychic structuralization resulting in the establishment of the ego and the id as separate psychic systems emergent from the undifferentiated matrix of earliest infancy proceeds concomitantly with the establishment of differentiated, affectively complex self and object representations. Stable self and object representations (internal objects) are normal components of the system ego. In emotional health, these images integrate the gratifying and frustrating aspects of experience and are differentiated from each other. In later development, structuralization of the psychic apparatus continues with the emergence of the superego. The formation of the superego is a complex process involving both differentiation from the ego and a series of identifications with parents and other mentors. The superego may be thought of as the repository of both the conscience and the ego-ideal. In many ways it is an internal parent which both loves and punishes, and it is vitally involved in self-regulation and the maintenance of self-esteem. (For a detailed discussion of ego, superego, and superego functions, the reader is referred to the standard psychoanalytic texts by Fenichel [1945] and Brenner [1955].)

Kernberg conceptualizes normal narcissism as the libidinal investment of the self. This self is a structure in the ego which integrates good and bad self-images. In other words, normal self-love predisposes successful completion of Kernberg's stage four of object relations development. Since most, if not all, alcoholics at the point of entering treatment have either regressed to or are fixated at more primitive levels of object relations, we can anticipate some degree of narcissistic disturbance in early-sobriety alcoholics. Kernberg delineates three levels of narcissistic pathology.

In his view, those who suffer from the most severe form of pathological narcissism, the narcissistic personalities, develop a pathological self-structure, which he calls the *grandiose self*. This grandiose self is a pathological condensation (fusion) of ideal-self, real-self, and ideal-object representations. It is not a stage of normal development. It is, however, a stable psychic structure, a characteristic which makes possible relatively smooth social functioning. Narcissistic personalities typically relate to others, not as separate people, but as extensions of themselves. They do not really experience others as others, but rather as projections of their grandiose selves. Hence what appears to be object relations are really relations of self to self. To make matters worse, this self is not a normal self, but is the grandiose self just described.

Characteristic defenses of narcissistic personalities include primitive idealization, projective identification, splitting, and devaluation. In one way or another, these defenses distort the object to meet the needs of the narcissistic patient. These mechanisms are thus in the service of omnipotent control. They also serve as defenses against real dependency on others. True dependence on another human being, experienced as separate and autonomous, would entail the risk of intolerable emotions of rage and envy toward the person depended on. Thus, what appears to be dependent relating in the narcissistic personality is, in reality, another aspect of their need for omnipotent control, in this case the control of a source of supplies. Such a pseudodependent relationship cannot possibly meet the real dependency needs which are part and parcel of the human condition, and which are most certainly present in the narcissistic patient.

Although most alcoholics would not meet Kernberg's technical requirements for diagnosis as narcissistic personalities, there are clearly many parallels between psychic mechanisms and behaviors prevalent in alcoholics, especially late in addiction or early in sobriety, and Kernberg's phenomenology of the narcissistic personality. Particularly relevant to and illuminating of alcoholic psychopathology are his analysis of pseudodependency in the narcissistic personality and his description of the grandiose self.

Kohut: Development of the Self

H. Kohut's (1971, 1977a) insights into the psychodynamics of addiction are directly relevant to our understanding and treatment of the alcoholic. Kohut sees narcissistic disturbance as central to the psychopathology of the addict. The core difficulty of these narcissistic personalities is the absence of internal structure; explicitly, there are deficits in the self's capacities for tension regulation, self-soothing, and self-esteem regulation. The alcoholic's pathological drinking is an attempt to make up for this "missing structure"; that is, the alcoholism serves to reduce tension and regulate self-esteem in the absence of adequate intrapsychic resources to achieve such regulation. Thus, in early sobriety these deficits in the structure of the self, with their concomitant psychological dysfunctions, will continue to disable the alcoholic until psychic structure can be built.

Kohut's view of narcissism differs from both Freud's and Kernberg's. In contradistinction to Freud's view of narcissistic libido as the precursor of object libido, Kohut believes that narcissistic and object-libidinal strivings develop along independent lines. That is, narcissism is seen not as a stage in the development of object love, but rather as an aspect of human life that has its own developmental history in which the self and its libidinal investments evolve from a fragmentary stage into a cohesive, archaic form (the nuclear self) and finally into a mature form. The development of mature object and idealized self-object love are parallel, but independent, processes.

Kohut differs from Kernberg in believing that the grandiose self (a term he coined) is a normal, albeit archaic, rather than pathological, structure. Kohut is particularly interested in two early self structures: the grandiose self and the idealized self-object (or idealized parent imago). These structures constitute the nuclear self, which Kohut views as bipolar.

Let us attempt to elucidate these concepts. Kohut defines the self as a unit cohesive in space and enduring in time, which is a center of initiative and a recipient of impressions. It can be regarded either as a mental structure superordinate to the agencies of the mind (id, ego, and superego) or as a content of those agencies. Although Kohut believed that these conceptualizations were complementary rather than mutually exclusive, he emphasized the self as a central or superordinate principle in his later theories. It is, so to speak, the organized and organizing center of human experience, which is itself experienced as cohesive and enduring. How does this sense of an I (self) which coheres in space and endures in time develop? According to Kohut, the infant develops a primitive (fragmented) sense of self very early. That is, each body part, each sensation, each mental content is experienced as belonging to a self, to a me, as mine; however, there is no synthesis of these experiences as yet. There are selves, but no unitary self. Nor are there clear boundaries between self and world. Kohut designates this stage as the stage of the *fragmented self*; it is the developmental stage at which psychotic persons are fixated or to which they regress. Although there are important differences, Kohut's stage of the fragmented self corresponds to Freud's stage of autoeroticism; it is another way of understanding the stage of human development that precedes the integration of the infant's experienced world.

At the next stage of development, an *archaic, nuclear self* arises from the infant's experience of being related to as a self, rather than as a collection of parts and sensations, by empathic caretakers. This self is cohesive and enduring, but it is not yet securely established. Hence, it is prone to regressive fragmentation. It is nuclear in the sense of having a center, or nucleus, and it is archaic in the sense of being a primitive (that is, grandiose and undifferentiated) precursor of the mature self. The archaic nuclear self is bipolar in that it comprises two structures: the grandiose self and the idealized self-object. That is, in this stage there is a differentiated self, which is experienced as omnipotent, but there are no truly differentiated objects. Objects are still experienced as extensions of the self, as self-objects. At this stage, the child's grandiose self attempts to exercise omnipotent control over his self-objects. In healthy maturity, all loved objects have a self-object aspect. However, here the experience of the object as a self-object is a reversible "regression in the service of the ego," which lacks the rigidity that characterizes the experience of objects as self-objects in pathological narcissism.

The internalization of psychic structure (albeit in rudimentary form) is codeterminous with the formation of the nuclear self. As Kohut puts it, "The rudiments of the nuclear self are laid down by simultaneously or consecutively occurring processes of selective inclusion and exclusion of psychological structure" (1977a, p. 183). Failure to adequately internalize functions originally performed for the child by self-objects results in deficits in the self. Addiction is a futile attempt to compensate for this failure in internalization.

> It is the structural void in the self that the addict tries to fill—whether by sexual activity or by oral ingestion. And the structural void cannot be filled any better by oral ingestion than by any other forms of addictive behavior. It is the lack of self-esteem of the unmirrored self, the uncertainty about the very existence of the self, the dreadful feeling of the fragmentation of the self that the addict tries to counteract by his addictive behavior. (Kohut 1977a, p. 197)*

Of crucial importance are the internalization of tension regulation, self-soothing, and self-esteem regulation, as well as the self-object's function as stimulus barrier. Kohut's stage of the archaic self corresponds, in some ways, to Freud's stage of (primary) narcissism. It does not develop into object love, however, but into mature narcissism, which is characterized by realistic ambitions, enduring ideals, and secure self-esteem.

Pathological narcissism is the regression/fixation to the stage of the archaic self. It is characterized by the presence of a

---

*Reprinted from *The Restoration of the Self*. Copyright 1977 by International Universities Press, Inc. Reprinted by permission of the publisher.

cohesive, but insecure, self which is threatened by regressive fragmentation; grandiosity of less than psychotic proportions, which manifests itself in the form of arrogance, isolation, and unrealistic goals; feelings of entitlement; the need for omnipotent control; poor differentiation of self and object; and deficits in the self-regulating capacities of the ego (self). Further, affect tolerance is poor. The tenuousness of the cohesion of the self makes the narcissistically regressed individual subject to massive anxiety which is, in reality, fear of annihilation (that is, fear of fragmentation of the self). Narcissistic personality disorders are also subject to "empty" depression, reflecting the relative emptiness of the self, or the paucity of psychic structure and good internal objects. In the condition of pathological narcissism, these manifestations of the grandiose self and/or the idealized self-object may be either blatantly apparent or deeply repressed and/or denied, with a resulting facade of pseudo-self-sufficiency, but they are never smoothly integrated into a mature self, as in the case of healthy narcissism.

In Kohut's formulation, the overtly grandiose self is the result of merger with (or lack of differentiation from) a mother who used the child to gratify her own narcissistic needs. It is a "false self" in the terminology of Winnicott (1960). Kohut envisions this false self as insulated from the modifying influence of the reality ego by a vertical split in the personality. The reality ego is in turn impoverished by the repression of the unfulfilled archaic narcissistic demands by a horizontal split (repression barrier) in the personality (Fig. 1). For our purposes, the salient point to be derived from Kohut's and Winnicott's theories is an understanding of the overt grandiosity of the alcoholic as a manifestation of a "false self," which is isolated, both affectively and cognitively, from the more mature reality ego, which is itself enfeebled by its inability to integrate the archaic self. Hence, some sense can be made of the coexistence of haughty arrogance and near-zero self-esteem so frequently seen in alcoholics.

We are using the term *pathological narcissism* essentially in Kohut's sense to mean a current failure (reflecting a fixation or a regression) to integrate the archaic nuclear self, with its compo-

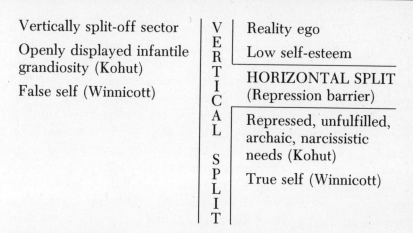

Figure 1. Self structure in pathological narcissism. (Adapted from Kohut 1971, p. 185.)

nent grandiose self and idealized self-object, into a mature self, whether such a failure manifests itself openly in the form of grandiosity (that is, arrogance, isolation, and unrealistic ambitions) and/or the need for omnipotent control of others, or covertly in the form of pseudo-self-sufficiency. Concomitant with such failure are ego and self deficits,* resulting from the inadequate internalization of the functions once performed by the idealized, omnipotent self-object. These deficits are included in our understanding of pathological narcissism.

We will also include in our concept of pathological narcissism certain phenomena described by Kernberg in his discussion of the borderline personality. These phenomena include the relative failure to securely integrate good and bad self and object representations into stable internal objects, along with the associated defenses of splitting, primitive idealization, projective identification, and denial. In metapsychological terms, Kohut's archaic, nuclear self is seen as affectively metastable—that is, as

---

*Structural deficits in the self are reflected in functional deficits in the ego. Hence, we do not consistently distinguish between ego deficits and self deficits. A rigorous metapsychology would require such a distinction.

constituted by a good grandiose self, a bad grandiose self, a good self-object, and a bad self-object. Although this synthesis of Kohut and Kernberg lacks metapsychological clarity, it does have the merit of accounting for the clinical phenomenon that early-sobriety alcoholics evidence both narcissistic and borderline characteristics, although in most early-sobriety alcoholics, narcissistic pathology predominates. It is perhaps no accident that the phrase "His majesty, the baby," which comes from Freud's 1914 essay *"On Narcissism: An Introduction,"* plays such a prominent role in the AA literature. Bill Wilson learned this phrase from his analyst, Henry Tiebout, and he incorporated it into his writings, which became canonical for AA members. Thus, AA also recognizes pathological narcissism as a central problem in alcoholism. Experience has shown that most alcoholics in the late stages of addiction and during the early stages of sobriety are regressed/fixated to the state of pathological narcissism. This is the minimal psychopathology usually encountered in recently sober alcoholics; some will be further regressed to unmodified borderline or psychotic states.

PATHOLOGICAL NARCISSISM AND THE CLINICAL ALCOHOLIC PERSONALITY

Let us see how the concept of regression/fixation to pathological narcissism as we have defined it can give coherence to our empirical knowledge and theoretical understanding of alcoholism. Elevation in the Psychopathic deviate (Pd) scale of the MMPI in both active and recovering alcoholics, probably the most consistent finding in the literature on the alcoholic personality, can be understood as a manifestation of the overtly grandiose self, with its arrogance, isolation, and lack of realistic goals. The elevation of the Depression (D) scale on the MMPI, which is also a consistent finding in advanced active alcoholism and early recovery, reflects both the psychopharmacological consequences of active alcoholism (depletion of available catecholamines) and the impoverishment of the self, riddled with structural deficits and impaired in its capacity for self-esteem regulation, found in pathological narcissism.

Developmentally, the depression reflects the disappointment which results from inadequate phase-appropriate mirroring of the child's grandiose self by self-objects. Additionally, active alcoholism gives one much to be realistically depressed about. Empirical findings, using adjective checklists and self-reports, of impoverishment of the self can be understood in the same way. The structurally deficient self of pathological narcissism is experienced as an empty depression, and it is reported as lack of interest in people, activities, and goals. Even the self is uninteresting to itself. The regression to pathological narcissism concomitant with the alcoholic process progressively strips the already enfeebled ego of its investments in objects and activities, leaving an empty self, an empty world, and an empty bottle.

Another consistent finding in alcoholics is field dependence. Field dependence entails a relative inability to utilize internal resources, as well as impairments in the differentiations of body image, of figure and ground, and of self and world. By definition, the field-dependent person experiences the environment as a self-*object*—which is precisely the way in which the person fixated/regressed to pathological narcissism experiences the world. Thus, our hypothesis well accounts for this datum.

Confused gender identity is a frequent finding in alcoholic populations. It also can be understood in terms of pathological narcissism. (Conflict over sex roles, a related finding, has both sociological and psychological determinants.) Developmentally, the archaic self arises before the establishment of firm gender identity. Hence, regression/fixation to the stage of the archaic self entails a blurring of gender identity. The failure to adequately internalize (identify with) the ideal self-object of the same sex, which is postulated as etiological in a vulnerability to pathological narcissism, would render difficult the establishment of a firm gender identity. The early psychoanalytic findings of latent homosexuality in male alcoholics may also reflect failure to internalize ideal self-objects, although they are expressed in terms of libido theory and the psychosexual stages.

Ego weakness is a construct which integrates several empirically confirmed characteristics of active and early-sobriety alcoholics: impulsivity, lack of frustration tolerance, lack of affect tolerance, and lack of differentiation of the self-concept. It overlaps many of the findings just discussed: confused gender identity, conflict over sex roles, psychopathic deviancy, and impoverishment of the self. In terms of pathological narcissism, ego weakness in the alcoholic is understood in terms of the structural deficits in the self. In other words, the failure to internalize by a process of selective and depersonified identification (designated "transmuting internalization" by Kohut) the functions of affect regulation once performed from the outside by mother and other caretakers results in ego weakness. In the case of weak or incomplete internalization, the self is subject to regression to pathological narcissism, with its accompanying ego weakness.

Stimulus augmentation, which has been found to be characteristic of alcoholics and which contributes to their ego weakness, can also be understood in terms of pathological narcissism, as a failure to internalize the mother's function as an auxiliary to the innate stimulus barrier. Although constitutional factors cerinly play a role in the alcoholic's stimulus augmentation, failures in internalization and structuralization just as certainly play their role.

PATHOLOGICAL NARCISSISM AND
THE ETIOLOGY OF ALCOHOLISM

The three main theories of the psychodynamics of alcoholism—the dependency-conflict theory, the need-for-personal-power theory, and the epistemological error theory—are given coherence by the concept of regression/fixation to pathological narcissism in advanced alcoholism. Developmentally, the archaic self, which is the fixation/regression point in pathological narcissism, is contemporaneous with the oral stage of psychosexual development. Regression/fixation to orality entails either overt dependency or intense conflicts around dependency. On the object relations side of development, objects are experienced, and related to, as self-objects. For our purposes, this experiencing of objects as self-objects is theoretically and clinically the most salient characteristic of pathologically narcissistic individuals. Because they experience others as a part of themselves, they are, by definition, dependent on those others, not only for external supplies but more crucially, for the very experience of being an integral self. Because they experience others as constituents of themselves, they can neither be really independent nor truly interdependent: There is no one apart from themselves with whom to be interdependent; there are no truly independent objects "out there" at the stage of the archaic self. This is the ultimate basis of alcoholic loneliness.

Further, because the very existence of the self is dependent on the object, experienced as a self-object, this dependency is fraught with the primitive, massive, panic-level anxiety induced by the threat of the dissolution of the self—hence the need for omnipotent control of the object. Any failure of the self-object to meet the needs of the archaic self is experienced as an injury to the self, which is reacted to with "narcissistic rage." This narcissistic rage has been conventionally understood in terms of psychosexual regression to orality (oral dependence) and denoted *oral rage*. Adding to this oral rage is the hatred that people so often feel toward those upon whom they are dependent.

Although this deep need for fusion with a self-object may be repressed from consciousness or dealt with by reaction formation so that it is not readily apparent in the form of excessive interpersonal dependence, the alcoholic has nevertheless found the "perfect" self-object with which to meet this need—the bottle. At the same time that dependency needs, or the need for self-objects, is being denied/repressed, it is being met through the pathological use of alcohol, which is simultaneously experienced as the perfect self-object and as a magic fluid (milk). Further, since the internalization of self-soothing, stimulus attenuation, and self-esteem regulation, which are originally performed by self-objects, have failed or are at least deficient in pathological narcissism, the pathologically narcissistic patient is necessarily *dependent* on external agencies to perform these functions. Pathologically narcissistic individuals may openly seek fulfillment of these needs in their interpersonal relations, or they may deeply repress them, or, as is more typical, they may be in intense conflict over meeting these needs, which are, in the very nature of the case, always present. However, open dependency is not acceptable in adult males and is increasingly unacceptable in adult females in our society. Hence, a conflict must ensue. Thus, dependency conflict is a necessary correlate of pathological narcissism.

Alcohol, through its pharmacological properties, readily performs the normal self functions of affect regulation, stimulus attenuation, and self-soothing by anesthetizing painful or uncomfortable drives, emotions, and sensations. It also raises self-esteem, at least initially. At the same time, its use is socially acceptable, even considered "manly," and is not considered dependent behavior. Therefore, pathologically narcissistic individuals can use alcohol to perform psychological functions of which they are not capable without appearing dependent to themselves or others. Thus the concept of regression/fixation to pathological narcissism well accounts for the dynamic of dependency conflict in alcoholics.

The fusion with the idealized, omnipotent self-object, characteristic of the stage of the archaic, cohesive self and of pathological narcissism, is driven in part by a wish to participate in the self-objects greatness and *power*. Alcoholics certainly idealize their self-object, alcohol, to which they attribute omnipotent powers. The need-for-power theory of the dynamics of alcoholism thus fits our theory of pathology of the self as the basic dynamic of alcoholism. Further, since the stage of the archaic self is developmentally a stage of egotism, the power sought in fusion with the omnipotent self-object is egotistic, not social. In terms of McClelland's theory, it is personal power, not social power, that is the goal of fusion with the omnipotent self-object. Hence, regression/fixation to pathological narcissism gives a rational basis to McClelland's empirical theory and explains why alcoholics drink to experience personal power. They do so because they are fixated/regressed to the stage of the grandiose self, and striving for personal power through fusion with powerful self-objects is the *modus operandi* of this developmental stage.

The epistemological error theory of the dynamics of alcoholism sees the driving force behind alcoholism as an impossible misconception of reality, which sets the alcoholic in opposition to the world and which allows no meaningful interaction with that world to be experienced. Rather than experiencing reality as an infinite set of interrelationships, interactions, and feedback loops—in short, as a necessarily interdependent field—the alcoholic experiences it as a reified subject acting upon a disjunctive world. Since this is incongruent with the nature of things, conflict must ensue. This is precisely the phenomenology of the experiential world of the pathologically narcissistic.

Although alcoholics, in their pathological narcissism, may have selves experienced as separate from the world (grandiose self), they do not have a world experienced as separate from the self. Thus, Bateson's theory also makes sense if the active and early-recovery alcoholic is seen as pathologically narcissistic. Again, there are no real objects "out there"; there is only a grossly inflated self constituted of objects experienced as self. This is the metapsychological structure of the famous inflated alcoholic ego. This inflated ego has no world with which to establish interdependency, or circuits of transformations of information in Bateson's terminology. Hence, the alcoholic's epistemology, or way of construing the world, must be false—that is, an inadequate account of that world. What is seen in structural terms as an archaic self composed of a grandiose self and an omnipotent idealized self-object is seen in cybernetic terms as an information system without feedback loops, as cognitive error.

Bateson actually says that the boundary between self and world in the alcoholic is too impermeable to account for the interdependent nature of reality; however, a self that experiences the world as itself is also radically cut off from the "real" (object) world—it comes to the same thing. Thus, our theory of regression/fixation to pathological narcissism can also account for the alcoholic's misconstruing of the world in such a way that he cannot receive corrective feedback from that world and winds up in opposition to it. Thus, the concept of experiencing objects as self-objects can serve as a rationale for Bateson's theory of alcoholism as epistemological error.

PATHOLOGICAL NARCISSISM AND COMPULSIVITY

Alcoholics who have achieved sobriety often manifest obsessive-compulsive personality traits. This compulsivity is usually of pathological proportions. This move from impulsivity to compulsivity is puzzling at first glance. Of course, any addiction is a compulsion, but we don't usually regard addicts as compulsives. By definition, they are suffering from an impulse disorder, and we regard them as oral or narcissistic characters, not as anal or compulsive ones. So how can this be?

At one level, the sober alcoholic's new-found compulsivity is a defense, a reaction formation, against the underlying impulsivity. As such, it performs a vital function in early sobriety, and the hope is that it is strong enough to do its job. However, there is a more profound reason for this phenomenon—namely, that both the impulsivity of active alcoholism and the compulsivity of arrested alcoholism are manifestations of the alcoholic's pathological narcissism. The bridge is the need for omnipotent control so characteristic of the grandiose self. In addiction, such power and control is sought in fusion with an omnipotent self-object—alcohol; in recovery, it is sought in ritual, rigidity, and other character defenses. AA rightly sees the modification, or treatment, of the underlying pathological narcissism as the key issue with the newly, and not-so-newly, sober alcoholic. Untreated, its outward manifestation quickly reverts from compulsivity to impulsivity, and the alcoholic is off and running.

USING THE THEORY

Perhaps the most important practical implications of the theory are the light it casts on (1) the newly sober alcoholic's needs for idealized objects and for omnipotent control; and (2) the newly sober alcoholic's psychological disabilities in the management of intense feelings, the quieting of anxiety, and the maintenance of self-esteem. The first forecasts the nature of our relationship with the patient, while the second specifies the nature of the reparative work that must be done. Our understanding of these needs and deficiencies in recently sober alcoholics gives us a cognitive structure and helps us gain insight into and tolerate our own feelings during our work with them. The theory is illustrated more explicitly in the case material that follows.

CHAPTER 7

Psychotherapy with the Early-Sobriety Alcoholic

Let us summarize our understanding of the condition of recovering alcoholics at the start of their sobriety. Organically, they are suffering from some degree of neurological impairment, which manifests itself as impairment of the ego functions of memory, new learning, sleep, and affect regulation; psychologically, they are suffering from some degree of narcissistic pathology, which also manifests itself in ego deficits; and socially, they are almost certainly suffering from serious conflicts with their environment. How can we use this understanding of the experiential world of newly recovering alcoholics to optimize their chances of remaining sober?

BUILDING RELATIONSHIP

The therapist's first task with the recovering alcoholic (and all other patients) is *building relationship*. Because the treatment

will end unless the therapist succeeds in establishing a meaningful relationship with the alcoholic, the building and preserving
of bonds between therapist and alcoholic *always* take prece-
dence in the therapeutic interview. Bonds are built by empathic
listening, supplemented by the clearing of resistances.

Very early in the history of psychotherapy, Freud realized
that the establishment of a relationship with the patient was
both central to the psychotherapeutic process and a prerequisite
for meaningful psychological work by the patient. In commenting on the beginning of treatment, he asked,

> When shall we begin our disclosure to the patient? . . .
> The answer to this can only be: Not until a dependable
> transference, a well-developed *rapport*, is established
> in the patient. The first aim of the treatment consists in
> attaching him to the treatment and the person of the
> physician. To ensure this, one need do nothing but
> allow him time. If one devotes serious interest to him,
> clears away carefully the first resistances that arise and
> avoids certain mistakes, such an attachment develops
> in the patient of itself, and the physician becomes
> linked up with one of the imagos of those persons
> from who he used to receive kindness. It is certainly
> possible to forfeit this primary success if one takes up
> from the start any standpoint other than understand-
> ing, such as a moralizing attitude, . . . or if one be-
> haves as the representative or advocate of some third
> person, . . . and so on. (Freud 1913a, p. 139)

This is as true now as it was then, and it is as true with
alcoholics as it is with other patients. It is the *attitude* of the
therapist which is crucial, especially with patients who are as
sensitive as alcoholics are in early sobriety. What is required is
active listening, the projection of interest and concern, and
nonjudgmental positive regard for the patient. However, the
situation with the newly sober alcoholic requires some modifi-
cations of Freud's excellent advice on conducting the early
stages of treatment. The modification essentially consists of
greater overt activity on the part of the therapist. Although

empathic listening and clearing of treatment-threatening resistances remain paramount, the therapist must also serve as an expert on the disease of alcoholism; he or she has an educative function to perform.

The therapist is also dealing with an impulse disorder that may be acted out at any time, possibly ending the treatment. Insofar as possible, this acting out must be anticipated and circumvented. It is intolerable affects which lead to the drink. Unconscious and/or disavowed affects are particularly dangerous. Any intense feelings, "postive" or "negative," conscious or unconscious, that remain unverbalized are a threat to sobriety. The therapist must therefore actively encourage the expression of feelings and must appropriately interpret some of the emotional discomfort as a symptom of recovery. In other words, the acting out of the resistance by drinking must be anticipated and dealt with before it occurs. Of course, this is not always possible; it is a goal, not a demand on the therapist. Therapy at this stage of recovery is so very difficult because the therapist has little time in which to deal with the patient's conflicts since those conflicts may be acted out by drinking and terminating the treatment. We do not have the luxury of waiting the patient out, however desirable this may be. Thus, what is required is a sort of bob and weave on the part of the therapist. Empathic listening, imparting of information, and the elicitation of feelings must be integrated into a coherent style. It requires a great deal of "therapeutic tact" for the therapist to sense when to do what in order to maintain the relationship. However, the growing attachment of the patient to the therapist provides the cement which holds both the patient and the therapeutic relationship together. Thus, Freud's recommendations for beginning the treatment remain pure gold which we must, however, necessarily alloy in order to successfully treat early-sobriety alcoholics. Let us look at how this works in practice.

THE CASE OF LARRY R.

Larry R. went to his internist in a state of intense panic. He was suffering from palpitations, racing pulse, and sensations of tightness in the chest, as well as intolerable anxiety. He was convinced that he was having a heart attack. Fortunately, he also told his physician that he had been drinking heavily for the past several months, although he was sober when he arrived in the doctor's office. After ruling out cardiac pathology, the internist told Larry that his drinking was contributing to his physical condition, the cause of which was anxiety. He urged Larry to accept a referral for psychotherapy for his anxiety and problem drinking. He prescribed minor tranquilizers for Larry to ease his withdrawal from alcohol and to reduce his anxiety.

The therapist was asked to see Larry on an emergency basis. He had "hit a bottom," requesting immediate help, and was open to therapeutic intervention. Although his impatience was symptomatic, this was not the salient point; on the contrary, it was clearly an occasion on which to "strike while the iron is hot."

Larry, a broad, well-muscled man arrived shaking and clinging to his wife. If the need for inpatient detoxification had not already been ruled out by the internist, the therapist would have suggested hospitalization. At Larry's request, the therapist agreed to allow him to bring his wife with him into the treatment room. He looked like a trapped animal; sheer terror radiated from his face. Larry concentrated on his somatic symptoms and his anxiety, which he described as intolerable. He was very open about his recent drinking. Since he was freely and meaningfully communicating, the therapist's stance was one of active listening, intervening just enough to demonstrate some interest and to obtain clarification. At this point, the patient was transmitting, not receiving. He needed to unburden himself.

At the end of the session, the therapist noted that it was not possible to tell how much of Larry's anxiety was being caused by alcohol. He asked Larry whether he would be willing to try an experiment—to stop drinking so that they could see just what was causing him such pain. Larry agreed and began twice-weekly individual psychotherapy. By the end of the first session, the seeds of rapport had been planted. Someone had responded to Larry's desperation; he had been listened to, and concrete steps to alleviate his pain had been suggested. The therapist accrued considerable relational capital from this emergency session. He was to have occasion to draw on it.

Larry's History

Larry was 33 years old. He had been married for 5 years to a woman 6 years younger than he, and they had no children. He had previously been married for 3 years at the age of 21. Larry was the oldest of two sons of Irish, working-class parents. He was 6 years older than his brother, who had had a "breakdown" in high school, for which he had been hospitalized.

Larry had been an athletic star in high school and had dropped out of college to try professional tennis. He had worked as a pro at a country club and had competed in tournaments, but failed in his bid to become a professional tennis player. Although he had been a heavy drinker from college on, it was at this point that his drinking got out of hand. He worked for 3 years as a bartender before going to work for a large manufacturer in the purchasing department. He had managed to hold onto his job in spite of his drinking and absenteeism. He was close to his maternal grandfather. His father was a problem drinker, and his mother disapproved of drinking. A lapsed Catholic, Larry had been raised in an observant home.

Larry's parents were social isolates, and he remembered little or no relationship with extended family members (with the exception of the maternal grandparents, who lived with the family). His mother was a highly anxious woman, a perfectionist, and a compulsive housekeeper. She worked as an office manager for a dentist. His mother was close to the grandfather, whom she idolized, and had a strained relationship with the grandmother, with whom she quarreled. She had often told Larry how much he reminded her of Grandpa.

Larry's father was shadowy in the patient's mind until late adolescence, when a modicum of closeness was achieved through their becoming "drinking buddies." His father would attend all of Larry's tennis matches, a "fanship" which Larry experienced ambivalently, enjoying the attention and admiration, while dreading what he felt to be an intolerable pressure to win. Larry was uncertain whether this pressure emanated from his father or from within. Although he wished to, Larry was never able to ask his father to not attend even one match. During Larry's latency years, his father had been ill with "stomach troubles" which made him a semi-invalid, unable to work for several years. Following surgery, Larry's father obtained a position with the manufacturer for whom Larry was working and supplemented his income by working as a bartender. In spite of his father's poor health, the family always seemed to have been economically comfortable.

Larry perceived his grandfather as strong, reliable, neat, and silent, a man who loved the woods and fields around their home. He shared this love with Larry, who idolized him. He died of heart disease when Larry was 14 years old. Larry remembered little sense of loss, which puzzled him. He had almost no relationship with his brother, although in retrospect he feels compassion for his brother's difficulties in living up to Larry's "star" status. His memories were hazy of his reaction to both his brother's birth and his brother's hospitalization for a psychotic break, an episode that had occurred while Larry was attending college and had not been discussed by his parents. Larry maintained minimal contact with his brother, who appeared to have fully recovered from his psychotic episode.

There had been an air of secrecy in Larry's home, and he hadn't known until the time of his divorce that both his parents had been married previously, and that his father had a child by his first wife. Nevertheless, Larry described himself as very close to his parents. He experienced their retirement to California several years earlier as traumatic. His drinking then accelerated and became out of control.

Larry's "fall from grace" occurred at a nearby university, which he had attended on a tennis scholarship. He felt lost, socially and academically. After an unhappy attempt to live with several other students, he returned home and became a commuter. He also began to drink heavily. He finally left the university, feeling like a failure in all areas. His first marriage followed shortly thereafter.

Larry had had considerable premarital sexual experience. However, he had always kept his affectionate and sensual feeling strictly separate. Women were "either mothers or whores." Larry had suspected that one of his college roommates, John, whom he had admired, was "bi." The suspicion made him intensely uncomfortable: "I can't help thinking that that's disgusting, although I understand that people can do what they like." His painfully ambivalent feelings toward this roommate contributed to his decision to return home. However, Larry maintained an off-and-on friendship with John, who had been hospitalized for alcoholism and had emerged a "cured alcoholic, who can control his drinking."

Larry had gradually lost sexual interest in his first wife, with whom he had been potent, orgasmic, and satisfied before their marriage. He drank more and more, and constant fighting, mostly about his drinking, ensued. His wife became pregnant during this period of marital strife, and they mutually decided on an abortion. Following the abortion, the remnant of Larry's sexual feeling for his wife died. She repeatedly pleaded with him to do something about his drinking. He responded with rage. His wife also objected to Larry's closeness to his mother. They soon divorced, and Larry again returned "home."

Following his divorce, Larry worked as a tennis pro at a country club. He also played on the local tournament circuit. At first he enjoyed this life and was moderately successful. However, his drinking ruined his game, and he lost his job. He then became a bartender at a bar near the tennis club. Now he could drink openly and more or less continuously, and he did. Some deeply buried instinct for self-preservation warned Larry that this life was the route to early doom, and he found enough strength to obtain his present job. However, he continued to tend bar and to drink on evenings and weekends.

It was at this point that he met his second wife in the bar, and they married after a short and wet courtship. Although Larry and his wife seemed mutually caring during their initial interview with the therapist, they reported that they had not had sexual relations for over a year and that there was much tension in their relationship. Larry experienced both his problem with alcohol and his failure to perform sexually as intolerable flaws for which he detested himself. He had always been highly demanding, holding himself accountable to expectations of superlative performance and moral perfection. He had been unable to live up to these expectations. For Larry, stardom on the high school football field and basketball court was a paradise lost. These early athletic successes provided Larry with narcissistic gratifications that later life had been unable to match. Like Biff in Arthur Miller's *Death of a Salesman*, much of his life was a futile attempt to recapture the "Ebbett's field experience."

Thus Larry, now tortured by anxieties that alcohol could no longer assuage, presented a history of both failure to live up to his high expectations, resulting in chronic narcissistic injury and rage, and failure to express and obtain satisfaction for his aggressive and sexual energies. It is a picture of an almost total damming up of basic human strivings, compounded by addiction to alcohol.

Diagnosis

Larry was clearly suffering from primary alcoholism. Alcohol abuse had been an accompaniment to his entire adult life. It was a major etiological factor in his academic failure, in the destruction of his career as a tennis pro, and in the breakdown of his first marriage. It was no longer an effective self-medication; on the contrary, it was contributing to his runaway anxiety.

In Jellinek's terms, Larry was a gamma alcoholic. According to DSM-III, he was suffering from alcohol dependence. The practical importance of this diagnosis cannot be overemphasized. It meant that Larry would have no chance at all to deal with his very real emotional problems unless his alcoholism could be successfully treated. It also meant that Larry could not drink alcohol safely. The data that confirmed the diagnosis was gathered over many sessions, but the very first session provided ample evidence for a working diagnosis of alcoholism. In addition, Larry's physical condition mandated a period of abstinence from alcohol. Given the blatant nature of Larry's psychopathology, it would have been easy to be seduced into treating the "underlying" personality problem. At this stage, however, that simply cannot be done; the treatment goal must be stable sobriety; and the therapist must use his knowledge of the patient's personality dynamics in the service of that goal.

The Beginning of Sobriety

Larry accepted the therapist's suggestion that he not drink so that a differential diagnosis could be established. He was initially able to maintain his sobriety, and some time to heal was gained. He was not able to accept his alcoholism, however. To Larry, to be an alcoholic, or even just a person who couldn't drink, was to be fundamentally flawed. His perfectionism could not even entertain the idea. It was impossible! The self could not be so damaged. Although this was a defense of the alcoholism based on fear— the stark fear that life without alcohol was not possible—it was also a defense against the intolerably deep narcissistic wound which Larry thought that the acceptance of his alcoholism would inflict. He was also defending against the loss of an internal identification and an external relationship with his father, which was based on their common devotion to alcohol. Not surprisingly, Larry was also unable to accept a referral to AA.

Education

The therapist's work in the early sessions therefore had a major educational component. He informed Larry about the physiological effects of alcohol and their relationship to his somatic symptoms and anxiety attacks. He also taught the disease concept of alcoholism in the hope that it would serve as a balm for the anticipated narcissistic injury. At the same time, careful attention was given to analyzing Larry's anxiety attacks, which were so terrifying that they threatened his sobriety. The common denominator proved to be repressed rage. Hence the focus of the sessions shifted to helping Larry recognize and express his feelings, especially his anger.

The Intense Feelings of Early Sobriety

The great threat to early sobriety is the very intensity with which long-anesthetized and/or repressed emotions are experienced. Anxiety, anger, guilt, and self-hatred cause the most difficulty, but the intensity itself, even of joyful feelings, is unfamiliar and can be overwhelming. Theoretically, ego weakness results in a failure to modulate intense affects, which then threaten to fragment a tenuously cohesive self. Metaphorically, the container (the self) is too weak to contain the contents (primitive feelings and unneutralized drives), and the container starts to disintegrate under the pressure. What is experienced is panic, the threat of the annihilation of the self. In Larry's case, rage was the threatening emotion to be repressed or denied at any cost. Unfortunately, the cost was a crippling somatization in the form of anxiety attacks which mimicked heart attacks. To complicate matters, to be angry for Larry was to be bad. Hence, angry feelings were not only potentially self-fragmenting; they were also a source of severe intersystemic (id-superego) conflict. What could the therapist do to help Larry escape this trap—either repressed rage, resulting in panic, or experienced rage, resulting in feelings of fragmentation? Both horns of this dilemma endangered sobriety.

A weak ego, like a weak muscle, is strengthened by exercise. The exercise for strengthening the ego's capacity for affect modulation is *verbalization*. Each time Larry was able to recognize, name, and talk about a feeling, a victory was won. Every time Larry was able to master—that is, experience and talk about rather than repress, deny, somatize, or act out—a quantum of anger, his ego grew stronger and his self-esteem rose. Hence, the therapist's intervention, over and over, was to ask "What are you feeling?"

Krystal and Raskin (1970) speak of affect regression to a developmental stage in which affects are experienced as massive, primitive, overwhelming, and undifferentiated.

Hence, *labeling the affects* is a crucial aspect of verbalization. It provides cognitive structure, starts the process of affect redifferentiation, and reduces the terror of the experientially primitive, unfamiliar, and chaotic emerging feelings. Affect labeling is a way station on the road from feelings experienced as mysterious happenings, as lightning bolts from above, inflicted on the alcoholic, to feelings experienced as consciously owned aspects of the addict's self. To recur to a classic metaphor, a little territory has been gained for the ego from the id. Initially, affect labeling must be done by the therapist: "You are angry" or "You are sad," and so on. Although these are interpretations, the feelings are usually near the surface and are transparent to a trained and experienced therapist. It is always the feelings that are close to consciousness that are interpreted, with the exception of sobriety-threatening feelings, such as Larry's rage. Krystal and Raskin's theory of affect regression makes sense of the ubiquity of automatic, maladaptive defenses, including drinking, against strong feelings in early sobriety.

Anxiety and Anger

Larry gradually learned to recognize and express his feelings, including his anger. Each episode of anxiety was carefully explored: "What was happening at the time?" "What happened earlier that day? The day before?" "Who were you with? What was happening between you?" "What were you thinking?" "What were you experiencing?" "What were you feeling?"

Angry feelings uncovered behind the anxiety were interpreted: "When you're angry and unaware of it, you become anxious"; "It is very difficult for you to accept your angry feelings."

The therapist told Larry that anger was a necessary emotion and that it is normal to have mixed emotions, including anger toward those to whom we are close. It was difficult for Larry to believe that his inability to experience and accept his rage led to devastating anxiety attacks; however, his attacks diminished in both frequency and intensity. Feelings of sadness, depression, fear, self-hatred, and guilt, as well as the "positive" emotions, were also ventilated, and Larry stayed sober.

Guilt and Self-Hatred

Guilt, anxiety, and self-hatred threaten sobriety and need to be uncovered and worked through. The disease concept of alcoholism, a potent alleviator of guilt and self-hatred that are secondary to the alcoholism itself, must be actively taught by the therapist. Here reality and an element of denial combine in a functional way to support sobriety. Anxiety is usually based on conflict or fear of fragmentation or both. Interpretation of these feelings is reassuring and can reduce the anxiety. Finally, painful emotions can be rendered tolerable by their interpretation as "growing pains" that are part of the healing process, organic and psychological, of early sobriety. Hence, some of Larry's early depression was interpreted as the effect of the alcoholism itself, which depletes one's neurotransmitters, emotional resources, and self-esteem; and some of Larry's early depression was interpreted as part of the healing process—explicitly, as a mourning process for a lost "friend" and an old identity and lifestyle. The therapist noted, "You're feeling depressed because you miss booze and your old life-style. It's like losing an old friend, and you are grieving." With

Larry, depression was also anger turned inward; when the anger was close to the surface, this was also pointed out.

How can this strategy of uncovering feelings be reconciled with the principle of supporting the defenses in early sobriety? The answer is essentially a practical one. Functional defenses, which protect the recovering alcoholic from pain he cannot yet handle, whether such pain be the potential consequence of new knowledge or of new emotion, are supported. Dysfunctional defenses, which are threats to sobriety, are analyzed and interpreted. However, denial that is appropriately protective is supported, as are successful repression and obsessive-compulsive behavior that does not threaten sobriety. For example, Larry's denial of homosexual feelings and of conflict around homosexuality was supported, as was his wish not to know the "family secret," whatever that might be.

Even though he was not drinking, Larry's denial of his alcoholism was not supported. Here the therapist had to walk a tightrope between "provisional" acceptance of Larry's decision (without an admission of his alcoholism) to not drink and his refusal to attend AA meetings, and reinforcement of Larry's denial of his alcoholism. The crucial issue was to buy time for healing, education, and relationship building. Long-term sobriety required acceptance of his disease, yet any sobriety at all was only possible if the loss of identity and the wound to self-esteem, which Larry feared that "surrender" to his alcoholism would inflict, could be postponed. So the therapist planted seeds of knowledge of alcoholism as he worked to strengthen Larry's ego. This is "therapeutic tack," an art difficult to teach, but acquired by the sensitive therapist through experience.

Although Larry's anxiety attacks decreased in frequency and intensity and his life settled down, he continued to "booze fight." This inability to accept his alcoholism made his sobriety provisional and unnecessarily uncomfortable. At a not-so-unconscious level, he was always waiting for the next drink; hence he was always living in the fear/hope/dread of pharmacological oblivion. Under these conditions, his pathologically high anxiety level could not completely abate. For all his wish to return to drinking, Larry also knew at some level that drinking meant psychic destruction and possibly death: a part of his anxiety was therefore quite realistic. Terror could necessarily never be far from the surface. Larry needed to maintain his anxiety to have a reason to return to drinking. As AA would put it, he was setting up his next drunk, and the therapist pointed this out. The need to maintain psychic discomfort as a rationalization for drinking is a part of the dynamics of symptom formation in early sobriety.

Overdetermination and Working Through

Larry's anxiety, like all psychological symptoms, was *overdetermined*. That is, it had many causes. It was necessary to examine Larry's anxiety from many perspectives. In Freud's illuminating simile, the boat cannot sail (the symptom cannot be alleviated) until the last cable tying the boat to the dock is cut (until every determinant of the symptom is made conscious and understood). Larry's anxiety attacks could thus be understood (1) as the unconscious fear of the eruption of repressed rage; (2) as a mechanism for setting up a 'slip'; (3) as a consequence of structural deficits in the self concomitant with pathological narcissism—explicity, the failure to internalize mechanisms for self-soothing and tension regulation; (4) as anxiety directly aroused by, and indirectly caused by the attempt to repress, narcissistic rage engendered by his inability to exercise omnipotent control over an environment still experienced as a self-object; (5) as separation anxiety

engendered by the progressive differentiation of self
and object intrapsychically and by separations in the
real world (such as his parents' move to California);
(6) as a direct physiological effect of alcohol abuse,
and later as part of the neurophysiological recovery
process; and (7) as a recapitulation, a somatic symbolization in the feeling of not being able to breathe, and
an attempt to master the trauma of his mother's prolonged and extreme smothering behavior, which resulted in yet more repressed rage with its concomitant
anxiety.

The anxiety attacks also served as avenues of
partial discharge for Larry's dammed-up libido,
which he could neither directly discharge nor subli-
mate. From this point of view, the rapid breathing and
other symptoms mimic orgasm and are substitutes for
forbidden satisfaction. They are simultaneously expressions of libidinal wishes and punishments for
those wishes. There is also a possible somatic aspect to
this: According to Freud's first (toxic) theory of anxiety, dammed-up libido is transformed into anxiety as
a kind of conversion process. In any case, Larry's
repressed sexuality was certainly contributing to his
anxiety. His anxiety attacks, with their chest pains,
palpitations, and shortness of breath, were also identifications with both his grandfather (who had died of
heart disease) and his mother (who suffered from
heart disease). Simultaneously, the anxiety attacks
were self-punishments for hatred of and hostility toward his mother and possibly also toward the idealized grandfather. An object relation, Larry to his
mother or grandfather, had regressed to an identification: Larry became his mother/grandfather and suffered their symptoms. The boundaries of self and
object, which were probably never very firmly established, had been lost in Larry's alcohol-mediated regression to an early developmental stage. This merger
of self and object were both wished for and feared. It

lessened Larry's separation anxiety by bringing him close to the longed-for objects of his childhood, but at the cost of a differentiated self, which is itself a cause of panic.

Finally, Larry's anxiety served as punishment for the alcoholism itself. In this sense it was a device, albeit a maladaptive one, for managing guilt. Some of these determinants of Larry's anxiety (those based on conflict or symbolization) could be worked through by interpretation and by making the unconscious conscious; others (those based on structural deficits in the self) could be worked through only by the slow building of psychic structure through the process of "transmuting internalization."

The Therapeutic Alliance

The therapy's primary goal during these early stages of treatment was to help Larry maintain his sobriety. This required a two-pronged attack: the recognition and verbalization of sobriety-threatening affects and breaking down of Larry's remaining denial of his alcoholism. This entailed buying enough time for the establishment of a meaningful therapeutic relationship and for the healing process to take hold.

Larry faithfully attended twice-weekly sessions. He worked hard, struggling with his fears, guilt, and depression. He partially internalized the therapeutic ethos of nonjudgmental understanding of the self; his self-hatred lessened and he was able to feel some compassion for himself. Slowly, he became aware of and experienced his rage and began to accept some of his "negative" emotions. Larry remained sober, yet basically miserable. He never really accepted his alcoholism. He continued to hope that the treatment would enable him to drink safely.

During these months, Larry and the therapist shared many painful moments of near-panic anxiety, murderous rage, and deep despair. The therapist consistently attempted to understand Larry's thoughts and feelings through empathic identification. He used Rogers's (1961) triad of desirable counselor traits— empathy, congruence, and unconditional acceptance—as a model. The therapist tried to feel with Larry, to understand in an affective as well as cognitive sense what was happening to him; to be genuine; and to convey acceptance of Larry at all times, whatever his feelings, thoughts, or behaviors might be.

At the same time, the therapist remained a separate person who was able to be objective. Understanding, and not judging, is the stance of the therapist, who must be able to "regress" sufficiently for an empathic merger to occur, without losing separate identity or objectivity. With experience and personal growth, the achievement of empathic/objective binocular vision becomes easier, although it always remains a goal toward which one strives. Paradoxically, therapists' acceptance of their inperfections is helpful to patients. It facilitates through identification the patient's self-acceptance of imperfections. Acceptance of one's self does not imply complacency. The therapist's self-acceptance is not verbalized, but instead is conveyed subliminally. The importance of these nonspecific aspects of therapy—regularity, reliability, empathic listening, unconditional acceptance, and the therapist's self-acceptance of feelings and limitations—must not be underestimated. They are curative. In fact, there is considerable empirical evidence (Truax and Carkhuff 1967) that attitudinal factors are more important than interpretive and other specific skills in determining counselor effectiveness. If the therapist succeeds in creating a "holding environment" (Winnicott 1952, 1956, 1960) in which the patient feels safe and secure, then the chances of the therapeutic process' being effective are greatly enhanced. The hope is that the patient will not be too damaged to achieve a predominance of basic trust over basic mistrust (Erikson 1950, 1968) and to enter into a "therapeutic alliance" (Zetzel 1956). Fortunately, Larry, who had always been a closed and fearful person, had enough capacity for trust and was hurting enough to establish a working relationship that was strong enough to enable him to stay in treatment and to endure painful insights.

What is the nature of a "working" (Greenson 1965a), or therapeutic, alliance? It is essentially the bond between the relatively healthy, rational, growth-seeking aspects of the patient's personality and the growth-promoting aspects of the therapist's professional self. It is facilitated by the patient's identification with the therapist's acceptance of and attempts to understand all that happens in the therapeutic relationship. The capacity to enter into a viable working alliance requires some basic health, some ability to objectively observe and evaluate the emotional storms that are always experienced in the course of therapy. The patient must have a rudimentary "observing ego," the germ of an ability to be nonpunitively self-critical. This rudimentary observing ego is the patient's analogue of the objective pole of the therapist's empathic/objective binocular vision. In fact, the working alliance may be viewed as a compact between the patient's observing ego and the therapist's professional self. Thus, the working alliance is the relatively rational, realistic component of the therapeutic relationship. Paradoxically, this rational component of the therapeutic relationship is, of necessity, highly emotional, an intensely affective substrate underlying all the work that goes on in the therapeutic process. Ultimately, it is made possible by memory traces of reliable caretakers in early infancy. In newly sober alcoholics, this capacity for relatively objective self-observation is weak and fragile; its nurturing is one of the critical tasks in treating such patients. We must help create that which therapists who work with better-integrated patients can often take for granted.

The therapeutic alliance also requires some capacity for basic trust; that is, patients must have had "good enough mothering" (Winnicott 1956) so that that positive early experience has lead to a conviction that the world contains some "good stuff" and that they have the capacity to acquire some of it. The more emotionally damaged the patient is, the more difficult it will be to establish a relationship characterized by basic trust.

The working alliance also requires the capacity for object constancy—that is, the ability to maintain a constant (internal) representation of an object in the face of frustration. The patient must be able to retain trust in the therapist during moments of rage induced by (perceived) frustration by the therapist. The patient who lacks this capacity will leave treatment. Unfortunately, these are the very capacities, the predominance of basic trust over mistrust and the achievement of object constancy, which are lost (or were never acquired) in the regression/fixation to pathological narcissism so common in early sobriety. The therapist working with "healthier" patients has the luxury of assuming the capacity to enter into a therapeutic alliance. For the alcoholism counselor, the achievement of a "working alliance" is the *goal*, not the precondition, of the treatment

In Larry's case, fear kept him coming for treatment until trust could be established. For a long time, Larry protected his relationship with the therapist by an outwardly compliant style that never risked open conflict or the expression of "negative emotions". He kept his distance for many months. Since this behavior was defensive, the therapist followed the principle of supporting defenses in early-sobriety as long as they threaten neither treatment nor sobriety. He accepted, rather than interpreted, this aspect of the therapeutic relationship. Since unexpressed anger toward the therapist can lead to the patient's terminating treatment, therapists must count on sensitive antennae and emotional attunement to the patient to know when to accept the surface and when to dig in. Larry's behavior was accepted because it was a necessary defense against both fear of abandonment by or destruction of the therapist (the object) if he openly expressed his rage at him for depriving him of alcohol (the therapist is usually experienced as a frustrator during early sobriety), and fear of annihilation of the self if he allowed himself to experience such intense feelings.

However, as treatment proceeded and his emotional pain persisted , Larry became increasingly frustrated with the therapist. At this point, the therapist decided to explore beneath the surface. He repeatedly offered interpretations to the effect that, "You are disappointed in me because you are still in pain." Because interpretations phrased as questions tend to arouse less resistance and are less likely to be experienced as blows to self-esteem, the therapist often offered interpretations in the interrogatory form—for example, "Are you frustrated with me because you are still anxious?" Interpretations are often not heard for a long time. This was true in Larry's case.

The therapist repeatedly introduced the idea that Larry was frustrated with the treatment and angry at him. One evening Larry came to his session in a rage. "What the fuck good are you; I still feel like shit," he screamed. "Why do I come here? I haven't been drinking, but nothing gets better. This is a crock." The therapist *merely* accepted Larry's rage; he did not try to explain or question Larry's frustration tolerance or indeed do *anything* but simply listen. Although he was frightened by his own outburst, Larry could not help but see that his relationship with the therapist was unimpaired. Thus, the therapeutic alliance was strengthened. This pattern recurred a number of times. Each time one of Larry's emotional storms was quietly accepted, there was an increase in his ability to trust. There were many other crises in Larry's life and treatment during the ensuing months. Whatever the provocation, Larry was neither criticized nor abandoned. The holding environment held. The nonspecific elements of therapy had remained a constant in Larry's anxiety-ridden existence.

Larry arrived at his session one day in a relatively peaceful state. During that session he said, and meant, "I trust you" to the therapist. A treatment milestone had been reached; Larry had achieved a relatively stable working alliance with his therapist.

Transference and Countertransference in Early Sobriety

In all human relationships there is both the "accurate" perception of the other person, based on what is actually happening in the here-and-now interaction, and the mutual distortions in perception by each of the other. These distortions arise from a tendency to try to fit current situations into earlier modes of experience. Early experiences with parents are particularly potent prejudgers of subsequent experiences. The anticipation that the behavior of others will be like the behavior of significant persons in our past are projected, distorting our perception of what is "really" happening now. Both of these modes of perception occur in the therapeutic relationship. The first is called the *real relationship*; the latter is called *transference* if it flows from the patient to the therapist and *countertransference* if it flows from the therapist to the patient. The hope is that there is also a *working alliance* between the patient's observing ego and the therapist's professional self (see foregoing discussion).

The *real relationship* is based on the actual traits and behaviors of the two parties; the *working alliance* is based on their mostly unspoken mutual agreement to work toward a common goal; and the *transference* is based on the projection of early childhood experiences onto the therapist. It is an unconscious recreation of an earlier object relation. It is the transfer, without awareness, of feelings originally engendered by an old relationship (say, the patient's relationship with the father) onto a new relationship (that with the therapist). The new person is responded to as if he were the former one. In Freud's words, the patient acts instead of remembering; that is, he acts out an old conflict, which he does not remember, in the new situation. He has no awareness that he is doing this. *Countertransference* is the same process in the therapist. The term is also used in a less technical sense to refer to all of the feelings, realistic or projective, that the therapist has toward the patient. We will use the term in this sense.

Transference is always present, in life and in therapy. In long-term, psychoanalytic, insight-oriented therapy, the development of the transference is fostered and exploited for its therapeutic potential. Transference also occurs in the psychological treatment of recently sober alcoholics, but here we are more interested in promoting the real relationship and the therapeutic alliance. Hence, we talk about the patient's relationship with us, but in here-and-now terms, and not in terms of the historical meaning of current behavior. There will be a time for this, but only after stable sobriety has been achieved. Since we are much more active than the traditional psychoanalytic psychotherapist, we are the objects of less transference projection. Nevertheless, it is important to be aware that much of what is going on in the therapeutic relationship is a new edition of an old story. We may not choose to interpret the historical basis of these misperceptions to the patient, but our understanding of the transference aspects of the relationship helps us deal with the feelings that the patient induces in us.

Larry's relationship with the therapist was real, in the sense that it derived from the personalities of the participants, the situation of their interactions, and the role expectations of the patient and the therapist. Thus, Larry's rather stiff, fearful, formal mode of relating reflected his beliefs about how one relates to a "doctor;" that is, it reflected a "set," or expectation, of social behavior. However, it was also, and perhaps predominately, reflective of Larry's fear of people in general, of his need to defend against the possibility of human intimacy, which might engender intolerable feelings. Hence, his demeanor reflected his perception of social roles but was also expressive of both character and defense. It was here-and-now behavior, a typical representative of Larry's behavior toward authority figures and to a great extent toward people in general. In addition to incarnating character and defensive style, however, Larry's manner of relating to the therapist was transferential; that is, it was a recapitulation or reenactment of his distant, fear-ridden, early relationship with his father. He was, at least partially, relating to the therapist as if he were his father, rather than a different person who might be different from the father of Larry's childhood. Much of Larry's defensive behavior in the therapeutic relationship could be understood as a reenactment of the archaic defenses of his childhood.

In treating an early-sobriety alcoholic like Larry, such transferential elements in the relationship are not interpreted; therefore, the therapist did not comment on the relationship between Larry's present and past behaviors. His distancing, a necessary defense, was left alone. Much later it might be useful for Larry to understand the genetic determinants, the connection between his early experience and his present reactions—but not during early sobriety.

Transference is complex. Many old relationships are activated and transferred to the therapist. At times Larry's reactions to the therapist were determined not so much by present realities or by his relationship with his father as by his early relationships with his mother and maternal grandfather. Insofar as Larry experienced the therapist as an interested, nurturing male, he was transferring his experiences of his grandfather. However, the unresolved trauma of his grandfather's death had taught Larry that it was dangerous to care too deeply for a loving man; this fear of being traumatically abandoned once again was another determinant of his detached relationship with the therapist. Similarly, his fear of being smothered by his mother was also transferred, becoming yet another determinant of Larry's emotional distance in the therapeutic relationship.

Developmental stages are also relived during the treatment. In the next chapter we will see how Kohut's (1971) theory of the narcissistic transference, in which early tendencies to idealize and/or control the parents are reenacted with the therapist, can be used to facilitate the treatment of alcoholics with stable sobriety. At Larry's stage of precarious sobriety, however, regressive transference reactions were not encouraged (although they occur to some extent anyway) and transference interpretations were not made.

The projection of loving feelings originally felt for parents, siblings, or caretakers onto the therapist is "positive" transference; the projection of hateful feelings originally felt for significant others onto the therapist is "negative" transference. In working with Larry, the therapist followed Freud's (1912a) advice to allow the positive transference to develop naturally, but modified Freud's advice to interpret negative transference by dealing with it if, and only if, it was threatening to the therapeutic relationship or to sobriety.

What about countertransference? Countertransference in the broad sense tells us something about ourselves and something about the patient. Our feelings while working with patients provide us with data about our own mental processes and unresolved conflicts, and with vital data about patients' mental processes and their effects on people; they are a unique source of information, providing us with insights not otherwise available. Working with a patient like Larry evokes all kinds of feelings, some of which are ghostly visitors from the past, and some of which are respon-

sive to the patient's actual presence. At various times
in his work with Larry, the therapist felt compassion-
ate, frustrated, angry, impatient, irritated, admiring,
depressed, left out, rejected, and lonely. It was his task
to try to understand these feelings and to separate out
what was coming from him and what was induced by
Larry. The most important lesson for the therapist is
that countertransference is always present and that it
is essential to be aware of these feelings; otherwise
they will be acted out, to the detriment of the treatment. Negative countertransference feelings of anger,
frustration, helplessness, depression, and anxiety do
not disable the therapist, but lack of awareness of
these feelings can be disabling. It is therefore essential
to have personal psychotherapy, clinical supervision,
and other insight-promoting experiences in training.

Alcoholic patients are notorious for the strength of
the countertransference feelings they induce. Larry
was no exception. In working with Larry, the therapist
made continuous efforts to become aware of his negative countertransference. He sought supervision and
consultation to help him better utilize those feelings to
understand his patient. Although we always see
through a glass darkly, and although the therapist was
far from perfectly understanding his reactions to
Larry, these countertransference feelings provided valuable clues to Larry's inner life. In particular, the therapist's feelings of isolation and rejection were induced
replications of Larry's experiential world. They told
the therapist how it felt to be Larry. The therapist's
experience of these feelings also revealed how others
must often have felt with Larry; they contributed to
the therapist's understanding of the bleakness of Larry's social experience. Occasionally, the therapist
would share his countertransferential feelings. Such
sharing provides the patient with immediate feedback
about his effect on others. The therapist's emotional
openness and risk-taking in expressing his feelings

served as a valuable model. In Larry's case, however, the therapist's predominant countertransference feelings were reactions to what for Larry was a necessary defense—emotional distance. Larry needed this distance in order to work therapeutically at all. The therapist therefore utilized his countertransference feelings sparingly as direct sources of intervention.

Larry, who felt overcontrolled by his mother, was particularly sensitive to feelings of being controlled. Hence, the therapist had to be particularly sensitive to and aware of his own need for omnipotent control. This kind of countertransference can be fatal to a therapeutic relationship if it is outside of awareness.

Slips

After about eight months, Larry picked up a drink. It was a deliberate act; Larry had decided to drink "socially." He had always found the idea of not being able to drink safely an intolerable imperfection. He did not so much seem to want to drink as to not not be able to drink. He had often described his misery at not being able to drink, his feelings of exclusion and deprivation, and his fantasized loss of his relationship with his drinking father. His meager self-respect was diminished even further by his being unable to "drink like a man." Since sobriety was not a value for him, the potential for positive self-regard inherent in overcoming an addiction was not available to him. To make matters worse, he projected his lack of respect for himself as an abstinent person onto others and believed that "people" had no respect for him because he did not drink. There was some reality in these beliefs, at least as applied to his barroom companions. But this would not have much mattered to him if he had not been using these people as targets for his projections.

At first, Larry drank moderately—an evening beer or two and a "few" beers on the weekend. He was visibly less resentful. He could *control* his drinking—or so it seemed. Alcohol was an aspect of the environment that he experienced as a part of himself—the archaic, grandiose self of infancy. He believed that he should, and did, have omnipotent control of that self and its extensions; ergo, he could control his drinking. Larry's relationship with alcohol could also be conceptualized as a relationship to an ideal self-object which must not fail him. Seen from Larry's point of view, it was perfectly logical that he could and should be able to control his drinking. He grimly set about trying to do just that.

What was the therapist to do? Larry's was not an impulsive slip, which could have been accepted, interpreted, and used as ammunition to further break down denial; rather it was a conscious decision (with many unconscious determinants) to try controlled drinking. Most slips are of the "fuck you" variety. They are a *drinking at* someone or something. They are impulsive expressions of rage or self-hatred. Other slips are equally impulsive attempts to anesthetize intolerable dysphoria. Larry's return to drinking was overdetermined; it included the expression of rage and the blotting out of dysphoric feelings among its determinants, but these were not the chief determinants of his slip. Impulsive slips are dealt with through acceptance and interpretation. Further, the therapist actively attempts to reestablish the patient's sobriety. "You were really pissed off at your husband when you drank those martinis, but you are sober today. Why don't you try to maintain your sobriety while we work to understand how you could be that angry and not know it" would be a typical intervention in the case of an impulsive slip. The patient is also urged to return to AA if a member and urged to join if not affiliated. The slip is later used in a reality-oriented, nonjudgmental way to illustrate the patient's inability to drink safely. But Larry's slip was not of this variety.

Although he firmly believed that Larry was a gamma alcoholic who could not drink safely, the therapist decided that the proof (no pun intended) was in the pudding and told Larry so. "Given your history, I do not believe that you can drink safely; however, you don't believe that, so you are trying to control your drinking and become a social drinker. Why don't we regard your current use of alcohol as an experiment; if it proves to be the case that you can drink safely, then fine; if not, then we will know that you will have to try something else, such as AA." This approach avoided a power struggle with Larry.

The therapist wanted to represent reality, not a punitive superego, in his attitude toward Larry's drinking. He was letting booze itself be the convincer. Many alcoholism counselors would have taken a stronger stand, and some would have stopped treatment at this point to avoid becoming an enabler. However, many alcoholics who become sober in treatment do not really believe that they cannot drink safely, and some of them are going to require experiential proof through yet another painful bout with alcohol before they can "accept" their alcoholism. Therefore, a strong argument can be made that the therapist, who has expended so much effort in building a lifeline in the therapeutic relationship, should stick with the patient and use the slips and their consequences to further break down denial. There are situations in which the therapist does indeed become an enabler; in such cases, a decision to terminate treatment as long as the patient continues to drink must be seriously considered.

Larry controlled his drinking for a month or so and continued to attend sessions. He seemed less angry, but more anxious. Then one evening he came in looking like a trapped animal. He was angry, anxious, and confused. Larry had returned to college part time. Although he was academically insecure, he had reported that he was enjoying college. This evening, however, he was upset with a history teacher, a Roman Catholic priest, who Larry somehow linked with his grandfather. Apparently, both men were too clean, too perfect authority figures, evoking a near-psychotic transference reaction from the grandfather to the teacher. Larry was unable to give coherent account of his rage at the history teacher. In the ensuing sessions Larry became increasingly irrational and experienced more severe emotional pain. The therapist moved in in a directly confronting way. He related all of this emotional chaos to Larry's return to alcohol, directly linking Larry's rising anxiety and deepening despair to his resumption of drinking. The therapist once again became didactic, teaching the effects of alcohol on mood and emotions. Although Larry never quite said so, it was clear that he had lost "control" of his drinking. Confronting Larry with his loss of control, the therapist again suggested AA. It took several such sessions before Larry decided to stop drinking again. Although he still refused to attend even one AA meeting, Larry seemed to have little difficulty reestablishing and maintaining his sobriety.

This cycle repeated itself several times. A few months of sobriety, subjective improvement, a decision to "have a few beers," growing irrationality, loss of control, confrontation, and a return to abstinence. Each time, Larry's condition deteriorated. The therapeutic relationship was now stormy and fragile: The therapist favored abstinence; the patient did not.

Then Larry unexpectedly decided that drinking was making him sick and he stopped once again. This time the initiative had come from him. During sessions, he related more of his emotional and interpersonal difficulties to alcohol abuse. It appeared that Larry's denial was unraveling. He still did not join AA.

He did, however, once again begin to improve. His emotional pain lessened and his self-esteem started to rise. This time his recovery had a more solid quality.

Then a crisis occurred. Larry received what to him was an unjust evaluation at work. His rage knew no bounds. His response was not the mature aggression of the adult who feels wronged and uses his energies to change his situation. Rather, it was the boundless, insatiable desire for revenge of "his majesty, the baby." It was a reaction of infantile narcissism, the infinite anger of the offended archaic, grandiose self. Now Larry drank with a vengeance; he drank *at* his employer and all the others—mother, father, grandfather, girlfriends, and wives—who had disappointed him. He would fix them. Because his weak ego boundaries did not enable him to clearly experience himself as separate from those others, it was inevitable that his aggression would also be self-directed. Unconsciously, Larry wanted to destroy the world and himself. A lifetime of repressed rage surfaced and overwhelmed him. Larry drank still more to assuage the intolerable feelings. This time Larry had not "decided" to drink socially; on the contrary, he felt that he had no choice, that he had to drink. The analyst would say that he was overwhelmed by unconscious forces; the alcoholism counselor would say that his disease relapsed.

After a week or so of round-the-clock drinking, Larry threw in the towel; he went to the Employee Assistance Program (EAP) at work and asked for help. At this point, Larry was too ashamed to call his therapist. The EAP counselor gave Larry a choice: either attend 90 AA meetings in 90 days or be admitted to a hospital for detoxification and rehabilitation. The EAP counselor apparently underestimated the severity of Larry's problem and pushed her first plan for AA attendance. Larry, however, thought that he could not stop drinking on his own. He now called his therapist in a state of panic and great confusion. He requested an emergency session.

It seemed that they were back at step one, the first night, when a shaking Larry had appeared at the therapist's office clinging to his wife. But they were not. For all of Larry's alcohol-induced regression, there was a still a balance of the trust so painfully accrued during the past year's work. Both Larry and the therapist drew on this capital—Larry in being able to turn to the therapist for help and the therapist in being able to be firm, directive, persuasive, and trusted when he told Larry that he must first go through detoxification and then enter the AA-oriented rehabilitation program that had been suggested. Fortunately, there was sufficient accrued trust to override Larry's fears of confinement; he entered the hospital.

Adjunctive Treatment Resources

Alcoholism is a total affliction, attacking every aspect of its sufferers' being. Medical, psychological, emotional, social, vocational, financial, and interpersonal damage are endemic in advanced alcoholism. In AA's words, "Alcoholism is a threefold disease of body, mind, and spirit." Rarely will individual or group therapy alone suffice in its treatment. In Larry's case, medical help was needed, first from the referring internist for his hypertension and other somatic symptoms and now for inpatient detoxification. Larry also required a prolonged period (ten weeks) in an inpatient rehabilitation program. Larry and his wife also required family therapy. More than anything else, Larry needed to affiliate with AA. Although there are alcoholics who recover on their own, or with the aid of psychodynamically oriented psychotherapy, most gamma alcoholics require the additional support offered by AA. Many patients simply won't attend AA, and some of these patients do "make it." However, active affiliation with AA is the best route to stable sobriety for the seriously afflicted alcoholic. Let us look at the part each of these adjunctive treatments played in Larry's recovery.

The Rehabilitation Program

Detoxification is primarily a medical procedure, but it should involve patients in as much alcoholism education and counseling as their physical condition permits. (Detoxification is discussed in more detail in Chapter 2). The program to which Larry was referred was medically sound and sophisticated, recognizing that detoxification in itself is not a treatment for alcoholism. Larry spent five days in detoxification and then proceeded into the alcoholism rehabilitation program.

Inpatient rehabilitation programs have several functions: (1) they buy time for sobriety to take hold by providing external controls until internal controls can be established; (2) they provide an opportunity for intensive education on the nature of alcoholism, emphasizing the disease concept of alcoholism since belief in it facilitates recovery even if it should turn out to be a metaphor or even a beneficient myth; (3) they provide a safe environment for the patient to experience and express the intense affects that have been anesthetized and repressed; (4) they create a therapeutic community in which patients have an opportunity to overcome isolation and gain self-esteem through a sense of common adventure; and (5) they introduce patients to, and compel attendance at, AA meetings. Alcoholic rehabilitation programs also provide many models of both illness and recovery with which the patient can identify.

Larry's program provided all of the elements just listed, as well as family counseling and an aftercare program. Larry proved to be a highly resistant patient. He was quite willing to face emotional problems, but he continued to deny the role of alcohol in causing those problems. Entering the program at all had probably exhausted Larry's capacity for "surrender." He needed to resist in order to prevent a loss of identity. As the weeks passed, however, Larry slowly became part of the "class." His denial broke down and some of his isolation receded. By the seventh week he was looking forward to AA meetings. It seemed that he was accepting his alcoholism emotionally, although he stated that he could not accept the disease concept of alcoholism intellectually.

Upon discharge, Larry was reasonably healthy both physically and emotionally. The therapist had been in close communication with the rehabilitation program, providing the counselors with information on Larry's history, character structure, and strengths and weaknesses; in turn, the program had provided the therapist with information on Larry's progress. Such open communication between professionals is essential in the treatment of alcoholics, who tend to use splitting as a defense and who are often expert at pitting would-be helpers against one another. Such communicating must always proceed with the patient's consent. Larry's aftercare plan included both attendance at a hospital aftercare group and resumption of individual psychotherapy. Larry also agreed to follow the AA suggestion "90 in 90"—to attend an AA meeting every day for the next 90 days.

Family Therapy at the Hospital

One of Larry's presenting difficulties was the lack of sexual activity in his marriage. He had met his wife in a bar and their social life had always involved heavy drinking. Stella had been raised in a drinking environment, and she was a heavy drinker herself. Larry's social life was centered around his in-laws' house, where drinking was more or less continuous. His father-in-law was alcoholic. One of Larry's fears in admitting that he was alcoholic was his fear that his wife would think him unmanly. It was important to him that his wife understand his alcohol problem, and he wanted her to be involved in his treatment. He welcomed the rehab hospital's family counseling program. His wife was less enthusiastic, but she was willing to participate.

The family program had several focuses: (1) it offered intensive education on alcoholism, stressing the disease concept of alcoholism and the necessity for abstinence from alcohol; (2) it provided individual and group counseling for family members, which gave them a chance to experience and express their feelings in an open and supportive environment; and (3) it worked with the family to improve communication and clarify conflicts. In Larry and Stella's case, the educational component of the family program was the most successful. Stella came to accept the fact that her husband could not drink alcohol safely and that he needed to attend AA meetings in order to maintain his sobriety. Unfortunately, she was much less able to use the program to talk about her own feelings, and the couple's sexual problem was too engrained to be unraveled in a few sessions of marriage counseling. However, their joint sessions had given Larry the sense that his wife was his ally and not his enemy (whatever her own ambivalence toward alcohol) in his struggle for sobriety. This was not a small contribution to his recovery.

Hospital Aftercare

The hospital provided an aftercare program of weekly group therapy sessions, as well as ongoing group therapy for family members. Larry attended seven or eight sessions but stated that he never felt comfortable. The therapist explored the soures of Larry's discomfort in the group during his individual sessions and encouraged Larry to talk about his feelings in the group. Working with a patient who is concurrently in a group is challenging. If the therapist serves as both individual therapist and group leader (cojoint therapy), the patient tends to blame the therapist for whatever the patient does not like in the group. Unless this is explored, the patient will act out his disillusionment. If, on the other hand, the individual and group therapists are separate persons, the patient may use the group as resistance to individual therapy and vice versa. The patient's statements about other treatment modalities can be treated like any other material; that is, their meaning and significance can be explored. However, the therapist must also be aware of the resistance and acting-out potential here. Therefore, patients should always be encouraged to take group issues back to the group. It is too dangerous to exclude *any* conflict-laden issue from individual sessions, yet at the same time the patient should make the best possible use of all the therapeutic modalities.

Some therapists will not work with a patient who is in a group led by another therapist unless they are free to communicate with the group leader, an arrangement which requires the consent of the patient and the cooperation of the group leader. However, this policy implies a lack of trust in the patient and is often experienced by the patient as demeaning. (Inpatient treatment is by definition a situation in which the patient is not capable of self-care, and in that particular situation, open communication and coordination of goals is essential.) This situation is rampant with countertransference potential. Hence, the therapist must be aware of feelings about the patient's being in treatment with someone else. The therapist may all too easily be tripped up by competitive feelings. After the second month, Larry decided that individual therapy and AA were all he could handle. Additionally, Larry was upset by the group's sexual explicitness, and he felt uncomfortable with the "overbearing, crude" group leader. After exploring the resistance side of Larry's decision, the therapist supported it. Larry was now working hard at recovery and the group did indeed seem to be too much. Following the principle of supporting defenses in early sobriety, stirring up Larry's sexual conflicts, as was apparently happening in the group, was premature. Larry also felt overcontrolled and needed some sense of his own autonomy, which was provided by his decision to leave the group.

Had Larry not been deeply engaged in individual therapy, his decision to leave the group would have had a quite different meaning. Aftercare groups are often central to an alcoholic's recovery. They provide a forum for the intimate sharing of feelings, give the alcoholic the feeling of being an active and valued member of a community, and serve as a bridge from a total-care situation to the (re)establishment of mature interdependency.

Larry Joins AA

Throughout his individual treatment, Larry had resisted visiting even one AA meeting. Neither during his eight months of sobriety nor during his five months of intermittent drinking was Larry open to the possibility of AA affiliation. Many alcoholics take this stance. Larry had attended an AA meeting some years earlier, and he remembered it as a horrendous experience. In Larry's perception, AA was comprised of nothing but utterly debilitated people who told hideous stories of crime and degradation, people with whom he could not and did not wish to identify. This view of AA as the earthly representation of the ninth circle of hell is common. It is closely allied with the image of the alcoholic as an utterly down-and-out, skid-row bum. It is inaccurate, but stereotypes die hard. Larry, who had attended a "high bottom" AA meeting in an affluent area, had misperceived that meeting. Objectively, most of the people at such a meeting would have looked and sounded pretty together. This is not to say they had not suffered from their alcoholism, but they would not have conformed to Larry's stereotype of the alcoholic.

It was exactly this stereotype which Larry reputed in his denial of his alcoholism. His image of the alcoholic both generated such horror in Larry that he could not identify himself as such a person and served as a defense against facing the possibility of living without alcohol. Larry brought such a powerful preconception with him that he was unable to perceive the reality of the meeting. He was not lying or consciously distorting; rather he was reporting the meeting as he had experienced and remembered it. This perception was powerfully determined by fear and denial—fear that AA might work, and denial of the depth of his alcohol dependence. This is an illustration of terror distorting perception to the point at which the nonpsychotic person loses contact with reality. Larry was also projecting his own self-loathing onto his image of the alcoholic and his own sense of doom onto the AA meeting. This was interpreted to him, but the interpretation did not "take" at that time.

Larry continued to use his memory of this AA meeting in the service of denial. To join AA meant admitting that he was alcoholic, and this he could not do, even during his periods of abstinence. Further, Larry knew that AA teaches total abstinence, a day at a time, and he did not wish to not be able to drink. Larry, like so many alcoholics, really hoped that treatment would allow him to drink safely. Larry also objected to the "holy-roller religious fanaticism" of AA. This, too, is a common complaint. It has some reality, but it is essentially a distortion of the "spiritual" aspect of the AA program. This too is used in the service of resistance. Alcoholics who are genuinely unable to tolerate the AA ideology must find another route to stable sobriety. The therapist should be suspicious of motive in such cases, however; this objection to AA is usually a defense thrown up by fear, the fear of losing the hope of being able to drink again.

The therapist has a multifaceted task in helping the alcoholic to affiliate with AA. The therapist must have a knowledge of the AA program based on both mastery of the AA literature and on attendance at many (open) AA meetings. Further, the therapist must be familiar with local meetings, which will vary in the interests and socioeconomic status of their members, and to some extent in the ideological slant of the group. Some meetings are more "hard line" than others. The therapist can then direct patients to the meeting where they will most likely feel comfortable. If patients are in the proper state of receptivity, it does not much matter to which meeting they are referred.

The AA program can be understood as a resocialization experience, an educational experience, a conversion experience, a transcendental community, a means of deliquescing guilt by sharing it, a constructive way of meeting dependency needs, a kind of Kleinian therapy (Segal 1964), in which the alcoholic works through the depressive position by making reparation (see AA's 9th Step, Making Amends), and a situation that induces a narcissistic transference (in those who are capable of it) to an ideal object (the AA program or the Higher Power), which allows repair of structural deficits in the self. When asked how the program works, AA members reply, "AA works fine."

In his early work with Larry, the therapist had felt the strength of Larry's resistance to AA and did not push attendance. At that point, Larry was sober and working hard in treatment. Once Larry had begun to drink again, the therapist confronted Larry with the relationship between his resumed drinking and each of his emotional crises; at these junctions he repeatedly suggested AA. The therapist now used his knowledge of the AA program to challenge Larry's perception of the program. Correction of cognitive distortion seldom suffices to change perceptions and beliefs maintained by deep-seated fear, however, and this was true in Larry's case. Explain as he would what AA meetings were really like, the therapist could not persuade Larry to attend. The underlying fear was addressed in these interventions: "You are afraid that AA just might work." "You don't really believe that you can live without alcohol, and you are beginning to doubt that you can live with it." "Your anxiety level is so high that you feel that you must have the option to drink if things get bad enough; that's why you won't go to an AA meeting." None of these interventions were effective, but patients hear more than is apparent, and an intervention may finally take effect months or years later.

When Larry finally entered the alcohol rehabilitation hospital, he was ready to face his alcoholism. Another layer of denial had been penetrated, although many layers remained. Now Larry had no choice but to attend AA meetings; they were mandated. As AA says, "Bring the body and the mind will follow." By the end of his ten-week stay as an inpatient, Larry's perception of AA had radically changed. AA was now a place where he received support and where he could talk about his feelings without being judged. The group "sharing" of AA deliquesced and made tolerable Larry's personal guilt. Larry still disagreed with AA's concept of alcoholism as a disease (as do many scientists), but he left AA meetings feeling that he had gotten something for himself.

After discharge, Larry decided to follow the suggestion that he attend 90 AA meetings in 90 days. Although he exhausted himself, he did so. His self-esteem rose as a result of his ability to follow through and meet his goal. Unlike his first period of sobriety,

Larry was not now "booze fighting," or at least it had lessened. The old ambivalence remained (as it always does in early sobriety), but the balance was tilted toward an acceptance of his alcoholism. Larry needed this intensive emergence in AA during the days and weeks following his reentry into the world. "Ninety in ninety" was an educational experience for Larry; he learned a great deal about AA and about alcoholism. It also structured his time, and it gave him so firm a supportive network that he could tolerate his anxiety. The therapist cannot be there every time the patient is in emotional pain, but the members of his AA group can be, and usually are, there when the alcoholic needs them.

"Negative Transference" Toward AA

In his early posthospital months, the therapist encouraged Larry to talk about his experiences in AA. If Larry didn't broach the subject of AA, the therapist did. Larry had ambivalent feelings about AA; The therapist accepted all of them.

All enduring relationships are ambivalent, and AA membership is, it is hoped, an enduring relationship which becomes central in the alcoholic's life. Like the relationship to a spouse, the relationship of the alcoholic to AA is up and down. One of the problems with AA is that it does not allow much room for the negative side of the ambivalence, nor does it sufficiently recognize the inevitability of negative transference. On the contrary, AA teaches members to "utilize, don't analyze" (the AA program); and that the "program never fails; people do." In other words, AA is an ideal object which must never be criticized.

Anger is unavoidable, however. Unexpressed, and particularly repressed, anger will be either internalized or acted out. In the case of the alcoholic, it is usually acted out. Alcoholics who are angry with the AA program and either do not know it or cannot express it may very well "vote with their feet" and leave AA. Therefore, it is essential that the therapist inquire into the patient's reactions to AA and not argue with the negative ones. On the contrary, the therapist listens, accepting the patient's feelings. As long as the patient continues to attend AA meetings, "negative" reactions to AA should not be interpreted. As long as they talk, they are unlikely to walk.

In theoretical terms, AA deals with the failure of many of its members to have reached or to maintain the developmental milestone of object constancy by supporting splitting, a defense native to the preobject-constancy stage of development. *Splitting* refers to the active separation of good and bad internal representations of objects to avoid the pain of facing the complexity of reality and the ambivalent feelings that that complexity engenders. AA is not alone in dealing with this problem by encouraging the use of the developmentally primitive defense of splitting. All ideological movements have their gods and devils. In this case, AA is the all-good object, while alcohol and to some extent "civilians" are the all-bad objects. The utility, indeed the necessity, of supporting defenses, including splitting, in early sobriety is not in dispute; however, the therapist must be aware of what is happening and must eventually confront the splitting and promote integration.

Sponsorship is an AA institution that can also present problems for the therapist. The AA sponsor is a more experienced member who takes the newcomer "under wing" and sponsors sobriety. Some sponsors (and some AA groups) are antitherapy, which puts the patient and sometimes the therapist in a bind. Further, sponsors, who share their own experiences and offer directive guidance to the neophyte AA member, not infrequently have their own countertransference reactions, including the acting out of unmediated power needs. Material about sponsor–sponsoree conflicts may require a somewhat more active response by the therapist than disparaging comments about AA. The therapist must be sensitive to the possibility of conflict for the patient between involvement in treatment and membership in AA. Some patients will use AA as a resistance to treatment and treatment as a resistance to AA. Individual psychotherapy is valuable treatment for alcoholism; so is AA.

The therapist's relationship to AA can conceal a virtual minefield of countertransference reactions. One may either over or under value one's own work. One may either accept AA too uncritically or be contemptuous of it. Therefore, it is essential that therapists have a clear awareness of both their professional role, and their feelings toward AA. The therapist must *always* be available to patients as an objective professional who will help them explore *all* conflicts, including conflicts with AA doctrine, AA members, and sponsors. There can be no forbidden topics. To do this well requires that the therapist have insight into self.

Larry affiliated well with AA during the early months following discharge. The therapist listened with interest and few comments to all Larry related about his experiences. The therapist encouraged Larry's active exploration of the local AA scene during his "90 in 90." Larry accepted the therapist's advice to pick a "home group" and to let himself be known there. He picked a small, "closed" (open only to AA members) meeting, where he tried to participate, but he found it difficult. The therapist told him, "Easy does it" (an AA slogan). Larry was unable to ask anyone to be his sponsor, but he did find people in his home group to whom he could speak, although without feeling comfortable. Given Larry's fears of intimacy and his involvement in therapy, the therapist did not raise the sponsorship issue until Larry brought it up. Larry may have had realistic reasons to fear approaching a potential sponsor. Sponsorship relationships can be destructive when they go badly. Some alcoholics seem to do quite well in AA without a sponsor, and Larry may have been wise in not acquiring a sponsor at that time.

Denial as Denial of a Defect in the Self

Most of Larry's negative comments about AA concerned the disease concept of alcoholism, which Larry regarded as a "cop out"; the therapist did not argue the point. He did, however, understand the emotional source of Larry's rejection of the disease concept as a manifestation of both Larry's self-loathing and his residual denial of his alcoholism. If he was morally flawed rather than diseased, then he had a reason to hold onto his guilt and possibly to punish himself for his "sins" by further drinking. Further, Larry could not tolerate the thought of having a "disease," a thought which implies the triumph of an external force over the self. Self psychology understands Larry's rejection of the disease concept as a manifestation of regression to pathological narcissism. The grandiose self is not diseased. Since analysis of this defense was not necessary to maintain Larry's sobriety, the therapist filed away his understanding of these dynamics for future use.

As the weeks and months went on, Larry spoke less of his involvement in AA. After the 90 days he attended fewer meetings, but his relationship with the AA program was becoming solid. Larry continued to be both an active member of AA and a committed therapy patient.

A Victory over Denial

Larry was settling down. After the 90 days he set up a routine of three AA meetings and a therapy session each week. There were fewer episodes of intense emotional conflict. He was less depressed. His anxiety continued to subside and he now rarely mentioned somatic symptoms. He spoke more of his work and of his desire to improve his relationship with his wife.

By now the reader must be tired of hearing that Larry's denial of his alcoholism had finally been overcome, only to be later told once more that Larry was now coming to terms with his alcoholism. Unfortunately, that is the nature of denial. For a moment, the alcoholic sees things as they are under the brilliant illumination of insight and rationality. Then the alcoholic once again pulls the blind. In Plato's (1961) famous myth, the prisoners released from their chains in a darkened cave emerge into sunlight and are so dazzled by what they see that they run back into the cave. Insight is often like that—a slow, erratic process. This is especially so when the insight requires the acceptance of a loss, and the alcoholic's acceptance of alcoholism entails grievous losses: the loss of a love object, the loss of a security blanket, and the loss of a way of life.

The breakdown of denial is a stage-wise process; one layer of denial is penetrated, a little light is allowed to enter, and then another layer of denial blocks further penetration by the light. Thus, the breakdown of denial is an extended process involving intense conflict, many reverses, and only tentative victories. It is a process in which anabolic forces battle with catabolic forces, the life instincts battle with the death instincts, fear battles with hope, and health battles with illness. The struggle to overcome alcoholic denial is indeed a fateful one. Freud said that we can only give up our love objects by making them part of ourselves (by internalizing them). Alcohol is most certainly the alcoholic's love object, but he cannot internalize that which is poisoning him; rather, he must replace it. What must be internalized is not alcohol, but the capacity to perform the functions that alcohol performed. The process of such replacement and internalization is what treatment is about.

The breakdown of Larry's denial was no exception; it was a long struggle in which his denial was penetrated layer by layer. At some ultimate unconscious level, the gamma alcoholic probably never accepts his alcoholism. That is why AA stresses that "nobody graduates" and "alcoholics have a built-in forgetter." By the time Larry finished his 90 in 90, he had come a long way toward accepting his alcoholism.

In the ensuing months he "worked through" some of his remaining resistance to that acceptance by recalling many events in his life, most of which he had previously discussed in therapy, but now there was a difference. *Larry now related his difficulties in those situations to his drinking.* Further, he did this spontaneously, without any urging.

Larry spoke about his first marriage and the role that his drinking had played in its failure. Larry was now able to concede that his first wife had been right when she said that he drank alcoholically. He also realized that much of his fighting with her had been in defense of his right to drink. He became more able to acknowledge the extent of his alcohol abuse and to see it as extending further back in time and spreading into every aspect of his life. The progression of his disease became real to him. Larry spoke of such unpleasant consequences of his alcohol abuse as the neglect of his personal hygiene.

Larry also began to see how he had used alcohol to dull his fear of people, of sex, and of his own feelings. He now clearly saw that he had to learn to deal with these things without alcohol, and although he was motivated to do so, he was bewildered as to how to go about it. His honesty took courage, and the therapist told him so. The more Larry saw how dependent on alcohol he had been, the more he felt unable to cope without it. But this was verbalized, not acted out, and Larry had no slips. The therapist assured Larry that he could do anything sober that he could do drunk, although it might take some time. Larry did not really believe this, but he was able to borrow the therapist's confidence in the healing process until he developed some of his own.

Larry came to acknowledge the role that alcohol had played in virtually every area of his life. He saw that it had been intimately involved with his academic failure in college. Slowly he came to grips with the damage that alcohol had done to his career as a tennis pro, a particularly painful insight. Larry stuck to his emotional task, and by the tenth posthospital month he understood and accepted that not only his tennis serve but his life had deteriorated as a result of his alcoholic drinking. The process had not been linear. The actual sessions often seemed chaotic. They were complex; they dealt with many issues; they were filled with conflicting feelings. There were moments of depression and discouragement. The therapist's most important function at this stage was being there—sticking with his patient as he struggled toward acceptance of his alcoholism.

One evening Larry came in looking subdued but calm. He stated, "I went to the cemetery and visited my grandfather's grave; I never did that before. I don't think I ever faced realities, like the reality of death. I don't know what I felt, but I cried a little. I spoke to him; I told him I was sober. I felt good when I left the cemetery. When I drank I never really faced anything."

Alcoholic denial is not only denial of alcoholism; it is denial of unpleasant reality. Larry's visit to the cemetery was a big step. It marked a transition from the period of "I can't drink," a teeth-grinding stage, to "I won't drink," a much more comfortable, less conflicted, inner conviction of the wisdom of not drinking. (See Zimberg 1978, 1982 for discussion of these stages.) Now Larry was truly out of the cave. Given that some denial will always endure in the unconscious and that no psychic victories are finally won, Larry had reached a state of, for practical purposes, acceptance of his alcoholism. He didn't like it, but he accepted it. This acceptance would require long term reinforcement, but it provided a solid foundation on which Larry could build a new life.

Acquisition of a New Identity

Larry had often stated that he did not know who he was. He felt like a chameleon; he tended to take on the coloration of his environment. He did not know his likes or dislikes, his goals, or his feelings. He gave an example of playing cards with his wife's relatives and not being able to tell whether or not he really liked to play cards. He related his confused sense of self to a split within him between two masculine ideals: the hail-fellow-well-met, hard-drinking father and the ascetic, controlled, meticulous, "perfect" grandfather. He felt empty, torn, and confused, controlled by the internal representations of father and grandfather, which he experienced as foreign bodies. He could not integrate them. He was neither father nor grandfather nor yet Larry. He was suffering from identity diffusion.

The state of identity diffusion is painful. It would take long-term psychotherapy to work through Larry's feelings of being torn between father and grandfather. However, a means was at hand to immediately reduce Larry's sense of identity diffusion. One advantage that Larry derived from acceptance of his alcoholism was that it gave him an identity: "My name is Larry and I am an alcoholic." This AA ritual in which the members say "My name is _____ and I am an alcoholic," serves not only to break down denial, but also to provide an identity—perhaps a negative identity, at least at first, but an identity nevertheless. Larry participated in this ritual every day for 90 days and several times a week thereafter. It is better to be something rather than nothing, better to have a core around which to organize a self rather than endure the catastrophic anxiety of nonbeing, the fragmentation of the self.

Identity diffusion, failure to feel centered, and the feeling of fragmentation are ubiquitous in early sobriety; they can be the cause of intolerable anxiety. The acquisition of the identity of alcoholic—or better yet, recovering alcoholic—assuages this anxiety. Eugene O'Neill, who knew alcoholism from the inside, wrote, "Man is born broken; he lives by mending. The grace of God is glue." (*The Great God Brown*, Act 4, Scene 1). Larry's acquired identity of *alcoholic*, painful as it was, provided the glue to hold together the pieces of a fragmented self.

The undefined self is a self of pure potential; its lack of content is experienced as emptiness, which the alcoholic futilely tries to fill with alcohol. The acceptance of alcoholism not only signifies the end of denial of a deadly disease; it also opens the possibility of organizing a firm sense of identity in place of a frightening emptiness. This identity is negative, but it has the potential to become positive. The *I am* in the ritual statement, "I am an alcoholic" is a performative utterance which reassures the alcoholic that he exists (a reassurance that may be badly needed), just as the *an alcoholic* specifies the nature of that existence. The alcoholic is more than an alcoholic, and identity will eventually encompass much more than being alcoholic. But at the beginning of sobriety, no matter how confused one may be as to who one is and no matter how inwardly split one may be, one *knows* that one is an alcoholic. This knowledge gives a sense of identity. Knowing who one is makes one more secure.

Larry now knew who he was, at least to the extent of knowing that he was an alcoholic. One dimension of his existence was no longer in doubt, and this further reduced his anxiety. He now had a core around which to build a new sense of self. That building would be long and laborious, involving new roles, behaviors, and values, and a new way of thinking about himself.

Dawning Self-esteem

All alcoholics suffer from near-zero self-esteem. Much of their bluster and reactive grandiosity is a cover for and denial of their abysmally low self-regard. This may be a consequence of rather than a cause of their alcoholism, or the causality may flow the opposite way, or most likely, the causal arrows point both ways. It probably works this way: There is a vicious circle of initially low self-esteem, an attempt to bolster that self-esteem pharmacologically, morning-after remorse leading to even lower self-esteem, leading to more drinking, which further lowers self-esteem. Be this as it may, the regulation of self-esteem is a crucial issue in early sobriety. The breakdown of alcoholic denial means acceptance of a dreaded flaw in the self and of a traditionally scorned social role. To make things worse, at the beginning of sobriety, alcoholics really have no hope of overcoming the addiction; they are sure they will fail and ambivalently wish to. The provision of realistic hope is the sine qua non of any therapy. It is particularly important in alcoholism counseling. The patient must borrow some of the therapist's hope that recovery is possible.

Larry suffered from abysmally low self-esteem. He felt that he was a failure in all areas of his life. Although he had some realistic reasons to feel this way, it was primarily his perfectionism and inability to take satisfaction in the partial, tarnished victories of everyday life that kept his self-esteem depressed. Psychodynamic factors further lowered his already tenuous self-regard. His repressed rage was turned against himself, and he continually punished himself by self-hatred for his unconscious hostility. His impotence also contributed to his low self-regard.

Early sobriety provided an opportunity for Larry to begin to build self-esteem. He was in a curious position; admission of his alcoholism, however tenuous, had delivered an enormous blow to his self-esteem, yet this very blow made possible the first steps toward regaining (or in Larry's case first acquiring) a healthy self-regard. For the alcoholic, sobriety is an achievement of no small magnitude.

Self-esteem comes with the victory over self that the recovery over alcoholism always entails. This was so for Larry. He knew that he had worked hard to overcome a devastating disability. He knew that he was continuing to struggle, a day at a time, against self-destructive forces within him. He slowly came to take pride in these accomplishments. His new sense of identity as a recovering alcoholic and his membership in a community of healers (AA) also added to his growing self-esteem. Self-esteem comes from struggling, a day at a time, with the tyrants within and without.

If the discrepancy between the ideal self, what one would like to be, and the perceived self, what one believes oneself to be, is too great, self-esteem must remain low. It is like being a pole vaulter who sets the bar so high that it can never be cleared. That was Larry at the beginning of therapy. Very slowly the gap between his ideal self and his perception of his real self narrowed. AA teaches that it is the effort, and not the outcome, that counts. The therapist shared these values and probably communicated them in subliminal ways. Larry came to partially share this point of view, and this change allowed him to view himself somewhat less harshly.

This is not to say that achievement in the real world is not an important ingredient of self-esteem.

AA paradoxically bases its philosophy that self-esteem should be dependent on the effort, not the result, on a real achievement, the achievement of sobriety. We all want success, material rewards, the respect of our fellows, sexual gratification, and love. When we get these things our self-regard tends to rise, when we do not it tends to fall. As one AA member put it, "Other things being equal, I'd rather be anxious in a Rolls Royce, than in the subway." The goal is not complete detachment of the level of our self-regard from events in the world—that is another impossible achievement; rather, it is a sufficient increase in the internal determinants of that self-regard to make life livable in the face of inevitable reversals and disappointments.

Viewed metapsychologically, the inability to maintain a relatively constant level of self-esteem is seen by the classical psychoanalysts as the failure to maintain a constant cathexis of the self-representation with libido. It is viewed by the self psychologists as failure to internalize the "gleam in mother's eye" (Kohut 1977a), her high regard, so that self-esteem never came to be regulated internally, but remained overly dependent on outside evaluation. The latter formulation is congruent with our theory of the regression/fixation to pathological narcissism in active and early-sobriety alcoholics. Seen from this point of view, self-regard was once the regard of others (mothers or other caretakers); in normal development, the capacity to maintain relatively stable levels of self-regard results from an identification with and internalization of the capacity of the caretakers to maintain relatively stable regard for us. If such regard was not present, it could not be identified with and internalized. The therapist's consistent attention, attunement, and caring initially supplies the self-esteem that patients cannot provide for themselves. This function slowly becomes internalized, and a relatively constant loving of the self becomes possible for the alcoholic. This process is usually uneven, fragile, and slow. This was so for Larry.

For the newly sober alcoholic, each additional hour of sobriety results in an increment in self-esteem. Later the units will be days, or weeks, or months, but the process will be the same. Each day Larry stayed sober, faced a feared situation, looked into a darkened corner of the self, or expressed a repressed emotion, his self-esteem increased. The process of increasing self-esteem is both a doing and a knowing—the maintenance of sobriety in the face of emotional pain, and the learning that self-love cannot be contingent on the attainment of impossible goals. Larry did some of each, and he did it in the presence of another, his therapist.

One evening Larry came in looking sheepish. "This is embarrassing, but there is a woman, Eileen, in my AA group, who has been having an awful time of it. Her life has been truly dreadful. She is in terrible emotional pain, depressed and frightened all the time. Sometimes she actually shakes. Yet she is always at the door welcoming newcomers. She stays sober in spite of her pain. I've admired her courage for months. Yesterday something happened; I walked in and saw Eileen standing there tormented, but sober, and I suddenly realized that I had been in emotional pain also and that I too had not drunk in spite of that pain. I thought, well maybe I have some courage too. When I left, I felt a little better about myself." Thus, a little self-esteem was won.

Object Relations in Early Sobriety

Psychoanalytically oriented theorists use the term *object relations* to refer to our relationships with both real and ideal others. They have in mind the distinction between subject and object. Thus, we are the subjects who experience all of our thoughts and feelings, while that to which those thoughts and feelings refer are our objects. Of course, we can be the object of our own thought. In that case, however, we do not speak of ourselves as an object, but speak of the self. Objects are all the things, with the exception of the self, that are intended by our cognitions and our affects. They are usually people, but they may be abstractions or ideals. Thus, Mother, Sally, and John are objects for us, but so are the Flag, God, and the Pursuit of Truth. Our relationships with Mother, Sally, John, the Flag, God, and the Pursuit of Truth are our object relations. However, we not only have relationships with Mother, Sally, and John, real people existing in the world, but we also have internal representations of Mother, Sally, and John, and we have a relationship with those internal representations. *Interpersonal relations* refers to our relationships with actual people, while *object relations* refers to our relationships with actual people, abstractions, and ideals, and our internal representations of those actual people and those ideals. It is the more general term.

Larry had difficulties in his object relations, whether those relationships were with people, ideals, or internal representations. He was terrifed of people; he had difficulties with intimacy, and he had conflicted feelings about God. He felt that he lacked ideals, and his internal representations of early significant others were conflict ridden. We will concentrate next on Larry's interpersonal relationships during early sobriety.

Larry's fear of people, particularly strangers, was extreme. He traced this fear back to his family's social isolation during his childhood. He remembered being afraid to ask a sales clerk for an ice cream cone and having his mother buy it for him. He expressed some anger that his mother had done this for him, rather than making him face his fear. His current fears were almost as strong. For example, he related how it was almost impossible for him to go around his office collecting for a football pool. This ordinary social task was overwhelming. The blotting out of this fear was one of his most important motives for drinking.

The therapist hypothesized that some of Larry's persistent, almost paranoid fears were based on the projection of repressed hostility. The mechanism is as follows: My rage is not dangerous, but the rage of others (the disowned and projected rage) is, so I had better stay away from them. Since Larry's fear of people did lessen as he became more aware of his own anger, this hypothesis received some confirmation. The therapist further hypothesized that part of Larry's fear of people had to be derived from his fear that they might discover what a horrible person he was: angry and alcoholic, among other disdainable qualities. This, too, was true. As Larry came to accept himself more, his fear of people decreased. As with so much else in therapy, this improvement came about by indirection; in this case, derepression of unacceptable aspects of self resulted in decreased fear of others.

During the first year of Larry's sobriety, however, there was only a moderate lessening of his fear of people. Too much remained repressed, and needed to remain repressed at this stage of his sobriety, for him to feel completely comfortable with himself. Since he mentioned several times how disgusted he was by homosexual practices or even desires, it was probable that repressed homosexual feelings were an important part of Larry's inability to accept himself. This inability was then projected onto other people, whose judgment now became feared. Larry was not yet ready to deal with his homosexual feelings, and this issue was not dealt with.

Larry made more progress in his relationships with those who were close to him than he did in his relationships with coworkers and acquaintances. He took significant steps to improve his relationships with his parents, his brother, and his wife. Sharing his hospitalization and his alcoholism with his parents was an important gain for him. For once he did not have to present himself as "perfect" to his parents; in his

words, "things are now more real." Their acceptance
and support were important to Larry, although they
did not really understand what was happening. About
four months after leaving the rehabilitation program,
Larry's mother developed dangerously high blood
pressure and was hospitalized. Larry flew to California to be with her. This entailed dealing with both his
fear of flying and his fear, partially based on identification, that he would develop the same illness. Larry
reported that he had felt adult and responsible in
California, and that he had communicated more
openly with both his parents. They in turn were more
open with him. He had taken a chance; he did something new and different in his relationship with his
parents, and it had paid off.

Unfortunately, this is not always the case. The
recovering alcoholic's new and healthier behaviors are
often not welcomed by significant others. The family
system has been disturbed. More ominously, significant others may have been heavily invested, usually
without being aware of it, in the alcoholic's alcoholism. The newly sober alcoholic is expecting that sobriety will be welcomed. Consciously or unconsciously,
the alcoholic expects love in response to that sobriety;
sobriety should be a cause for celebration. The recovering alcoholic may also unconsciously expect to exercise omnipotent control over significant others
as the "price" for sobriety. Reality can be cruelly dis-
appointing. The significant others may respond
negatively, or at least differently than the alcoholic
expected. The hurt and rage induced by this disappointment can be devastating and often leads to slips.
Therefore, it is usually best to take an active, educational role in explaining to the newly sober alcoholic
that things may not go as expected with friends, family, coworkers, and bosses. The alcoholic needs to
understand that change, even for the good, is always
threatening, and that a period of readjustment, with

uncertain outcome, in inevitable. Anticipatory educational interventions and strong support by the therapist are *vital* in this area to cushion the disappointment
which so often comes with attempts to relate in new
ways, and which is the result of unrealistic expectations, others' unconscious motivations, and recalcitrant reality.

Larry also began to separate from his parents.
Paradoxically, as he felt a more "real" connection with
his parents, he felt less tied to them. In part this reflected Larry's beginning to work through the developmental stage of separation-individuation. Some of
his anger toward his parents had facilitated this separation, by providing the driving force, the energy,
necessary for the work of establishing an independent
existence in both the real, external world and the internal, representational world. His bond with the therapist and with AA gave him the security to experiment
with a more autonomous relationship with his parents
and to experience his internal representation of himself as less a function of his internal representations of
them. When his mother expressed a desire to move
back East and to buy a two-family house with him,
Larry was able to say, "No! I don't want to do that."
He now recognized his wants and desires. He felt
more separate and autonomous, and he did not feel
guilty about it.

Larry's relationship with his wife remained
maimed by his fear of approaching her sexually. This
overwhelming fear would require long-term treatment to overcome. However, Larry and Stella made
strides in establishing more open communication.
They now disclosed their feelings, and the more they
were able to acknowledge their "negative," angry
feelings, the closer they felt. As Larry experienced,
and in some cases expressed, his anger toward Stella,
he became more aware of his loving feelings toward
her. We cannot selectively repress feelings: When we

repress anger, we necessarily repress love. At Larry's request, the therapist conducted several sessions with the couple. These sessions proved helpful. Larry and Stella began to enjoy the new shared activities that replaced their old life of bars and drinking. Although he was in near despair at times over his sexual fears, and the thought that he might lose her, Larry increasingly reported warm feelings for his wife.

An important event in Larry's recovery occurred when Larry confronted a disturbed member of his AA group, who had come to dominate it. Larry was able to tell him, "I don't like the way that you chair meetings and try to run the group"—a seemingly small action which reflected a significant internal change for Larry, who was a "people pleaser." His self-esteem improved, and he felt closer to the members of his group.

Internalizing the Therapist

Internalization, for all its widespread discussion in the psychological literature, remains a mysterious process. Somehow that which once came from the outside, from other people, becomes part of us. There is an identification by one person with another, and this identification somehow enables that person to "take in" attributes of, qualities of, and functions performed by the other person and to make them his own. The normal psychological and emotional development of the child is thought to be dependent on such identifications with and internalizations of parents and other caretakers. It is thought that healthy identifications are not gross and total, but rather that they are partial, selective, and depersonified.

When the identification is depersonified, it is the quality, the attribute, the function, or the activity that is identified with, rather than the person who possesses those attributes or qualities or who performs those functions or activities. Thus it is the attribute, quality, or function that is internalized. This is not to say that an emotional bond between the identifier and the object with whom he identifies is not important; on the contrary, such an emotional bond is a necessary condition of identification and internalization. Identifications that are too gross make us clones, or leave us feeling controlled by a foreign object, rather than feeling that we have integrated something valuable. Either of these feelings is usually unconscious.

Kohut (1971), in an attempt to understand the process of internalization, spoke of *transmuting internalization,* by which he meant a slow, incremental taking in of functions once performed by others, which he thought was a concomitant of "optional frustration" during normal development. For example, the attuned mother soothes her unhappy child, but she cannot be present every time the child needs soothing. If the frustration is not too great, the child will acquire a particle of mother's ability to soothe. Many such particles must "get under the baby's skin" before they are "transmuted," or changed into a functional capacity for self-soothing. Too much or too little frustration prevents such transmuting internalization. Kohut believed that a similar process took place in psychotherapy, in which the therapist's ability to soothe, for example, came to be internalized, a particle at a time, until the patient could soothe himself.

Behaviorally oriented theorists, who are contemptuous of such talk of identification and internalization, hold that such theorizing is neither parsimonious nor explanatory, and that learning theory can account for developmental changes. From the behavioral viewpoint, it is all conditioning, the linking of stimulus and response, or of stimulus and reward. However, the connection between the stimulus and the response is every bit as mysterious as the process of internalization. Self psychology's account of the development of a separate self through the selective depersonfied internalization of others is a more fruitful way of looking at changes that take place during development.

When alcoholics come for treatment, they have regressed to or are fixated at the stage of pathological narcissism. Identification with the therapist facilitates resumption of the developmental process; it enables growth. The hope is that the patient will identify with the therapist's sobriety (which does not necessarily entail abstinence from alcohol by the therapist), tolerance for human frailty, desire to understand and not to judge, hope, unconditional acceptance, and belief that each alcoholic is a human being worthy of attention. It is this professional stance that the patient must internalize. This occurs in the manner that Kohut described—that is, slowly, incrementally, and concomitantly with many small frustrations in the course of the relationship. Kohut believed that what ideally happens is "the building of psychic structure"; the patient comes to possess capacities for internal regulation that were lacking at the beginning of the therapeutic process. These new capacities are what are gradually internalized through identification with the therapist.

Larry resisted identification with the therapist. He remained distant. But identification need not be conscious. The process has its own momentum, and after two years of therapy, Larry had seemingly internalized many of the therapist's therapeutic values and many of the functions that the therapist had initially performed for him. Larry was now more tolerant and less judgmental of himself; he was now better able to modulate his anxiety and to soothe himself; he now accepted himself, if not unconditionally, then at least to a much greater extent than he previously had; he was now better able to maintain his self-esteem at a reasonably constant level; and he was now sober. All of these gains were the result, in part, of Larry's identification with and internalization of the therapist.

The therapist's hope was that Larry would take these things with him when he left therapy. Whether we understand this process as a transfer of learning, as do the behaviorists, or as an internalization of the therapist, as do the psychoanalytic theorists, something very precious had been gained. Larry would go away with much that he did not have when he began therapy.

The Beginning of Stable Sobriety

Larry was no longer an early-sobriety case. He had been sober for a year and now had no desire to drink. For most alcoholics, the early-sobriety stage lasts one to two years and is reached when the patient feels that he does not want to drink. Larry had reached this point. It was not merely that he could not drink; he now chose not to drink. Although he would always be "one drink away from a drunk," Larry now had the resources to stay sober "a day at a time."

Larry had many residual problems: sexual conflict, repressed rage at grandfather for dying and abandoning him, repressed homosexual impulses, fear of people, and continuing difficulties with self-esteem and anxiety. And yet, how far he had come. He no longer lived in terror; he was neither symptom ridden, nor depressed. He had hope and he was sober.

The issue of termination has not occurred in Larry's case since he decided to remain in treatment to work on his remaining problems. (Termination is discussed in more detail in Chapter 8.) If he had decided to terminate at this point and continue with his AA activity, the therapist would have been satisfied with the treatment process. Larry and the therapist would have agreed upon a date for termination. During the termination phase, the therapist would have directed

Larry back, time and again, to his feelings about leaving therapy, thereby giving him an opportunity to work on the issues of separation, loss, abandonment, and autonomy.

Since growth is an open-ended process, the therapist would have told Larry that he was welcome to return at any time, regardless of whether or not he was in acute distress, to recommence that mysterious process by which two people connect in such a way that one can grow and the other can experience the awe that one always does when confronted with the resilience of the human spirit.

CHAPTER 8

Psychotherapy with the Stably Sober Alcoholic

Alcoholism is a serious and potentially fatal illness. Psychological authorities have long stressed the severity of the emotional derangement that is a concomitant of alcoholism, whether such derangement be understood as a cause or as a consequence of the alcohol abuse. Alcoholics are not neurotic individuals who happen to drink too much; rather, they are people who suffer profound psychological disablement. As they say in AA, nobody is there for hangnails. The psychological disablement is usually less severe than that found in the psychoses, but it is almost always more severe than that found in the neuroses. The emotional disablement in gamma alcoholism is the regression/fixation to pathological narcissism. The first step in the recovery process must be control of the alcohol abuse. For gamma alcoholics, that control can only be achieved through abstinence—sobriety. The most recent and by far the most comprehensive longitudinal study of drinking behavior (Vaillant 1983) supports this view. It may be the case that other problem drinkers can return to asymptomatic controlled drinking, either through behavioral therapy or through their own efforts. This chapter does not deal with their treatment.

Gamma alcoholics are those who have become physically and psychologically dependent on alcohol, usually with grave damage in more than one of the life spheres of physical health, emotional well-being, interpersonal relations, and social and vocational functioning. Often the damage extends to all of these areas. In lay terms, they suffer from severe advanced alcoholism. For these patients, the achievement and maintenance of sobriety is first and always the primary treatment goal; abstinence from alcohol is the alpha and omega of treatment with the gamma alcoholic. A certain number of gamma alcoholics will be able to achieve stable sobriety, either by their own efforts or, more usually, through some combination of professional treatment and AA participation. (See Chapter 4 for techniques for the treatment of active alcoholics.) Those who reach stable sobriety are referred to as recovering alcoholics.

This chapter is addressed to improving the quality of the recovering alcoholic's life against a backdrop of continued and continuous abstinence from alcohol. Some recovering alcoholics reach a stable, more or less satisfying adjustment without formal help; many others find that the AA program and other self-help groups meet their emotional needs. However, many recovering alcoholics do turn to psychotherapists and psychoanalysts for additional help. Often, but not always, they are members of AA.

Although alcoholics with stable sobriety seek professional help with every sort of problem, two syndromes most commonly bring the stably sober to treatment. The first is that of the recovering alcoholic with considerable ego strength and growth potential who finds that AA participation has resulted in stable sobriety, but who feels stifled in an important area of life. Most commonly this area is either work or love; often it is both. The other syndrome is that of the alcoholic who has the ego strength to achieve stable sobriety, but who continues to be afflicted with severe emotional conflict and psychological pain. Those who suffer from the latter syndrome usually require long-term treatment.

Stably sober patients may be the same patients that we helped to reach sobriety, or they may be people who turn to therapy after they have become sober. Although the treatment of these patients has many parallels with standard psychotherapeutic procedures, there always remains a unique dimension in work with the recovering alcoholic, a dimension which importantly affects the therapeutic relationship. For example, transference reactions are often acted out in psychotherapy. This acting out is later interpreted and the understanding resulting from the interpretation is utilized to facilitate growth. With the recovering alcoholic, however, the acting out of a transference reaction may very well mean a drink—hardly a desired step in a growth process. The therapist must *always* keep this possibility of a return to active alcoholism in mind when treating the stably sober. Both the therapist and the patient may act as if this danger were not always present. As AA says, "Alcoholics have a built-in forgetter." Since sobriety is the sine qua non of recovery, let us begin by discussing the process by which sobriety is internalized.

INTERNALIZATION OF SOBRIETY

Virtually no chronic alcoholic wants to get sober. The pain is too great. The regressive pull is too great. That is why either actual external events—such as the loss or threat of loss of a job, or the loss or threat of loss of a mate—or events experienced as external—such as the loss or threat of loss of health—are so often the precipitants of the emotional crisis that results in the alcoholic's becoming sober. These external events furnish the apparent motives for sobriety. At this point the alcoholic is "doing it for them." Such motivation is often not sufficient, and external controls such as those provided by hospitalization are necessary to achieve sobriety of any duration. After leaving the hospital, the alcoholic may remain sober out of fear of losing something valued. It is still being done for "them." This is the stage of "I can't drink" (Zimberg 1978). The hope is that a gradual process is initiated at this point by which remaining sober comes to be something that the alcoholic wants to do rather than something that must be done.

If this process is sucessful, the stage of "I won't drink" is reached. The controls which were originally external or experienced as external are now internal. Now, no asylum walls or chemical barriers are necessary. In the last chapter we looked at this process in some detail as we followed Larry's struggle to become and to remain sober. By the time we left him, he had internalized controls which enabled him to maintain his sobriety.

It is not known exactly how this control becomes internalized. Identification helps; in fact it may be the key. This is one reason that AA and peer counseling can be so effective in establishing stable sobriety. The alcoholic is provided with figures with whom to identify. They too are alcoholic, but they are no longer active; they are recovering. It is not with Bob or Jane or John or Sally that the alcoholic must identify, but with Bob's or Jane's or John's or Sally's sobriety. The alcoholic may also identify with his nonalcoholic therapist's sobriety, although here the identification is less direct. At first the identification is with the sobriety of the other, but slowly that sobriety is drawn within. It is as if the sobriety of the other is mentally ingested, digested, metabolized, and assimilated until it becomes part of the mental world of the newly recovering alcoholic. Although this is only a simile, it comes as close as we can get to an understanding of the process of internalization. Through this process the controls which allow others to remain sober become the controls of the newly sober one.

With time, sobriety becomes more rewarding. The pain of early sobriety recedes, the residual pain is endurable, and the alcoholic wants to remain sober. Sobriety becomes part of the recovering alcoholic's ego-ideal—of the ideal self. Living up to one's ego-ideal increases self-esteem and that feels good; hence, it is a behavior one tries to maintain. This is the case with the recovering alcoholic's sobriety. Remaining sober is no longer a struggle; it is an increasingly comfortable decision.

Finally sobriety becomes a way of life to which the recovering alcoholic need give no thought. At this stage there is no conscious conflict over alcohol, although unconscious conflict remains. AA believes that this is as good as things get for alcoholics—that the unconscious conflict, which AA understands as the disease of alcoholism, always remains and that this unconscious conflict can erupt at any time, threatening sobriety. AA therefore teaches as part of its folk wisdom that, "Nobody graduates," that "alcoholism is the disease that tells you that you don't have it," and that "the alcoholic is always one drink away from a drunk." Their belief is that the drink response to stress is a groove cut so deeply into the alcoholic's brain that group support and active education in AA is a life-long requirement for the maintenance of sobriety. Although it does not speak in these terms, AA has its doubts about both the security of internalization and the transfer of learning when it comes to sobriety. Zimberg (1978) believes that insight therapy can lead to conflict resolution, resulting in the stage of "I don't have to drink" and in the removal of the causes for drinking. Our belief is that secure sobriety depends not so much on conflict resolution, however important that may be, as on the building of psychic structure, so that the alcoholic can perform the psychic tasks apparently performed by alcohol. We also believe that the external reinforcement and group support of AA are an excellent insurance policy, even for the alcoholic with long-term sobriety.

In this chapter we will follow the stories of two people who were stably sober. For both, sobriety had become a part of their ego-ideal. Both were active in AA; return to drink was not a manifest issue in their treatment.

HENRY: A STIFLED YOUNG MAN

Henry had been sober for a little less than two years when he came for therapy. He was an unusually tall, rather awkward, soft-spoken, almost withdrawn young man in his late 20s. In spite of his shyness, Henry was articulate. He had come to Chicago from a

small town in the midwest. He told the therapist that
he loved AA and that he felt secure in his sobriety;
however, he was still afraid of people and found it
difficult to go out for coffee after a meeting with the
members of his AA group. He gave the following
reasons for seeking therapy: "I am nowhere when it
comes to sex and career. I am still isolating and afraid
of people. I just work and hide out in my apartment—
except for AA meetings—the meetings help. I don't
know where I'm going. I'm gay I think, but I don't
know how to find a lover; I'm afraid to approach
people. At work I do all right; I work in an archive,
but I have no goals. I feel blocked in about every area
of my life, so I thought that I would try therapy."

Henry had grown up in a depressed, alcoholic
household. His older brother, Bernard, had drowned
at the age of 16, when Henry was 6 years old. Bernard
had been idolized by the father, who had wanted him
to be his successor as head of the family business.
After the brother's death, his room was turned into a
shrine and the home took on a tone of perpetual
mourning. The father, who had a drinking problem of
long standing, now openly displayed alcoholic behavior. When he was visibly drunk, which was often, he
would engage in violent, but mostly verbal, quarrels
with Henry's older sister, Carol. This sister became a
compulsive overeater and later married an alcoholic.
The father had been a successful architect who had
drunk himself out of a good job. He now had a small
design firm which he ran from the basement of his
home with his wife's assistance. Henry's parents spent
most of his childhood working alone in the basement,
emerging periodically to stare worshipfully into Bernard's room. A more powerful model of isolation
would be hard to imagine. The therapist could not
help thinking of Miss Havisham's embalmed wedding
banquet in Charles Dickens's *Great Expectations*.
Henry's mother was apparently in a deep and long-

lasting depression. She was a withdrawn, silent enabler of her husband's drinking. She rarely spoke.

The 6-year-old Henry was more or less forgotten
by his parents, although he lived in constant fear of his
father's drunken rages. The father eventually became
"dry," with occasional lapses. He did this with neither
professional help nor AA participation, however, and
in Henry's words, "There was no spiritual growth."
The atmosphere in the home did not change. Henry
had to find a way to survive in this highly pathological
environment; his solution was withdrawal, both psy-
chically, by repressing his feelings, and physically, by
hiding as far away from the constant quarrels as possible. By repressing his feelings, Henry avoided even
the possibility of expressing those feelings. One cannot express, at least not directly, feelings of which one
is unaware. The only feelings that Henry saw expressed were the angry ones between his father and
sister, which resulted in nothing but pain. He could
not risk that. Thus, he hid his feelings from both himself and others. Later Henry would also withdraw
chemically, through the use of alcohol. Henry had
sought to avoid any conflict with his sullen but explosive environment by almost literally not being there.
Although the chemical withdrawal had ceased, the
rest of this pattern was still operative when Henry
entered therapy. Helping Henry to modify this once
life-saving but now dysfunctional defense became a
major objective of his treatment.

The ghost of Henry's brother dominated his
childhood. It is hard to compete with an idealized
memory. Bernard was remembered as a "real man,"
who had been interested in and proficient at sports,
hunting, fishing, camping, and things mechanical.
These were the father's interests as well. From time to
time his father would come out of the basement and
out of his shell to try to interest Henry in these activities and in the family business. He especially tried to

interest Henry in guns and hunting. However, Henry
sensed that he could never replace the dead Bernard
in his father's affections and he did not try to excel in
these activities. Henry also had a clear perception of
his father's enormous rage and potential for violence;
accordingly, he had no wish to play with guns with his
father. Instead Henry pursued his own interests. Fortunately, he had a great deal of innate talent. As he
grew up, he became a fine piano and horn player
and an outstanding student of languages. As he rather
bitterly put it, "So now I couldn't communicate in
four languages." The angry, depressed atmosphere at
home did not change. Mother continued in her deep
depression. Bernard's room remained a shrine. When
Henry gave concerts at school his parents did not
attend. Henry, like all adolescents, was confused by
his emerging sexuality. Since he felt attracted to men
in an environment which denied or scorned such feelings, he felt even more isolated and different. His
alienation increased.

Henry went off to college in a "dry" town, but
this did not stop him from developing almost instant
alcoholism. We have never met an alcoholic who did
not manage to find a way to drink in spite of being
broke or living in a dry county. In such cases necessity
is truly the mother of invention. Although he had
drunk only once in high school, becoming ill on that
occasion, Henry started to drink daily as soon as he
left home and started college. The alcohol took away
his feelings of shyness, fear, and alienation, and he
loved it. The quantity and frequency of his drinking
escalated rapidly. He majored in French because the
French department served wine. He also developed
an interest in sociology. As he put it, "I had always felt
like a visiting observer of a strange country, so becoming a sociologist felt right." He developed an interest
in the Indians of Canada and Alaska. The therapist
suggested that being a sociologist in the Yukon would

feel much like being gay in Iowa, but that he would then be a member of the dominant culture observing the exotics instead of the reverse. Henry agreed. Thus, Henry's choice of a career had been determined partly by interest and partly by his need to master an old trauma by turning a passive experience into an active one.

Henry spent his junior year in Europe. In Germany Henry felt that he had social sanction to drink beer all day (and into the night); in Norway he felt that he had social sanction to drink aquavit all day (and into the night); in France he felt that he had social sanction to drink wine all day (and into the night). He loved Europe. By the time he returned to the United States, he was a full-blown alcoholic. Like many alcoholics, Henry managed to find the "heavy hitters." In his senior year he shared a house with three other students, all of whom drank and drugged on a regular basis. His drinking allowed Henry to emerge from his social isolation to the extent of being able to drink with his roommates, but this proved to be a short-lived benefit. By the time he joined AA at age 25, two of his roommates were dead—one as the result of drunken driving and one by his own hand. The third is still an active alcoholic. Although Henry's memory of his senior year is hazy, he graduated with honors. By then he was experiencing blackouts and horrendous hangovers.

Following graduation Henry went to Chicago, where he obtained a job with a university archive. His life consisted of work and solitary drinking in his one-room tenement apartment. He used the facts that he never missed work and that he received promotions as parts of his denial system. "If I am able to work and to support myself, then I cannot be an alcoholic. Besides, I'm too young." Nevertheless, Henry began to distrust his own denial. His physical health was deteriorating. He developed asthma and multiple allergies. More ominously, he developed infections that would not heal, a sign that his immune system was being damaged by his drinking. Nevertheless, his denial held and he was able to keep his underlying awareness that he had a problem with alcohol out of consciousness. After several years of this life, Henry was barely functioning. Even the work performance in which he took such pride was crumbling.

Finally, Henry awoke one morning and found water throughout the halls and stairwells of his apartment building. When he went down to the corner liquor store, the owner asked him if he had been affected by the fire in his building last night. He asked, "What fire?" Finally Henry realized that he had been unconscious during a fire, in which he could very easily have died. This was Henry's "bottom." He called his brother-in-law who was in the AA program, and he joined. He stopped drinking within a few days and has been sober ever since. By the time he began therapy, he had lost the desire for alcohol and seemed to have no difficulty maintaining his sobriety. His health problems had resolved.

EVELYN: A DAMAGED WOMAN WHO FOUGHT FOR HEALTH

Evelyn had been sober for seven years when she came for therapy. She had had no desire for alcohol for many years. Although there was much she did not like about it, she was active in AA. Shortly before calling the therapist, she had picked up the telephone and smashed it over her husband's head. She did this without any immediate provocation or obvious motive. This loss of control terrified her. Almost simultaneously, her AA sponsor, to whom she was deeply attached, suddenly dropped her. Evelyn was bereft. When she arrived in the therapist's office, she was in a state of great agitation and panic. The first task was to help Evelyn reduce her anxiety to more manageable proportions.

Evelyn was married to a withdrawn man who could neither read nor write and who was also a recovering alcoholic. In spite of his illiteracy, Martin was successful in the home improvement business. He was ashamed of his illiteracy and sought to conceal it. Evelyn would cover for him, taking responsibility for all of the paperwork, ordering, and recordkeeping. Although she loathed him, Evelyn felt that she needed Martin to "take care of her." Martin had an equal, if not greater, need for her to take care of him and his business. Their relationship could be viewed as a mutually beneficent symbiosis or as a case of mutual parasitism. Their lives were seemingly inexorably intertwined, and they both hated their mutual dependence. Evelyn disclosed, "I have a sex problem; it disgusts me. I sleep with my dogs; Martin sleeps in the back bedroom. I also have two cats. (Nervous giggle) I hope you like animals."

Evelyn was a rigid, extraordinarily tense woman in her mid-30s, who looked as if she was about to snap in half. The therapist had rarely seen a stably sober alcoholic whose anxiety level was so high. Evelyn said that she had not had one comfortable sober moment. As she spoke, her tension would visibly increase until she broke it with a mirthless smile; she giggled frequently. Evelyn was beginning to hate AA and that both scared her and made her feel guilty. She stated, "If I hear another person in AA say, 'It just keeps getting better' or 'If you can't handle it, turn it over to the Higher Power,' I think that I'll kill him." And then, with a giggle, "I'm only kidding." The repressed rage of a lifetime was breaking through and threatening to overwhelm her.

Many recovering alcoholics complain about AA's seemingly too facile optimism, its Pollyannaish side.

They also complain about the aspect of AA's teaching that is emotionally suppressive, especially its tendency to advise its members not to express angry feelings. In the words of the AA text, *Twelve Steps and Twelve Traditions*, "Anger is a luxury that we alcoholics cannot afford." The therapist must take these complaints seriously and not dismiss them as symptoms of alcoholic denial.

Although Evelyn was terrified by her impulsive slugging of Martin, she was even more upset by her rejection by Bonnie, her sponsor. The two women had been close for five years, and Evelyn had idolized Bonnie. Just before she entered therapy, Evelyn had called Bonnie to tell her that she was considering having a baby with Martin in the hope that a child would bring them closer together. Bonnie reacted coldly; she said that their relationship was based on AA and since this decision had nothing to do with AA, there was nothing further for them to talk about. Evelyn, who had "shared" everything with Bonnie, could not believe that Bonnie really meant what she had said. Evelyn made several attempts at reconciliation, all unsuccessful. She was devastated. Evelyn was in a crisis. She was fragile to begin with; she felt out of control; and she had lost her best friend, the main pillar of her support system.

Evelyn had been brought up in a rural area of Cape Cod in a house surrounded by farmland. She was an only child. Her father was an alcoholic fisherman who frequently became publicly drunk. Her mother, the daughter of a rich farmer, looked down on her working-class husband and further scorned him for his drinking. There were constant and sometimes violent quarrels; it was Evelyn's mother who would be violent toward her father.

Evelyn's mother was socially pretentious and looked down on almost everyone. She was compulsively clean, always scrubbing and polishing. Everything was filthy, dirty, disgusting, especially Evelyn. Her usual tone with Evelyn was sarcastic; she frequently hit and punished her. When Evelyn was 16 years old, she failed all of her subjects at school. Although her mother had never taken any interest in Evelyn's school work, she hit Evelyn with a hairbrush until she was bruised. Evelyn remembered another incident from her high school years: She was talking to a friend at the dining room table and said something her mother did not like. Her mother slapped her face so hard that she flew off her chair and sprawled on the floor. She felt utterly humiliated in front of her friend. Amazingly, Evelyn described herself as "spoiled," and she would defend her mother's "strictness." It took many sessions to elicit the facts of her upbringing, let alone her feelings about these facts. Occasionally she would smile her smile, giggle her giggle, and say, "It was awful, really awful." Evelyn had been terrified of her mother, and she was still terrified of her mental representation of her mother, of the mother she had introjected. This introject constantly threatened to "put her down," and this threat was the basis of much of the fear that was her constant companion. Evelyn's mother was probably psychotic, and the voice of this psychotic mother, now inside her head, would not allow her to enjoy her sobriety.

Evelyn's mother eventually started to drink with her husband; she too became alcoholic. As the years went by the parents' drunkenness worsened. Evelyn's memories were of constant, violent fights, of her mother's hitting her father, of her father's anxiety and fear when he was sober, of her father, and later her mother, passing out, of her father's falling down and splitting his head open, and of her mother's unrelenting sarcasm and sadistic punishments. What probably saved Evelyn from psychosis was a close and enduring relationship with a neighboring egg farmer and his wife. Evelyn frequently visited this childless couple, who served, in effect, as the healthier and more nurturing parents she so desperately needed. This farmer loved nature and taught Evelyn the names of all the plants and animals in the neighborhood, about the heavens, the stars, and the names of the constellations. Evelyn developed the deep love for nature and animals that probably saved her life.

After failing in school, Evelyn was sent to a Catholic boarding school (Her parents were nominal Protestants.)The school seemed strict but provided individual attention. Evelyn's academic progress was taken seriously. For the first time she did well in school.

After graduation, Evelyn studied the care of the elderly in a one-year training program in a Boston hospital. Although she did well in the program, Evelyn began to drink during that year. After graduation, she returned to her parents' house, found a job caring for the elderly in a local hospital, and started drinking in earnest. She went to work each day and drank each night. Within two years Evelyn was drinking to oblivion daily and could have been accurately diagnosed as alcoholic.

Some time during her early 20s, Evelyn started to date. She had sex with various men, but always while blind drunk, and without pleasure or even memory of the act. Most evenings she stayed home and got drunk with her parents. After a number of years of this death in life, Evelyn's mother developed cancer. Evelyn remembered this as the worst period of her life. "As my mother got worse, she would cry out like an animal. I rather enjoyed it." Then a giggle, "I'm only kidding. Her suffering was horrible, really horrible. My father drank really bad then, really bad, and I would come home and get drunk right away. My drinking had become real bad too."

After her mother died, Evelyn continued to live with her father and drink with him. She had always felt close to him. "He was a good man, but he lived with terrible fear—that's why he drank. No matter what he did, I loved him." Evelyn identified with him, with his fear and his alcoholism. Evelyn "enjoyed" living with her father after her mother's death, but he quickly remarried. She felt rejected and hated her stepmother, yet she continued to live with them. Her father stepped up his drinking and Evelyn followed suit.

At this point she met Martin, who was also drinking alcoholically; she married him "to get out of the house." Evelyn said that she had always found him disgusting because he was uneducated, but that sex was not "too bad as long as we were both drinking." Shortly after her marriage, her father was found dead in the bathtub. He left everything, including the house, to the stepmother. Evelyn said that this was the worst hurt she had experienced. She couldn't believe that her beloved father could have done this to her. He had signed a new will shortly before his death, but Evelyn maintained that brain damage from the alcohol had caused her father to be unaware of what he was doing. She also fantasized that her stepmother had murdered her father, or at least assisted in his exit. Now her drinking knew no bounds. She lost her job.

Finally, Evelyn joined AA. Surprisingly, once she got over the shakes, Evelyn had little desire for alcohol. Apparently she simply had had enough of drinking; she did not miss it. She was always tense, however, and she suffered from crippling anxiety. Her husband joined AA and became sober a year later. Although they both take pride in the success of the business, in sobriety their marriage had been torture. "Martin is a good man and a hard worker, but he disgusts me." Evelyn had never found AA very satisfying, and an earlier attempt at therapy was not helpful.

She had tried various jobs, but was unable to function comfortably in any of them. Her enrollment in a local college gave her some pleasure, but brought out all of her insecurities.

SETTING GOALS

The treatment of choice for the still disturbed, stably sober alcoholic patient is self-psychological psychodynamic therapy, a treatment which aims at expansion of self-awareness and repair of structural deficits in the self. Treatment goals are co-determined by the patient and the therapist. The patient's conscious wishes and desires must be integrated with the therapist's professional judgment. There is usually no conflict; however, therapists have a responsibility to use the insight and foresight that experience, training, and objectivity impart. It is for these that people come to us. Sometimes there is obvious conflict between the patient's and the therapist's goals—as in the case of the gamma alcoholic whose goal is "to learn to drink safely," a goal which the therapist knows to be impossible. Such flatly contradictory purposes are unusual, however. A more common discrepancy arises when we are able to see possibilities for patients, to which their fears and long experience of defeat render them blind.

Treatment goals should be realistic, taking into account the patient's values, potential, ego strength, character structure, and life situation. Treatment goals are provisional; they are subject to change throughout the course of treatment. Henry's goals were to make a career choice and to overcome his fear of people so that he might have friends and a lover. Evelyn's goals were to regain control of herself and to feel less anxious. The therapist concurred with both patients.

The treatment of the stably sober alcoholic proceeds, as does all psychodynamic therapy, with the establishment of the therapeutic alliance, the building of trust, the unfolding of transference reactions, the interpretation of defenses and unconscious conflicts, and the slow accretion of psychic structure through "optimal frustration." Catharsis and insight are the poles around which growth accretes. Treatment involves the weaving of a tapestry in which the woof of the release of hitherto repressed emotions is bound with the warp of understanding. The figure in the tapestry is the new self of the patient. When asked in what mental health consists, Freud replied, *"Zu arbeit und zu liebe"*—to work and to love. Perhaps because we live in a more hedonistic age, we would add to play, so that the goal of treatment becomes the enhancement of the patient's capacities to work, to love, and to play.

REMEDIATION OF STRUCTURAL DEFICITS IN THE SELF

Psychotherapy weaves between amelioration of developmental arrests and the resolution of conflict. If Kohut is right in believing that the addictions, including alcoholism, are futile attempts to overcome deficits in the self, then the psychotherapeutic rehabilitation of the alcoholic must remediate these deficits. The question is, how is this to be done? Kohut offers an answer in his recommendation that the narcissistic personality and behavior disorders, including the addictions, are amenable to self-psychological psychoanalytic treatment. Perhaps few alcoholics, recovering or otherwise, are candidates for full-scale analysis, be it classical or Kohutian; the regression is too deep and the risk of setting off a slip too great. Rather, psychoanalytic psychotherapy that incorporates the insights of self psychology is the treatment of choice for stably sober alcoholics.

Self psychology concerns itself with the development, pathology, and treatment of the self. Let us review its tenets. The self is defined as "a unit, cohesive in space and enduring in time, which is a center of initiative and a recipient of impressions" (Kohut 1971, p. vii). This self is both an endopsychic structure and an experience. That is, we have a self, of which we are only partially aware, which allows us to be ongoing enterprises with cohesion in space and continuity in time. This self has both conscious and unconscious contents; our self-awareness reveals only a small part of this self. At times Kohut speaks of the self as a content of the mental apparatuses of id, ego, and superego. The self in this sense is a self-representation which may reside in any of the components of Freud's tripartite model of the mind. These self-representations may be unconscious, preconscious, or conscious. Alternatively, Kohut regards this self as a "superordinate" concept which becomes the overarching conceptual representation of the personality, and Freud's apparatuses of the mind become breakdown products of a healthily unitary and cohesive self. Here Freud's structural model of the mind is put aside, and the patient is understood in terms of the development and viscissitudes of the superordinate self.

The self as a superordinate principle serves as an explanatory myth that makes sense of human experience. The self in this sense is both a real, albeit endopsychic, "thing," the container of psychic experience which gives meaning and cohesion to that experience, and an explanatory concept which gives an account of both normal and pathological development. Kohut regards these two conceptualizations of the self as complementary, citing the principle of complementarity in physics, which regards electromagnetic energy, such as light, as both a wave and a particle. For our purposes, these theoretical discriminations are not too important. To understand the practical applications of self psychology to the treatment of alcoholism, we need to know more about the development and morphology of the self, whether that self be conceived of as a self-representation which is a content of the mental apparatuses, or as a superordinate structure which serves as a primary explanatory hypothesis.

Most psychoanalysts have maintained that the self has a history, a regular sequence of development in which a primary chaos is slowly organized into a coherent whole. They have felt that an organizing principle as intricate as the self cannot possibly exist at the beginning of life. On the contrary, the self is seen as a complex achievement dependent on the successful transversing of a treacherous developmental course. Freud (1914b), in his essay "On Narcissism," said that a "structure as complex as the ego cannot exist from the beginning." Glover (1956) postulated that there were "ego nuclei" which coalesce, in the normal course of development, into a unitary ego. Kohut thought that selves, in the sense of islands of awareness, exist from the beginning, but that the building of an "archic nuclear cohesive self" is a developmental achievement. In the beginning, there is the stage of the fragmented self—a stage which is reminiscent of James's (1890) description of the world of the neonate as a "blooming, buzzing confusion." It is to this stage of the fragmented self that the psychotic is fixated, or to which he regresses. According to Kohut, this fragmentation is overcome by being related to as a whole self, a person rather than a collection of body parts, by empathic adults. The cohesion of the self comes about through the internalization of the experience of being treated by others as a whole, in such experiences as being securely held. Children also gain feelings of coherence through maturation and the discovery that their fingers, toes, mouth, anus, and genitals are all their own. It is this experience of the formerly isolated body parts and functions as *my* parts and functions that is alluded to in the story of the man who goes to the doctor and says, "Doctor, my head aches, my muscles are stiff, my bowels are upset, and to tell the truth, I myself don't feel so well either." It is this "I myself" that is the developmental achievement called the cohesive self.

At this stage there is not yet a secure distinction between the self and its objects, so that the child experiences the human environment as a world of self-objects. The emphasis may be on *self*-objects—the world and other people as an extension of me—or the emphasis may be on self-*objects*—me as merged with the world and with other people. This is a stage of normal development—the stage of the archaic nuclear self. If this development from a fragmented to an archaic, cohesive self is successful, it results in a self which is secure from the danger of irreversible fragmentation, but which still experiences itself as a *self*-object and others as self-*objects*. This archaic cohesive self remains immersed in its self-objects. Kohut cites the game of "This little piggy went to market" as a playful way of temporarily regressing to the stage of separate body parts, the individual toes, followed by a joyful reintegration of those body parts into a cohesive self. He sees this game as an activity by which children master the trauma of earlier fragmentation though a symbolic repetition of the trauma.

The archaic nuclear self has two constituents: the grandiose, exhibitionistic self and the idealized self-object; it is therefore described as "bipolar." The exhibitionistic, grandiose self stage appropriately requires "mirroring"—that is, perfectly empathic confirming responses from the environment. Optimally, the parents will be able to enjoy the child's grandiosity and exhibitionism. What is needed is the "gleam in mother's eye" at the child's emerging delight in self. If the parents react to the child with pride, then the groundwork for secure self-esteem will be laid. However, the stage of the grandiose self has its dark side—in which the child expects to perfectly control objects, who are still experienced as a part of the self. When these objects refuse to be controlled, the response is narcissistic rage. It can be murderous and unquenchable. Regression to the stage of the grandiose self, with its concomitant narcissistic rage, is one of the most ominous manifestations of human aggression. Often the rage is turned against the self, leading to self-destruction. The grandiose self corresponds to Freud's "His Majesty, the Baby." When it is thwarted, the response is the cold fury of narcissistic rage: "Off with their heads!" The clinically useful concept of narcissistic rage makes sense out of much of the irrationality of both alcoholism and alcoholics.

The other pole of the archaic nuclear self is the "idealized self-object"—that is, the child's merger with an idealized, omnipotent environment, his participation in mother's and father's power. If these stages of grandiose exhibitionism and the need to partake of the felt omnipotence of the self-objects is responded to empathically, then these archaic structures will be assimilated into the mature self and will provide that mature self with a sublimated form of their primitive energy and with a feeling of fullness and inner richness. If, during the course of development, the inevitable frustration is not too great and is phase-appropriate, then the grandiosity becomes realistic ambition and the omnipotent self-objects are internalized as ego-ideals. There is a process of gradual and natural disillusionment with ideal self-objects and their replacement by "real" objects. Further, the functions of the self-objects as stimulus barriers, tension regulators, soothers, anxiety modulators, and self-esteem maintainers are internalized and become part of "the psychic structure of the self."

The mature self has the capacity to act as its own stimulus barrier, to self-soothe, to modulate anxiety and react to it as a danger signal rather than as an augury of annihilation, and to maintain a reasonably constant level of self-esteem. The mature self still has a bipolar structure, with a tension arc between the pole of ambitions and talents and the pole of ideals and admirations. This tension arc is a source of energy which Kohut compares to the flow of electrons between the negative and the positive poles of a battery.

In the narcissistic personality and behavioral disorders, there is a regression/fixation to the stage of the archaic self. This self has enough cohesion to prevent the irreversible fragmentation of psychosis, but its cohesion is sufficiently tenuous to allow episodes of temporary, reversible fragmentation which are experienced as annihilation of the self—as psychic death. The pathologically narcissistic also suffer from a paucity of internalized functional capacity—a paucity of psychic structure—which results in feelings of "empty" depression. It is escape from the panic terror of annihilation and the feeling of unbearable emptiness that the addict, including the alcoholic, seeks in his drug. Kohut writes:

> The addict . . . craves the drug because the drug seems to him capable of curing the central defect in his self. It becomes for him the substitute for a self-object which failed him traumatically at the time when he should still have had the feeling of omnipotently controlling its responses in accordance with his needs as if it were part of himself. By ingesting the drug he symbolically compels the mirroring self-object to soothe him, to accept him. Or he symbolically

compels the idealized self-object to submit to his merging into it and thus to his partaking of its magical power. In either case the ingestion of the drug provides him with the self-esteem which he does not possess. Through the incorporation of the drug he supplies for himself the feeling of being accepted and thus of being self-confident; or he creates the experience of being merged with a source of power that gives him the feeling of being stronger and worthwhile. And all these effects of the drug tend to increase his feeling of being alive, tend to increase his certainty that he exists in the world.

It is the tragedy of . . . these attempts at self-cure that . . . they cannot succeed . . . no psychic structure is built, the defect in the self remains." (Kohut 1977b, p. vii)

By achieving sobriety, the alcoholic has gained much, perhaps even life, but he has not filled in the gaps in psychic structure nor cured the defect in the self. This self-pathology is both causative of and consequent upon the alcoholism. Once stable sobriety has been reached, an effort must be made to remediate these deficits in the self. It is through the formation and working through of the narcissistic, sometimes called the self-object, transferences that the rehabilitation of the self takes place. Let us look at these narcissistic transferences.

THE NARCISSISTIC TRANSFERENCES

The reader will recall that *transference* refers to the reenactment in the therapeutic relationship of early object relations. Patients respond to therapists as if they were mother or father or brother or sister. These transferences may be of love or of hate: If the former, we speak of *positive transference*; if the latter, we speak of *negative transference*. Although the transference can be regarded as resistance, as an acting instead of a remembering and reexperiencing, it is therapeutically invaluable because it provides both the patient and the therapist with a here-and-now replication of the patient's conflicts with first objects. Those conflicts are not of merely historical interest; on the contrary, they are causing the patient conflict, both intrapsychic and interpersonal, in current life. This new edition of old loves and hates provides a safe arena in which powerful emotions can be experienced, modes of relating can be placed under a microscope, and the unconscious can be made conscious.

Classical transferences develop when people who possess securely cohesive selves, but who suffer neurotic conflict (that is, unconscious conflict between desire and conscience) engage in psychoanalytically oriented treatment. These classical transferences are characteristic of the psychoneuroses such as those found in hysterical and obsessive-compulsive personalities. Such transferences occur not only in treatment situations; they also occur in life.

Classical transference is about relationships with objects experienced as separate from the self. *Narcissistic transferences*, on the other hand, are about relationships with objects experienced as part of the self. In the narcissistic transferences, the therapist is experienced either as an extension of the patient's self or as an omnipotent self-object into which the patient merges. Kohut first called these relationships "narcissistic transferences"; he later referred to them as "self-object transferences." They are characteristic of narcissistic personality disorders and narcissistic behavior disorders such as addiction. What are the varieties of narcissistic transferences and how do they develop?

There are two principle narcissistic transferences: the mirror transference and the idealizing transference. Both are manifestations of the archaic, nuclear self. *Mirror transferences* develop when the *grandiose self* becomes activated in the therapeutic regression of an analytic relationship. *Idealizing transferences* develop when the *idealized self-object* (archaic parental imago) is activated in the therapeutic regression of an analytic relationship. To speak of the activation of the grandiose self or idealized self-object is to reify and concretize a *process*. Stated more accurately, the patient relives the developmental stage of the archaic cohesive self in the relationship to the therapist. Both manifestations are frequently present. According to Kohut, the therapist need only "let the transference unfold." The principle to follow is nonintervention. Because transference simply "happens" if the therapist allows it to, the transference that does develop will reflect the developmental level of the patient. The principle transference will be congruent with the mode of relating characteristic of the patient's level of object relations, which is in turn determined by the developmental stage to which the patient is fixated or has regressed. If the therapeutic regression is carried far enough as a treatment technique, then the patient will regress through all of the object-relational and psychosexual developmental stages. However, we are talking here about the transference that develops spontaneously during the early and middle phases of treatment and that reflects the patient's highest level, rather than the deepest level, of object-relational and psychosexual development.

In the case of patients who have developed to the point of experiencing others as separate objects, the classical transference neurosis will develop. Here the conflicts characteristic of the oedipal stage of development emerge, and the themes of jealousy, rivalry, and passion will be played out in the therapeutic relationship. These themes, and the conflicts arising from them, are fought out with objects experienced as separate and autonomous, whether such objects be intrapsychic representations or projective re-creations of early relationships. With patients who suffer from narcissistic behavior or character disorders, however, the transference that spontaneously develops will not be a repetition of early conflictual relationships with significant others experienced as separate people, but rather will be a relationship in which either the therapist is experienced as part of the patient or the patient merges with the therapist.

These relationships are not relationships between a self and an object; rather, they are self-object relationships. The degree of merger will vary with the patient's developmental level. The grandiose self is more archaic than the idealized parental imago; therefore, the mirror transferences reflect more regression than the idealizing transferences. The most primitive type of mirror transference is the *merger*, in which the boundaries between self and object are lost and reality testing is impaired. This type of transference is rare in narcissistic patients; it is more characteristic of borderline and psychotic patients.

At the next level is the *twinship* transference; the patient assumes that the therapist is a twin who shares interests, values, knowledge, skills, and abilities. The patient treats the therapist accordingly. The twinship relationship is not uncommon in narcissistic patients.

At a higher level is the *mirror transference proper*. Here the grandiose self is manifested in all of its glory. These patients are grandiose and exhibitionistic in the manner of a small child. They expect, indeed demand, that the therapist mirror them— that is, confirm and endorse their every action. The expectation is of total control of the therapist. This is phase-appropriate behavior in the stage of the grandiose self. However, it can be pretty tough on the therapist; the patient's constant demands for admiration and approval are wearing. The patient is looking for the "gleam in mother's eye." According to Kohut, *all* that the therapist must do is enjoy the patient's grandiosity and exhibitionism in much the same way that parents enjoy their children's narcissism (see Freud 1914b). If the patient's behavior is accepted and not criticized, it will be spontaneously "outgrown," not in the sense of being completely relinquished, but in the sense of being transformed and assimilated into more mature forms of being and behaving. The archaic grandiosity is slowly integrated into the reality ego and becomes the source of realistic ambitions.

If the primitive grandiosity of the grandiose self is merely repressed, resulting in a horizontal split, its energies will be effectively lost and unavailable to the reality ego (the mature self), which is thereby impoverished. A form of split-off, disassociated grandiosity, which Kohut conceptualizes as separated from the reality ego by a vertical split, will characterize the patient's overt behavior. Kohut believes that the patient's overt grandiosity is isolated from the reality ego by the vertical split in much the same way that affect is isolated from thought in obsessional patients. This overt grandiosity is not a manifestation of the very real power of the grandiose self, which is lost to the patient through repression; rather, the overt grandiosity is a residual of the parents' narcissistic cathexis of the child. In nontechnical language, the overt grandiosity is an identification with the parents' use of the patient, in childhood and beyond, to fulfill their needs for exhibitionism and display. The "stage mother's" investment in her child's performance is an extreme example of such parental behavior, and the former child actor's adult overt grandiosity would be an example of such an identification.

If the idealized parental imago (idealized self-object) is activated in the therapeutic relationship, then an idealizing transference will develop in which the patient creates an ideal, omnipotent object, the therapist, into which to merge. (An imago is an endopsychic representation of an object—in this case, a self-object.) In the stage of the grandiose self, the patient believes, "I am perfect." In the stage of the idealized parental imago, the grandiosity is given over to the idealized parent and the patient believes, "You are perfect, but I am part of you." Once the grandiosity is given over to the parent (therapist), the wish is to participate in the greatness and omnipotence of the idealized self-object. Once again the therapist's job is to accept the transference. The patient needs to idealize the therapist in much the same way that small children need to believe, and do believe, that their parents are the smartest, strongest people in the world. Many therapists are intensely uncomfortable when put on such a pedestal. They know, at least in their saner moments, that they are not so wonderful, wise, or all-powerful. They also sense the need to control that is inherent in the patient's idealization—"because you are so powerful and wise, you will fulfill all of my wishes"—and rebel against it. The therapist must learn to be comfortable with such idealizations; they are usually followed soon enough by disillusionment and rage. The therapist should not take idealizing transferences, any more than any other transference, personally. They aren't about the therapist.

According to Kohut, if the therapist uncritically and acceptingly allows these narcissistic transferences to develop, to unfold, then the narcissistic patient will form a stable and enduring bond based on either mirroring of the grandiose self or idealization of the omnipotent self-object. These transferences are then "worked through" as the therapist inevitably disappoints and frustrates the patient's expectations. If these disappointments and frustrations are not too severe—that is, if they are not traumatic—then they will set off intense, but manageable, reactions. It is through sticking with the patient through these transference storms that growth occurs and the archaic, nuclear self is assimilated into the reality ego, resulting in a mature narcissism characterized by realistic ambitions and enduring ideals. Eventually the transference has to be interpreted, but the trick is not to do this prematurely. The therapist must not take a "maturity morality" stance, which will cut off the unfolding transference and prevent the emergence of all of the patient's exhibitionism, grandiosity, and idealizing tendencies. In the narcissistic as in the instinctual realm, that which is repressed does not disappear; on the contrary, it gets enacted in various indirect and dysfunctional ways. The more that narcissistic as well as instinctual needs are expressed during treatment, the better.

Self-psychological psychoanalysis is not the treatment of choice for most recovering alcoholics. Rather, what is indicated is once- or twice-weekly intensive, insight-oriented psychodynamic psychotherapy that is informed by Kohut's insights into the viscissitudes of narcissism. These patients have an intense need for mirroring, or approving confirmation, as well as a need to idealize the therapist. They are also particularly narcissistically vulnerable. The treatment should therefore focus on blows to the alcoholic's low self-esteem (alcoholism inflicts such terrible narcissistic wounds); failures of the childhood environment to supply sufficient phase-appropriate mirroring and opportunities for idealization; and the alcoholic's experience of much of the world as an extension of self. Anxiety is usually understood and interpreted as panic fear of psychic death, rather than as a manifestation of intrapsychic conflict; and rage is usually understood and interpreted as narcissistic rage, fury at the failure of the self-object to perfectly mirror or protect, rather than as a manifestation of mature aggression.

Much seemingly irrational behavior can be understood in terms of both the alcoholic's need for omnipotent control and the rage that follows failure to so control. The grandiosity and primitive idealization of the archaic, nuclear self also explains the perfectionism of alcoholics and the unrealistic standards that they set for themselves. Most alcoholics have not developed realistic ambitions or livable ideals—these are characteristics of the mature self. The alcoholic's depression can be understood in terms of the paucity of psychic structure, which was never built up through the normal process of transmuting internalization. This empty depression also reflects the repression, rather than the integration, of the archaic, nuclear self and the failure to integrate the split-off grandiosity of the vertical split. The emptiness does not abate with sobriety. Further, the narcissistic rage to which the alcoholic is so prone can be turned against the self, resulting in intensely angry depression, sometimes of suicidal proportions. Failure to internalize the stimulus barrier and poor resources for self-soothing render the alcoholic especially vulnerable to psychic injury. Therefore, events in daily life threaten the alcoholic's already tenuous self-esteem.

The insights of self-psychology into the dynamics of pathological narcissism are relevant and helpful in working with stably sober alcoholics. Further, Kohut's technique can be used in a modified form in which the narcissistic transferences (attenuated in psychotherapy) are allowed to unfold, the patient's need to control and to participate in greatness is accepted, and a slow working through is used to help integrate components of the archaic, nuclear self into the reality ego.

AA intuitively diagnoses and treats the alcoholic's pathological narcissism. Its statements that "alcoholism is self-will run riot" and that "the alcoholic is under the domination of 'His Majesty, the Baby'" allude to the activities of the grandiose self and are diagnostic of the pathologically narcissistic character structure of so many of its members. In its treatment of this pathological narcissism, AA utilizes both the development of narcissistic transferences and the techniques of educational and moral persuasion. Both mirror transferences and idealizing transferences develop within AA and are, to a limited extent, worked through.

The ideology of the program, which stresses the commonality of its members, the sameness of the alcoholic experience, and the underlying similarity of the "alcoholic character," tends to pull a "twinship" mirror transference. "Identify; don't compare" and "identify with the feelings" are, among other things, injunctions to form a twinship transference. The Fellowship becomes a band of brothers and sisters who share a set of experiences, hurts, strivings, and values that are seen as unique to them. They form, in effect, a community of twins. The members' pathological narcissism predisposes them to form such a transference. Thus there is an ideal fit between character structure and treatment modality. AA works best for precisely those alcoholics who are capable of entering into a narcissistic transference with the program. Failure to form such identifications is seen as "denial" and resistance. This concurs with analytic experience, in which resistance to entering into a transference and fear of the concomitant regression are common. The bond between the "twins" can also be seen as identification with their common ego-ideal, the Twelve Steps of AA (see Freud 1921).

AA also offers opportunities to develop a mirror transference proper. Speaking at meetings gives the AA member a socially useful and acceptable arena in which to express the exhibitionism and grandiosity of the grandiose self, which is mirrored (that is, accepted and confirmed) by the assembled members. The speaker does indeed elicit the gleam in many mothers' and fathers' eyes. AA members also develop idealizing transferences toward the AA program. The "program" itself becomes the ideal object that cannot fail. "The Program never fails; only people do" and "Principles before personalities" are AA slogans that define the "program" as an ideal object. AA's "Higher Power" is also the subject of an idealizing transference for many of its members. The ability to enter into an idealizing transference with either the program or the higher power or both is probably the "secret" of successful affiliation with AA.

The sponsorship relationship also offers an opportunity both for the expression of the grandiose self and for the development of an idealizing transference. In fact, sponsoree–sponsor relationships are frequently characterized by idealizing transferences and not infrequently by mirror countertransferences. Thus, AA also allows—*encourages*—the narcissistic transferences to unfold. It then partially gratifies and partially works through these transferences. Generally speaking, AA tends toward the long-term or permanent maintenance of the idealizing and twinship transferences, while taking a mostly educational stance toward the mirror transference proper, which it also partially gratifies.

AA, unlike self-psychological psychotherapy, takes an educational stance, preaching a "maturity morality" as a way of helping its members overcome their pathological narcissism. When AA says that its members did not know how to live and that they are learning how to live in the program, it is referring to the paucity of psychic structure, resulting in impaired and disabled ego functioning, in active and early-sobriety alcoholics, and to the use of directive educational techniques and the therapeutic building of psychic structure through the working through of narcissistic transferences within AA.

Some authors, including Kernberg (1975), have noted the same phenomenon: the need for mirroring and the need to idealize in narcissistic personality disorders. However, they understand and approach it differently. Kernberg interprets the need to control early and directly. He takes a more confrontational stance. Not surprisingly, this approach stirs up much anger, which Kernberg interprets as "oral rage." Transferences are partly iatrogenic—caused by the treatment—and Kohut's empathic stance pulls a different transference than Kernberg's confrontational stance. By and large, Kohut's technique leads to better results and more enduring change. However, Kernberg's methods also have their uses. There are times when it is therapeutic to interpret the controlling aspects of an idealizing transference or to point out to patients that they are enraged because we are not "following their scripts."

Evelyn's initial transference was seemingly object relational. She re-created her fear-saturated relationship with her mother and then spent a great deal of time and energy placating the therapist in an effort to avert the anticipated blows. However, after about six months of twice-weekly treatment, a mirror transference developed. Evelyn became increasingly demanding. She wanted all of the therapist's attention and control of his life. She wanted admiring confirmation. Once she heard the therapist breathe as she left a session; interpreting this as a sigh, she came to the next session enraged. Some time later, the therapist telephoned a patient who had undergone surgery. Evelyn knew this patient and reacted with rage because the therapist was paying attention to someone else. This was not a sibling rivalry reenactment, in which the patient's transferential jealousy recapitulates the relationship with parents and siblings experienced as separate objects; rather, it was a rage reaction of the unmirrored grandiose self. From Evelyn's point of view, the therapist should have known that his call would hurt her and should not have made it.

During another session, there was a car accident outside the office. The therapist's eyes went to the window. Evelyn experienced the therapist's behavior as a traumatic failure of empathy in which her *self*-object failed to mirror her. The therapist *merely* accepted Evelyn's rage in each instance. He felt that Evelyn had had insufficient opportunity to live out the stage of the grandiose self and that she needed to do so in the therapy. She had had very little loving confirmation from her highly pathological parents. Her rage reactions to the therapist's failures to adequately mirror her were transferences of the rage of her grandiose self when both mother and father traumatically failed to phase-appropriately mirror her. Accordingly, the therapist thought that there would be time enough for interpretation; acceptance and the unfolding of the transference were more important now.

After a long time, Henry developed an idealizing transference. For many months, Henry did not seem to have any relationship with the therapist, although he faithfully appeared for

sessions and some sort of therapeutic alliance was clearly oper-
ating. As time went on, however, Henry increasingly looked
toward the therapist as an all-powerful, all-knowing source of
wisdom. The therapist was supposed to know all about academic problems, the ins and outs of thesis development, and the
worlds of sociology and administration. This idealization was
never interpreted. Nevertheless, there was a gradual disillusionment, and the therapist came to be perceived as a humanly
limited and flawed "real object." Although Henry occasionally
became intensely angry at the therapist when the inevitable
failures to protect revealed the therapist's lack of omnipotence,
he expressed his rage only indirectly, through emotional withdrawal. Initially, Henry was unaware of these rage reactions;
instead he experienced depression. This was interpreted, and
after much therapeutic work he was able to experience his rage
directly. As the idealizing transference was worked through,
these rage reactions became less frequent. Henry needed to go
through an idealizing transference and to experience his rage
and disappointment in the inadequacies and nontraumatic failures of his self-*object*.

TRANSMUTING INTERNALIZATION

Kohut states that once a narcissistic transference has been established, each nontraumatic failure of empathy (imperfect mirroring) or nontraumatic failure to protect (lack of omnipotence in
the self-*object*) leads to the internalization of a grain of psychic
structure. A small measure of that which had been done by
the therapist for the patient—tension regulation, for example—
now becomes part of the patient's psychological equipment.
The working through of a narcissistic transference consists of
hundreds or thousands of such small failures, the emotional
reactions to them, and the piecemeal taking on by the patient of
the function that the therapist has failed to perform adequately.
Thus, psychic structure, the ability to do for oneself what was
once done by others, is slowly accrued. The outcome of successful therapy is that the patient feels "full"; the empty depression

dissipates; the reality ego is strengthened; and the patient is far better able to maintain a reasonably stable level of self-esteem, to modulate anxiety, to regulate tension, and to self-soothe. Transmuting internalization is a depersonified, selective identification with the functions, rather than the personality, of the therapist (parent). This selective identification builds structure. It is the process by which the structural deficits in the self are remediated.

In summary, the remediation of structural deficits in the self is a two-stage process: (1) the development of one of the narcissistic transferences, and (2) the gradual internalization of psychic function through the working through of nontraumatic failures of empathy by the therapist.

RESOLVING INTRAPSYCHIC CONFLICTS

Although alcoholics suffer profoundly from deficits in the self, from developmental arrests, which must be ameliorated through the techniques of self psychology, they also suffer from unconscious conflict between desire and conscience. In traditional terms, there is conflict between the id's instinctual drives and the superego's prohibitions. When conflict is conscious, one can make a choice, however painfully; but when conflict is unconscious, then no resolution is possible. The conflict is either acted out or symptoms develop. It is the therapist's business to make the conflict conscious. In Freud's (1933) evocation phase, "Where id was, there ego shall be." This is done through interpretation—of genetic material, of the transference, and of the patient's behavior. Self-knowledge comes from derepression through free association, revival of early conflicts in the transference, and interpretations of the meaning of current behavior.

In addition to their problems with pathological narcissism, alcoholic patients also have object-instinctual conflicts; they too wanted to slay their fathers and marry their mothers, kill off their siblings, and so forth. Many events in their adult lives have offered opportunities to replay these conflicts and stir up the profound emotions associated with them, but their ego weaknesses gave them scant chance of resolving these conflicts. Since much of this book is about the making conscious of and resolution of psychic conflict, the topic will not be further purused. The point to be made here is that narcissistic problems and deficits in the self neither obviate conflict with objects experienced as truly separate, nor do away with conflict among the id, the ego, and the superego. They merely impoverish resources for dealing with such conflicts. It is not a matter of either/or, but of both/and. (See Wallerstein 1983.) The therapist must weave back and forth between building psychic structure and increasing self-awareness.

Work without Alcohol

Both Henry and Evelyn had grave difficulties in the area of work. Henry had a job in which he was able to function, but he felt frustrated and inhibited. He had no clearly defined vocational goals. Although Evelyn was a competent manager of her husband's business, she lacked self-confidence and had been unable to function in any job that she had held in sobriety. Her current efforts at the local college were so anxiety provoking that she was in constant torment, despite her objectively fine performance.

Henry

Henry was endowed with an unusual array of talents; he was an excellent linguist, a fine musician, a skilled writer, and a good student. In a way he was suffering from a "tyranny of talents," which inhibited him from selecting a goal, investing it with libido, and pursuing it with consistency and passion. Part of the problem consisted in Henry's failure to eroticize many of these activities; he did them well, but they gave him little or no pleasure. This was part of the price Henry paid for repressing his feelings. Since he tried to "not be there," it was necessarily the case that he could not fully be there emotionally in his many activities. This had been a life-saving defense in Henry's highly pathological home, but it was now crippling him in his attempts to be a full participant in life and in love.

The therapist knew that emotional investment in Henry's aesthetic and intellectual interests would be an inevitable byproduct of the derepression of buried feelings that was one of the main purposes of Henry's treatment. Henry could not have accomplished as much as he had if he had been totally unable to become emotionally involved in his work. The trick was to get more juice flowing. Helping patients to experience their feelings at a deeper level is always a part of self-psychological therapy.

A large part of Henry's vocational problem went back to his parents' almost total lack of interest in his activities and ambitions. His early excitement over music, for instance, was not mirrored by his parents. They did the "right" things: They bought a piano and provided him with lessons, but they were unable to respond to his performances. Henry's parents were still mourning for their dead son, and they had no energy left over for Henry. Henry's early efforts took place in an atmosphere of deep depression. This depressive tone colored those efforts and cast its shadow on all of his interests and activities. His parents' lack of interest in him persisted into his adult life. Henry nevertheless managed to sustain most of his interests, but the life had gone out of them, and he had become a rather dead, obsessive-compulsive worker.

The therapist, soon recognizing the damage that had been wreaked by Henry's unresponsive environment, took an interest in Henry's aesthetic, academic, and work activities, both current and past. He asked many questions: "What do you actually do? What is a typical day at the archive like for you? What happened at work that you were so depressed? What kind of music did you play? What were your relationships like with your teachers?"

Therapists are often reluctant to inquire about or show interest in the patients' activities. Somehow, it does not seem "dynamic" enough; it is not "really" therapy. This is a profound mistake. A therapist will *never* go wrong in showing interest in the patient's interests, whatever they may be. This is especially true when working with alcoholics, whose worlds are so often impoverished and who so desperately need to have their interests rekindled. When the therapist evidences such interest, relationship is strengthened, ego strength is enhanced, and the therapist receives the fringe benefit of a free education. In a case such as Henry's, in which the parents were unwilling or unable to take an interest in the child's activities, the need is particularly acute for the therapist to make repeated and detailed inquiries into the patient's educational and vocational activities. In so doing, the therapist is not trying to "make up" for what has been missed; this is not possible. Rather, the therapist is meeting a need which continues to exist in the here and now of the therapeutic situation.

The first step in helping Henry deal with work in sobriety consisted of *simply* asking many questions and listening attentively when Henry replied. This technique also served to build a relationship with Henry, who was shy and found it difficult to deal with more conflictual material. Early discussions of music, school, and French became the basis of a therapeutic alliance that proved to be durable. As Henry became more secure, he ventured into conflict-laden areas such as his repressed rage toward his unresponsive parents and his "survivor guilt" as the son who did not drown. (It was not accidental that he had attempted to "drown" himself in alcohol.)

Henry's administration job at the archive involved keeping track of artifacts and organizing traveling exhibits. He did this job well. When he was drinking, he had grimly held on, never missing a day and functioning adequately, if not brilliantly, on automatic. Fortunately, both Henry's self-image and his denial system mandated this zombie-like functioning, so he arrived at sobriety with a job. Very often that is not the case. Zombie-like functioning on a job that perpetuates alcoholic denial is not necessarily a blessing. Unlike so many alcoholics, Henry did not find it difficult to work when sober. The more usual pattern is for newly sober, and sometimes not-so-newly sober, alcoholics to experience anxiety and self-doubt on the job. Even though they may not have drunk on the job, the thought that alcohol-induced cessation of pain was only hours away would often make work tolerable, and the thought, much less the reality, of not having the possibility of such relief completely changes recovering alcoholics' perception of the work situation. Consequently, many recovering alcoholics have difficulty readjusting to work without the anticipation of the magical, soothing effects of alcohol.

Henry's experience was atypical in this regard; what little anxiety he experienced working sober soon diminished. He found, however, that he didn't really like his work once he became sober. While he was drinking, he was so fearful that he would be unable to continue to function that he could not even contemplate changing jobs or taking another career direction. Now all sorts of possibilities occurred to him. This new-found freedom made him anxious. Suddenly there were choices, possibilities, decisions to be made. Henry considered leaving sociology to obtain an M.B.A. and "go after the money." He considered "something" with music; he considered 15 different specializations within sociology. All of this was exhilarating, but it confused, almost bewildered, Henry. He sounded very much like a confused adolescent. The therapist carefully explored each of the options with Henry. The possible effect of a given career choice on his sobriety was a paramount consideration. During this period, Henry was volatile and fragmented, but he was becoming very much alive.

The therapist enjoyed Henry's second adolescence. Although it took many months of "playing" with vocational possibilities, it became clear that Henry had a deep love for sociology. Henry had needed to feelingly explore both his inner resources and the opportunities that the world offered in order to find out that he had made the right choice in the first place. "Thought is trial action," and the therapy sessions had served as trial actions in which Henry had learned "who he was." They had been a vehicle for the discovery of the self. Now the focus started to narrow. Having settled on sociology, Henry had to make some practical decisions. He eventually decided to continue in his present job while he pursued a graduate degree in sociology.

Although Henry's circumstances were somewhat unusual, with his relative youth and multiple talents, vocational problems are virtually ubiquitous in early sobriety, and they continue to be common in later sobriety. The nature of the problems vary, ranging from those of the skid-row alcoholic who has destroyed all life chances to those of the imaginative worker who finds that "creativity" is blocked in sobriety. Henry's pattern, that of the alcoholic who grimly holds on to his job through compulsive work and does not quite know what to do in sobriety, is freqently seen by therapists who treat alcoholics.

Alcoholism can be viewed as an "escape from freedom" (Fromm 1941), with its progressive impoverishment of the self and loss of human potentiality. From this existential point of view, the achievement of sobriety is a reclamation of freedom. Fear is always concomitant with this new-found freedom, with its choices, decisions, and responsibilities. The result is a sort of ontological agoraphobia, which can arouse such intense anxiety that sobriety is jeopardized. The intense anxiety that accompanies the realization that one has choices occurs in relation to all life areas. It is one reason that AA advises its members not to make major decisions during the first year of sobriety. This postpones the necessity of dealing with this particular kind of anxiety until more stable sobriety is attained, and it prevents impulsive actions during a period of rapid change. Nevertheless, there are cases of major decisions made in early sobriety bringing beneficent results. In any case, a time comes for the stably sober recovering alcoholic to take advantage of whatever life chances are there.

The alcoholic's relationship to work, like everything else in his life, changes with sobriety. For Henry, this process involved a sequence something like this: "I must hold on to my job or perish"; "hitting bottom" and becoming sober; early contentment with simply being sober and being alive, a contentment which included his job (the pink cloud); growing discontent with the job; a sort of vertigo, the dizziness of freedom, which came with the realization that he could do many things and work many places; the exploration of self in order to make a choice; and finally the actual making of that choice. Our choices are, in essence, definitions of ourselves. Consequently, one must have a self in order to choose. Many alcoholics do not have a firm sense of self; therefore, much of the therapeutic work must center on helping these patients consolidate a separate and autonomous self. They must complete the arrested developmental task of separation-individuation (see Mahler, Pine, and Bergman 1975). Becoming aware of their likes and dislikes, their strengths and weaknesses, including those in the vocational area, is part of this process. The self is, in part, what we define it to be through our choices. In spite of his disturbed childhood, Henry did have a sense of self, but it was a self in hiding (Guntrip 1971). Therapy helped this hidden self to emerge.

Conners's (1962) research on the self-concept of alcoholics (see chapter 6) is especially noteworthy here. You will recall that Conner found that the self-concept of the active or newly sober alcoholic lacks definition and extension. These subjects checked very few self-descriptive adjectives. Their self-concepts were empty and virtually barren, with the exception of a few "primary relationship qualities" such as "nice guy" and "friendly," and neurotic qualities like "anxious" and "depressed." It was the "secondary relationship qualities," precisely those attributes such as "skilled" and "capable" that are required to function well in the modern work setting, that were missing from these alcoholics' self-descriptions. Conners found that the self-concept became elaborated and enriched with sobriety. Our work is to facilitate this elaboration and enrichment.

Paradoxically, the making of choices itself entails the loss of freedom. Some potentials are actualized, but everything is not possible. We become this rather than that. This is a restriction on the claims of the grandiose self, which recognizes no limitations. Since the grandiose self experiences itself as omnipotent, there should be no limitations of its power. Thus, regression/fixation to the stage of the grandiose self (pathological narcissism) will render decision-making difficult. To some extent, we are what we do and we are not what we do not do. This actualization of one out of the many, with its consequent relinquishment of the rest of the many, is agonizing for many alcoholics. They prefer the pure air of potentiality to the more nourishing, but more restrictive, ground of actuality. Thus, helping the patients overcome their fear of making choices is an essential part of therapy. The therapist's recognition that part of the difficulty lies in the inability of the grandiose self to accept limitations on its power gives some clues as to the nature of the reparative work that must be done before the patient will be able to make choices without excessive anxiety.

> Once Henry had thought and felt his way to a career decision, he once again began to work hard at both his job and his graduate program. Although these activities retained a compulsive coloration, they were now more spontaneous than they had been when he was drinking. Henry now knew that he could quit and get another job and that his present choices were "for today." He became excited when he talked about his work, especially his work in graduate school. The therapist shared his excitement and mirrored Henry's growing self-satisfaction. The therapist must become the "gleam in mother's eye" without being perceived

as a parent who will only approve of or who demands success. Rather, the therapist must project (and genuinely feel) interest in the patient's activities regardless of their outcome. Given Henry's depressive, unsupportive background, the therapist became more actively involved with Henry's efforts than would normally be the case.

Henry did well during the ensuing year. He was now close to finishing the course work for his graduate degree and was working on a thesis proposal. At that juncture, he was asked to take a traveling exhibit to China. This would mean a six-week trip halfway around the world with no AA meetings and no sessions. Henry was torn; he really wanted to go on that trip, but he didn't want to do anything that might jeopardize his sobriety. On one hand, bringing an exhibit to China would be a major accomplishment, and the travel opportunity was thrilling in itself; on the other hand, the thought of being so far from home base was frightening. Henry was not sure that he could maintain his sobriety without his support system, although he was not conscious of any desire to drink. The job itself also engendered anxiety. Henry was unwilling to take chances with his sobriety. His immediate response, which included relinquishing the trip if it was a possible threat to his sobriety, was itself a "sober" response. He was really putting "first things first," as the AA slogan would have it. Henry had not been so anxious in a long time. The therapist encouraged him to explore his feelings about the trip in detail: "Will there be drinking?" "Yes." "How do you feel about being around alcohol?" "Okay, I think." "Will you be traveling with others?" "Yes." "Are they drinkers?" "Yes. In fact, one probably has a problem." "How do you feel about that?" "I don't care if people drink around me; it doesn't make me want to drink. But I'm afraid I'll be embarrassed if there is a toast at a banquet or something like that." "How might you handle that?" "I don't know; I'll have to think about it." "Will being so far away tempt you? After all, who would know?" "No." "What will you do if you get uptight?" "Call you. Is that Okay?" "It sure is."

The therapist also encouraged Henry to talk the matter over with his sponsor, and to bounce it around at AA meetings. After much consideration, Henry decided to go on the trip, but provided himself with safeguards. He arranged for friends in AA to write to him; he arranged for telephone contact with both his sponsor and the therapist if the need should arise; he took AA literature with him; and he gave himself an "out," in that he agreed to return home at once if his sobriety should be threatened or if his anxiety level should become too high. Once alcoholics give themselves the freedom to withdraw from sobriety-threatening or anxiety-arousing situations, they almost never have to do so.

Henry made the trip. It was a success. He returned with a new self-confidence and self-assuredness. He had handled a difficult assignment well, maintaining his sobriety while far from home and under stress. Henry received letters from AA friends while in communist China, and he believes that the Chinese secret police are still trying to decipher such strange code phrases as "turn it over," "keep it simple, stupid," "only for today," "a day at a time," and "don't drink if your ass falls off." The therapist suggested that ideological purity could be maintained by translating "a day at a time" into the Chinese for "A journey of a thousand miles starts with a single step."

Although a trip to China presents unusual problems in regard to alcohol and work, all recovering alcoholics must come to terms with the fact that they live in a drinking society and that drinking accompanies many work-related activities. Generally, alcoholics are initially defensive and insecure in work-related drinking situations; however, with time, they usually get to the point that they can participate in work-related social functions without either drinking or feeling self-conscious about not drinking. It is *mandatory* that the therapist explore with the patient feelings about the availability of alcohol and its consumption at social occasions. Some patients need guidance on how to handle themselves in this situation, but most merely need to express their feelings. The guiding principle here is that the patient should never do anything that jeopardizes sobriety; the longer the patient is sober, the fewer will be the situations that threaten that sobriety. If the patient is not in AA, it becomes especially vital that the therapist and the patient work on this problem. Generally, recovering alcoholics radically overestimate both the prevalence of drinking and the pressure to drink. They need the therapist to acknowledge the reality behind their fears while correcting the distortions and identifying the projections contained in those fears.

Henry's trip had been a success, but he soon had a disappointment to counterpose it. Shortly after his return, his thesis advisor rejected his proposal, commenting that it was poorly written. Henry came to his next session more depressed than the therapist had ever seen him. Throughout his emotional difficulties and his alcoholism, Henry had remained an academic "star." For this to happen in sobriety seemed unbelievable. The advisor's comment about his writing particularly rankled. He was "overreacting" to a transient failure. The therapist realized that Henry had experienced his advisor's comments as a deep narcissistic wound. His disproportionate reaction indicated that this issue had more meaning than met the eye.

Whenever there is such a disparity between a patient's reaction to an event and the seemingly objective importance of the event, the therapist can be sure that there are latent meanings behind the manifest content. In traditional language, the unconscious has taken advantage of some conscious conflict or event to break through the repression barrier and obtain conscious representation, in a disguised and distorted form, of unconscious material. We must help patients uncover, or become conscious of, the unconscious thought or feeling. Unconscious material generally falls into one of two categories: (1) repressed forbidden wishes, or (2) the claims of repressed archaic psychic structures. In other words, we must deal with either intrapsychic conflict or developmental arrest.

In Henry's case, the unconscious content that found representation in his depression was a manifestation of an archaic psychic structure—his repressed, undeveloped, and unintegrated grandiose self. In essence, Henry's grandiosity (as opposed to his pleasure and satisfaction in his very real abilities and accomplishments) had been offended; he had run into a wall that simply was not supposed to be there for him. Remembering that regression/fixation to pathological narcissism is the usual psychological outcome of alcoholism, the therapist understood that Henry's grandiose, archaic self—Freud's, "His Majesty, the Baby" —had been offended and was responding with limitless rage, the murderous rage emanating from narcissistic wounds, which Kohut has labeled "narcissistic rage" to distinguish it from mature aggression. In this case, the rage was turned against the self, resulting in a depression of almost suicidal proportions. Many a slip is set off by such a mechanism.

The first task was to help Henry experience his rage; he was unaware that he was even angry. Since Henry had always repressed his anger, which did not go away even though he was unaware of it, the experience of coming to feel his deep-seated desire to wipe out his advisor was genuinely liberating. Henry really experienced his rage as he ranted about his advisor. Thinking of himself as "highly civilized," Henry was amazed by the primitiveness and strength of his rage.

However, there is potential for growth in the kind of self-honest that comes from acknowledging how ready one sometimes is to torture, maim, and kill those who offend one, even in trivial ways. At first Henry was shocked by this realization of the intensity of his anger; however, over the course of five or six sessions, Henry was able not only to experience his rage, but also to "own" it. At first the therapist "merely" accepted Henry's rage in all of its intensity. As Henry felt his anger, his depression lifted.

Much later, the therapist pointed out the tenuousness of Henry's self-esteem and the blow that his professor's response had delivered to that self-esteem. The therapist commented on Henry's perfectionism, here reflected in his difficulty accepting the fact that even a fine writer is inevitably uneven and unable to satisfy every audience. However, the therapist did *not* discuss offended grandiosity nor "His majesty, the Baby"; rather, he was highly empathic toward Henry's hurt and rage. At this point in treatment, it was most important for Henry to experience his rage, and to criticize him for it would be to double bind him. For Henry, who had so little capacity to allow himself to feel, much less to express, anger, this experience with owning an episode of narcissistic rage was a breakthrough. As time went on, Henry became capable of expressing his anger in appropriate ways. Henry's archaic grandiose self would be integrated into the mature self (reality ego) indirectly. AA takes a more confrontive and educational stance on this issue. With patients who are not functioning as well as Henry, it is sometimes necessary to confront the grandiosity more directly.

Therapeutic strategy is determined by the patient's personality structure and emotional state. If drinking seems to be a likely result of the narcissistic rage, then the therapist must confront the patient with the unrealistic quality of the response; otherwise such confrontation should be left to AA and the grandiose self allowed to emerge. It can then be dealt with psychotherapeutically. In Henry's case, acceptance of his grandiosity worked well; he quickly recovered his equilibrium and decided to transfer to a doctoral program. After exploring the possibility that Henry was running away from a painful situation, which it would be better to face, the therapist supported Henry's decision.

Henry now seemed aware of much hitherto hidden inner strength. The expression of his rage at the thesis advisor not only alleviated his depression; it also served to start a process of derepression of a vast store of repressed rage. It was not only the expression of anger but also the therapist's acceptance of Henry's anger that was liberating. Henry now had more available energy, which he poured into his job, doctoral program, and an adjunct college teaching position, which he had aggressively sought.

Now a new problem arose: Henry would work himself to the point of exhaustion without knowing it. This was the result both of Henry's lack of awareness of his feelings and of a failure to internalize the self-care functions of the mother, which had never been phase-appropriately optimal and were probably barely adequate during the crucial early years of his life. (See Mack 1983.) The claims of the grandiose self to be exempt from bodily limitations probably also played a role here. The therapist had to teach Henry to recognize fatigue, but Henry slowly learned to attend to internal cues, rather than to rely on the therapist to tell him when he was over doing.

This failure to recognize fatigue can be seen as a structural deficit in the self, resulting from a failure to internalize the protective functions of early caretakers. Failure to adequately internalize self-care is common in alcoholics (Mack 1983), and therapists must be attentive to these needs. The failure to provide adequately for basic biological and emotional needs can also be seen as a form of *denial*, denial that the alcoholic has ordinary human needs. Since denial is the quintessential alcoholic defense, this is hardly surprising. AA addresses this issue in its rubric, *HALT*—"Don't get hungry, angry, lonely, or tired." Although this is not a suggestion to be taken literally, the folk wisdom of the group here clearly points to the failure to learn adequate self-care.

As Henry advanced at work, he was promoted to the position of supervisor of five employees. He was not comfortable as a boss. These difficulties were an expression of his low self-esteem, inexperience, and extreme inhibition in expressing anger or even disapproval. As a result his subordinates took advantage of him, and the work of his department suffered. In AA language, Henry was being a people pleaser. In a work situation in which he was expected to be in charge, this was a disaster. The therapist focused on Henry's fears of what might happen if some of his subordinates were displeased with him.

A turning point occurred when his assistant, Carol, to whom Henry had assigned the job of writing part of a catalogue, was unable to finish her task. She kept finding excuses for not doing the job. Henry was enraged, but he did not know it. Instead he became anxious. After much probing, Henry began to experience his frustration with, and anger at, Carol. The fact that Carol, his sister, of whom he had been afraid, had the same name as his assistant did not go unnoticed. Henry gradually became more assertive with his staff. He reassigned the writing task and began making realistic demands on Carol, which he insisted that she meet. As he had anticipated, Henry's staff did not like his increased assertiveness. He learned that he did not need his subordinates' constant approval. By the time he terminated treatment, Henry was comfortable being authoritative (not authoritarian) and assertive with both subordinates and superiors, but this did

not come easily and required rehearsal and exploration.

Part of Henry's difficulty in his supervisory position was the result of his still low self-esteem; he felt
that he had no right to make demands. Shortly after
he confronted Carol with her failure to produce the
catalogue, Henry remarked, "I knew that I had very
little self-esteem, but I never realized *how* little. I
remembered something: Do you know that when I
was drinking, and for a while afterward, I was afraid
to pull the cord on the bus at my stop because I didn't
want to call attention to myself? I thought I had no
right to make demands on the driver or inconvenience
the other passengers. So I had to wait for someone else
to pull the cord, and sometimes I'd have to ride way
past my stop before anybody pulled it. I've been like
that at work, afraid to pull the cord, but I'm going to
start pulling it." Henry saw the connection between
his problems as a supervisor and his low self-esteem.
He did indeed start to pull the cord at work, and his
self-esteem rose in consequence.

Henry also had difficulty delegating work. One
day he said, "Today I discovered why I do so much. I
realized that if I gave John the task of arranging an
exhibit, he might, God forbid, do it differently than I
would." Henry laughed in recognition of his need for
omnipotent control, gaining insight into the price he
had paid for his attempts to exercise such control.

Promotions engender conflict in many people,
not only alcoholics. Transference is not limited to the
therapeutic situation, and work situations often elicit
transference reactions. Promotions to supervisory positions intensify those reactions. With alcoholics, who
are by definition self-destructive, the stress of success
is particularly dangerous. Promotions to supervisory
positions often stir up oedipal conflict and guilt; in the
unconscious, to surpass the parents is to slay them,
which leads to guilt and fear of retaliation. For a man,

to become the boss is to become the father, which is a consummation both dreaded and desired. Becoming a supervisor also evokes feelings of sibling rivalry. In Henry's case, since his brother was actually dead, these unconscious fears of, and wishes to, kill the brother and take his place were particularly intense. The avoidance of such conflict was one reason that Henry chose a field so far removed from his brother's interests. Henry therefore had a particularly acute need to repress the expression of anger toward subordinates (symbolically defeated siblings), so that he could prevent himself from slaying them and possibly being retaliated against. The therapist interpreted this deeply unconscious material to Henry.

Success also means separation; therefore, promotion often stirs up separation anxiety. In addition, it is objectively dangerous to be the "point man." This dynamic did not seem to be an important determinant of Henry's difficulties as a supervisor. However, the more assertive a supervisor he became, the more he was differentiated from the other members of the department, and in that way separation anxiety may have inhibited Henry's growth as a leader.

Work inhibitions seem to be of two types: conflict based and drought based. Freud (1926) said that if to walk means to stomp on Mother earth, then there will be an inhibition in walking. Here a conflict embedded in a forbidden wish, stepping on Mother, has become associated with the performance of a normally unconflicted task, walking. Hartmann (1939) spoke of a conflict-free sphere of the ego, which he believed was a necessary condition for the successful performance of work. Although the work area of personality does need to be relatively conflict free, work interests also need to be invested with instinctual energy (erotized) or else they are dead, and such investment always brings a certain amount of conflict with it. The other problem, the dried up, unfulfilled

and unfulfilling work self, results from a withering of
the unmirrored self. This self needs the water and
sunlight of interest and reflected joy in its accomplishments. In working with alcoholics' work problems, we
need to address both areas: the resolution of conflict
and the facilitation of growth. In Henry's case, the
conflicts primarily involved the repression of anger
and fear of assertiveness; the expression of interest by
the therapist helped him achieve more career satisfaction.

Evelyn

Evelyn's anxiety permeated her every activity. Work
was no exception. She had never been able to function
comfortably nor well in school or at work, and this
dysfunction was both a cause and a consequence of
her frequently intense, chronic anxiety. Her self-con-
sciousness was crippling. Nothing was effortless and
automatic. Rather, she was like the centipede who
forgot how to walk when he looked at his legs.

How can we understand such radical educational
and vocational disablement in this alert, intelligent,
sensitive woman? Certainly alcoholism can so disable. However, Evelyn's difficulties both anteceded
her alcoholism and continued long after her attainment of stable sobriety. The answer to this question
is complex. It involves pathological introjects, lack of
opportunity, the effects of alcohol itself, feelings of
estrangement, and cripplingly rigid standards of perfection. Let us trace Evelyn's school and work history.

When Evelyn began treatment, she was a student
at a local college, where she was studying for a degree
in nutrition. She was only able to handle one course
each term, and she agonized over each assignment
and examination. She could spend days trying to read
a single chapter. She stated that it had always been
like that. Learning had always been difficult, if not
impossible. Evelyn had first pretended that it didn't

matter, that she did not care, but later, when she allowed herself to care, things did not get much better at school, and learning never came easily. From kindergarten on, she had never felt comfortable in a school or work environment. Evelyn's feelings of isolation, uniqueness, and estrangement had a social dimension and a psychological, almost existential one. The therapist thought of Heidegger's (1926) notion that man experiences the world as *unheimlich*: uncanny, strange, and sinister. Evelyn lived with a gnawing, persistent sense of estrangement, alienation, of never really feeling a part of the life around her.

It has been suggested that alcoholics are especially sensitive to the tragic aspects of human life. In this sense they are existential heros who live, at a deeper level than ordinary human beings, the terrifying apartness and radical finitude of human existence. Their alcoholism is then seen as a response to, and an attempt to transcend, their exceptionally clear perception of the human condition. This may be the case for some alcoholics; nevertheless, the alcoholic response to this "insight" into the human condition is pathological. The alcoholic does see something that is really there when he experiences himself as different and disconnected, but he ignores the possibilities for human relatedness. The alcoholic experience of aloneness, difference, and isolation reflects both ontological factors (the human condition) and psychopathology (pathological narcissism). It is important that the therapist neither be seduced by what can be a very persuasive rationalization of the alcoholic life-style, nor be insensitive to the lonely aspects of human experience to which the alcoholic is so often attuned.

The alcoholic experience of differentness, of not belonging anywhere, of never feeling at home, of uniqueness is part of the collective self-description of the alcoholic contained within the folk wisdom of AA. Many, if not most, AA speakers comment on this sense of uniqueness. There is both pride and pain in this sense of isolation and apartness.

For Evelyn, the pain predominated, although she took certain bitter, almost perverse, pride in it.

The alcoholic experience of aloneness and difference can be best understood as a consequence of the pseudo-self-sufficiency of pathological narcissism. Not having differentiated from the idealized self-objects of infancy, the nondifferentiated self remains inflated with the omnipotent power of those self-objects, and experiences itself as radically different from and not in need of others. Unfortunately, this "splendid isolation" is terribly lonely: "There is nobody here but this chicken." Further, almost all of the pathologically narcissistic individual's psychic energy, or libido, is invested in the archaic self-objects, leaving little or no energy available for investment in new, differentiated objects. There is also insufficient energy available for current life tasks. Therefore, the world of objects remains inadequately cathected. The world is experienced as strange, foreign, sinister, and unreal. There is no way to feel at home in such a world. This was the case for Evelyn.

Evelyn's rural elementary school experience set the pattern for her experience of the world of work. She was miserable. She felt that she did not understand teachers, nor they her.

"I was stupid; the teachers got fed up with me. I could never learn. I had the hardest time with reading and I still can't do math. My mother didn't much care—at least I thought she didn't. It didn't matter to my parents. She was a good mother, though—always had milk and cookies when I got home from school. She was a good mother; those horrible things didn't happen, at least not all the time. She was a good mother, it was just that she . . . didn't really like me. Not when I got older, she didn't like me; whenever I tried to do something, it was always the wrong way. I can still hear her: 'That's no way to do it; you're stupid.' But, she was a good mother, really she was; it was just that she didn't like me."

In spite of her fearful defense of her, Evelyn knew that her mother's oft stated opinion that she was stupid had come to be a crippling part of her. Evelyn had internalized her mother's hatred of her. Mother had become a pathological introject. In Evelyn's words, her mother "put her down" whenever she attempted to accomplish anything. "Put down" were also Evelyn's words for euthanasia of an animal. Hence her fear that her mother would "put her down" was a fear that her mother would kill her. Although she was not aware of it, Evelyn was terrified that her now internalized mother would kill her if she dared to be "smart." Any kind of achievement would thus set off intense anxiety. On the other hand, her mother might also "put her down" for being stupid. In chess terms, she was *zug zwang*: Any move she made would bring her closer to checkmate, to annihilation. Given the persecution of this terrifying introject, it was a wonder that Evelyn attempted anything at all.

Evelyn's school career continued as it had started. She got by, but she considered herself stupid, disliked by the teachers, and different from the other students. In her junior year of high school, she openly rebelled; if she was supposed to be stupid, then she would be. She stopped doing any work and failed every subject. Evelyn was deeply shocked when her mother beat her. It was not that she was unaccustomed to being beaten by her mother; rather, she never (consciously) anticipated that her mother, who had never showed any interest in her school work, would react so strongly to a school failure. Evelyn's mother was apparently reacting to the hostility behind Evelyn's rebellion.

The therapist saw Evelyn's deliberate failure as both a cry for help and an expression of anger. Evelyn

did get help. Her parents sent her to a Catholic boarding school. This act on the part of an economically
marginal, educationally indifferent, nominally Protes-
tant family is difficult to explain. Evelyn had learned
of the school from a friend, and she herself had requested that her parents send her there. She had not
really expected them to comply with her request,
however, and she was ambivalent when they did. This
active seeking of escape from her unhappy, alcohol-
drenched home was indicative of hidden strength and
a nascent drive for health. Sending the child to boarding school was in some ways a rejection, but it was
also, to some degree, an expression of caring and
concern. It also allowed Evelyn's mother to express
her feelings of superiority and contempt for the people in her community: *Her* daughter was away at
boarding school.

Evelyn and the therapist spent much time discussing her school failure and her parents' response to
it. In many ways, her subsequent failures were reenactments of this episode. There was something positive in being able, however indirectly, to scream for
help. Her school failure also served as an expression of
the disdain she felt toward the "educated people," the
teachers toward whom she purported to feel so inferior, and of whom she was fearful. Her failure was
also an expression of anger and hostility. Some of this
hostility was directed at her mother, an effort to hu-
miliate her mother by being a failure and a public
disgrace. Evelyn received both negative and positive
attention in response to her failure. It was both punished and rewarded. It also settled matters; to be a
clear-cut failure was at least to be something, to have
an identity, and it put an end to a painful struggle. In
many ways it was better than marginally getting by.

The therapist suggested that Evelyn's subsequent
failures were reenactments that were (1) cries for
help; (2) demands for attention; (3) ways of resolving

and ending painful struggles; (4) expressions of anger, contempt, and hostility; (5) attempts to elicit the masochistic, guilt-alleviating satisfaction of punishment; and (6) an anticipation of and search for the love that Evelyn had experienced as implicit in her parents' sending her to boarding school. These unconscious reasons to fail accompanied Evelyn's overwhelming unconscious fear that her mother would kill her if she succeeded. Many sessions were necessary to work through this overdetermined behavior. Evelyn and the therapist also worked on helping her express her needs and hostility more openly, so that she would not have to express them indirectly and self-destructively.

Boarding school was an important experience for Evelyn. For the first time, interest was shown in her academic performance. She received a great deal of individual attention and responded by becoming a passing student. Evelyn came to love the consistency and discipline of life at school. It was the first order in her chaotic life. She was attracted to Catholicism and seriously considered converting, but Evelyn dropped the idea when her mother became enraged. Evelyn continued to improve in the small classes. Learning was linked with caring and being cared about, to some degree learning came to be associated with love. It was perhaps no accident that the AA sponsor Evelyn came to idealize had once aspired to become a nun and had attended a similar school. Evelyn had started boarding school with many educational deficits, and she did not entirely overcome them, but she did graduate with a respectable record.

Evelyn went on to attend a training program in the care of the elderly. She was never able to explain this odd vocational choice; she had no special interest in old people or their care. But the academic demands were minimal, and it gave her a chance to get away from home. She was anxious and inefficient, becoming overly involved with her patients. She also began

to drink. After graduation she returned home and
went to work as a nursing aide. Evelyn's decision to
return to her parents' home at the point at which they
were entering the terminal phase of their alcoholism is
diagnostic of a developmental failure to separate and
individuate. She did not establish a life of her own.
Instead, she merged with her parents, identifying with
their deep depression and alcoholism. Her drinking
escalated during the ensuing years, but she always got
to work on time, functioned minimally but adequately, and avoided conflict with her superiors.
Evelyn relied heavily on Valium and other minor tranquilizers to control the alcohol-induced morning
shakes and emotional tension.

Even after Evelyn finally joined AA and became
sober, she continued to take Valium to function at
work. There came a time when she had absorbed AA's
disapproval of mood-changing drugs and went off the
tranquilizers. She fell apart. She would tremble, become confused, make serious mistakes, and at times
be unable to function even minimally at work. Her
supervisors suggested counseling, but when her functioning worsened, they dismissed her. Evelyn became
severely depressed and was treated with antidepressant medication. She remained bitter about this period
in her life: "At least I functioned when I was a drunk.
After that I couldn't function at all."

Although the anxiety persisted, Evelyn's depression gradually lifted. She continued to attend AA
meetings, which she "hated." Hated or not, they kept
her sober. At the end of her drinking she had married
Martin, an older man who was also alcoholic. After the
acute phase of her depression, Evelyn did not try to
work at a "job" for a long while. Rather, she became
the manager of her illiterate husband's business. She
functioned well in this capacity, perhaps because she
felt superior to Martin. She could also be successful
because she considered this Martin's success, not hers,

and thereby felt no fear that her mother would "put her down" for her success. Martin was tyrannical in his demands, yet he was utterly dependent on Evelyn, and he often deferred to her judgment. This arrangement was clearly a pathological symbiosis, but it did provide Evelyn with a success experience—even though they both considered the venture "Martin's business."

How could the therapist assist Evelyn vocationally? Many alcoholics have trouble functioning when sober, but her case was extreme. She was long sober and she had been off tranquilizers for years; yet she was still unable to hold a job. She was a "nervous wreck." The therapist might have made a judgment that Evelyn did not have the emotional resources to work and helped her to accept this, but he did not believe that to be the case. He therefore decided to try to help Evelyn understand her crippling anxiety.

Evelyn's anxiety at school and at work was multi-determined. She was terrified of her internalized mother, who threatened to destroy her for both success and failure. What this internalized mother meant in practice was that Evelyn was *literally* expecting her mother to step up and strike her if she dared to "act superior." Evelyn's mother was not dead for her; it *felt* as if she was dangerously alive. When she began treatment, Evelyn was almost conscious of this. One aim of therapy was to make her fully conscious of her fear of her mother and of the connection between this fear and her repeated failures. This malignant introject could then be overcome through identification with and internalization of the therapist as a good object.

Another source of Evelyn's anxiety was the fear that success would mean separation from Martin. This was both a reality threat—could she support herself?—and a psychological threat—could she exist as a separate person? Martin, like her mother, resented her "acting superior" and disapproved of her going to college; success in school would mean separation from him. Insofar as Martin represented her mother, college success also meant separation from her. Here again the solution involved a long-term working through of a developmental arrest and completion of the separation-individuation process (see Mahler, Pine, and Bergman 1975). Because it often represents differentiation and separation, both intrapsychically and interpersonally, success can arouse intense separation anxiety. This is a central issue in working with recovering alcoholics who are vocationally inhibited.

Evelyn's anxiety also derived from her fear that forbidden sexual and aggressive impulses would break through her rigid defenses. She felt that any form of assertiveness was equivalent to release of the terrifying murderous rage that she had so deeply repressed. Since achievement is not possible without aggression, it was crucial that Evelyn feel more comfortable with her aggressive impulses. Her repressed aggression and sexuality were also projected onto others, which imparted a paranoid flavor to her fear of other people. School and work provided both sexual stimulation and provocation to aggression. Evelyn's anxiety was also a self-punishment for those forbidden aggressive and sexual thoughts and feelings; it was simultaneously a compromise expression of that aggression and sexuality. Her anxiety served as both a disguised sexual discharge and a passive-aggressive means of expressing hostility. Evelyn was unaware that her anxiety-induced "stupidity" and inefficiency infuriated those around her, and part of her treatment consisted in making her aware of the hidden satisfactions in her anxiety. In particular, the therapist pointed out the aggressive uses she made of her anxiety-related ineptitude. The long-term answer was derepression—putting Evelyn in touch with her forbidden feelings and impulses. This major task was accomplished by interpretation of her dreams, fantasies,and behavior both in and out of session.

Evelyn's anxiety also made her feel alive. Anxiety, painful as it was, was at least a feeling, a defense against deadness and emptiness. Evelyn's anxiety functioned in much the same way as the self-mutilation of the schizophrenic or the head-banging of the autistic child. Both are ways of feeling alive. The treatment here was indirect: As derepression enabled her to feel more alive and less empty, her need to feel anxious in order to feel alive would diminish.

Some of Evelyn's anxiety resulted from skill deficits. It was necessary to explore classroom and work problems to sort out skill deficits from emotional blockages. The treatment of skill deficits is remediation. A closely related aspect of Evelyn's anxiety involved not so much her not knowing how to function as her not knowing how to function without alcohol or drugs. Evelyn had had little adult experience with drug-free functioning. Here the treatment was a reeducation in the management of her feelings without alcohol or tranquilizers.

Evelyn's perfectionism also made her anxious. She had to be the best. This identification with her mother's sense of superiority and scorn for other people was interpreted to her. Her need to be the best was one reason that she could only take one course each term—that way she was fairly sure of an A. This was ideal for Evelyn: She could simultaneously be the best—get the A—and fail as a college student—only pass one course. It was an ingenious unconscious compromise solution to a psychic conflict.

Evelyn's anxiety was also a defense against intimacy; it served to maintain her isolation. The answer here was also by indirection—the gradual lessening of her fear of people through the therapeutic process. Evelyn was also anxious because she did not possess a securely cohesive self. When her feelings became too strong, therefore, she was threatened with fragmentation. In this sense her anxiety was a fear of psychic annihilation. Here the treatment was through transmuting internalization and the building of psychic structure.

Evelyn related many of her work and school problems to her slowness, a function of her perfectionism. It took her "forever" to write a paper, to read an assignment, to complete a task. The therapist remembered a rather bizarre comment Evelyn had made early in treatment: "Saying F is like taking an enema." Evelyn, who always said "F" and blushed and giggled when she wanted to say "fuck," had meant that cursing was emotionally purgative. However, the therapist made an unconscious connection between Evelyn's slowness and her comment. The therapist asked whether she was slow in the bathroom. She blushed and said, "Yes."

Thereafter, much material surfaced concerning her slowness in the bathroom as a child and her mother's giving her enemas when she was too slow to evacuate her bowels. It became clear that Evelyn's slowness was, in part, a delayed victory over the enema-giving mother. Her anal retentive behavior indeed had a spiteful, stubborn quality. It was an unconscious attempt to master, through repetition, a childhood trauma. As Evelyn became aware of her memories of the bathroom of her childhood, the therapist got a sense of the depth of the power struggle between mother and daughter for control of the child's physiological functions, and of the intensity of the helplessness and rage that the child had felt when her mother forcibly invaded her body with the enema, thus robbing her of self-control and what she experienced as a body part. The child experienced the enemas as both painful and exciting. Insofar as they were eroticized, they were an expression of, albeit sadistic, maternal love.

Thus, paradoxically, Evelyn's slowness was also an unconscious attempt to provoke an enema from her mother, which would enable her both to master a trauma through repetition and to reexperience an anal erotic pleasure. There are no contradictions in the unconscious. It is of the uncovering of such unlikely, unconscious memories, or at least unconscious connections, that insight-oriented therapy consists. This particular insight enabled Evelyn to make sense of one of her most baffling and self-defeating symptoms, her slowness, and allowed her an opportunity to experience and work through the long-buried rage that her mother's treatment had engendered.

Love without Alcohol

As we have seen, recovering alcoholics suffer from all sorts of work problems, ranging from Henry's insecurity as a supervisor to Evelyn's free-floating anxiety. We encounter the workaholic and the work-inhibited; the supercompetent and the underachievers. Some of their problems stem directly from their alcoholism; some are only tenuously related to it; and some have no direct connection. The same is true of love in sobriety. Recovering alcoholics demonstrate every possible problem in their love relationships. We encounter the frigid or impotent and the compulsively promiscuous; the bold lovers and the fearful wallflowers. Again, some of their difficulties stem directly from their alcoholism and some do not. In every case, however, they must learn to love without alcohol. Let us look at this process in Henry and in Evelyn.

Henry

One of Henry's reasons for entering therapy was "my love life is nowhere." Henry described himself as gay, but his gayness was mostly theoretical, since he had practically no sexual experience. He had no doubt that he was homosexual and wanted to stay that way, but he did not really understand his sexuality. The therapist encouraged Henry to explore his sexuality, from his first fantasies to his current frustration. Henry was unable to uncover any heterosexual yearnings or fantasies, nor could he remember ever having had any.

All people are bisexual, at least in the sense of having sexual feelings for members of both sexes. Many theorists, including Freud, Jung, and Erikson, have postulated that humans are inherently bisexual, and they have offered biological, embryological, hormonal, and behavioral reasons. For our purposes, *bisexual* means that both hetero- and homosexual love are possible for all humans. In the course of therapy, heterosexual patients usually become aware of some homosexual feelings, and homosexual patients, of heterosexual feelings. Although this can be anxiety provoking, it is ultimately liberating. No further energy need be expended in repressing such feelings, and no anxiety need be felt from the threatened return of the repressed. The uncovering of such thoughts and feelings need not, and usually does not, result in changes in the patient's sexual preference.

The fact that Henry remembered no such feelings was indicative of very deep repression. There was something overwhelmingly fearsome about heterosexuality. The repression was successful, however, and this was an area in which he felt no conflict, so it was unnecessary to pursue the issue. Since this topic can arouse anxiety, it must be approached with caution; the therapist must take into account the possibility that homosexual (or heterosexual) panic may lead to a drink. This is not an issue for early sobriety.

Henry remembered growing up in a house in which sex was never mentioned. There was no display of affection between the parents or between the parents and children. Touching, if not expressly forbidden, was not practiced. Eros did not flourish in the arid soil of Henry's home. Nevertheless, the sap began to flow in Henry's pre-pubescent body. Henry remembered feeling attracted to men and boys during his first year in junior high school. These feelings continued and intensified, and Henry was confused and frightened by them. He could share them with no one. Henry survived high school by withdrawing. He had no meaningful emotional contact with his peers. It was an almost schizoid solution to his sexual conflict. Fortunately, Henry continued his involvement with music, which provided him with a little social contact. He did try to date a few times, but when he kissed a girl, he "felt nothing." His dates were futile attempts to conform, empty gestures. Henry was feeling both the panic of the inexperienced adolescent, and a serious sense of alienation.

Although Henry knew that he was attracted to men, he had no idea of what he might do with a man. The mechanics of gay sex were a mystery he did not attempt to elucidate. Rather, as he said, he turned from solving the problem of being gay in a small town in the Midwest to solving the problem of being a sociologist in an alien culture. Henry's incipient sexual research was soon to be brought to an end by his love affair with alcohol. During and following his college years, alcohol was the object of his longings and the source of his satisfactions. As long as he was drinking, Henry never had to come to terms with his sexuality. At the end of his drinking there were a few meaningless sexual encounters during greyouts. However, by that point Henry mostly wanted to be alone with his bottle.

Henry attained sobriety, but nevertheless remained ignorant of the physical aspects of homosexual love. Maintaining this ignorance was indicative of massive emotional blocking. During early sobriety, Henry met and became involved with an AA member, an older, rather depressed man. This man, with whom Henry had an informal sponsor-sponsoree relationship, initiated Henry into the "13th Step." (AA has 12 steps of recovery; the "13th" being AA slang for the seduction of a "pigeon," or newcomer.) Henry neither regretted nor resented being seduced by his sponsor.

On the contrary, he found the relationship freeing. Sexual seduction of a sponsoree by a sponsor is usually damaging to the sponsoree. It is an abuse of trust, and it carries incestuous overtones.

Henry used his relationship with John to explore his own body in order to discover its erotic possibilities. Although he found that he enjoyed all forms of gay sex, Henry discovered that he preferred being the passive partner in anal intercourse. Henry ultimately tired of John's chronic depression, however, and by the time he entered therapy, he was rarely seeing him. However, he had nobody else and felt lonely.

Although the therapist had not indicated his sexual preference, Henry assumed that he was heterosexual, and it seemed important to Henry to have the approval of a "straight" male. The therapist encouraged Henry to talk openly about all aspects of his sexuality: his memories, his early fantasies, his experiences, his current desires. Silent acceptance of all that Henry disclosed helped him to feel more free in his sexuality. Since Henry wished to remain gay, the therapist was minimally interpretive in the area of sexuality. What was addressed in sessions was Henry's fear of people and closeness. Henry was looking for a stable relationship, but could not have one if he remained terrified of intimacy.

With the support of therapy, Henry began to date. He and the therapist discussed how Henry could meet people. Henry (wisely) did not want to go into gay bars in the city. Instead, he started going to gay AA meetings. He spent a few casual evenings with the men he met at these meetings, but his loneliness persisted. He spent a session discussing how to serve a dinner for a potential lover. Having grown up in a depressed, asocial household, Henry had little knowledge of how to entertain. The sessions spent discussing the rudiments of entertaining and socializing may not seem "psychotherapeutic," but they were of great help to Henry. Many alcoholics, despite their seeming social sophistication, have severe soical deficits and require some degree of socialization. Being sane entails knowing how to be sane. The introduction of didactic elements into the therapeutic process does not prevent or interfere with more dynamic, insight-oriented psychological work; on the contrary, it facilitates it.

Recent years have seen an advent of well-attended "specialty" AA meetings: gay men's meetings, lesbian meetings, women's meetings, men's meetings, and occupationally specialized meetings, such as those for policemen. "Sectarian" AA meetings are at variance with the universalistic ethos of the AA movement; however, there can be no doubt that they help many people who are better able to identify in such "special" settings. Henry attended gay meetings.

After an extended period of social and sexual isolation Henry met Gary, a divorced professor with five children. It was love at first sight. Gary was gregarious and unafraid of people. Much of the next year of therapy was spent in helping Henry deal with the vicissitudes of intimacy. Each step closer was fraught with fear for Henry, but he was able to talk it through. The two men were happy together; they were sexually compatible, and they shared many interests. A controversy arose when Gary demanded that Ruth, Henry's cat, be placed elsewhere. Ruth had shared Henry's darkest moments, and Henry feared giving up his oldest friend for a new, relatively untried relationship. However, Ruth moved to the country and Gary moved in with Henry.

Relationships between people and their pets are important object relationships. Love for an animal has been known to prevent patients from committing suicide. There is growing evidence that love for a pet can improve physical and mental health and prolong life. Patients should therefore be encouraged to talk about their relationships with their animals. This material should be taken seriously and analyzed in much the same way as any object relationship. For many alcoholics, their relationship with their companion animal is the only, or the most important, relationship in their lives. If there are regressive, defensive, or schizoid aspects to the patient's relationship with the companion animal, this too must be discussed. All meaningful and nurturing relationships must be supported, however; relationships with animals are no exception.

It became apparent that Henry was often unaware that he was angry at Gary; he would have been afraid of expressing that anger even if he had been aware of it. This repression and inhibition stemmed from his early experiences with anger, which were uniformly negative. His basic fear was that he would lose Gary if he expressed anger. A related problem concerned Henry's lack of assertiveness.

Therapy helped Henry begin to realize when he was angry, but expressing anger to Gary was even more difficult than expressing anger at work had been. The imagined loss was more intolerable, and Gary, being an older man, was in some ways a symbolic father. Henry's actual father had been an unpredictable, frightening man. Although Henry's fear of his father was partly a projection of his own hostility toward his father, it was also a reality-based response to the potential for violence that Henry sensed. Henry also harbored a fear/wish that his father would punish him for forbidden sexual and aggressive thoughts and feelings; this part of his fear of his father was motivated by guilt. The connection between these feelings and Henry's fear of expressing anger was repeatedly interpreted.

Working through—this process of examining a problem from every possible angle—requires patience and persistence on the parts of both therapist and patient. A problem must be viewed in terms of both its current meaning (here, fear of loss of Gary's love) and its genetic meaning, or source (here, fear of the father's wrath). Transference reenactments of the problem can also be interpreted. Henry ultimately worked through his fear of recognizing and expressing angry feelings toward Gary, and by the time he terminated, he was capable of expressing anger toward those he loved.

Henry's lack of assertiveness was caused partly by his unawareness of his own desires and preferences. Therapy, with its emphasis on introspection and self-understanding, made him more aware of his needs, desires, and goals. It was a process of differentiating a self and establishing an identity. One reason for Henry's difficulty with intimacy was his fear of losing his identity by fusing or merging with another. Thus, the more separate and individual Henry felt, the more he could risk intimacy with others. We seek relationship in order to overcome our separateness, but we must be separate before we can relate. In this sense, human development is paradoxical: The emergence of psychic separateness from the original symbiosis with primary caretakers serves only to prepare us for new unions with those we love.

Telling his parents that he was gay was another painful issue for Henry. He needed to "come out" to affirm his identity, even if it meant losing whatever love he received from them. He brought many versions of the letter he was composing for them to his therapy sessions, seeking and almost demanding concrete advice. But the therapist did not allow himself to be trapped into giving such advice. Rather, he explored the issue and its ramifications with Henry. The letter was finally mailed; the response was a long silence, and then rage.

Henry became deeply depressed, and for the first time the therapist was concerned that Henry might drink. The therapist suggested that Henry step up his AA attendance and discuss the experience at gay AA meetings. Henry's anger at his parents for their silence and rejection was first denied, then gradually admitted, and finally really felt. The therapist asked if

Henry was not enraged at him for failing to protect him from this catastrophe.

Patients frequently blame therapists for disappointments in their lives. In the unconscious, the therapist is omnipotent and omniscient. Narcissistic patients in particular relate to therapists as omnipotent self-objects, as all-powerful parents with whom they wish to fuse. As we have noted, regression/fixation to pathological narcissism determines the alcoholic's psychic structure. When the omnipotent sef-object, whom they experience as part of themselves, disappoints them, they react with narcissistic rage. This rage is often unconscious and is frequently acted out by the patient's leaving treatment. It is the small child's rage at his parents for not preventing him from stubbing his toe. Whenever the patient experiences a setback, it is important to explore the possibility that the patient is angry at the therapist. Patients usually deny this; they do not wish to appear so childish. On a conscious level it *is* childish; nevertheless, it is frequently true.

After a time, Henry's depression lifted, and he no longer seemed to care so much about his parents' rejection. As painful as it was, the experience was liberating; for the first time Henry was separate from his parents, his own man. His anger helped him to separate from them both interpersonally and intrapsychically. Their mutual survival of Henry's expression of his rage at the therapist helped Henry along the path of separation-individuation.

Eventually, Henry's parents decided to patch things up, and Henry passively agreed. They did not fully accept Henry's sexuality, but they did, more or less, accept Henry. He was satisfied with this rather thin relationship. His affair with Gary, who had more than his share of what AA calls "character defects," went through several stages and crises, but on the whole it was constructive and mutually sustaining. Henry had learned how to love in sobriety.

Abraham's 1908 paper, "The Psychological Relations Between Sexuality and Alcoholism," was the first to suggest a connection between alcoholism and homosexuality. What Abraham saw was the socially acceptable expression of usually forbidden male homoeroticism in the camaraderie of the tavern and in drunkenness in general. More broadly, he saw that alcohol was used to "dissolve the superego" and permit the expression of all sorts of forbidden sexual impulses; in alcoholism, the search for such release had become chronic. In our society, these forbidden wishes are frequently homosexual in nature. Here the connection is between heavy drinking, which can lead to alcoholism, and *repressed* homosexuality.

How does this apply, if at all, to overt homosexuality? Abraham saw that alcohol could be used as a pharmacological facilitator of psychosexual regression in a broader sense, ending in a regression to orality and a withdrawal of object love. That is, there is a withdrawal of interest in other people (except as a source of supplies) and a fixation on the self and the bottle. Here alcohol itself becomes the love object, and the regression is from object love to self love and self absorption, or narcissism. We have noted the relationship between alcoholism and narcissism. Some theorists have also proposed a connection between homosexuality and narcissism. If that should be the case, then there would be an organic connection between alcoholism and homosexuality, with pathological narcissism being the bridge. Let us see if that is the case.

Freud (1905a, 1914b) theorized that homosexuality was a narcissistic object choice, in that homosexual love is love of someone like us, someone of our own gender. In effect, the homosexual falls in love with what he once was, what he is now, or what he would like to be. He is not really in love with another person, but with himself, or with his ideal self (ego-ideal). (Heterosexual love can also be narcissistic in this sense.) Homosexual love provided Freud with one clue to the nature of narcissism. Viewed from another angle, homosexual love results from the male homosexual's identification with his mother's love for him, rather than the development of a love for her and her psychic successors. In other words, the male homosexual loves as he was loved or wished to be loved by his mother, instead of loving someone *like* his mother. Thus he loves, at one remove, himself instead of a woman. This provocative theory is consistent with our hypothesis of regression/fixation to pathological narcissism in alcoholism. The only trouble is that it does not seem to fit the facts in Henry's case.

Henry's love for Gary did not *seem* to be of this type. Perhaps this issue was not explored in sufficient depth, but the existing evidence does not support Freud's hypothesis. Perhaps Gary was a father substitute, but he was not merely a reflection of Henry, nor an ideal Henry. Of course, the "loved one" is always, to some extent, idealized and represents what we would like to be. As Plato (1961) pointed out in the *Symposium*, Eros is the child of Plenty and Poverty, and love is always a search for that which we have not. It is all a matter of degree. Although Henry's love for Gary certainly had narcissistic aspects, it also had aspects of true object love, of love for Gary as a separate person. The therapist understood Henry's homosexuality as a search for a father's love.

Kohut (1971, 1977a) believed that "perversions," including homosexuality, are futile attempts to compensate for missing psychic structure through fusion with omnipotent self-objects. Here the sameness of the object is necessitated by the fragility of the self, which requires "mirroring" by one of the same gender. In Kohut's view, developmental deficits leave the self insecure and subject to regressive fragmentation. Bonding with a member of the opposite sex arouses too much anxiety in such a fragile self, while bonding with one of the same sex is reassuring. This is Kohut's self-psychological restatement of the classical psychoanalytic theory that male homosexuality is a defense against the castration anxiety evoked by the sight of the female genitals. This may well have been the case with Henry, who had so deeply repressed his heterosexual feelings. Here regression/fixation to pathological narcissism also acts as a bridge between alcoholism and homosexuality, but in a different way. In Kohut's view, both alcohol abuse and homosexual object choice are means of maintaining the cohesion of, or preventing the fragmentation of, an insecurely cohesive self. Kohut's theory, which has virtue of also applying to female homosexuality, adds to our understanding of Henry's homosexuality. Whatever biological predisposition may have existed, the need to be "mirrored" by a similar body to reinforce the cohesion of a tenuous self and the search for a father's love were the most important psychological determinants of Henry's homosexuality.

The therapist can apply whatever theory seems to illuminate a particular case. The etiology of homosexuality is not yet known, nor is it necessarily pathological. Patients should be helped to understand this aspect of their lives, just as we would try to help them understand any other. The real damage comes from denial, guilt, and repression associated with homosexual impulses, feelings, and behaviors. Humans are constitutionally bisexual, and which sexual potentials become manifest is the result of an unknown and complex interaction of constitutional factors and environmental influences. As to the connection between homosexuality and alcoholism, broad, sweeping theories should perhaps be applied cautiously. Not infrequently, however, alcohol *is* used to permit the expression of homosexual feelings, and Kohut's insights into the use of drugs and homosexual object choice to maintain the cohesion of the self are impressive. However, this best fits cases in which the homosexuality is promiscuous and compulsive.

In Henry's case, the treatment served to reinforce the cohesion of the self; the object relational aspects of his relationship with Gary were discussed, and both its transferential and self-object aspects were interpreted. In other words, the treatment dealt with both Henry's need to take in male strength and power through anal incorporation and Henry's search for the love of a father. For all its complexities and overtones, Henry's relationship with Gary was satisfying for both of them.

Evelyn

When she began treatment, Evelyn had completely disavowed and disowned her sexuality. Her instinctual needs had been almost completely repressed. If they occasionally surfaced, they were instantly reassigned to the depths. As Evelyn put it, "I have a problem with sex; it disgusts me." Her affectionate feelings were almost as completely repressed. Evelyn was far from dead, however, and her sexuality was very much alive, albeit entombed. In fact, it was the threatened failure of her repressions that occasioned so much of her unbearable anxiety. In her insightful words, "My life is a secret from me." She lived in constant fear of discovering that secret, and the enormous energy she expended in keeping the secret a secret left her feeling tired all the time.

Alcohol allowed Evelyn some instinctual release, and she had had love affairs in her drinking days. As she said with an embarrassed giggle, "Oh God, I did everything when I was drinking. But I don't really remember; I was drunk." Evelyn had met and married her husband when they were both drinking. She had found intercourse with him tolerable, if not really pleasurable, as long as she was drinking. "I married Martin to get out of the house, to have someone to take care of me. It was all right as long as I was drunk." When she became sober she discovered that, "Martin was repulsive to me." She could no longer tolerate the physical side of her marriage. She moved into her own room and slept with her dogs. She was close to them and Martin deeply resented it. Her marriage had remained sexless for years.

Evelyn's near-psychotic mother was obsessed with the "disgusting" nature of "filth." The usual object of Evelyn's mother's abhorrence of dirt was her father. Evelyn grew up hearing her father called dirty, filthy, and disgusting by her mother. Evelyn understood that "filth" meant something other than dirty hands. Although it was never mentioned, Evelyn realized that what was meant was sex; what was filthy was one's body, men, and sex.

As a child, Evelyn was often witness to her drunken father's clumsy sexual advances toward her rejecting, contemptuous mother. Evelyn found this "disgusting." "It was awful; it really was. I pitied him."

Evelyn's mother would sometimes turn on her father and beat him; he would not retaliate. These frequent, ugly scenes were traumatic, but they were also exciting. The drunken, dirty man's attempts at lovemaking with his wife were Evelyn's first exposure to sex. The situation was complicated by her love for her father. She saw her father, drunk and ineffectual as he was, as a kind and loving man. She also saw him as an inhibited, fearful man. She both pitied and loved him.

Evelyn identified with her father and with his fearfulness. This identification was conscious, and she stated in therapy that she had been aware of this identification as far back as she could remember. By comparison with her mother, her father was warm and loving. He was only capable of expressing his feelings when he was drinking. In her love for him, the child was responding to some real traits in her father. When he had been drinking, but was not yet drunk, his shyness disappeared and he was able to express warmth, concern, and love. With further drinking he became sloppy, and the good moments ended. This was thin gruel indeed, but it was all Evelyn had. Out of desperate need, Evelyn had idealized her father; flawed as he was, he was the most available object for idealization.

Idealization is a complex phenomenon. Evelyn created a father who could, at least partially, fulfill her needs. The process was similar to the one in which children endow their teddy bears with qualities not resident in inanimate objects. This is the earliest use of the creative freedom of the human mind. It is the model for all of the artistic and cultural products of human maturity. It is also a delusion, but in the sense that all cultural creations—art, myth, and religion—are delusions. Winnicott (1951) called such creations as the teddy bear—not in its cuddly self, but as suffused with human meaning—*transitional objects*. Linus's blanket in the *Peanuts* comic strip is a familiar example of a transitional object. Objects are transitional in that they are transitions between pure fantasy (hallucinatory wish fulfillment) and attachment to "real" objects in the external world. In this sense, the teddy bear is, in Wordsworth's (1850) words "half created and half perceived." It is both reality and illusion.

People can also serve as transitional objects. Evelyn's father had become one. He was her teddy bear, and her ideal. Children need to look up to and love powerful, reliable adults, and if the adults around them are not lovable or powerful or reliable, they make them so in their minds. Evelyn did this by idealizing her father. Tragically, the discrepancy between Evelyn's "real" father and her idealization of him was too great, and she became traumatically disillusioned. In normal development, such disillusionment takes place gradually and phase-appropriately, leaving the child with an internal representation of a good object. In traumatic disillusionment, the child is left bereft and empty—without a feeling that there is something good inside them.

Evelyn defended as best she could against this disillusionment, largely through denial. She was still doing this when she began treatment. As the years went on, however, and her father deteriorated, Evelyn had little choice but to turn away from him. But she could not do this without "taking him with her," which she did through identification with him and through introjection. Her father became part of her. This introjection differs from the process of healthy internalization of good objects. Pathological introjection is more like swallowing the object whole, so that it is like a foreign body, whereas healthy internalization implies the digestion, assimilation, and metabolism of the object, which then becomes "food" for psychological growth and development. Healthy internalization is always selective and depersonified.

That is, it is not the person that becomes part of us; rather, we internalize their attributes and some of the functions they had once performed for us. Freud (1926) said that the id never really gives up its objects, and that the ego can only give them up by making them part of itself, by incorporating them. Evelyn did just that. Her alcoholism was, among other things, an identification with her father. Drinking was not only a way of feeling close to him; it was a way of being him. When Evelyn drank, she became her father: dirty, sloppy, clumsily lustful, falling-down drunk.

Insofar as Evelyn felt like her father, she felt her mother's hate for him, directed against herself. This was intolerable, and as she grew older and her father's deterioration became undeniable, she turned away from her father and, out of necessity, identified with her mother. This was an identification with the aggressor (A. Freud 1938). Identification with the aggressor is a common defense mechanism; it is also the basis of much self-hatred. Since alcoholics most certainly hate themselves, it is reasonable to postulate that they commonly use identification with the aggressor as a defense mechanism. Through this identification, Evelyn now also became contemptuous of dirt, filth, and "inferior people." Here, too, she was *zug zwang*. If she identified with her father, it was identification with degradation; if she identified with her mother, she had to hate herself.

To make matters worse, her mother's craziness entrapped her in yet another double bind. If she was too "superior," too identified with her mother's contempt for "inferior people," she was then denounced as a "phoney." The child was truly in a terrible trap. Evelyn dealt with this by intensifying her identification with the aggressor. She did this in spite of the ferocious rage that her mother directed at her. This identification made it impossible for Evelyn to learn to love or to express herself sexually.

Evelyn entered adolescence developmentally crippled and gravely handicapped when it came time to date. The convent school saved her from having to deal with the interpersonal aspects of her sexuality, but the internal conflicts did not go away. As soon as she left the convent school to study in the city, she began to use alcohol to dull that conflict. In the succeeding years, Evelyn relied increasingly on alcohol. She had sex with many men, but always when severely intoxicated. She developed crushes on several, who used and then dropped her. None took her seriously, and she always ended up home, drinking with her parents. Finally she met Martin—in a bar.

In a strange way, Martin echoed both her father and her mother. In his alcoholism, crudeness, lack of education, and "dirtiness," he was her father, who she could both love and disparage. She identified with her mother and related to Martin the way her mother had related to her father. She could be contemptuous and critical. Since she regarded Martin as beneath her, she could bolster her chronically low, tenuous self-esteem by feeling superior, just as her mother had tried to bolster her self-esteem by looking down on her scorned husband. The difference was that Evelyn knew that she was doing this and felt guilty about it. To complicate matters, Evelyn had come to feel some genuine affection for Martin, much as she had for her father. In therapy, she repeatedly stated that Martin was a "hard worker," "a good man," "decent; he cares, he does," and "basically kind." That was her view of her father. However, she went on to say, "There is nothing to him; he has no interests. He comes home and sleeps or watches TV, just like my father came home and drank."

Their relationship was made even more complex by a strange twist in which Martin played the role of her mother. As Evelyn's sobriety consolidated, she became more ambitious; she returned to college. Martin was ambivalent about this, but his attitude was mostly hostile. He started to attack her as a "phoney," just as her mother had done. Now he was both the scorned father and the cruel, ridiculing mother. A more thorough entwinement of past relationships with a current love relationship could hardly be imagined. Evelyn's marriage thus satisfied all kinds of regressive psychic needs, and it became an impossible bond to sunder. Additionally, there were here-and-now ties: Martin needed Evelyn to help run his business, and Evelyn needed Martin to support her. Evelyn characterized their relationship as a "sick dependency on both sides." The therapist challenged the reality of this mutual need. Could not Martin hire somebody to help him, and could not Evelyn manage to earn a living?

Evelyn had little awareness of the "transferential" bonds tying her to Martin. Therapy increased her awareness. She arrived at "Martin is just like my father" by herself, while the therapist interpreted the ways in which Martin was similar to her mother. At first Evelyn resisted seeing how she related to Martin as if he were her mother. Eventually Evelyn came to see that she was reenacting her relationship with both parents in her marriage. Her own insights, coupled with the therapist's interpretations, freed her intrapsychically; that is, they made her feel less dependent on and less emotionally entangled with Martin, but they did not lead to a separation in reality.

Martin served Evelyn as both an object and a self-object. She, therefore, could not leave him until she had internalized the self-object functions performed by him or developed and worked through a self-object transference to the therapist.

Since Martin was a self-object for Evelyn, she expected him to mirror her. When he did not she responded with narcissistic rage. This was an outlet for her dammed-up hostility and rage. He became the recipient of both rage over his here-and-now behavior and rage at her parents. It was this unconscious increment to her conscious rage that explained the vehemence of her seemingly irrational attacks on him. The more she got in touch with and expressed her rage at her parents, the less she needed to act it out with Martin.

Insofar as Martin represented both her parents, Evelyn's relationship with him was an attempt at mastery of a trauma through repetition. Evelyn's entire upbringing had been traumatic, but her reaction to being exposed to her parents' sexuality was singularly intense. If her relationship with Martin was a repetition, then her disgust at his sexual advances was also a repetition. This suggested that her drunken father might have molested her. The intensity of her repugnance reinforced this suspicion. Consciously, Martin's sexual advances reminded her of her father's sexual advances toward her mother and of the sounds she had heard coming from their bedroom. Perhaps, these sights and sounds were sufficiently traumatic, but the therapist sensed that there was more there.

Since this issue was fraught with so much anxiety, the therapist approached it with caution. Evelyn responded with denial to the therapist's gingerly exploration of the possibility that her father had molested her. The therapist retreated, but one goal of treatment remained to make conscious any memories Evelyn might recover of real sexual experience with her father. The recovery of such memories is not possible before the therapist is internalized as a good object, because only then can disillusionment with the defensively idealized objects of childhood be risked.

Evelyn was traumatized by her exposure to her parents' sexuality; another goal of treatment was to help her overcome that trauma. Evelyn's flat sexual rejection of Martin after they became sober resulted in constant tension and smoldering hatred. Martin was in perpetual rage and Evelyn lived in constant fear of him. Although Martin was suspicious of therapy, he hoped it would warm her up. When this failed to happen, his free-floating rage became focused on her going for therapy. This complicated the therapeutic relationship.

What had happened to Evelyn's libido? Neither gratification nor sublimation seemed possible, yet the claims of Eros had to be met somehow. At first Evelyn denied having any sexual feelings at all. Later she stated that sex might not be so disgusting with an "educated man." The therapist pointed out that he was an "educated man," but Evelyn blushed and quickly replied, "Oh, not you. I didn't mean you." If there was an erotic transference it never became explicit.

What did emerge was Evelyn's mostly fantasy relationship with a minister to whom she had turned at the nadir of her drinking. He had spent a great deal of time with her, and she had become sober under his influence. She remained troubled during early sobriety, and their relationship had continued. Evelyn began to have sexual fantasies about him, but when he put his arm around her and hugged her, she fled. Evelyn was deeply shocked and hurt by the minister's advances, but she was also flattered and secretly pleased. ("My life is a secret from myself.") It took a great deal of therapeutic work before she could talk about this exciting but traumatically disillusioning relationship. Evelyn became aware of her disappointment, disillusionment, rage, and sexual feelings for the minister. Her relationship with him was primarily an idealizing transference, but the therapy chose to focus on Evelyn's sexual feelings for the minister since repression of her sexual desires was causing so much anxiety. Evelyn blushed and stammered, but she was eventually able to discuss feeling attracted to this "educated man." This was liberating, as was venting of her rage at him; her anxiety level noticeably decreased.

Evelyn's relationship with the minister influenced her relationship with the therapist. It made it harder for her to trust and dangerous to allow positive feelings to develop. She kept her distance and defended against positive feelings for the therapist. Her fears of closeness in the therapeutic relationship were discussed. The more conscious these fears became, the easier it became for Evelyn to overcome them.

Early sessions had focused on Evelyn's hurt and shock at her sponsor's rejection of her. As time went on, she mentioned Bonnie less frequently. After almost a year of twice-weekly sessions, Evelyn once more became preoccupied, if not obsessed, with Bonnie. Bonnie had been Evelyn's mentor; she was interested in education and ideas. She had "sponsored" not only Evelyn's AA career, but also her return to school and her career as a college student. Evelyn had discussed each of her many crises at school with Bonnie, had shared her disappointments with her, and had looked to her for praise and approbation. Then this woman, who had meant so much to Evelyn, dumped her. She was devastated.

Evelyn had idealized Bonnie. Once again we see the emergence of the need for ideal objects, which is just as much a part of the immemorial claims of the unconscious as are the claims of the instinctual drives. Evelyn had tried to meet this need with her grossly inadequate parents, with the egg farmer down the road, with the nuns at boarding school, with the bottle, with the minister, and, in an odd way, with Martin. All had failed her. Like all needs that are not stage-specifically met, it remained in the unconscious and was enacted whenever the opportunity presented itself. The therapist first concentrated on helping Evelyn recognize and express some of her rage at Bonnie for her rejection. Getting in touch with how deeply hurt she had been was an extremely painful process. Later Evelyn recognized the regressive, transferential aspects of their relationship. "Bonnie is my mother; I know that. I want her praise and sometimes I get it, but other times she puts me down just like my mother. She needs to be superior to me."

Evelyn's bond to Bonnie was so powerful, and her repudiation of heterosexuality so vehement, that the therapist asked whether she had ever had sexual feelings toward or fantasies about Bonnie. She had vehemently denied such feelings or fantasies and had left the session offended.

Months later, during the period when Evelyn and the therapist were working on her feelings toward Bonnie, Evelyn said that she had been thinking about the therapist's comment and had realized that she did have sexual feelings for Bonnie. Her anxiety during this session was extraordinary; at times the chair in which she sat shook. Believing that she needed to fully verbalize her fantasy, the therapist asked Evelyn if she could be more explicit. Evelyn blushed and said, "No, no, I can't take any more." Then she stammered, "I want to go down on her—Oh, no! Yes, no, yes . . . I, I, I want to satisfy her."

During the succeeding weeks, Evelyn reestablished contact with Bonnie. Although Bonnie was reserved, she too seemed to want to reestablish the relationship. Evelyn arranged a meeting with Bonnie. She went to Bonnie's house, spent some time in small talk, and then blurted, "I love you; I want to eat your pussy." Bonnie became indignant, angrily rejecting Evelyn's advances. Evelyn, having done what she needed to do, left feeling relieved.

In the next session, Evelyn related the incident. She concluded, "I never knew I had all these feelings. I don't like them—I don't know if I can live like this. I almost—no—like it. It's good in a way, isn't it? I feel good. I guess it means that I'm alive. I am alive." The therapist replied, "Yes, you are alive." For the first time, Evelyn left a session smiling a real, rather than a forced, smile.

Evelyn has not yet known love in sobriety. She is still afraid of intimacy. But having dared what she dared, she no longer feels inferior to her friend. In fact, in some ways she feels superior for having deeper insight. Her marriage is calmer, and Evelyn feels less bound to Martin, although she is still afraid to leave him. Nevertheless, Evelyn has come a long way in recognizing and accepting her sexuality, and this has reduced her anxiety and freed her to be productive in other areas of her life.

Play without Alcohol

Huizinga (1944), In *Homo Ludens* (Man the Player), argued that the ability to play was the essence of being human. Although he may have overstated the case, there is no question that play enriches and sustains life. It is as if whatever human freedom may reside in the chinks of necessity manifests itself in play and playfulness. Without play there could be no creativity, no aesthetic activity, no culture. Art is play, as is ritual and, perhaps, one side of science. Play is action without "reality" consequences, and in this sense all thought is playful. In Freud's words, "Thought is trial action."

Kohut (1977a) is explicit about the playful aspect of science when he says, "All worthwhile theorizing is tentative, probing, provisional—contains an element of playfulness." One must be able to play before one can be creative, whether such creativity be manifested in scientific theorizing, in philosophical speculation, in aesthetic creation, in humor, or in lovemaking. Play frees us from the here and now, provides respite from the requirements of reality, redeems and revitalizes—re-creates us, yet, paradoxically, involves us in the intense immediacy of an "eternal now." Although play is close to the core of human creativity, it is not uniquely human. Animals also play, although the meaning of their play may differ from that of human play.

By *play* we mean human activity that is not utilitarian in any narrow or obvious sense, and that is normally accompanied by a feeling tone of exuberance and joy. Paradoxically, play may be, and frequently is, serious. It is usually a self-absorbing experience which has no referent outside of itself. The poet Rainer Maria Rilke wrote in his *Duino Elegies* (1922), "Man only sees his death before him; the beast has his destruction behind him, . . . and when he steps, he steps into eternity." The chess player concentrating on his next move or the skier negotiating a narrow turn is "stepping into eternity"; he is not "looking behind him," and in this sense play unites us with the beasts, brings us close to our animal heritage. Work that is not merely drudgery, love that is not merely obligation, is playful. Play is joyful; it gives us the inner strength to once again go out and meet the world in all its grimness and complexity. Play partakes of and puts us in contact with "Joy, the daughter of Elysium" (Schiller 1785).

The alcoholic is rarely able to play. Pathological drinking is grim and serious business, and increasingly so as the disease progresses. Yet drinking is associated with relaxation, recreation, playing. Perhaps this is so for some drinkers, but in a tragic paradox, the alcoholic has gone on searching the bottle for joy, for the release of playfulness, long after that bottle has ceased to supply even cessation of pain, let alone pleasure. To play, one must be able to let go, to "regress in the service of the ego" (Kris 1952), to be spontaneous, to take chances, to relax one's vigilance. To do this, one must feel safe. Alcoholics do not feel safe; they do not possess the serenity that would allow them to let themselves go. One needs a secure sense of self in order to lose oneself in an activity. In other words, one needs relatively impermeable ego boundaries in order to engage in those temporary, reversible, creative, and re-creative mergers in which one "becomes the music" or the game. Paradoxically, alcoholics' too permeable ego boundaries result in overly rigid defenses which do not allow them to engage in just those reversible, temporary mergers that complete engagement, the loss of "self" which is so truly re-creative, requires. Alcoholics are simultaneously too connected with and not connected enough with the environment. One cannot escape the isolation of the self by relating to the world as *self*-object, for then the world becomes but an extension of the self. Thus, pathological narcissism condemns alcoholics to both inappropriate and disastrous misperception of the world as an extension of themselves and a crippling inability to experience momentary escape from self in "blissful activity." The alcoholic's inability to play is truly disabling, and at least one type of alcoholic drinks in order to play. Tragically, whatever capacity for play the alcoholic may retain is lost in the bottle.

To play, we must be able to get in contact with the child within us. Most alcoholics know, although they will deny it, that their behavior is childish, so they are unable to allow themselves to be childlike. The result is a pseudomaturity, based on denial and hypocrisy, that is unlivable and must be undone through that parody of childlikeness we call drunkenness. Regression there must be; nobody can live purely rationally. The reality principle is, after all, in the service of the pleasure principle, and the ego is in service of the id. If there cannot be "regression in service of the ego" in the form of temporary loosening of ego boundaries, defenses, and reality constraints, which permits relatively unmediated expression of the instincts, there will be regression, not in service of the ego, but in the form of permanent loss of ego boundaries and dominance by the instincts. Hence, no therapeutic task is more important than learning to play.

If we are correct in our belief that many alcoholics drink in order to play and that in drinking they engage in a kind of pseudoplay, then sober alcoholics will still be gravely disabled by their inability to play. After all, nothing has changed beyond the cessation of drinking. Indeed, experience supports the truth of this notion. Sober alcoholics usually find it easier to work than to love or play. That was true of both Larry and Henry; Evelyn was gravely handicapped in all three areas.

How can therapists help patients learn how to play? To begin, play requires security and a sense of safety. The more we can build ego strength through the therapeutic process, the easier it will be for the patient to play. Rigid defenses come from fear—fear both of the external world and of forbidden internal desires. Therapy loosens defenses by making the unconscious conscious in the context of a safe relationship. Therapy provides both the security and the safety that playfulness requires. Further, internalization of the therapist as a good object moves the feeling of safety and security inside.

What are the genetic roots of play? Our first toys are our own bodies; we play with ourselves before we play with others. Autoeroticism remains the prototype of all play; it has no extrinsic purpose. Infants are, in Freud's words (1905a), "polymorphous perverse." That is, they play with and derive pleasures from the entire body—its surfaces, its interior, and its orifices. These pregenital pleasures later become subservient to the genitals and are organized in the service of reproduction. They now have a "purpose," an "economic" function. The primordial autoerotic pleasures are now relegated to "fore*play*." In *Love's Body* (1966), the philosopher Norman O. Brown has criticized Freud's emphasis on "genital primacy" as a criterion of mental health and maturity, and has suggested that a return to the "polymorphous perverse," to playfulness, would be true liberation.

The therapist is accepting of autoeroticism and infantile masturbation, and in that acceptance gives the patient permission to play. Infantile masturbation is less forbidden by parents, hence less repressed, than it was, but patients still have deep conflicts over autoeroticism, pregenital impulses, and infantile masturbation. Here, as elsewhere, derepression is liberating, and in this case indirectly facilitates the ability to play.

Language is also playful. Huizinga (1944) considers the use of language a "play activity." Metaphor is play, and so is poetry. When in therapy we teach a patient to verbalize feelings and conflicts, we are teaching how to play. Further, we speak of "plays on words," and much interpretation, especially dream interpretation, turns on plays on words. Patients learn that they have been "playing" all along. They are like the character in the Moliere (1670) play who learns that "he has been speaking prose all his life." This too is liberating.

The patient and the therapist play with each other. Patients move in the therapeutic process from playing with themselves—

private fantasy—to playing with others—sharing fantasy creations with their therapists.

In his closest approximation to a theory of play, *Jokes and
Their Relation to the Unconscious* (1905b), Freud stresses the
"economic" motives behind play (here, wit) and its function as a
means of obtaining partial gratification of forbidden impulses.
In his words, "jokes are tendentious"; that is, they have a purpose—the veiled expression of aggressive or sexual thoughts.
Freud was probably being too "realistic" here. Although play,
including verbal play, can certainly gratify aggressive and sexual needs, Freud seems to have missed the main point: Play is
precisely that activity which needs not be purposeful, needs not
have an economic motive.

Therapy is itself a "playful" process. The demands of reality are suspended during the therapeutic hour. The transference
is also playful. Freud (1914a) stated, "We admit it [the patient's
conflicts] into the transference as to a *playground*" (italics
added). Here in the "playground of transference," the patient
has a "harmless"—that is, not real—format in which to work
through conflicts. Further, the formal structure of therapy is like
that of play: It has a special time and place; it has its own rules; it
is unique; it is demarcated from "ordinary" life; it is simultaneously highly intense, deeply engaging, yet not quite "real."
Hence, engaging in therapy is, in one sense, playing, and patients learn to play by playing. Of course, therapy has its "serious side," but so do many forms of play. In helping patients
learn to play, we must separate those aspects of play inhibition
that are a result of conflict from those aspects of inhibition that
are a result of skill deficits. In other words, we must address
both fears of playing and not knowing how to play.

Henry

Henry had lost his ability to play. It had never
been very fully developed, although music had allowed him some opportunity to play. Unfortunately,
most "play" in Henry's home was associated with the
outdoor activities his father had shared with his
brother. After Bernard's death, the father had made

some attempt to engage Henry in these activities, but Henry knew that he was "second best." Further, Henry was not about to "play with guns" with his violent father. Henry must have been additionally inhibited in playing by the fact that his brother had drowned while "playing." To make matters worse, how could a child yell and scream and laugh, as children need to do, while his parents were in deep mourning? Hence, many inhibitions prevented Henry from enjoying play. Each of these factors was discussed, and when Henry did not make the connection, the therapist pointed out the relationship between Henry's early environment and his inability to play. Henry gradually became less inhibited and more capable of playfulness.

Alcohol had progressively narrowed Henry's horizon and impoverished his ego. Nowhere was this impoverishment more apparent than in the loss of his already limited ability to play. When Henry began treatment, he could not even relax enough to chat over coffee after an AA meeting. Henry was acutely aware that he never played, and one of his motives in entering therapy, although he didn't phrase it that way, was to learn to play. Not only did Henry regain his original limited capacity for playfulness, but he far transcended his original limitations.

AA, itself a form of play, helped. AA speakers telling their stories echo something primeval, both phylogenetically and ontogenetically. They touch something deep in human memory of the tribal story teller, the shaman, telling tales around the campfire. This is probably the origin of literature and of drama, and in our formulation it is play, as is the whole realm of the aesthetic. Further, story telling is, hopefully, part of our growing up, with Mommy or Daddy telling us a story, and this too is evoked by the AA speaker. Here we are passive, the recipients; AA provides both a symbolic recapitulation of this experience and an opportunity to turn the passive into the active, to become the storyteller instead of the listener. To be an AA speaker is to be an artist, to be a player in a symbolic reenactment that induces "purgation through pity and terror" in the audience. Further, AA emphasizes humor, and laughter is the essence of playfulness. Kohut (1977a) cites humor as a manifestation of healthy narcissism. To laugh, especially at ourselves is liberating as is all true play. Simultaneously, Henry was "playing" with his therapist. Here, in the give and take of therapy, was an opportunity to tease, to be counterteased, to try our new behaviors, to play at them, without reality consequences. Henry learned to play by playing in a safe environment.

Balint (1969) tells the story of a patient who had not been doing well. One day, she suddenly got off the couch and turned a somersault. The analyst realized that the patient had broken through and was on her way to getting well. Henry never turned somersaults, but he gradually loosened up. Henry's first approximation to a somersault was buying a concert subscription with his brother-in-law. This was not easy for him, and he could not do it until he felt that he deserved some pleasure. His guilt had to be manageable before he could allow himself to enjoy a concert. Everything that happened in therapy—making the unconscious conscious, unconditional acceptance, and conflict resolution—contributed to the reduction of his guilt. Explicitly, the working through of Henry's "survivor guilt," of which he initially was not even aware, gave him the freedom to engage in pleasurable activities. Another component of Henry's play inhibition was his fear of people. Here again the cure was by indirection; the more Henry accepted himself, the less he feared others.

Henry's relationship with Gary also helped him to play. Gary was able to play and he was unafraid of people. He took Henry under his wing, dragging him to the beach, on madcap rides in his dilapidated car, to coffee shops, and finally up in a skyrider. As Henry learned to play with Gary, he became more relaxed, and it became easier for him to let down his defenses in therapy. An upward spiral toward health was initiated.

As Henry became less guilt ridden, as his ego boundaries became more secure and he felt more autonomous, he became capable of that joyful reconnection with the child within that makes play possible. Since he had many interests, the therapeutic work in this area focused on removing inhibitions. Henry also had skill deficits, but they were remedied more by Gary than by therapy. By the time he terminated, Henry was attending concerts, going to the gym, entertaining and being entertained by friends, enjoying sports and outdoor activities, and laughing.

Evelyn

Evelyn had not been allowed to be a child, so it was not surprising that she did not know how to play. The few memories she had of playing as a child were with her friend the egg farmer. Alcohol had allowed her to "play around" and to have some fun, but most of this had been in a near blackout state and lacked the joy and spontaneity of true play. There was a grimness even to her hell-raising. Evelyn had taken flying lessons with her father, and this had been an important pleasurable experience. Martin was also interested in flying and this was a bond between them. When she became sober, however, she could no more fly than she could make love. Evelyn was so fear ridden in sobriety that she could not take pleasure in anything; if she did, her (internalized) mother might kill her. Hence Evelyn had to search for pleasure around the edges.

For example, she enjoyed school and being with her fellow students, but she could not allow herself to admit it. She could at times be intellectually playful, an activity she shared with her friend Bonnie, who gave her permission to engage in intellectual playfulness. But even here she could allow herself very little. Evelyn was so shaky that she could allow herself neither instinctual regression (her rage and lust might get out of hand) nor the sort of regression that allows us to "lose ourselves" in an activity.

The one exception was with her dogs. Evelyn could play with her dogs without fearing criticism or retaliation. She would throw sticks until both she and the dogs were exhausted, or she would run with them through the fields near her house. Evelyn was ashamed of her intimate playfulness with her dogs and expected the therapist to ridicule her for her closeness to them. The therapist, on the contrary, supported this relationship. Approval of this "regressed" behavior was liberating. Determining that Evelyn would not benefit from the "technical neutrality" of the classical analyst, the therapist was openly supportive of Evelyn's ego-enhancing activities. She needed and responded to this kind of approval. Even more important than support was her growing insight into the hatred her mother had felt toward her and any pleasure she might have, and into how she had defensively identified with and internalized that hatred.

Evelyn also had skill deficits; she had no sober experience with play and scant knowledge of play activities. Evelyn was in such desperate straits in the other areas of her life, however, that little therapy time was devoted to overcoming these deficits. Evelyn has not yet learned how to play, but she has made a modicum of progress in allowing herself some pleasure. She is no longer ashamed of playing with her dogs; she can allow herself some schoogirlish fun with friends, and she has developed a rudimentary capacity to play with ideas.

REGRESSIONS AND DISAPPOINTMENTS

Regression can be pathological or therapeutic, self-destructive or self-enhancing, permanent or reversible, harmful or adaptive. Regression is the return to an earlier, less differentiated, more primitive mode of functioning. Freud (1900) described three kinds of regression: temporal, formal, and topographical. That is, we can return to that which is earlier in time, that which is simpler in structure, or that which is closer to the unconscious.

Topographical regression refers to Freud's first model of the mind (see *The Interpretation of Dreams* 1900, Chapter 7), in which the mind is mapped into three regions: the realm of consciousness, the realm of the preconscious, and the realm of the dynamic unconscious. These are the "organs" of the mental apparatus. Topographical regression is the movement from that of which we are aware, the conscious, to that of which we can become aware by an act of volition, the preconscious, to that of which we have no awareness, the unconscious. Temporal regression is the return to that which is earlier in time; formal regression is the return to a preceding developmental stage, whether that stage be prior in the order of psychosexual development or prior in the order of object relations development.

Since that which is earlier in time is developmentally antecedent and is closer to the unconscious, all regression entails all three types of regression; in fact, temporal, formal, and topographical regression are but aspects of one regressive process. For example, the 5-year-old toilet-trained child who returns to soiling upon the birth of a sibling is regressing temporally (absence of sphincter control is temporally prior to control), formally (by retreating from the genital stage to the anal stage), and topographically (by retreating from conscious control to unmediated discharge by the unconscious).

Regression is usually pathological. It may be adaptive, however, in the sense that it is a defense against unresolvable and unmanageable conflict at a higher developmental level, which allows one to reorganize and to function on a lower developmental level. However, such regression always entails

loss of flexibility and functional capacity. In some cases—
chronic schizophrenia or far advanced alcoholism, for example—the regression may be irreversible. Most regression is reversible, but such reversal is not easy. Alcoholism is the epitome
of a regressive illness; the alcoholic regresses both from the
genital stage to the oral stage and from emotional investment in
objects to narcissism. One may be fixated rather than regressed,
never having progressed to genitality and love of others. Freud
postulated that we are prone to regression to stages at which we
were either excessively indulged or excessively frustrated.

It is possible that for some alcoholics their alcoholism was a
therapeutic regression. That may be the reason that some recovering alcoholics do so well. They do not return to their pre-morbid
level of functioning, but rather use the opportunity to reorganize
that their alcoholism has afforded, indeed necessitated, to grow.
For these fortunate few, the loosening of defenses and character
structure by their alcoholism allows a reintegration at a level of
development not previously obtained. Needless to say, the "side
effects" of alcoholism render it useless as a "therapy."

There are also healthy regressions—the kind of revivifying
and life-sustaining, easily reversible retreats to earlier and
simpler modes of functioning. We described such regression,
which Kris (1952) described as regression in service of the ego,
in our discussion of play. Regression may be psychosexual or it
may be object relational; that is, it may allow either unmediated
discharge of the instinctual drives or a return from separateness
to symbiosis. Usually it is both. The feeling of union experienced by lovers in orgasm or the mystic in ecstasy are additional examples of such healthy regression. Kris also postulated
that the artist has a unique capacity for contact with the unconscious through such a regression, and that creativity requires a
heightened capacity for regression. It is just this ability to journey through the dark realm of the unconscious and return intact
that makes the creator a hero. Perhaps that is why genius and
madness are close relatives.

Psychoanalytic psychotherapy is a regressive treatment.
The patient is invited to regress, to relinquish ego controls, to
free associate, to allow the contents of the unconscious to

emerge, and to rediscover the child within during the analytic hour. We also invite a regression to the dependency of early childhood in the transference. Such a radical treatment can therefore be undertaken only by those who have the strength to limit the regression to the treatment hour. It is for this reason that we avoid or modify analytic modes of treatment with active and early-sobriety alcoholics. Alcoholics with stable sobriety and reasonable ego strength can proceed to work more analytically and can be invited to regress in order to allow the relinquishing of maladaptive defenses, the gaining of a deeper knowledge of self, and an opportunity for a reorganization at a more optimal level. It is as if the patient were a puzzle whose parts were assembled such that they formed a coherent but vague picture with numerous gaps, and that only by disassembling the puzzle could the missing pieces be fit in and the puzzle reassembled into a more complete, vivid, and satisfying picture. The disassembly is the analysis; the state of being disassembled is the regression; and the reassembly depends on the synthetic power of the patient's ego. Such a process must not be undertaken unless the patient has the capacity for resynthesis. Many recovering alcoholics do have the capacity to safely undergo and benefit from long-term psychodynamic, insight-oriented psychotherapy. It is not this type of therapeutic regression that we are concerned with here, but rather regression to the highly pathological modes of functioning characteristic of alcoholism.

The therapist working witth stably sober alcoholics must navigate between insufficiently deep regression in the treatment session and the dangerous regression that spills over into the patient's life. The regression to be most feared is the slip. It requires much experience to develop the "therapeutic tact" and "clinical judgment" that allow one to sense how much the patient can take without endangering sobriety. The therapist should err, if at all, on the side of caution. If the patient is regressing too rapidly or dangerously, the therapist should become more active, directing the patient toward here-and-now reality issues. Therapists working with recovering alcoholics should take a conservative stance, returning to "the depths" when the patient is more secure.

Sometimes what appears to be regression because it is so distressing is actually growth and the pain is growing pain. We tell patients this. The working through of a previously unconscious abandonment depression is an example; so is the relinquishment of splitting as a defense, with the concomitant experience, for the first time, of others and oneself in their full richness and ambiguity. Therapy is inevitably associated with regression in another sense. Progress in therapy is never linear; it is often two steps backward and one step forward. The therapist must expect this. Hence, regression, not in the sense of therapeutic regression in the session, but in the sense of movment backward in the patient's emotional condition, is part and parcel of therapy. This can be discouraging for both patients and therapists. The therapist must provide hope when the patient has none and is close to despair. The therapist's role is to help the patient *understand* the reason for this particular regression at this particular time. If the regression becomes dangerous, then the therapist must move from an analytic stance to a more active, openly supportive one. Knowing how to time such a move is the art of psychotherapy with recovering alcoholics.

At one point Henry gave up on his job and impulsively went on part-time status. This decision made no economic sense and led to social withdrawal and the kind of isolation Henry had experienced during the last days of his drinking. Analysis revealed that Henry was very angry at the archive's director, who had been highly critical of him. Instead of experiencing and expressing his anger, Henry retreated and regressed to the sort of sulky, withdrawn behavior that had characterized him at the beginning of therapy. This "fuck you" leave of absence in fact hurt Henry and did nothing to communicate his displeasure to the object of his anger. Once this became conscious, Henry was able to reverse this regression both in reality, by returning to full-time work, and intrapsychically, by experiencing his anger instead of acting it out. He also gained insight into the genetic roots of this behavior in his childhood fear of expressing anger toward his irrational father.

Evelyn also went through regressive periods, in which she stopped talking to people and retreated to her room. The therapist considered these regressions dangerous, and, although he tried to help her understand them, he also took an active stance in support of her "return to the world."

Alcoholics take disappointments badly. Nontherapeutic regressions are usually set off by disappointments. For example, Henry's disappointments at work and Evelyn's disappointments in her relationship with Bonnie set off regressions. The therapist and the therapy are frequently blamed for real-life disappointments, and the patient often becomes enraged at the therapist. The unspoken, usually unfelt message is, What good is this therapy if I don't get the promotion, the lover, or better health? Such rage, usually unconscious, is particularly characteristic of pathological narcissism. If this narcissistic rage is not made conscious, the patient will act it out in life or by terminating therapy. We must deal with both the discouragement and with the rage.

CHANGING ROLES: INTERPERSONAL CONFLICT AS A NECESSARY CORRELATE OF HEALTHY ASSERTIVENESS

Although we have not taken a family systems approach to alcoholism, it is necessary to realize that alcoholics do live in a human environment, however impoverished, and that they interact with and react to that environment, which in turn interacts with and reacts to them. In the course of their alcoholism, their relationships with that environment inevitably become distorted and pathological. It is within such a distorted, pathological environment that roles and power relationships are established and become fixated. This can be viewed as an adaptation of the system to the illness of one of its components. Such an adaptation always involves a loss of functional capacity; it is a downward adjustment. In other words, the system reaches equilibrium at a lower level of adaptation. Recovery of the "sick" member threatens that equilibrium; sobriety changes and challenges the established roles and power relationships. The status quo is threatened for all concerned, and humans do not change easily or gladly.

As alcoholics become healthier, they are more considerate of others, but they also demand more for themselves. The chaos of active alcoholism is usually followed by a "honeymoon" period during early sobriety. With the establishment of stable sobriety, however, the honeymoon ends and the stage is set for a new kind of conflict—the clash of interests that is an unavoidable part of the human condition. The question is, can the alcoholic and the system accommodate to or creatively resolve this conflict of interests? Often they cannot, and either the system dissolves or the alcoholic returns to drink.

One of the most common causes of relapse is the alcoholic's inability to handle the narcissistic rage and disappointment that results from the failure of significant others to be thrilled by new-found assertiveness and maturity. Sobriety leads to change, and if the marital partner or significant other cannot also change, the growing maturity of the recovering person ineluctably jeopardizes the relationship. The slowly dawning recognition that this is so is a very painful experience for the recovering person, who naturally expects that recovery will please "them." This is not necessarily so. Significant others may even actively undermine the recovering alcoholic's sobriety. Coming to terms with these realizations is one of the toughest tasks confronting the sober alcoholic. The alcoholic's pathologically narcissistic character structure may result in sobriety being used as a means of control of others, and this worsens the situation. However, all of the pathology does not lodge intrapsychically within the alcoholic; on the contrary, much of it resides in the "others" and in the system. The early-sobriety alcoholic needs to be warned that disappointments may well be ahead. With stable sobriety we focus more on helping the alcoholic work through the conflict and endure the pain of being a separate person interacting with other separate persons who may have different goals and values, and who are not always beneficent, loving, or helpful.

Although active alcoholics are often argumentative, willful, and aggressive, they are rarely assertive. Underneath the sound and fury is passivity. Alcoholism is a progression from active involvement in the world to passive receptivity. This turn from activity to passivity is marked by a progressive impoverishment of the personality so that interest and involvement diminish toward a vanishing point, with the sole exception of protecting the source of supply. Recovery is the reversal of this process. As long as drinking is not interfered with, the alcoholic is usually "easy to manage." In a process parallel to the inward impoverishment, the alcoholic's human relationships become progressively thinner. By the time sobriety is reached, the potential for what Buber (1937) called *I-Thou relationships*—that is, relationships in which the other is treated as an end, not as a means—has long passed, and the alcoholic treats significant others as things, means of being taken care of and remaining besotted. Relationships are now "I-It." Reciprocally, the significant others have, out of necessity, also come to treat the alcoholic as an It, a problem to manage. To make matters worse, both sides have inflicted deep wounds that are not easily forgiven or forgotten. The degree of pathology in surviving relationships, if there are any, varies with the severity of the case.

Early-sobriety alcoholics are usually focused on maintaining their sobriety; often they are hanging on by their fingernails and are not likely to stir up conflict with the environment. Significant others are usually grateful for the possibility of lasting sobriety, although they may mistrust it. At this stage they are likely to make endless allowances in their relationship with the recovering alcoholic. Employers and fellow employees are also likely to make few demands on the recovering alcoholic during this "era of good feelings." This is both realistic and appropriate in the stage of early sobriety. Sometimes, however, the alcoholic's sobriety is so threatening to the others that they overtly undermine it.

With recovery, the alcoholic discovers the self and its needs and wants. Self-esteem rises. Anger is expressed rather than obliviated with alcohol or acted out in grossly inappropriate ways that, although difficult to endure, are easy to dismiss. The recovering alcoholic becomes less fearful of people and more ready to engage them in struggle; he ceases to be a people pleaser. The alcoholic also experiences mature aggression, which may now be used to modify the environment and strive toward the fulfillment of goals.

The recovering alcoholic becomes increasingly capable of I–Thou relationships, in which the other is treated as an independent center of initiative. However, alcoholics also discover themselves as "thous," as real persons; and the new I–Thou relationships, which are relationships between subjectivities, between persons, inevitably involve conflict. Separation and growth lead to treating oneself as worthy, deserving, and important at the same time that one comes to treat others as worthy, deserving, and important. These independent centers of initative, however mutually respecting, do not have identical self-interests, and interpersonal conflicts are inevitable. Clashes of interest occur between persons of good will. These healthy conflicts occur over and above the clashes that result from the pathologically narcissistic propensity of alcoholics to treat others as an extension of themselves. Health has its own kinds of conflict.

Larry's wife did not like the changes in him. He was more demanding, more assertive, and more sure of himself. Larry was also "more uptight," unable to get the kind of release, sexual or otherwise, that alcohol had permitted him. At times Stella told Larry that she had liked him better when he was drinking, and she would sometimes suggest that he take a drink. Her attitude hurt and enraged him. Although he was able to work through these feelings in therapy, the survival of their marriage remains in doubt.

Henry experienced conflict on his job and in his relationship with Gary as he became more assertive. The conflict was both painful and unfamiliar. With the help of therapy, however, he was able to overcome his fear that he would be abandoned. His increased assertiveness paid off. Henry learned to tolerate people not liking what he did, being angry at him, and challenging him. He learned that he did not need pseudoharmony in order to survive.

Evelyn also developed a greater sense of herself with sobriety. Her first assertion of self was her refusal to sleep with a man she realized she did not love. Later she discovered her intellectual interests and returned to school. Although her husband disapproved, she was able to continue despite the conflict it caused. A similar conflict ensued when she decided to enter therapy. Again she was able to make a move toward self-fulfillment in the face of opposition. The more she becomes herself, the further she gets from Martin. Her marriage will probably not survive her growth as a person.

FEAR OF SUCCESS, FEAR OF FAILURE

Alcoholics are failures by definitions. Their crippling, overwhelming feelings of failure do not go away easily or quickly. Alcoholism can be seen as a choice to fail. There are powerful reasons for this choice. Gaining an understanding of these reasons is one of the most important goals of psychotherapy with the alcoholic. Since the need to fail has not disappeared, recovering alcoholics are, with reason, terrified of failing again. At the same time, they also wish it, since failure is familiar and continues to meet some psychic need. The alcoholic's first experience of success may be sobriety. This success is frightening. Success often means separation, moving away from one's peer group, and this evokes intense separation anxiety. Further, success may symbolize a forbidden victory over siblings or parents. Hence, success may also stir up oedipal guilt and castration anxiety as well as guilt over "killing off" an ambivalently hated sibling. If success means killing a hated rival, be it a sibling or the same-sex parent, then there will be guilt and fear of retaliation. The alcoholic is caught in a trap. Failure is an intolerable blow to self-esteem, but success is forbidden and anxiety-provoking.

This universal human conflict is present in an intensified and unmediated form in recovering alcoholics, although the nature of the intrapsychic conflicts and their dynamics vary with the individual case. For Henry, success meant, among other things, surpassing his hated rival, the drowned brother, Bernard. Henry's death wishes toward Bernard were unconscious, as was his need to punish himself for these unconscious wishes. It was vital that this unconscious conflict be rendered conscious. Failure, though feared, was also wished for by

Henry. It meant "not being there," so that nobody would want to attack him. For Evelyn, both failure and success activated the critical, hating introjected mother. Therapy aimed at helping her overcome this malignant introject.

Freud (1926) listed five resistances to recovery in psychotherapy: the conservatism of the instincts (id resistance); repression, the transference, and secondary gains (ego resistance); and self-punishment (resistance from the superego). The resistance from the superego is what makes success so dangerous. Therapists underestimate the dangers of success for the recovering alcoholic. Many a slip is set off by a success. This is usually the result of self-punishment, however, not arrogance. It is also a way of escaping the anxiety that the success engenders. It is therefore vital that therapists be attuned to these dangers and understand the meaning of both failure and and sucess for the patient.

TERMINATION

Termination refers to both the actual ending of therapy and the process leading to that ending. In a sense, the process leading to termination begins at the very first session; however, as the term in usually used, the termination phase of therapy is the period that follows the therapist's and patient's joint decision to end therapy on a given date. One of the most important phases of treatment, termination is a mourning process, a time of saying goodbye. Like all endings, except death, it is both a completion, the finish of something already existing, and a beginning, a prelude to something new. The ending of the relationship with the therapist evokes memories and feelings of every significant separation or loss in the patient's life.

Life is a series of separations and losses, starting with physical separation from the mother, continuing with psychological separation from the symbiotic union with the mother, progressing through life's stages, and ending with separation from life itself. Throughout our lives we differentiate and reintegrate. Separation is the price of individuation. To refuse to, or to be unable to, pay that price means stagnation and psychic death. As Bob Dylan put it, "He who isn't being born is busy dying." In fact, one might say that life is about risking closeness and then suffering the pain of saying goodbye. So is therapy. Often the saying goodbye is both the most painful and the most meaningful part of therapy. *Termination* refers to the actual ending of therapy, to the mutual agreement between patient and therapist to end it, to the setting of the date of the final session, and to the process and the emotional reaction that that decision sets in motion. Just as each analysis is a crystallization of the universal and the unique, each termination both shares elements with all other terminations and is unlike any other psychotherapeutic termination.

For many patients, termination is a period of sadness and even despair. Others, experiencing termination as a rejection, feel angry and consciously or unconsciously blame the therapist for agreeing to their request for termination. Still others feel a sense of joyful release. And some defend against their feelings of separation and loss by denial; they report no special feelings. Most patients, at one time or another during the termination process, have all of these reactions and experience all of these feelings. There are also those who can not bear the pangs of separation, and who simply announce that they are terminating that very day; sometimes they do this after years of intensive work and closeness with the therapist. All of these reactions to termination are, in one sense, transference reactions; that is, they are both recapitulations of earlier stages of therapy and reenactments of the patient's early experiences with interpersonal and intrapsychic separation.

When do we terminate with an alcoholic patient? In the case of the stably sober patient, the goals are the ability to work, love, and play joyfully without alcohol.

This is a descriptive definition of an essentially behavioral criterion. From an intrapsychic point of view, the goals are repair of the structural deficits in the self and resolution, or at least attenuation, of psychological conflict. However, these are ideals. No one has a perfectly mature, firmly cohesive self; no one has uniformly and completely internalized the psychic functions once performed by others; and conflict, interpersonal and intrapsychic, is an ineluctable part of life. No one is either completely whole or completely aware of the psychic determinants of behavior. As Freud (1895) realistically, if somewhat cynically, stated it, "the goal of therapy is to change neurotic misery into ordinary human misery."

Since we always "see through a glass darkly," self-knowledge is necessarily fragmentary and incomplete, and we can never be certain that the most auspicious time for termination has been reached. Hence, the criterion must be pragmatic. Is the patient in good enough shape to "get by" preferably with some pleasure in the process? Has the patient learned as much, grown as much as he is likely to in this particular therapy, with this particular therapist, at this particular time? With the alcoholic patient, the ability to maintain sobriety without therapy is also a criterion.

Termination is negotiated between the therapist and the patient. We tell patients that since growth is open ended they may stay as long as they wish. This undercuts the resistance that comes from the fear of getting well, when getting well means losing the therapeutic relationship. Thus, when a patient asks the therapist how long the treatment will take, the therapist can tell the patient, "As long as you find our relationship facilitating and helpful, you can continue to come; and when you no longer find it helpful, you will leave, and that will be fine." This intervention both invites the patient to stay as long as desired and gives freedom to terminate without guilt. Part of the genius of AA lies in its insight into the dilemma of the alcoholic who fears losing the best thing he has found if he "gets it all together." AA cuts through this particular Gordian knot with its slogans "Nobody graduates!" and "Once an alcoholic, always an alcoholic." Hence, AA members feel free to grow as much as they are able, without feeling that their vital relationship with "the program" is endangered.

Patients with stable sobriety come to treatment for all sorts of reasons. Some are looking for advice on how to deal with a particular problem or crisis, or for highly focused help in a circumscribed area. These patients usually stay for only a few sessions, and termination is not really a part of their treatment. However, most alcoholics with stable sobriety who come for therapy have more ambitious goals; they are looking for emotional growth. Although they may not know it, they are looking for deep-seated change, what psychoanalysis calls "structural change." Accomplishing such a goal entails undergoing long-term, intensive psychotherapy. These patients become involved in intense transference reactions, slowly become familiar with the repressed or disavowed parts of themselves, and both internalize the therapist as a good object and transmutingly internalize the abilities to self-soothe, modulate anxiety, screen stimuli, and maintain a constant level of self-esteem. This process usually takes two to five years. When the patient has reached such an approximation to these goals that both patient and therapist are satisfied that their work together is finished for now, then it is time to set a termination date. It is usually preferable to wait for the patient to broach the issue of termination.

Since "growth is open ended" and the unconscious is inexhaustible, any request for termination is, in one of its aspects, a resistance. The decision to terminate is always a resistance to the discovery of whatever aspects of self remain unknown, and the desire to terminate must be partially understood as such. Therefore, it is the job of the therapist to explore this resistance with the patient. The therapist must be equally sensitive to the growth aspect of the patient's desire to terminate. Every properly timed termination is both a resistance and an act of individuation and growth. The desire to terminate, like everything else in psychotherapy and mental life, is overdetermined. It takes a great deal of accurate empathy and understanding for the therapist to shift these conflicting forces and help the patient to reach a sound decision to terminate or to continue in therapy. Working with patients to determine whether or not they are ready for termination is notoriously difficult. On one hand, the therapist may push a difficult, or otherwise unrewarding patient toward premature termination; on the other hand, the therapist may try to hold on to an enjoyable or satisfying patient after that patient is ready to terminate. The therapist's dilemma is parallel to that of the parent who must neither reject a child by phase-inappropriately pushing a precocious maturity nor impede phase-appropriate strivings for autonomy and independence. The therapist's countertransferential reactions to the patient's desire to terminate are often completely, and always partially, unconscious. Therefore, this is a good point for the therapist to seek supervision or consultation.

Exploring the possibility of termination is like exploring any other issue. It must be looked at from as many angles as possible, and the patient's experiencing of the associated feelings must be facilitated through free association and interpretation. This is a time for the therapist to ask time and again, "What are you feeling?" The decision to terminate is extremely important, and it should not be reached precipitously. The patient should be instructed to think about the tentative decision to terminate and urged to discuss the issue for at least several sessions before making a final decision. The issue of termination can be viewed pragmatically: When it works, don't fix it. The trick is to determine when it (the patient) does indeed work. Once a decision to terminate has been reached, the patient and the therapist discuss a date for a final session. This is often determined by practicalities, but if possible, four months to a year should be allotted for the termination phase of therapy. Other things being equal, a longer period is better.

Some patients are so damaged that they will require life-long, or at least very long-term, psychotherapeutic support. For some, the relationship with AA will suffice, but many others will continue to need additional help in the form of professional psychotherapy. Patients with chronic physical illnesses need life-long medical help; we accept this. Patients with chronic emotional illnesses may also need life-long help—in their case, psychological help; we tend not to accept this. There is no rational reason for this distinction. Keeping an alcoholic patient sober and optimally functioning is no mean feat and is a most worthwhile therapeutic goal. The therapist must be capable of distinguishing the growth-capable case, who will eventually terminate, from the maintenance-requiring case, who probably will never terminate from some form or other of therapy. Some "maintenance cases," after a long time in therapy, become growth cases. The therapist must always be alert to the possibility of such changes.

Henry

Henry worked very hard in therapy for three and a half years. The therapist had sensed emotional withdrawal on Henry's part over a period of several weeks. He had wondered what it was about. Then Henry came in and stated that he thought he had reached his goals and wished to discontinue therapy. The therapist asked him to elaborate.

Henry's goals had been the development of a gratifying relationship and the making of a career decision. He said, with a self-effacing smile, "I think I've reached those goals." The therapist inwardly agreed: Henry had indeed made progress. He had a satisfying relationship and he had found stimulating, enjoyable work. But had the intrapsychic goals been achieved? They discussed the decision over the next several sessions. The more they explored the issue of termination, the more the therapist felt that Henry had indeed achieved "structural change": The most disabling of the structural deficits in his self had been "filled in" through transmuting internalization; object constancy had been reached; and Henry's self-knowledge had been significantly broadened and deepened. Most important, he no longer repressed or disavowed his anger. Further, Henry had developed the capacity for fruitful introspection and he would continue to examine his motivations and try to understand his feelings. In short, he had become capable of self-analysis. In addition, he would remain involved in AA. Therefore, the therapist supported Henry's decision to terminate and said, "The process of saying goodbye is very important, and a great deal of growth is possible during this period. So why don't we continue until our usual summer break in five months? I think you'll get a lot out of it." Henry agreed, and a date for the final session was set.

Evelyn

Evelyn is doing surprisingly well in therapy. Given her traumatically pathological history, it is a wonder that she functions at all, much less as well as she does. She is a persistent and courageous patient, and her struggle for health inspires respect and admiration. She has turned out to be capable of considerable emotional growth. However, Evelyn is not near termination. She still needs help and will be a long-term patient, but she too will "make it."

It cannot be said too often that termination is a mourning process. Freud (1917) described mourning as a two-stage process. In order to mourn a lost object, the mourner must first identify with and internalize that object, and then withdraw libidinal investment from that object. According to Freud, "Each single one of the memories and hopes which bound the libido to the object is brought up and hypercathected, and the detachment of the libido from it accomplished." The mourner must recall with intense feeling and deep emotion every significant bond with the lost one. It is as if the mourner were tied to the lost object (a person, a goal, an ideal, a life stage, or a part of the self) by a bundle of rubber bands, each representing an emotional tie to the object; by recalling a given emotional tie with sufficient intensity, the mourner stretches that rubber band until it snaps, and when each of the emotional ties has been reexperienced with this degree of intensity and the last rubber band has been snapped, the mourner can recollect the emotional investment in the lost object and become free to reinvest it in a new object. In short, the mourner is then capable of loving again. Freud called this process "mourning work," and indeed it is work. Termination is just such a "working through." Since the therapeutic relationship is both real and transferential, the mourning in termination is both a mourning for the therapy and the therapist, and a mourning for the lost objects of childhood.

Freud was talking about mourning for lost objects experienced as truly separate; however, this is only part of the process. Narcissistic patients, including alcoholics with stable sobriety, must also mourn the loss of the self-objects of childhood, the grandiose self and the idealized parental imago. In a sense, the whole process of working through a narcissistic transference is a mourning process; it is a mourning for the loss of these ideal objects. In a successful therapy, the ideal objects are replaced by real objects, by the therapist or the parents with all their human limitations, and these real objects are in turn internalized and the patient's emotional investment in them slowly relinquished. Only then are patients free to reinvest their love in the world and in those they find worthy of that love.

In practical terms, helping patients mourn is like taking them through a mental photograph album and allowing the feelings elicited by each photograph to emerge. Many feelings around separation and loss surface during termination, but the focus is usually on the anticipated loss of the therapeutic relationship. These painful feelings are often defended against, so the therapist must bring the patient back again and again to feelings about the approaching termination of their relationship.

Some theorists (Miller 1974) believe that the dynamics of masochism, depression, and self-destructive behavior may importantly involve refusal to or an inability to mourn. Since alcoholics are by definition masochistic and self-destructive and are always depressed by the time they reach treatment, it is reasonable to hypothesize that the inability to mourn is an important dynamic in alcoholism. Clinical experience confirms this hypothesis. Therefore, it is particularly important to teach alcoholic patients how to mourn and to go through the mourning process with them. Termination gives the therapist a unique opportunity to engage the recovering alcoholic in an intense, here-and-now mourning process.

Generally, the more successful the therapy, the more intense the mourning during the working through of the decision to terminate. The termination phase of psychotherapy is often stormy and emotionally intense; it usually involves regression and a return to the symptoms that brought the patient to treatment. The patient is likely to become anxious and depressed. This should be expected, and the therapist should stay empathically close to the patient during this painful process.

Despite its many satisfactions, psychotherapy with alcoholics is a frustrating business. So many patients come and go through the revolving doors of our clinics and offices. We lose more than we save. Too few are those who achieve stable sobriety; fewer still are those who both achieve stable sobriety and grow emotionally; and yet fewer are those who achieve stable sobriety, grow emotionally, and reach a point at which they are joyfully productive, capable of sustained love, and able to take satisfaction in themselves and their sobriety.

As Spinoza (1677) said long ago, "All things excellent are as difficult as they are rare."

References

Abraham, K. (1908) The psychological relations between sexuality and alcoholism. In *Selected Papers on Psychoanalysis*. pp. 80–90. New York: Brunner/Mazel, 1979.

Alcoholics Anonymous World Services (1952). *Twelve Steps and Twelve Traditions*. New York: World Services.

—— (1955). *Alcoholics Anonymous*. New York: World Services.

Amark, C. (1951). A study in alcoholism: clinical, social, psychiatric, and genetic investigations. *Acta Psychiatrica Neurologica Scandinavica*, 70:1–283.

American Psychiatric Association (1980). *Diagnostic and Statistical Manual of Mental Disorders*, 3rd ed. Washington, D.C.: APA.

Balint, M. (1969). *The Basic Fault: Therapeutic Aspects of Regression*. New York: Brunner/Mazel, 1979

Barnes, G. (1979). The alcoholic personality: a reanalysis of the literature. *Journal of Studies on Alcohol*. 40:571–633.

Bateson, G. (1951a). *Communication: The Social Matrix of Psychiatry*. New York: W. W. Norton.

—— (1971). The cybernetics of "self": a theory of alcoholism. *Psychiatry*. 34:1–18. Reprinted in *Steps to an Ecology of Mind*. New York: Ballantine, 1972.

Bion, W. (1959). *Experiences in Groups*. London: Tavistock.

Blane, H. T. (1968). *The Personality of the Alcoholic: Guises of Dependency*. New York: Harper & Row.

Bleuler, M. (1955). Familial and personal background of chronic alcoholics. In *Etiology of Chronic Alcoholism*, ed. O. Drethelm, pp. 110–166. Springfield, Ill.: Charles C Thomas, 1955.

Brenner, C. (1955). *An Elementary Textbook of Psychoanalysis*. New York: International Universities Press.

Brown, N. O. (1966). *Love's Body*. New York: Random House.

Buber, M. (1937). *I and Thou*, trans. by R. G. Smith. New York: Charles Scribner's Sons.

Butz, R. (1982). Intoxication and withdrawal. In *Alcoholism: Development, Consequences, and Interventions*, 2nd ed., ed. N. J. Estes and M. E. Heinemann, pp. 102–108. St. Louis: C. V. Mosby.

Cahalan, D., Cisin, H., and Crossley, H. (1969). *American Drinking Practices: A National Survey of Behavior and Attitudes*. Monograph 6. New Brunswick, N. J.: Rutgers Center for Alcohol Studies.

Chein, I., Gerard, D. L., Lee, R. S., and Rosenfeld, E. (1964). *The Road to H*. New York: Basic Books.

Child, I., Bacon, M., and Barry, H. (1965). A cross-cultural study of drinking. *Quarterly Journal of Studies on Alcohol*, Supplement 3.

Cloninger, C. R. (1983). Genetic and environmental factors in the development of alcoholism. *Journal of Psychiatric Treatment and Evaluation* 5:487–496.

Conners, R. (1962). The self-concepts of alcoholics. In *Society, Culture, and Drinking Patterns*, ed. D. Pittman and C. Snyder, pp. 455–467. Carbondale, Ill.: Southern Illinois University Press.

Cox, W. M. (1979). The alcoholic personality: a review of the evidence. In *Progress in Experimental Personality Research*, vol. 9, pp. 89–148. New York: Academic.

Durkheim, E. (1897). *Suicide*. Glencoe, Ill: The Free Press, 1951.

Erikson, E. (1950). *Childhood and Society*, 2nd ed. New York: W. W. Norton, 1963.

—— (1968). *Identity, Youth, and Crisis*. New York: W. W. Norton.

Fenichel, O. (1945). *The Psychoanalytic Theory of Neurosis*, pp. 375–386. New York: W. W. Norton.

Field, P. (1962). A new cross-cultural study of drunkenness. In *Society, Culture, and Drinking Patterns*, ed. D. Pittman and C. Snyder, pp. 48–74. Carbondale, Ill.: Southern Illinois University Press.

Freud, A. (1938). *The Ego and the Mechanisms of Defense*, rev. ed. New York: International Universities Press, 1966.

Freud, S. (1900). The interpretation of dreams. *Standard Edition* 4/5: 1–628.

—— (1905a). Three essays on the theory of sexuality. *Standard Edition* 7:1–231.

—— (1905b). Jokes and their relation to the unconscious. *Standard Edition* 8.

—— (1912a). The dynamics of transference. *Standard Edition* 12:97–108.

—— (1912b). Recommendations to physicians practicing psychoanalysis. *Standard Edition* 12:109–120.

—— (1913a). On beginning the treatment. *Standard Edition* 12:121–144.

—— (1913b). Totem and taboo. *Standard Edition* 13:1–161.

—— (1914a). Remembering, repeating, and working-through. *Standard Edition* 12:145–156.

—— (1914b). On narcissism: an introduction. *Standard Edition* 14:67–104.

—— (1917). Mourning and melancholia. *Standard Edition* 14:237–256.

—— (1920). Beyond the pleasure principle. *Standard Edition* 18:1–64.

—— (1921). Group psychology and the analysis of the ego. *Standard Edition* 18:65–144.

—— (1923). The ego and the id. *Standard Edition* 19:1–66.

—— (1925). On negation. *Standard Edition* 19:235–240.

—— (1926). Inhibitions, symptoms, and anxiety. *Standard Edition* 20:75–172.

—— (1928). Dostoevsky and parricide. *Standard Edition* 21:173–194.

—— (1933). New introductory lectures on psychoanalysis. *Standard Edition* 22:1–182.

—— (1937). Analysis terminable and interminable. *Standard Edition* 23:209–254.

—— (1938). Moses and monotheism: three essays. *Standard Edition* 23:7–140.

—— (1940). Splitting of the ego in the process of defense. *Standard Edition* 23:271–278.

—— (1985). *The Complete Letters of Sigmund Freud to Wilhelm Fliess,* trans. and ed. J. M. Masson. Cambridge: Harvard University Press.

Freud, S., and Breuer, J. (1895). Studies on hysteria. *Standard Edition* 2:1–318.

Fromm, E. (1941). *Escape from Freedom.* New York: Rinehart.

Glover, E. (1928). The aetiology of alcoholism. *Proceedings of the Royal Society of Medicine* 21:1351–1355.

—— (1956). *On the Early Development of the Mind.* New York: International Universities Press.

Goffman, E. (1961). *Asylums.* Garden City, N.Y.: Anchor.

Goldstein, K. (1939). *The Organism.* New York: Schocken.

—— and Scheer, M. (1941). Abstract and concrete behavior: an experimental study with special tests. *Psychological Monographs,* vol. 53.

Goodwin, D. W., Schulsinger, F., Hermansen, L., Guze, S. B., and Winokur, G. (1973). Alcohol problems in adoptees raised apart from alcoholic biological parents. *Archives of General Psychiatry* 28:283–243.

Greenson, R. (1965a). The working alliance and the transference neurosis. *Psychoanalytic Quarterly* 34:155–181.

Gross, M., and Hastey, J. (1976). Sleep disturbances in alcoholism. In *Alcoholism: Interdisciplinary Approaches to an Enduring Problem,* ed. R. E. Tarter and A. A. Sugerman, pp. 257–308. Reading, Mass.: Addison-Wesley.

Guntrip, H. (1968). *Schizoid Problems, Object-Relations, and the Self.* New York: International Universitites Press.

—— (1971). *Psychoanalytic Theory, Therapy, and the Self.* New York: Basic Books.

Harris, L., and Associates, Inc. (1971). *American Attitudes Toward Alcohol and Alcoholism,* study no. 2138. A survey of public opinion prepared for the National Institute on Alcohol Abuse and Alcoholism. New York: Louis Harris.

Hartmann, H. (1939). *Ego Psychology and the Problem of Adaptation.* New York: International Universities Press, 1958.

—— (1964). *Essays on Ego Psychology: Selected Problems in Psychoanalytic Theory.* New York: International Universities Press.

Hartocollis, P. (1968). A dynamic view of alcoholism: drinking in the service of denial. *Dynamic Psychiatry* 2:173–182.

Hartocollis, P., and Hartocollis, P. C. (1980). Alcoholism, borderline, and narcissistic disorders: a psychoanalytic overview. In *Phenomenology and Treatment of Alcoholism*, ed. W. E. Fann, I. Haracan, A. D. Pokorny, and R. L. Williams, pp. 93–110. New York: SP Medical & Scientific.

Heidegger, M. (1926). *Being and Time*, trans. J. Macquarrie and E. Robinson. London: SCM Press, 1962.

Hewitt, C. C. (1943). A personality study of alcohol addiction. *Quarterly Journal of Studies on Alcohol* 4:368–386.

Hillel. In *The Living Talmud*, ed. J. Goldin, p. 69. New York: Mentor, 1957.

Horton, D. (1943). The functions of alcohol in primitive societies: a cross-cultural study. *Quarterly Journal of Studies on Alcohol* 4:199–320.

Huizinga, J. (1944). *Homo Ludens: A Study of the Play Element in Culture*. Boston: Beacon, 1950.

Husserl, E. (1929). *Cartesian Meditations: An Introduction to Phenomenology*, trans. D. Cairns. The Hague: Martinus Nijhoff, 1960.

Huxley, A. (1954). *The Doors of Perception*. New York: Harper & Row.

Irgens-Jensen, O. (1971). *Problem Drinking and Personality: A Study Based on the Draw-a-Person Test*. New Brunswick, N.J.: Rutgers Center of Alcohol Studies.

Jacobson, E. (1964). *The Self and the Object World*. New York: International Universities Press.

James, W. (1890). *The Principles of Psychology*. Cambridge: Harvard University Press, 1983.

––––– (1902). *Varieties of Religious Experience*. New York: Longmans.

Jellinek, E. M. (1952). Phases of alcohol addiction. *Quarterly Journal of Studies on Alcohol* 13:673–684.

––––– (1960). *The Disease Concept of Alcoholism*. New Haven: College & University Press.

Jones, M. C. (1968). Personality correlates and antecedents of drinking patterns in adult males. *Journal of Consulting and Clinical Psychology* 32:2–12.

––––– (1971). Personality antecedents and correlates of drinking patterns in women. *Journal of Consulting and Clinical Psychology* 36:61–69.

Jung, C. (1961). The Bill W.–C. G. Jung letters. In *The AA Grapevine*, January 1963.

Kaij, L. (1960). *Alcoholism in Twins: Studies on the Etiology and Sequels of Abuse of Alcohol.* Stockholm: Almquist & Wiksell.

Kammeier, M. L., Hoffman, H., and Loper, R. G. (1973). Personality characteristics of alcoholics as college freshmen and at time of treatment. *Quarterly Journal of Studies on Alcohol* 34:390–399.

Kant, I. (1781). *The Critique of Pure Reason,* 2nd ed., 1787, trans. M. K. Smith. London: Macmillan, 1929.

Kernberg, O. (1975). *Borderline Conditions and Pathological Narcissism.* New York: Jason Aronson.

—— (1976). *Object Relations Theory and Clinical Psychoanalysis.* New York: Jason Aronson.

—— (1980). *Internal World and External Reality: Object Relations Applied.* New York: Jason Aronson.

Khantzian, E. J. (1981). Some treatment implications of ego and self-disturbances in alcoholism. In *Dynamic Approaches to the Understanding and Treatment of Alcoholism,* ed. M. H. Bean and N. E. Zinberg, pp. 163–188. New York: The Free Press.

Klausner, S. (1964). Sacred and profane meanings of blood and alcohol. *The Journal of Social Psychology* 64:27–43.

Knight, R. P. (1937). The dynamics and treatment of chronic alcohol addiction. *Bulletin of the Menninger Clinic* 1:233–250.

—— (1938). The psychoanalytic treatment in a sanatorium of chronic addiction to alcohol. *Journal of the American Medical Association* 111:1443–1448.

Kohut, H. (1971). *The Analysis of the Self: A Systematic Approach to the Psychoanalytic Treatment of Narcissistic Personality Disorders.* New York: International Universities Press.

—— (1972). Thoughts on narcissism and narcissistic rage. In *The Search for the Self,* vol. 2, ed. P. H. Ornstein, pp. 615–658. New York: International Universities Press, 1978.

—— (1977a). *The Restoration of the Self.* New York: International Universities Press.

—— (1977b). Preface to *Psychodynamics of Drug Dependence.* National Institute on Drug Abuse Research Monograph 12, pp. vii–ix. U.S. Department of Health, Education, and Welfare. Washington, D.C.: U.S. Government Printing Office.

—— (1984). *How Does Analysis Cure?* Chicago: University of Chicago Press.

Kris, E. (1952). *Psychoanalytic Explorations in Art.* New York: International Universities Press.

Krystal, H., and Raskin, H. (1970). *Drug Dependence: Aspects of Ego Function*. Detroit: Wayne State University Press.

Levin, J. D. (1981). A study of social role conflict in chronic alcoholic men affiliated with alcoholics anonymous. Ph.D. diss., New York University. Ann Arbor, Mich.: University Microfilms International 8210924.

Loper, R. G., Kammeier, M. L., and Hoffman, H. (1973). MMPI characteristics of college freshman males who later became alcoholics. *Journal of Abnormal Psychology* 82:159–162.

Ludwig, A. M., and Wikler, A. (1974). "Craving" and relapse to drink. *Quarterly Journal of Studies on Alcohol* 35:108–130.

MacAndrew, C. (1965). The differentiation of male alcoholic outpatients from non-alcoholic psychiatric outpatients by means of the MMPI. *Quarterly Journal of Studies on Alcohol* 26:238–246.

MacAndrew, C., and Geertsma, R. H. (1963). An analysis of responses of alcoholics to Scale 4 of the MMPI. *Quarterly Journal of Studies on Alcohol* 24:23–38.

Mack, J. E. (1981). Alcoholism, AA, and the governance of the self. In *Dynamic Approaches to the Understanding and Treatment of Alcoholism*, ed. M. H. Bean and N. E. Zinberg, pp. 128–162. New York: The Free Press.

Mahler, M., Pine, F., and Bergman, A. (1975). *The Psychological Birth of the Human Infant: Symbiosis and Individuation*. New York: Basic Books.

Masters, W. H., and Johnson, V. E. (1970). *Human Sexual Inadequacy*. Boston: Little, Brown.

McClelland, D. C., Davis, W., Kalin, R., and Wanner, E. (1972). *The Drinking Man: Alcohol and Human Motivation*. New York: The Free Press.

McCord, W., and McCord, J., with Gudeman, J. (1960). *Origins of Alcoholism*. Stanford, Calif.: Stanford University Press.

Menninger, K. (1938). *Man Against Himself*. New York: Harcourt, Brace.

Millay, E. St. V. (1917). Renascence. In *Collected Poems*, ed. N. Millay, pp. 3–13. New York: Harper & Row, 1956.

Miller, A. (1949). *Death of a Salesman*. In *The Portable Arthur Miller*, ed. H. Clurman. New York: Viking, 1971.

Miller, C. (1974). Depression as a consequence of the failure to mourn. Paper delivered to the American Association for the Advancement of Psychoanalysis on October 8, 1974, at the Karen Horney Clinic, New York.

Moliere, J. B. P. (1670). *Le Bourgeois Gentilhomme*. In *Eight Plays by Moliere*, trans. M. Bishop, Act II, Sc. 4, p. 346. New York: Random House Modern Library, 1957.

O'Neill, E. (1929). The Great God Brown. In *The Plays of Eugene O'Neill*. New York: Random House, 1967.

Park, P. (1973). Developmental ordering of experiences in alcoholism. *Quarterly Journal of Studies on Alcohol* 34:473–488.

Petrie, A. (1967). *Individuality in Pain and Suffering*, 2nd ed. Chicago: University of Chicago Press, 1978.

Pitts, F. N., Jr., and Winokur, G. (1966). Affective disorder–VII: alcoholism and affective disorder. *Journal of Psychiatric Research* 4:37–50.

Plato. Symposium. In *Plato: Collected Dialogues*, ed. E. Hamilton and H. Cairns. Princeton, N.J.: Princeton University Press, 1961.

—— Republic. Book VII. In *Plato: Collected Dialogues*, ed. E. Hamilton and H. Cairns. Princeton, N.J.: Princeton University Press, 1961.

Rado, S. (1933). The psychoanalysis of pharmacothymia. *Psychoanalytic Quarterly* 2:2–23.

Rilke, R. M. (1922). *Duino Elegies*, trans. D. Young. New York: W. W. Norton.

Robbins, L. N., Bates, W. N., and O'Neil, P. (1962). Adult drinking patterns of former problem children. In *Society, Culture, and Drinking Patterns*, ed. D. J. Pittman and C. R. Snyder, pp. 395–412. Carbondale, Ill.: Southern Illinois University Press.

Robbins, L. N., and Smith, E. M. (1980). Longitudinal studies of alcohol and drug problems: sex differences. In *Alcohol and Drug Problems in Women*, ed. O. J. Kalant. New York: Plenum.

Rogers, C. (1951). *Client-Centered Therapy: Its Current Practice, Implications, and Theory*. Boston: Houghton Mifflin.

—— (1959). A theory of therapy, personality, and interpersonal relations. In *Psychology: A Study of a Science*, ed. S. Koch. New York: McGraw-Hill.

—— (1961). *On Becoming a Person: A Therapist's View of Psychotherapy*. Boston: Houghton Mifflin.

Sadava, S. W. (1978). Etiology, personality, and alcoholism. *Canadian Psychological Review Psychologie Canadienne* 19:198–214.

Sandmaier, M. (1981). *The Invisible Alcoholics*. New York: McGraw-Hill.

Schiller, J. C. F. von (1785). *An die freude* (Ode to joy). In *Friedrich Schiller: An Anthology for Our Time*, ed. and trans. F. Unger. New York: Fredrich Ungar, 1949.

Segal, H. (1964). *Introduction to the Work of Melanie Klein*, rev. ed. New York: Basic Books, 1971.

Simmel, E. (1929). Psychoanalytic treatment in a sanatorium. *International Journal of Psychoanalysis* 10:83–85.

—— (1948). Alcoholism and addiction. *Psychoanalytic Quarterly* 17:6–31.

Spinoza, B. (1677). The Ethics (*Ethica Ordine Geometrio Demonstrata*). In *The Chief Works of Benedict De Spinoza*, trans. R. H. M. Elwes, vol. 2, pp. 44–272. New York: Dover Publications, 1951.

Szasz, T. (1958). The role of the counterphobic mechanism in addiction. *Journal of the American Psychoanalytic Association* 6:309–325.

Tarter, R. E. (1981). Minimal brain dysfunction as an etiological predisposition to alcoholism. In *Evaluation of the Alcoholic: Implications for Research, Theory and Treatment*, ed. R. E. Meyer et al. NIAAA Monograph Series. Washington, D.C.: NIAAA.

Tarter, R. E., Alterman, A. I., and Edwards, K. L. (1985). The vulnerability to alcoholism in men: a behavior-genetic perspective. *Journal of Studies on Alcohol* 46:329–356.

Tiebout, H. M. (1944). Therapeutic mechanisms of Alcoholics Anonymous. *American Journal of Psychiatry* 100:468–473.

—— (1949). The act of surrender in the therapeutic process. *Quarterly Journal of Studies on Alcohol* 10:48-58.

—— (1957). The ego factor in surrender to alcoholism. *Quarterly Journal of Studies on Alcohol* 15:610–621.

Truax, C. B., and Carkhuff, R. R. (1967). *Toward Effective Counseling and Psychotherapy*. Chicago: Aldine.

U.S. Department of Health, Education, and Welfare, National Institute on Alcohol Abuse and Alcoholism (1971). *First Special Report to the U.S. Congress on Alcohol and Health*. Washington, D.C.: U.S. Government Printing Office.

—— National Institute on Drug Abuse (1977). *Psychodynamics of Drug Dependence: National Institute on Drug Abuse Research Monograph 12*. Washington, D.C.: U.S. Government Printing Office.

Vaillant, G. E. (1983). *The Natural History of Alcoholism: Causes, Patterns and Paths to Recovery*. Cambridge, Mass.: Harvard University Press.

Wallerstein, R. S. (1983). Self psychology and "classical" psychoanalytic psychology: the nature of their relationship. In *The Future of Psychoanalysis*, ed. A. Goldberg, pp. 19–63. New York: International Universities Press.

Whitehead, A. N. (1933). *Adventure of Ideas*. New York: Macmillan.

Wilsnack, S. C. (1973). Sex role identity in female alcoholism. *Journal of Abnormal Psychology* 82:253–261.

——— (1974). The effects of social drinking on women's fantasy. *Journal of Personality* 42:43–61.

Wilson, G., and Lawson, D. (1978). Expectancies, alcohol, and sexual arousal in women. *Abnormal Psychology* 85:358–367.

Winnicott, D. W. (1951). Transitional objects and transitional phenomena. In *Through Paediatrics to Psycho-analysis*, pp. 229–242. London: Hogarth Press, 1958.

——— (1952). Psychoses and child care. In *Through Paediatrics to Psycho-analysis*, pp. 219–228. London: Hogarth Press, 1958.

——— (1956). Primary maternal preoccupation. In *Through Paediatrics to Psycho-analysis*, pp. 300–305. London: Hogarth Press, 1958.

——— (1958). The capacity to be alone. In *The Maturational Processes and the Facilitating Environment*, pp. 29–36. New York: International Universities Press, 1965.

——— (1960). Ego distortion in terms of true and false self. In *The Maturational Processes and the Facilitating Environment*, pp. 140–152. New York: International Universities Press, 1965.

——— (1971). *Playing and Reality*. London: Tavistock.

Winokur, G. (1974). The division of depressive illness into depressive-spectrum disease and pure depressive disease. *International Pharmaco-psychiatry* 9:5–13.

Winokur, G., Reich, T., Rimmer, J., and Pitts, R. N., Jr. (1970). Alcoholism III: diagnosis and familial psychiatric illness in 259 alcoholic probands. *Archives of General Psychiatry* 23:104–111.

Winokur, G., Rimmer, J., and Reich, T. (1971). Alcoholism IV: is there more than one type of alcoholism? *British Journal of Psychiatry* 18:525–531.

Witkin, H. A., Karp, S. A., and Goodenough, D. R. (1959). Dependence in alcoholics. *Quarterly Journal of Studies on Alcohol* 20:493–504.

Witkin, H. A., and Oltman, P. K. (1967). Cognitive style. *International Journal of Neurology* 6:119–137.

Wordsworth, W. (1850). The prelude. In *The Poetical Works of Wordsworth*. New York: Oxford University Press, 1910.

Wright, B. A. (1960). *Physical Disability: A Psychological Approach.* New York: Harper & Row.

Wurmser, L. (1978). *The Hidden Dimension: Psychodynamics in Compulsive Drug Use.* New York: Jason Aronson.

Yalom, I. D. (1975). *The Theory and Practice of Group Psychotherapy.* New York: Basic Books.

Zetzel, E. (1956). Current concepts of transference. *International Journal of Psychoanalysis* 37:369–376.

Zimberg, S. (1978). Principles of alcoholism psychotherapy. In *Practical Approaches to Alcoholism Psychotherapy*, ed. S. Zimberg, J. Wallace, and S. B. Blume, pp. 1–18. New York: Plenum.

—— (1982). *The Clinical Management of Alcoholism.* New York: Brunner/Mazel.

Index